Contents

To our fantastic Wives who by now probably think we are mad, we thank you for letting us continue with our ridiculous hobby. We thank you for supporting us throughthe long days and lonely nights when we had deadlines to adhere to and pages to submit. None of this would be possible without your continued love and support.

To Lee, the true engine room behind the scenes at everything 5 Yard, we sure as hell couldn't do anything we do without so we truly are thankful every day. We alsocould not be happier with this year's cover and look, so a million thank you's right there.

To Stocks' Sister who spent twice as long editing this as she did last year we are forever in your debt and our thanks will never be enough. What you've done to helpus to get these books out is inspiring.

To the whole 5 Yard Family, each and every one of you holds a special place in our hearts and we couldn't be prouder of the crew we have assembled. If a Football Thanos does descend on planet earth, then we know we have got him beat for sure.

Finally to each and every one of you Rush Nation, who has listened, read, watched,interacted or bought something from the store we are just blown away by the continued love for all things 5 Yard Rush and from every member of the 5 Yard Family we all say a huge thank you to you all.

CHAPTER 1

Foreword

Written by **Chris Mitchell & Adam Murfet**

A year and a bit ago we decided to collate all our notes on Fantasy Football together and create the Fantasy Football Playbook for 2020. When all was said and done and our digital quills had stopped writing we looked back on what we had achieved and we'll be honest Rush Nation, we were super proud of what we had managed to put together. Lee then took the words and created the beautiful cover and pages that all made the 2020 Playbook. Even if we never sold a copy we had all grown as Fantasy Football players and had helped each other to grow not only as Fantasy players but as people as well, that was enough for us. What we did not expect though was just how successful the book would be and how many people would support 5 Yard Rush and just how many people read, enjoyed and benefited from the book.

So what did the 2020 book mean for 5 Yard going forward? Well, as soon as Draft season proper had started, we instantly knew we were going to write another Playbook. It became not only a personal passion project for us because it helped us to get better at the hobby we all love but it also helped others with knowledge about the game or with players coming into the League that perhaps they didn't know. The fact that people took knowledge out of the book was one thing but to have so many players send us thanks because we helped them in one way or another was truly amazing and we will never be able to thank you enough. We knew that what we gained from the 2020 edition meant that we wanted to write the 2021 edition for ourselves and then for you Rush Nation. As we always say, we wouldn't be where we are without not only you guys but also the Fantasy Football and NFL UK communities. The love for the game grows with every day here in the UK and we absolutely adore being part of the communities and the groups on social media.

Whilst 2020 was a brutally tough year for the entire human race, we at 5 Yard continued to press forward with expanding our brand and bringing you even more great content. We started the sister show, 5 Yard College which Tom and Ash have taken from strength to strength and even now have added dedicated writers Mark and Jordan who have added to an already expansive and exciting College Football arm of our Family. Simmo also adds his College history knowledge to the 5 Yard College team with his series about each year in College Football History which will eventually end up with him creating an Index of College Football which will allow you to deduce all sorts of information about College ball going forward.

We also added a DFS show to our armoury which Nick and Mark have started all guns blazing and have been cashing bank for you DFS players since the show started mid season. Whilst DFS for Football is over the guys are deep in their bunkers working on formulas for next season already and they will be back in your ears with show on DFS tips, tricks and strategies in the not to near future.

Pittsy and Rob started the Fast Action Friday show, where in season they bring you right up to date with the week's news on a Friday just before the weekend starters with a bite size and fun show to get you up to speed to get those lineups right heading into the weekend.

Finally and most recently we have added Rich to the team who brings a wealth of Dynasty Football Knowledge and along with this he also hosts the 5 Yard Dynasty Podcast. Rich regularly has some of the biggest names in Dynasty Football on as guests to talk about all things Dynasty.

We have also added Nath to the team who specialises in IDP. Nath and 5 Yard are striving to create a common scoring format for IDP that can be the gold standard in the UK and eventually the world when it comes to IDP scoring. IDP scoring is notoriously different and can make starting or joining a League difficult, we aim to make it easy and fun for all.

So what can you expect from the 2021 edition of The Fantasy Football Playbook? Well let's go back to the 2020 edition. If you read that and own it then great, that is the foundation for what we build going forward. If not then there is a QR Code at the back of the book that will enable you to download the book in a PDF file for just one British pound. There is also a copy in the shop should you wish to get it that way. The 2021 edition builds on what we set out last year. This year there are more tips and tricks to building the best roster. Murf has updated his PAS metric to include last year's data and this further cements the need and way to stream players from the waiver wire. The PAS metric ties in nicely to Murf's Value of each round in a Fantasy Football Draft. Knowing where the values are and when to pull the trigger can help get out in front early. There are our consistency charts to help you see who was consistent last year and who wasn't. There are some big surprises and knowing these could save you from taking the L on a week to week basis. We give you an insight into our Draft Strategies and the top mistakes players make when drafting.

Stocks then dives into this year's incoming Rookie class and gives his thoughts on the guys he thinks are most important for Fantasy Football this year. There are double the guys there were last year and again if there is anyone you feel we have missed out then get in touch @5yardrush and we can chew the fat on the player you want to chat about.

Once again Rush Nation we couldn't do this without your huge support, after all we are just a bunch of guys chatting about the sport we love and you give us the platform to be able to do bigger and better things year in and year out. So we hope you enjoy what's about to come from this book and as Stocks says "Let's go win those ships."

Murf & Stocks

CHAPTER 2

5 Things That Will Change in Fantasy Football in 2021

Written by *Adam Murfet*

It is fair to say that 2020 was an extremely challenging year for the NFL and for fantasy football owners. COVID wreaked havoc on the Draft, OTA's, Training Camp. There was no pre-season because of the pandemic. We had cancelled games, teams changing or not having allotted bye weeks. Also, there was the challenge of last minute COVID designations, entire position rooms like the Broncos QB room and the Browns WR room to name just two instances due to COVID close contact rules.

However, the season got completed. Every game got played and most had their key players available for most of the time. There were a lot of big injuries early. However, there were also a lot less injuries as the season tailed off.

With this hopefully once in a lifetime experience behind the NFL, it is our job to take what is meaningful from last season's data and to try and not overreact to unique circumstances. However, we saw some significant changes in the game that we need to be aware of. Some will counter the advice of the 2020 version of the Fantasy Football Playbook. What worked in 2020 might not work in 2021? That is why this is a yearly publication as opposed to a one-off bible about how to win Fantasy Football Leagues.

So, let us look at the top 5 trends you need to think about changing your approach for 2021.

1)   *Draft an Elite QB Earlier.*

Yes, you are reading this right. In last year's publication, as well as also looking at the history of late round QB, the game has changed significantly. That is because there is a new refined tier of elite QBs in Fantasy Football. Instead of having 1 or 2 elite guys, there are now as many as 6 elite threats in 2021 to pick. And realistically, when there are that many difference makers, it means half the league will have an elite option, and half the league will not. Since it is the largest scoring position, not getting one of these elite options is going to make it very difficult to succeed and win a league. Not impossible, but harder. For those of you wanting to know who these elite options are, they are:

Patrick Mahomes
Josh Allen
Kyler Murray
Dak Prescott
Deshaun Watson
Aaron Rodgers

Notice in this list, there is no Russell Wilson or Lamar Jackson. Wilson had a season of two halves. However, the commitment of Pete Carroll to fire his Offensive Coordinator Brian Schottenheimer in January as "we need to run the ball more often" means perhaps they won't "Let Russ Cook" in 2021. There is also the concern about Deshaun Watson and whether he has a different landing spot, as the NFL saga of the year continues to drag on. However, Watson will be an elite option.

And I know some people will be shocked not to see Lamar Jackson on this list. He could positively regress. However, we have 2 years of data on Lamar Jackson, and they are wildly different in terms of passing numbers. That lack of consistency scares me just enough to not be one of these elite options. That is not to say I will not be drafting him at all. He could become an incredible value.

So, how soon is early? Well, I am still not advocating a 2nd 3rd or 4th round pick in a 1QB league for these players. If you look at the research in the 2020 Fantasy Football Playbook and later in this book, you will see the value is just not there, compared to what you are giving up in other positions. It does not pay to take Mahomes in the 2nd round, the same way you did not get the payoff to take Jackson in the 2nd round in 2020. Avoid that.

Looking at ADP data, you are looking at the 5th/6th round for most of these players. Not Mahomes, but the rest of the elite tier will more than likely be there.

If you have a preference in players, such as Josh Allen or Kyler Murray, then make sure you get your man in the 5th round. However, I would watch the board and see what happens to the pool. I can see you getting an elite option in the 6th round in most drafts.

Will a late round option make the top 5 in the QB for scoring in 2021? Most probably. Usually, a late round option will run it close or get in there. Tannehill, Brady, and Herbert were late round QBs that made the top 9 in scoring. Jackson was undrafted the year before, Mahomes was undrafted or late drafted the year before that. It can happen. But it is a riskier approach to win that we saw in 2020. I grabbed Josh Allen in the 9th round in a lot of drafts and he won me a fair number of leagues. And he has consistency on his side with a couple of years of valuable numbers.

Do not make the game harder than it needs to be. Take one of these elite guys in the 5th/6th round and you will be well on your way to having a good draft and a good season.

2)   *Do all you can to get an Elite Running Back.*

What we saw in 2020 was a move back to years past, where the bell cow back was just a handful of guys, whilst the rest of the league moved to a more Running Back by Committee (RRBC) approach. As more and more great Running Backs enter the league, as we have seen in the last few draft classes, teams are happy to stockpile these backs, or take the heavy workload off them in the regular season and save them for the late season push/playoffs. In 2020, four elite Running Backs entered the draft in Clyde Edwards-Helaire (CEH), Jonathan Taylor, J.K Dobbins and D'Andre Swift. Let us use the baseline of 66% (2/3rds) of snaps in a game as the level to achieve consistent production.

CEH achieved 5 such weeks of 66% or over, in Weeks 1,3,4,6, and 14. Jonathan Taylor had 3 such weeks, in Week 2, in Week 15 and the week hardly anyone plays Fantasy Football, Week 17. Swift had just two in Week 10 and Week 16, whilst Dobbins had 1 in Week 8. Meanwhile Undrafted Free Agent (UDFA) James Robinson had 10 such weeks over the 14 games he played, before injury curtailed his season. In fact, the top performers in Fantasy Football all had significantly more than these talented rookies. Alvin Kamara had 10 weeks of over 66% of snaps. Dalvin Cook had 11. And Derrick Henry also had 8.

The amount of time they play directly correlates to how many opportunities they must score fantasy points. This point seems simple but is not widely accepted amongst fantasy owners.

They believe even now for the most part that talent trumps opportunity. They will cite the exceptions such as Aaron Jones massively outperforming his snap share in 2019 or Ezekiel Elliot severely underperforming against their opportunity (Zeke had 9 games where he played on 66% of snaps or more). These outliers can be explained. However, they are outliers. You cannot reason with opportunity. Christian McCaffrey was not the number one Running Back in Fantasy Football on talent alone. It was because he also played on 97% of his teams snaps in that season where he broke a ton of records. Rule number 1 should always be Opportunity over Talent. That is why James Robinson, who went undrafted in the NFL draft, outperformed his rookie class, including the four elite options. It does not mean he is a better Running Back. He just proved he is good and made the most of his opportunities.

So, what is an elite Running Back? Well, in simple terms, it is someone who has both the talent and the opportunity. Who are these elite Running Backs? Well, if we look at the above, we want players who have demonstrated their talent who also have a great opportunity to perform most weeks. These players are, in no particular order:

- Christian McCaffrey
- Saquon Barkley
- Alvin Kamara
- Dalvin Cook
- Derrick Henry
- Ezekiel Elliott

You have people like Nick Chubb who clearly have elite talent but perhaps not the same opportunity as the others. Joe Mixon has injuries to contend with, but he could also be in this next tier, as well as some of the rookies we mentioned from last year.

The reason why your drafts had anywhere from 9-12 Running Backs go off the board is because these players are extremely valuable, and rare. The tiers below the top 2 tiers are scary. Do not get 2 of the top 15 QBs and you will fall behind the rest of the league. Some owners will have to take two top two guys to make up on missing out on an elite Running Back. And that is ok.

Basic Roster construction is having winning players across your team. You will always have a gap. However, you need to make sure your gap is in a position where the cost of having a gap is far less than if it was in a more valuable spot on the roster. Having an elite QB and pairing them with an elite RB is a great way to ensure your team can ride the bumps and keep you competitive through the season, in a lot of cases.

If you cannot get one of the elite Running Backs in the draft, try and work out a trade that makes sense. Try and get a couple of guys who make the sum of whole parts. And if an elite RB goes down, pay through the nose with your Free Agency Acquisition Budget (FAAB) to get that next man up. I blew my FAAB on James Robinson and Mike Davis in a lot of places last year, and it worked out well. Do not be afraid to blow almost all your budget on these guys. Remember, opportunity trumps talent. The difference between the RB1 and the RB12 is on average 12 points a game over the past 5 years. That is too much to give up without an equaliser somewhere.

3)   *Wide Receiver is deeper than ever. However, that does not mean you can afford to sleep on the position.*

The Wide Receiver position is deeper than ever before. With an outstanding rookie class in 2020, that saw Justin Jefferson become the WR8, as well as top 36 performances from Brandon Aiyuk, CeeDee Lamb, and Chase Claypool, as well as Tee Higgins, Jerry Jeudy and Laviska Shenault also showing what they can do, the pool of Wide Receivers is deeper than ever. 48 Wide Receivers averaged over 10 PPR per game. That means you should hammer WR in the middle rounds.

However, you also cannot afford to abandon the position until then. If you were picking up an elite Running Back (if he did not get injured of course) and followed that up with Wide Receiver/Wide Receiver you were onto a winner. That strategy can be stretched to Round's 3 and 4 this year if you need to start RB/RB at the end of round 1, start of round 2, to make up for the lack of an elite Running Back.

Very few of the Round 2 and 3 Wide Receivers missed in 2020. And with the likes of Stefon Diggs and Calvin Ridley seeing their ADP jump into this range, it is hard to see many misses again in these rounds. So, take advantage of the situation. Especially if you bagged a rare elite Running Back.

4)   *You must make sure you take a second Quarterback if others are.*

Taking two Quarterbacks was not the normal, done thing to do, until 2020. With COVID and the uncertainty of availability of Quarterbacks, especially at the last minute, meant fantasy owners took two Quarterbacks. This meant the Waiver Wire was thinner than ever, making it harder to stream or play matchups. Therefore, you are going to have to consider taking 2QBs in your drafts this year.

The pandemic is not going to go away overnight. And there is no guarantee COVID will not affect the NFL in 2021. Not to mention, having the safety of a competent back-up if your elite QB goes down could make the difference. Watch your draft very carefully. If you start to see QBs coming off the board, you will need to adapt and take a QB before you are stuck with an unplayable option that will cost you a shot of a title if your QB remains side-lined. Dak Prescott killed a lot of teams last year. Do not make the same mistake this year and get caught streaming poor lower end league options.

5)   *Tight End is less important than ever before. You either go for Kelce or you leave the position until the last 4 rounds.*

Last year more than every proved that Tight End is just a position that is either worth going big or going home. Kelce justified his ADP selection. Kittle, Ertz, Andrews did not. Kittle was injured so he gets a pass. However, outside of Travis Kelce, only Darren Waller returned in a big way on a top 7 round investment. To demonstrate the position fully, Darren Waller finished the year as the TE2 with 278.6 PPR Points. Logan Thomas and Robert Tonyan, who were the TE3/TE4 overall (separated by 0.02 of a point), scored 176.62 and 176.6 PPR Points. That is a full 102 PPR points behind the TE2.

The strategy for the position is very clear for next season. Pay up for Kelce or wait until the end of the draft to take a Tight End. The gap between the TE3 and the TE12 was just a measly 1.96 PPR Points per game. You are not losing out owning a low end TE if you cannot get Kelce. So just ignore the position and grab one of the guys at the end of your draft. Drafting a Tight End in rounds 4-8 are a pure waste of a pick. Personally, unless someone like Tonyan or Thomas are available in round 9, I am prepared to wait until the 12th round for my Tight End. I have taken Gronk in the 13th round this offseason already, and I am more than happy with that.

These are the five key adjustments we need to make to our draft strategy and our play in 2021 to be successful. If we do not adapt as fantasy owners, the sharks will eat us up, and we will become the fish in the pod. At the end of the day, we all want to win. And these adjustments will open up the opportunities to win even more. These are not hard and fast rules. However, we want to maximise our returns on every draft pick, and the above should be considered as part of your strategy.

Bonus) 17 Game Season in 2021.

In late March it was confirmed the NFL would be moving to a 17-game season from the 2021 season onwards. This was not a massive surprise, considering the ground work to extend to a 17-game season was done in the latest Collective Bargaining Agreement signed in 2020.

However, what does this mean for fantasy football seasons, now we have an 18-week season in 2021 and beyond? Well, there are a few different things leagues can do for 2021 amid all of this uncertainty. Here are some options you can consider.

1) Do Nothing.

This one should not surprise many people. Those who play in week 17 seasons should absolutely do nothing and leave their league as is. However, if, like most of you, you play in 16-week seasons, then you might be hesitant to change. And that makes sense. What if teams start rotating players more towards the end of the season? What if it affects the dynamic of the whole league and opens up a lot more complaints if we do something? That makes complete sense. Remember the old adage "If it ain't broke, don't fix it!". It does have merit here. The only downside to doing nothing is that people will not be playing fantasy football for the last two weeks of the regular season. If that upsets enough people, then you can always change it in 2022 and beyond.

2) Add an additional game to the fantasy regular season.

This one is probably the easiest change to make. You simply move your playoffs to start in Week 15 instead of Week 14 and you give everyone one extra regular season game to try and get into the playoffs. However, this change will probably come with the greatest whinging at the end of the season. I can almost guarantee that someone will do at least 1 of these 3 things 1) Moan they had to play a harder schedule than everyone else. And, as a result, they missed out of the playoffs. 2) If it had ended in Week 13, they would have been in the playoffs. However, (Insert lame reason) happened and now they missed the playoffs. It is not fair! Or 3) Because of the extra week, the fantasy playoff fixtures got messed up and they lost to someone who would not have even been in the playoffs. They would have won the league had it been under the old format.

I can nigh on guarantee that if you do make this change, someone will be unhappy at the end of the season. The best way to appease this is to change who makes the playoffs. So instead of having the top 6 on Win/Loss record for example you could do the top 4 on Win/Loss record and have 5th and 6th get into the playoffs on total Points For (PF) that are not in the playoffs. That negates the schedule argument and undeserving arguments. There will still be a change, but it is a fairer way of determining who should be in the fantasy playoffs.

3)   You make the Championship game a 2-week affair.

You amend nothing other than changing the final to a 2-week playoff. There are a lot of people, me included, that advocate this approach. The reason for it is you want the season to occur as normal. However, you want the final to be won on merit. And a 2-legged final is the best way to do that. Imagine all the Fantasy Football Championship games in 2020 that were decided by Alvin Kamara in one of the first games of the weekend. Whilst it should be rewarded for drafting him and getting to the final, to have that be the deciding factor in 70%+ of finals would have been harsh on the players who lost that final as a result.

I appreciate that result does not happen every year, or even most years. However, having a 2-week final still gives that player an advantage, without it being impossible to overcome. Especially for those that play in money leagues, it will make it more meaningful and more worthy as a fantasy championship.

The downfall to this is one less week of the fantasy season that people will play in unless they are in the final. Some others might object as "It's not what happens in real football". Especially with money on the line, it adds the most skill and is likely to have a worthy winner.

4)   11 Week Fantasy Season, each playoff game is 2-week matchups.

This is the most out there proposal. It means everyone plays everyone in the league once (if it is a 12-team league) and then the top 6 will all play in 2-week playoffs. The positives are that it does make the fantasy playoffs more intense and more skilful. The downside is 2-fold. First, half the league will not be playing for anything meaningful unless you create something meaningful in the losers bracket. And second- if you earn a bye, you will be sitting for two weeks. As a lot of people play to enjoy playing, missing time for 2 weeks could put people off. It is an out there format, but it does put more onus on the playoffs and having to go through a gruelling schedule to win. This is certainly a format that should be considered for cash home leagues.

There are probably many more ways to navigate the 17-game season. However, these are the four most popular scenarios I have seen out there amongst fantasy players. If you want to bounce any ideas at me or ask questions, hit me up on twitter @murf_NFL.

CHAPTER 3

10 Things You Can Do to Have a Good Fantasy Football Draft

Written by Adam Murfet

I get asked a lot as someone who has played fantasy football for 20 years and won lots of leagues, "how do you make sure you have a good draft?". Well, it is not easy. In fact, a lot of the time I walk away and think I did not have a good draft. The Scott Fish Bowl X Draft in 2020 for example. I walked away from that draft and I hated it. It just did not look good at all. And guess what, it was not!

When I look back at the drafts, I was not happy with, I can most of the time relate it to the fact I did not do enough of the below things to allow me every chance of success. To be honest, in a snake draft, most of the work is done before the draft has even begun. The outcome, for the most part, should be predetermined. By this statement, I do not mean that you should get the players you expect. What I mean by this, is that if you are prepared, you should have a good idea what is coming up, and you should be able to anticipate which players should be available in the appropriate rounds.

Ok, sometimes people throw a spanner in and select a QB high that causes a panic. Or there is an irrational run of Running Backs in the 3rd round as people are scared they are going to run out. However, most of the time, the trends are predictable.

That means, if you have done the work before the draft, you can be prepared and make the selections you kind of expect. It also means that you can potentially influence the draft and cause people to panic also.

Now, I will preface this whole segment with the age-old adage, "you cannot win your league at the draft". And this statement has never been truer today than it was 10, 15, 20 years ago. However, you can certainly lose your league at the draft. Meaning, if you do not draft well, you could really struggle to take down the title.

Draft day is the best day in the fantasy calendar. So why not enjoy it more by following these top 10 tips to ensure you crush your draft and get yourself off to the best possible start.

1)   Do some research and get some great resources from people you trust.

Can you believe it? By buying this book, you are already 1/10th of the way there to having a good fantasy draft. You bought this book because you want to win. You will probably listen to podcasts from great analysts. You will read tons of material from great people, and you will be informed and ready to crush your draft. You will be amazed at the amount of people who do not do this. Their draft will be in 2 days and they will print off Adam Rank's rankings or print off something from ESPN and expect that will be enough.

Believe it or not, you need to do some work. You might get lucky with printing off rankings one year. Maybe even a couple of years. However, it is not a sustainable model for success.

By doing research on strategy, where professionals have players ranked, what some mock drafts look like, doing mock drafts, or even just listening to and reading about the new rookies, changes in teams from 2020 to 2021 is a massive leg up on probably 50% of the people in your draft (I mean, not if you are in a hardcore league where everyone is consuming information everywhere. Or if you are in an expert's league either. But for most home leagues, this will certainly be the case).

By buying this book, and reading it, you are already ahead of half the people in your home league. Congratulations.

2) Understand your league mates and garner insight from them in league chats.

This one appears to be hard. However, it is easier than you think. For starters, it is not that tough to get the takes and opinions out of your league mates. There is a whole period of the offseason that is dedicated to help you find out what your league mates think of certain players. It is called off-season hype! And I love it!!!

First, you need to get a notebook (or use the margins of this book if you prefer). Make a list of the teams and owners. And work out what you know about them. Who do they support? Who are their favourite players? Who do they really hate? Who burned them last year and is therefore on their do not draft list ("Chris Godwin and his 4.5 PPR Points in Week 14 cost me my match-up and a chance to get into the playoffs! I'm never drafting him again!" This sort of thing). Once you have this information, then look at their previous drafts. Who did they take every year? What positions do they go for in what round? Do they go QB early? Do they go QB late? Do they go RB/RB? Or do they like a TE in the opening 4/5 rounds?

Fantasy players, for the most part, are creatures of habit. They want their favourite players, and they follow what has worked for them in the past. It makes sense. At the end of the day, it is all fun is not it. I always tease Stocks about drafting A.J. Green. He is one of his favourite players in fantasy football. I respect that and appreciate it. I loved A.J Green too; 5 years ago, when he was good and did not have the injuries. But I do not want A.J. Green on any of my rosters anymore. You cannot rely on him. Try and break those habits and safety blankets. It will lead to more success. Remember, it is more fun if you are winning.

Now, I mentioned off-season hype. This is the best bit. Make sure you have a WhatsApp group or a league chat with everyone. Then, find a bit of news on some players. And off-season hype news is the best kind of news for this. Why? Because it is not actually news at all! It is all fluff. "Denzel Mims looks 'on fire' in practice!" I mean, where is the news in that? What does it tell us? Sweet FA!

However, that is why it is so good for fantasy football. I do not want to give my opponents useful, actionable information. I do not want them to see that so and so has got hurt, unless it serves a wider purpose to me, or its months before the draft.

If you play on Sleeper, this insight is even easier to get. It comes via app notification! I do not even need to look for it. If you do not play on Sleeper, Rotoworld is also good for this. So, let us go back to Denzel Mims. I want to see where people are on Mims. He has a new Head Coach, maybe a new Quarterback, and he is a top 60 pick from 2020. So, I will just drop this "news" into the chat and say something like "ooo Mims looking good." And that is it. Do not over-sell it. And then wait for the reactions. Who are the ones citing the breakout? And who are the ones citing he is a bust because he plays on the Jets? Jot some notes.

You can probably drop this kind of information 2-3 times a week without raising suspicion (unless they have bought this book). So be selective. This is a bit like playing poker and showing your hand. You are showing either a bluff or showing you had the hand. Why do it? You are giving away a tiny bit of information, to gather a lot back. And, to paint a narrative that you might be high on a player you are not on, or vice versa. That little bit of information could give you a slight edge in the draft. If you like a player and you are not sure who else likes him, this allows you to potentially see who else is in the market for him.

This is next level stuff, but it absolutely works. If you are not doing this, maybe someone in your league has been? And when you thought you were the shark; you were the fish. Let us change that today. Go be a shark.

3)   *Throw people off your strategy and rankings. Change it up.*

If you are one of those people who was a fish based on the last point, you need to change it up. Most people going into 2020 drafts when drafting against me kept taking Buccaneers players, Robert Woods, and Quarterbacks in the 8th/9th round before I could get who they thought I wanted.

I got people taking Robert Woods in the 3rd round (too high for me despite my projection), people taking Godwin/Evans from me (I didn't have them in my WR1's so I wasn't bothered at all). And I slept on QB because of the value.

I did not go into a draft with a set RB/RB strategy, or married to getting a QB extremely late (I was grabbing Josh Allen on the 7/8 turn in some drafts). I let the board do the talking and my rankings and tiers tell me who to draft.

This allowed me to get Keenan Allen in the 5th/6th round, Brandin Cooks in the 8th round etc. And it really allowed me to be flexible with who to take.

I knew my opponents in many drafts. And I knew who was going to take a certain player where. I was able to "snipe" my opponents time and time again by getting a player I wanted, that they also wanted. If I had to take him 1 round higher to get him, so be it. That is the benefit of information and mock drafts/actual drafts.

To avoid being the fish, and be a shark, you need to do the work and practice. However, you also need to look at your trends and draft history. Do you always go Running Back in round 1? If so, are you going to get sniped for "your guy?" Or are you someone who always goes QB late, so people will also wait and thus allow a premium player to fall down the board far lower than they should go (If Kyler Murray is there in the 6th round as everyone is waiting on Quarterback, you must ask yourself if he is worth it there. He very well could be).

Do people know your favourite players? I love Mike Evans. But if I do not get him and get Adam Thielen instead, I am not bummed out at all. You can still enjoy fantasy football if you do not have your favourite players. Do not let anyone tell you different.

Now, for the extra sneaky bit. Start getting tells on others and throw people off your tracks in terms of strategy. And again, off-season hype is perfect for this. "Cooper Kupp 'looking explosive' in camp". This is a great blurb to share. You took Kupp last year. However, you realise Robert Woods is probably the man to own in that WR room. He is cheaper and has out-produced Kupp the last two years. And he still has positive Touchdown regression in his future.

So, you throw out there "my boy Kupp! Look at him go". Again, do not over-sell it. This looks completely plausible. You drafted him last year. You talked about him. So, people start to get on the hook. Maybe someone is planning to move off their strategy to "snipe" you and get their own back for last year. Excellent! You have your league mates drafting to your tune, forcing them into potential mistakes, and you can get the guy you really want at a cheaper price. Thanks!

I have been doing this for years. Somehow, after this book comes out, I am not going to be able to do it much anymore. Or everyone will be far more cynical. But that is ok. It adds to the strategy. Who wants to just leave the excitement for Draft Day? Why not have fun with the strategy weeks, months before the draft.

If you love poker, these strategic pieces will really appeal to you. Start messing with your league mates, give away false tells, and get their tells. If you nail this, you can really ruin someone's draft, cause them to make mistake after mistake, and laud it over them for years! Who would not want to do that?

4)   Follow NFL Beat-Writers on Twitter.

I talk about this a lot. However, I find people still do not do it. Or know how to do it. NFL beat-writers attend every practice (if team specific, which is the best kind), attend every presser, and know the inside track when it comes to what is "Coach Speak" and what is true news.

So, how do you find out who to follow? Well, if you search The Athletic and look at the beat writer of every team. And then follow them on twitter. This is the single best way to get information about all 32 teams. Want to know who is getting the carries during practice at Running Back? The Athletic beat writer will know. Want to know who is winning the QB competition? The Athletic beat writer will know.

They are also amazing at answering questions via tweets. Want to know an injury prognosis? Send them a tweet. If they know, they will reply and share. Greg Auman, the Athletic beat writer for the Tampa Bay Buccaneers is especially good at this.

I can guarantee you very few people are doing this in your league. However, these 32 people (sometimes more if more than 1 covers a team) have the answers to about 80% of your questions. Is it that much of a shock about James Robinson getting the job and excelling? Not if you followed the beat reporter.

At the end of the day, making good decisions is about having good information. And these people have almost all the information you need from a team perspective. And they want to get the information no one can. That is their job.

I cannot stress the edge doing this will give you. This could be the difference between taking a James Conner or James Robinson with your last pick in the draft instead of a kicker and ending up winning the league as a result.

5)   Do Rankings and Tiers, do not rely on others.

This is another one I have talked about at length. Nobody is expecting you to be an expert and project the future. Nor is anyone expecting you to become a fantasy football analyst.

The very simple way to do this, away from doing your own projections, which requires a lot more work, is to narrow down the analysts you like, and look at their rankings.

You have bought this book. Therefore, you must trust our analysis. Thank you very much! I love and appreciate you for it. However, you should not just use our rankings and tiers. You need to look at other people you trust.

Get a list of 4-6 people in the fantasy football industry you really love and look at their rankings and tiers side by side. Now, start to look at the players who are consistent in a spot. However, also look at the big discrepancies. These are the players who perhaps do not have a solidified consensus.

You can also look at Fantasy Pros and their expert consensus rankings. My rankings are part of this group. They take all the experts and throw together a consensus. However, many people draft off these so do not use these exclusively otherwise everyone will do the same thing and you lose your edge.

The clever thing to do now is to take the compiled expert rankings you have made, look at the consensus between them. And now, you look to see if you agree or disagree based on your research. "I think James Robinson is too high, so I am going to move him down below Miles Sanders". It is your rankings. You are not wrong if they are yours and you are happy.

Once you have done this, do you know what you have created? Your very own rankings. They are personal to you and unique. There will be similarities. However, there will also be some unique differences.

Now, you need to look at their points from last year, their probable points from this year, and design some tiers. That way, you can make snap decisions between where the value in the draft is. I talk about this in a lot more depth in the 2020 book.

Now you have this, do some mock drafts. See if you are happy with the results? Do you like your team? If not, then change your rankings. You will find that doing mock drafts is testing your rankings to see if it produces a reaction, an overpay, etc. This last point is extremely important as it makes your rankings battle hardened and you have tested them to ensure you are happy.

Now, you may have noticed these first five points are done before the draft. As I mentioned, the prep allows you to ensure you carry an edge and get a desirable outcome into your fantasy draft. However, you can still influence the draft, at your draft.

So here are numbers 6-10 that are reserved for Draft Day.

6)   Throw people off their game either right before or during the draft.

This one is much harder if you have never met the people you draft against and have never drafted with them before. Because, you might not have the important information you need.

However, if you play in a regular home league, or have managed to get some great information out of people before the draft. Or, you have drafted with these people before, it is time to be the master of disruption once again.

I have gone to great lengths with this. When I have done live drafts in the past, I have retold stories of extreme failures of league mates. I have started exaggerated rumours about a player before the draft that could be construed as true. I have had coasters made of a bad pick from the draft before and put them on the table for people to enjoy. I have made videos; I have shown previous draft boards.

This is all to get in the heads of those you are drafting against. Draft day is amazing. It is great fun to catch-up and enjoy being with friends and share stories. But it is also about winning a war! That is probably your goal because you have bought this book. So, it is time for the Fergie/Mourinho (look up Premier League Football Managers for this one) mind games.

Here are some tips that will help:

•   Talk about historically bad picks. "Hey, remember you picked David Johnson 1st in 2017 and he went down in the 1st Quarter of the first game, never to return. And now all these Running Backs with the first pick getting injured. Didn't you come last that year?" "Ha remember when you drafted Lev' Bell 3 days after he had opted out for the season. That was funny". Stuff like that.

•   Have your team name reference something about someone else that causes a funny/embarrassing reaction. I once called one of my teams the Red Wine Disaster Wearers after a friend of mine had red wine poured over him chatting up a girl in a bar. Someone asked me what inspired my name, and so I told the story. My mate was so flustered with his first pick he ended up attempting to take Antonio Brown, who had gone, and instead took the first name he could think off, T.Y Hilton. Who, whilst not a disaster, was a massive reach for a player who ended up WR24?

• Bring props. I told you about my coasters. But do t-shirts, printouts, bunting etc… I have heard about hundreds of stories of people messing with other players by bringing all sorts to the draft. The best one I have heard of for a long time is some people drafting in a pub and they drafted on a big projector screen visible to the whole pub. The league was going to make a day of it. So, they decided to use the projector and then spend the rest of the day in the pub. So, one fantasy owner got on the phone to the league champion's mother and managed to get about 150 different baby and toddler photos of the league champion. They then split the screen in two, running the draft on one side of the screen and running the baby pictures on the other half of the screen. So, how did the league owner manage to stop the pictures being run for 4 hours straight? He agreed to take a kicker in round 1. Truly brilliant!

• Do a running commentary of picks and get others to join. This is truly great if you want to plant seeds of doubt into people.

In truth, there are many creative ways to get at people during the draft and on draft day. Share some of your favourites with me at 5yardrush@gmail.com.

7) *Be very fluid in your draft. Do not have a defined strategy.*

I talked about this in the 2020 book a lot and on the podcast. Do not shoehorn yourself into a strategy. It will leave you with limited options, open to others working out your strategy and means you are likely to be disappointed in your draft. By allowing the draft to you, you can control the board, get excellent value in draft picks, and have a strong and deep roster.

8) *Do not bring your notes/be engrossed in your notes during the draft.*

This one is massive for me. I see a lot of people, and I did this years ago, bring cheat sheets, iPad, laptops, magazines, handwritten notes to the draft. This is giving the league a massive tell one way or the other. But it also gives away a significant advantage.

First off, you are bringing the notes to the draft because you cannot remember them/have not really prepared. This is bad because it shows the other owners that you are not prepared, and they will take advantage. Or you are showing off because you are so well prepared. Again, this tells the rest of the league you know your stuff and are more ready than ever before. Thus, giving away your advantage.

The other point is you cannot see what everyone else is doing/how they are reacting to the draft in progress. Having your rankings on your phone and checking it on your phone on your pick is not the end of the world. It is your pick. And 200 names are a lot to remember the order of. However, do not be thinking about your pick when it is not your pick. Watch the board, look at the trends. Look at what the other teams are doing. Look at their reaction to each pick. Who is bummed they missed out on Justin Jefferson in Round 2? That means they probably want a receiver next. That is valuable information. Being buried in your notes and missing that is giving away an advantage to everyone else. As they all saw it and you did not. Watch the draft, watch the players. Pick up the tells. Fantasy football is a lot like poker in that regard.

9)   *Do not go on tilt.*

This should really be covered if you follow point 7. If you miss a player you want, do not react. Just move on. There are plenty of players.

Do not go on tilt. For those of you not familiar with the term, it essentially means do not panic and go and chase the draft. You missed out on a Running Back, and so instead of drafting the best player on the board, who might be a Wide Receiver, you panic and take a Running Back who is nowhere near as good and you end up over-drafting. All because you are set on one player and therefore one position. This is a criminal move and one that will end your league season before it starts, if you let your tilting get out of hand. You should be the one to make other players tilt. If you have done the work, followed these steps, laid the groundwork, it will be them tilting, not you.

If, however, you feel like you are panicking and you do not know what to do next, do the next best thing. Refer to your rankings. I know I said do not look until it is your pick. But if you are tilting and you are floundering, regroup. Take a time out, refer to your rankings, get familiar with where you are and relax.

Yes, you will miss a few picks, and some tells. However, if you do not get back on the path of value-based drafting, you will lose this draft anyways. So, it is better to give up a few minor tells that might or might not happen, so you can execute and nail your draft. However, if you have done the work, done the mock drafts, followed this guide, you will not tilt. You will be fine.

10)   *Have fun!*

This sounds like a copout doesn't it? But I swear to you it is not. Do you know the amount of people who go to great lengths to win the draft that they get so fed up with the end of the process and do not enjoy it?

Winning is fun. But being with friends, especially after the year we have had, and doing something you all love to do, together, is special.

We all take so many things for granted. But not being able to do a live draft in 2020 really was horrible. And it looks unlikely we might be able to be in the same room and do it for 2021. Which means when you do get to draft together, do not take it for granted and have it be special.

Also, you make better decisions when you are relaxed and having fun. If you can live in the moment, do your prep work, have fun making your picks and winding up friends, you will draft better. You just will.

If you are stressed about it, worrying about every pick because you have not made the playoffs in 8 years, then you are probably going to miss out again this year.

Draft day comes once a year. Embrace it, enjoy it. But most importantly, smash it. If you do the work beforehand, you will be halfway there. You still need to navigate the season, injuries and all those other challenges. However, at least you will be on the front foot and not the back foot this year when Week One rolls around.

CHAPTER 4

10 Steps to Help You Make the Playoffs

Written by Adam Murfet

This book is starting to sound like a self-help book isn't it. Top 5 things here, top 10 things there. I guess it kind of is through it. You have bought this book because you want to win at fantasy football, or you are friends of Stocks and I and you are supporting us (thanks!).

This section is more for in season management. You do not need to pay too much attention to some of this until halfway through the season.

I wanted to write a chapter that was actionable for you during the season. So, you do not just get to Week One and never look at this book again. I wanted to ensure it could remain a living breathing in season guide.

The inspiration for this chapter was a solo podcast I did on 25th November 2020. It is titled very similar to the title of this chapter. And ultimately, it has the same tips. If you want the audio version of this chapter, go back, and listen to it.

The reason it is in the book is because it works. I have followed these principles religiously over the past few years and refining these principles. But they do turn losses into wins and wins into playoff berths.

I would say that these tips come into play from Weeks 6/7 onwards. So, without further ado, here are the top ten things you need to do to help you make the playoffs.

1)   Look at your remaining schedule and who you are playing in your league.

This does not mean much in the opening weeks of the season. However, when you have played half the league, have some meaningful stats, and should have an idea who the good teams are in your league and who is not.

The best way I do this, when I get to Week Eight onwards, is to draw a four-box grid for each team, and mark those boxes with:

- Strengths

- Weaknesses

- Bye weeks of players

- Opportunities to get an advantage

Here is an example one from one of my leagues last year. In this example, it shows the team who was my rival for the 1 seed in the playoffs.

Strengths	Weaknesses
<ul><li>Wide Receivers (Hill, Boyd, Adams, McLaurin, Shenault, Agholor)</li><li>Tight End (Jonnu Smith, Cole Kmet)</li><li>Defence (Browns and Steelers)</li></ul>	<ul><li>QB- (Trubisky, Tua)</li><li>RB- (Conner, RoJo, Fournette)</li></ul>

Byes	Where can I gain an Advantage?
Trubisky (11) Fournette/Rojo (13) Kmet (11) Hill (10), Slayton (11), Perine (10)	• Stop them gaining a viable QB as a streaming option (keep picking up best QB streamer) • Make sure a major RB streamer does not come available for them to pick up

This is a real example. I can map out how they get their wins and where their losses come from. In this league, they did secure the 1 seed but bombed out in the semi-finals as I was able to keep rotating QB and RB pickups on my roster, making it harder for them to upgrade. This ties into point three when it comes up, as to how I was able to do that.

By mapping these out for all your opponents, you can start to see how you can get a guide as to how you can win and how you can change your own destiny. This is something fewer than 5% of players will do. But it works. In the leagues where you can gain an advantage, this is the first step to changing your fortunes if you are struggling in the middle of the pack.

2)   Manage your byes. If you have late byes, get cover week in advance.

We have all done it. You get to set your lineup and you see you have 3 to 4 players on bye. The Waiver Wire run has already gone that week, meaning you have missed the top players to cover for a week. Therefore, you either accept the loss or you pick up bench fodder to put in your starting lineup, dumping usable pieces in the process. This happens at some point to most people every year.

Do you know how you avoid that? Preparation. Knowing when you have your bye weeks and stashing players a week or two in advance is a real keyway to get prepared, avoid the scenario as described above, and to avoid paying through the nose in Free Agent Acquisition Dollars (FAAB) if your league has them.

Some good ways to make sneaky roster moves is to pick up players who are on bye one week before the players who you have on bye. Not many people will pick up a player and sit them on their bench for a bye unless they offer major upside. So, you should have low competition for these players. Low competition means you can put them lower on your priority claims or bid less FAAB dollars. Plus, you have your cover.

It is remaining smart about things. If you look at the box above, you can see the above team needs Wide Receivers in Week 11 to cover byes and Running Backs in Week 13. So, you want to be getting these in for a week or two before. If you can find Week 10 bye week Wide Receivers who can sit on your bench in this scenario, that would be ideal.

Ultimately, fantasy football requires planning to be good. It requires a lot of luck too. But planning is key. Not having too many players on bye weeks is crucial. Then you only must manage with a couple of transactions. So, stay ahead of the curve and get ahead with your bye week covers and identify Free Agents with favourable matchups in the week you need them sooner rather than later.

3)   Trim your roster of dead weight, you need every roster spot.

I have already alluded to this point in point one. Most people stash players on their bench for emergencies or the hopes that a player will be good. Some people draft a bust in the third round, but because they drafted him in the third round, they cannot possibly drop him. "I can't drop James Conner, who I spent a 3rd round pick on, for James Robinson!". Err… yes you can, and probably should have done.

Here is a secret nobody ever wants to admit. Average Draft Position (ADP) and Draft Capital (what round you took a player in) mean absolutely nothing from the very second your draft ends. You will not draft again, therefore what you spent is irrelevant. Those players no longer hold any form of draft value (unless you are playing in Dynasty, then they do), because you will never judge them on their draft position. Rather, you judge them on their performances.

The most stupid thing I hear in trades every year is "I'm not trading you player X, I drafted him in the second round. You didn't even draft player Y, he was a free agent!". So! What does that matter? Let us go back to James Robinson and James Conner. Would you have refused a trade for James Robinson if you had James Conner because Robinson was not drafted? No! Robinson was a top 5 back before he was injured in Week 14. James Conner was 24th after 14 weeks.

So why do fantasy players continue to hold onto players who are producing nothing for them? Hope. That is why. "A.J Green is a potential Hall of Fame receiver; he could come good again". He COULD but he probably will not. He has not done anything of merit for a few years now due to injury. You can hope for a very long time. However, you need to be smart.

It is ok to keep high upside players on your bench. That is the whole point. But you must know their upside. If Nelson Agholor, who is so hit and miss as a fantasy option, has a great match-up the week one of your studs has a bye, then I understand why he is on your bench. There's logic and a plan to it. If you are just keeping Nelson Agholor in the hopes, he becomes a week-to-week strong play, then that is not going to pay off for you in the long term.

As you get over halfway through the season, and as you see off your bye weeks of your key players, your roster starts to carry players who are not needed. I guarantee you most players will carry a spare Quarterback and a spare Tight End and probably never play them for the rest of the season. Why? Insurance? Desperation? Why keep Cole Kmet if you have Travis Kelce? There is literally no point!

"But Murf, what if Kelce gets injured?" I hear you ask. Well, that is a good question. What if he does? Is Kmet that good that he demands a spot on the roster? Probably not. Because, after the top 3 Tight Ends, the rest are a much of a muchness. Go look at the scoring. If you lose Kelce, it doesn't matter who you get to replace him because 1) you cannot replace Travis Kelce and 2) if you get almost anyone, they will do about as well as all but 3 or 4 Tight Ends in the league. Logan Thomas was a streamable option until Week 10/11 last year and he finished at the TE3 on the year. So again, why have a backup Tight End?

The same goes for Quarterback. The only reason to have a second QB after week eight is either to match-up proof your own Quarterback (if you do not have an elite option), or because your back-up is far superior to the rest of the back-ups on the Waiver Wire. If you are in the latter camp, well then you need to ask yourself how much value there is to that. Is your back-up QB going to help you in the playoffs if your QB goes down? If the answer is no, then cut them loose.

I like to have fluid bench spots from about Weeks 8/9 onwards. People who I can cut at a moment's notice and not care. If you have ever played in a league with me, I average between 60-100 transactions a year per league. And that is because I chop and change players a lot. I cut people who end up going off. And I end up grabbing players before others who end up becoming studs on my team. I own the Waiver Wire.

I like to have a bench that is so fluid, I can stash players just out of spite. Go back to the example box under point 1. If I am playing this person later in the season, I am stashing good QB options and good RB streaming options against him for a week, to ensure I increase my chances of winning. If Taysom Hill scores 32 points on my bench, that is great! Because it means Taysom Hill does not score 32 points against me! What a great bit of insurance.

I also do this against rivals for bye weeks. Really simply, if they need a piece and are in a close match-up, I will try and pick up the pieces they need and try and stop them from getting a win. I am constantly told you cannot influence the results of rivals, but is that true? If Trubisky is going against the number 1 ranked defence in the league and I can stop my main rival for the number 1 seed from getting a better option at QB by taking the best streaming options that week and stashing them on my bench, and he loses by a handful of points, I have cost that person a win, right? It is rarely that cut and dry. However, it can happen. If I get the 1 seed on a tiebreaker or by one game, it is because I helped create the opportunity.

It is a next level strategy. However, if you become good at this, you will be amazed at how many of your "average" teams will make the playoffs.

4)   Look at the NFL schedule for weeks 14-16(17 if you play in a 17-week league). Who has favourable match-ups vs touch schedules?

You will hear a lot of talk towards the end of the season about strength of schedule (SoS). What does this mean?

Well Strength of Schedule is important to understand, as if you end up having lots of players in the Fantasy Football Playoffs (Weeks 14-16/17) with great schedules, you can end up having a good advantage and a great opportunity to top score.

Why don't we do this for the draft? Well, simply put, we do not know what teams are good and what teams are bad. Pundits think they know. But they do not know the true value of good or bad, and what it means for fantasy football.

It is safe to say that Strength of Schedule does not really become meaningful until weeks 11 onwards. Because then you have enough data to really analyse who is a good defence to target by position for fantasy purposes and who must avoid matches.

Last season, I went on for weeks for everyone to buy David Montgomery at whatever cost they could. Why? Because he was playing the easiest Running Back schedule remaining. And by some way. In Weeks 12-16 he scored 126.2 PPR Fantasy Points and was the RB1 over that time. By contract, Weeks 1-122 he scored 110.4 PPR Points. Montgomery did not just become a great Running Back overnight. He played teams with really poor run defences. The schedule opened up for him. If you bought David Montgomery over those weeks prior to Week 12, he probably won you a championship or at least a championship berth.

The Strength of Schedule will look at, and rank who the best and worst teams are at giving up points to all positions. From next season, there will be a tab for you to view this on our site from Week 10 onwards.

This matter, so that you can start to make Waiver Claims or trades based on Strength of Schedule. I will say that it is not the end all or be all. Great players will make plays and points against anyone, the same way bad players will not score many regardless of who they play. But, as you saw with David Montgomery, it can turn ok players into fantasy stars for a few weeks of the year. It is just important you end up on the right side of those rising stars and not the wrong side.

Strength of Schedule for me is more a tiebreaker when looking at players of similar skill set when making line-up decisions. For example, I have a start/sit decision between Marvin Jones Jr. and John Brown. Marvin Jones is up against the 9th worst defence at allowing Wide Receiver fantasy points (they give up the 9th the greatest number of points) vs John Brown who is up against the 2nd best defence at allowing Wide Receiver fantasy points (they give up the second least number of points). I look at that and go "OK! Marvin Jones in my flex this week".

5)   Pick up Running Back Handcuffs.

This seems slightly counter-intuitive to point 3. However, there is a reason why this is important. Running Backs are still probably the most important roster position in fantasy football. Because the scarcity of genuine league winners is real. There are not that many leagues winning Running Backs. Therefore, it is important to be ready if one of these elite backs comes down with an injury or a sickness.

It makes little to no sense to draft a handcuff at the start of the season. But as each week goes on, Running Backs take so much punishment. They are one of the most injury prone positions. Therefore, if you have Tony Pollard on your bench, and Zeke Elliott goes down, you are immediately in the position to play a strong RB1 every week whilst Zeke is out.

Mike Davis became one of the Waiver Wire darlings of 2020. Because, whilst he was only supposed to fill in for a few games, he ended up starting 13 games for the Carolina Panthers. He dropped off at the end, but he was still putting up decent, starting numbers in fantasy football.

Therefore, as bench spots open up, having these handcuffs is like holding onto a lottery ticket. It requires skill, luck, and patience. However, if a player goes down, and you are holding the winning lottery ticket for his replacement, you are probably going to end up doing very well in the playoffs. You only need to look at Damian Williams, C.J Anderson, Raheem Mostert, and Mike Davis as recent examples over the last few years of playoff winning Running Backs who would have been on almost nobody's roster after the draft.

So why not pick up a lottery ticket or two. You just never know right?

6)   Take Lineup risks. Unless you are a favourite, shoot for upside.

This one is for those of you hovering around .500 with the playoffs fast approaching. Most people tend to follow the projections on their app, play it safe, and then a close one by a handful of points because their app projected Sammy Watkins would outscore Darius Slayton, only for that not to happen.

The idea of this book is to not rely on the projections. It is to help you make smart decisions. If Slayton has the better match-up, has less competition for targets and is likely to be more involved, why start Watkins over him?

You cannot afford to play safe with line-ups when the playoff berths are on the line. You have probably played safe all year and you are hovering around .500. It means that strategy is not really working. Start to take some risks. Shoot for the guys who could score 20+ but who could also only score 3. Shoot for the moon. What is the point of starting a player who scores 7-11 points every week and you are projected to a statistical tie? You will not have the players to break the tie, and your opponent probably will. Instead, go for the player who could score 3, but who might also score 20. If that player has an average or better match-up, and is seeing more opportunity in recent weeks, then play him. Look at how many targets, not catches, he has had in his last 4 games. If the targets are there, but the catches are not, it probably means he has been covered or been unlucky. But it means the Quarterback is looking his way. So, ride that and hope it lands.

If you play the safe option, you are just readying yourself for defeat. Do not come and moan to anyone that you lost by 2.4 points because you left a 22-point Wide Receiver on your bench. If you had the visibility to see how he could get to 22 points (and you must have done, because he is on your bench), then you need to ask yourself why you did not start him. Learn, and move on.

Do not lose due to apathy or laziness. If it does not work, at least you went down swinging.

7) *Use season averages to see projected scores.*

People rely on projected scores in their apps too much. And it makes sense because it is easy. But they are rarely right. They are projections after all.

A really quick way to see where you are is to look at all your players and work out their projected averages based on their season to date. John Brown has 150 points over 10 games played, meaning he is averaging 15 Points per Game (PPG). I bet his projection in the app is 11/12. Why? IF you use your own players PPG and work out your opponents, you get a much clearer view of where you stand.

This advice is not full proof. You still have variance available. However, it is probably more accurate than the projections you are looking at. And it is based on real metrics and numbers, not hypothetical projections.

If your projected scores are close, but when you look at season PPG totals for each player, and see that if the average plays out, you are going to lose by 10-12 points, probably best to take some risks. If the opposite happens and you average out all the players and are expected to win by 10-12, then you can play more cautiously. At least you have a process and reason for your method. And it is not hard to work out. The formula is total points / number of games played. Simple enough.

8) *Play mind games. Start posting messages in group chats and putting opponents off.*

This has been covered off a bit with the draft tips, but it applies mid-season as well. Mentioning "news" that players are coming back from injury or who have mysteriously landed on the injury report can force fantasy owners to add some additional cover off the Waiver Wire, and maybe drop a useful piece in exchange. It could force line-up changes. It could do so much.

Do what you can to cause panic. It is part of the game. Do it too often and you will lose the effect of this. Do not do it enough, and you will fall behind the trend and others will beat you to the punch. Get this right, and people will take you seriously and it will throw them off their game. That is an edge you are creating.

If nothing else, it paints the picture you are really on top of things and therefore people will not try this on you. Because, if you are posting most of the breaking news and injury stuff, the feeling will be you are 1) taking this seriously and therefore you are going to be a formidable opponent this season. You can therefore live in their head rent free for a while. And 2) when you want to pull a loose thread and spin it into bigger news than it is, you have earned the credibility to tell a slight exaggeration. You can also walk it back and say you got it wrong. If you post 15 things right and 1 thing wrong, the game will not be up, unless they read this book.

9) Interact with 5-yard Rush plus others for ideas and group think.

The best way to make a possible decision, whether that's trade, waiver claims, starts and sits, whatever, is to have as much information as possible. The best way to do this, talk to us, and others. The more you group think an idea, the more validation you get for that idea. Information is power. Make sure you harness it and use it to make the right decisions more often than not. Remember, making the right decision 60% of the time in fantasy football will probably yield a playoff berth and a winning record. Unless your wrong decisions were catastrophic.

10) Follow beat reporters. Be the first person with the information and out work your league.

Once again, this is another point I mentioned in the draft chapter. But just because the draft is over, it does not mean the work has stopped. If anything, by Week 8, unless you are sitting on 2 wins or less, or 8 wins, you are very much in the period where whoever works the hardest and smartest will probably make the playoffs. It is as simple as that. Therefore, follow the beat reporters and get the information before everyone gets the NFL.com or Sleeper alert. Do not leave anything to chance. If it is on NFL.com or on Sleeper, assume your league probably knows or are about to know. Having a thirty-minute advantage could mean you can pick up a replacement off free agency before someone else even sees the news.

If you follow all ten of these steps, you will massively increase your chances of making the playoffs. Try it this season in your home league and see.

CHAPTER 5

How to Avoid Being in Too Many Leagues this Season

Written by Adam Murfet

Here we are, at the start of 2021. I am writing this chapter just eight days after my Tampa Bay Buccaneers have been crowned World Champions in Super Bowl LV. I am already seeing many people inviting me into new dynasty start-ups and new leagues already. The season is 7 months away.

I did cave in and joined one. The league had too many fun friends for me not to join. But that will be in for dynasty start-ups for me this year.

Due to lockdown and COVID last year, people were going crazy for drafting, it was something to do. People got massively excited. So much so, that people massively over-committed themselves. People loved the draft aspect but struggled to manage 10/20/30 or even the 50 plus teams they drafted.

This led to so many people dropping out of leagues either mid-season or after the season, many dynasty start-ups being very dead for action throughout the year, as people were over committed, or people just not being active. None of these scenarios are cool or fair on league-mates. I left several dynasty start-ups this offseason that were drafted last year because people did not put the time and energy into them, meaning they were not that fun or exciting. A lot of people also treated these like a redraft league, and I would have months without a trade response. That is just not fun or fair.

As the UK remains in lockdown and will probably do so until just before this book is released, how do we all stop getting into too many leagues.

Most people think the answer is easy. Mock draft. The problem with that is mock drafts are boring. It is typically against a computer or random people, and they are not massively realistic. People make a silly pick, and it ruins the whole draft.

Therefore, I am on hand to provide you with two very workable solutions to ensure you can still have all the fun of drafting, without any of the rubbish of maintaining too many leagues come August/September.

1) *Play in or start-up some Best Balls.*

What is Best Ball? It is a draft only league? You complete your draft and then you just watch the results. Typically, these are point leagues and the highest scoring players on your roster get put into the active spots. It is all automated, meaning there is literally no management from after the draft.

There are no waivers, no trades, no lineup setting, nothing. You draft and then you are done.

What are the benefits?

It is still competitive. It is still a league with 1 winner and 7/9/11/13/15/19 losers. There is a league table based on cumulative points. You can still do prizes, commit cash to a pool, forfeits for losers etc because it can all be hosted on a platform.

And, once your draft has ended, that is essentially the end of your commitment. You can log in once every couple of weeks to see how you are getting on. You can post on a league board, boast about picks, and mock others. But you do not need to do anything other than that.

It is also great practice for the real draft season. I do about 50 of these best balls during the offseason. It means come July, I have done a lot of prep and have had a lot of draft experience. It is effectively like pre-season for me. I do a few drafts, gather some data, look at what is going on from an Average Draft Position (ADP) perspective and I start to know player values and where I can expect to see players come off the board. It is great practice and a great time killer in the offseason. It also keeps fantasy football alive all year round for me.

What is the downside?

The first is the platforms available to do these one. The only 2 platforms that do this kind of format for free entry are My Fantasy League (MFL) and Fantrax. Both are platforms that require some getting used to from a draft and usability perspective. They do require some patience and perseverance that some people just will not put up with.

To explain to those in the US who are reading this book, most people in the UK draft from their smartphones. They rely on slick and smart apps to draft. A minority will draft from a laptop unless it is a live draft. For timed, slow drafts, expect most picks to come via Smartphone.

Neither of these platforms have slick mobile apps or sites, meaning the experience can be clunky. However, if you can overcome these, then that is fine.

There is the ability to use an API to get the results from sleeper and draft in there. However, that requires management, and manually checking and sorting results. If you plan to do this for a league, it is a lot of work just to have a nicer draft experience. There are some places where you can buy sheets to help, but it is still slightly labour intensive. And if you are not looking for that, maybe stick to the above options.

The second is draft fatigue. I am not going to lie, when August comes around, I am almost on draft autopilot and the drafts become a lot less fun. Especially when it comes to just online, slow drafts. If the chat is slow, and the draft is slow, it is not as much fun. Last season I did close to 125 drafts and drafted every day from March until September. Signing up for too many Best Ball drafts is another problem. However, doing one every couple of weeks or less is certainly fine. Have a nice slow clock and a good, lively chat room.

2)   Do Mock Drafts with friends or league-mates.

Mock drafts can be fun. You all need practice, right? So why not do a few together. You can do live ones and simulate the draft day experience, get on a zoom, and have a few beers. Or you can get creative with mock drafts and do formats you have never tried like Auction or Superflex. At the end of the day, it is just practice.

This option is massively underutilised in my opinion. People hate it as its just practice. But why not make it fun. You can control the other elements of this. It is entirely down to you and the group you bring along to do this.

You can even use a draft analyser like those on Fantasy Pros to see which of you won and which of you lost, with a forfeit for the loser and a prize for the winner. The ceiling is only limited by your creativity, or lack of it. If you need any ideas about how to jazz up a mock draft- email me 5yardrush@gmail.com. You never know, we might even join you in one, whether it is myself, Stocks or one of the writers. Make it interesting and we might just do it!

At the end of the day, the amount of people who bailed on leagues or did not give the league the right time or attention absolutely sucked. Too many of my friends who are commish's did not have the best of years last year due to the lack of activity.

For the first time in my life, I understood the value of entry fees more than ever. It forces you to commit and be more a part of the league if you commit your own money to it. Personally, I do not like to play for money. I play for the fun and skill of it. And I would prefer to leave money out of it. Which is why 5 Yard Rush puts on free leagues. However, those that do not take our leagues seriously risk no entry the following year.

I am genuinely pleased we easily had a 99% participation rate in our leagues as a result. They were challenging, hard, and good fun.

So, this year, decide in advance how many leagues you can handle, set a hard count, and stick to it. Use Best Ball's and mock drafts to scratch your itch, not real leagues, if you cannot commit to them. Do not be that person who lets down everyone else because you are over-committed. Instead, find new ways to get your fix. I respect people a lot more if they turn me down for leagues, than if they accept and do not give it their best effort. Nobody will ever hold it against you for turning them down. I guarantee it.

So, do not oversubscribe and just draft instead.

CHAPTER 6

The Impact of COVID-19 on Fantasy Football

Written by Adam Murfet

COVID-19 has changed the world forever. For what has been a shocking and unimaginable twelve months or so at best for some of us, and a truly unforgettable and painful twelve or so months for others, it has left a truly lasting impact on our lives.

Wearing masks, keeping away from crowds, not taking for granted time with loved ones are all impacts that have been made on our everyday lives.

But what about Fantasy Football? At the time of writing this, many of us are still awaiting our vaccinations to keep us safe from COVID-19. However, we do expect there to be a season to be played in 2021. What is likely to occur, in terms of offseason schedule and routines, no one is sure currently.

However, the one thing I can assure you is just like our lives, the NFL, and in particular, fantasy football will have changed forever because of this pandemic.

So, I thought I would expand on a couple of thoughts of what has changed from 2020-2021 and focus on some of the ways fantasy football might have changed forever. Or, at the very least, recommend some changes to the way it is played now. Most of this will be relevant more for redraft leagues, however it might also carry over into dynasty, depending on the rules in place in your league. Dynasty is a lot more personal and has a lot more rules and safeguards built in that redraft does not. Hence why this chapter is taken more from a redraft point of view.

1)   Injured Reserve (IR) Spots.

For the most part, it seems that most leagues do not allow IR spots in redraft. Or, if they do, it is limited to one spot at most. I understand the thinking of this. Due to the nature of redraft, with an 8-week IR, it was rare that an exceptional player would go down injured and possibly make a return. This means, if this happened to you, like say a Michael Thomas this year, you would get a roster spot opening up that perhaps others might not. Therefore, it was deemed unfair by many to offer IR spots in redraft.

I understand this line of thinking. 100%. However, I do think a couple of things might now change in the NFL, which will make it more applicable to have an IR spot than ever before.

For those of you not familiar with IR spots, they are usually designated for players who land on the official Injured Reserve List in the NFL. In order to go on the Injured Reserve List, it meant that you were going to be out of action for at least eight weeks, with your injury potentially being season ending.

That meant a player could go down in Week One with an injury, be out for eight or nine weeks and be scheduled to return off IR by Week Nine at the earliest. However, they might not come off until Week Ten, or Week Fourteen, or even Week Sixteen. So, as I mentioned previously, if you had a stud that went on IR, you could hold on to them by stashing them on IR. If they were out for six weeks and did not go on the official Injured Reserve list, you could not move them into an IR spot.

However, in 2020, the league moved to a three-week Injured Reserve timetable. This was mostly for those who had COVID to start. However, it was also used for injuries. Then, an official COVID- Injured Reserve List happened that was separate from the original IR. This was to give teams extra roster flexibility in terms of bringing players in.

It is safe to say that the 3 Week IR was very popular with teams and coaches. So much so, that I do expect it to be a thing in the league moving forward.

Having a 3 Week IR means more players are likely to end up on it, and therefore having an IR spot or two in leagues from next season makes sense. It is no longer going to be a function that only a few owners in leagues will use. Instead, it will be used by almost everyone (unless you escape the curse from the injury fantasy football gods). So, moving forward, having 1-2 IR spots makes a lot more sense than it ever did.

In 2021, it might still make sense to have additional IR spots to what you would normally have. The United States is far vaster and has far more people than the United Kingdom. Not every adult is likely to get vaccinated in 2021. And maybe most NFL players might. But their families and friends are unlikely to get the same treatment. Therefore, do not be shocked if COVID close contacts and isolations are still required in 2021 by the league. They might not be needed at all. But it is better to be prepared and have extra spots when you set it up, than to get caught short and not be able to put players on IR due to COVID.

2)   Fantasy Commissioners need to update their rules and be more robust.

This season has taught us to take nothing for granted. You cannot assume that the rules you put in place in 2016 or earlier are still a good fit today. The game has changed, and, more importantly, the landscape has changed. If your commissioner has not updated the rulebook in a few years, it is time to approach them and get it updated.

Your league rules need to be more flexible. Trying to guess potential outcomes and preparing rules for it is tedious and means there are a lot more pointless rules that reduce the flexibility of the league.

The need for a backup plan in case games are called off is essential. This could still happen due to weather, natural disaster etc. so if you do not have a contingency plan in case a game or two gets called off, then you should probably do that. I do not think a "well tough luck" approach should apply in circumstances that could not be foreseen. Having a backup plan should be top of the things added to your rules for 2021 and beyond.

The easiest way to do this is just by having a nominated back-up player clause. That means should a game get called off due to COVID, weather, natural disaster, a player can be nominated to come off the bench. If you use sleeper, you can ask players to nominate by using player nicknames. Take a screenshot of all the rosters before kick-off, and you are good to go if the unthinkable happens.

It is a very simple thing to put in, but one your league-mates will be forever grateful for. It takes the stress out of most situations and means you will not have a ton of bickering coming your way should the worst happen.

If you are not on sleeper, try using Google Forms. If you miss the deadline and do not do it, then tough.

The other thing fantasy commissioners should do is add a clause allowing them to make a change to the rules or make a ruling for "the best interest of the league".

There are going to be some things that cannot be foreseen. You need to trust your commissioner to make the best decisions for the league. If you do not you probably need to question why you are playing in that league.

This clause should not be abused. It is purely for the purpose of dealing with situations that could not be seen ahead of time. There is no way we could anticipate all the different things that can happen. Therefore, having a clause or rule like this is vitally important. If COVID-19 and 2020 has taught us anything, it is to expect the unexpected.

3) Expect more drafts to happen online and potentially with a slow draft element.

As we have had these uncertain times pressed upon us, many people are now weary of travel or being able to do something for hours at a time without disruption.

It is very hard to expect people to draft at home if they have families, especially young children. Therefore, finding one night that works for everyone, if live drafts are still not an option, could mean it is very difficult to get an evening where everyone can make a draft.

Also, COVID-19 has changed people's priorities and re-shaped the way people do things. For some, the desperation to draft will be greater than ever. For others, it might be much lower down the priority list. They still want to play and be part of the league but dropping everything for the draft is just not as much an option or priority anymore. These are all possible outcomes, and league-mates will need to be sensitive to this. Therefore, talk about all options weeks and months in advance. Listen to all the options and agree as a consensus. There is nothing stopping a live draft meet-up for those who want to do it, with those who are worried to join a zoom call remotely.

There is nothing wrong with a slow draft with maybe an opening night draft get together for those who want to still do things the more traditional way.

At the end of the day, leagues are sacred. Especially those home leagues. Do not kick people out or be unsympathetic because they have spent the better part of eighteen months inside, and their world has changed. Bring these issues to a head weeks/month in advance and try and find a way to accommodate everyone.

Believe it or not, the best drafts I have ever done have been done exclusively online. The pranks were flowing, and the chat was better than ever. Do not fear change. Embrace it. And you can still do meetups for those who want to do things more old-school.

4) Preseason games will probably see fewer starters than ever.

The NFL has no preseason games in 2021. And what happened? The league survived. The league did not get off to the slow start that many expected. Quite the opposite. There was a ton of fireworks in Week One with a renewed excitement for players to get to work.

What does that mean going forward? Well, for 2021, we are not even certain, at time of writing, that we will even have preseason. However, for future years, there will certainly be, if there is not any preseason 2021. Typically, you would only see starters in the second and third preseason games. The time they play in the preseason seems to get shorter and shorter every year.

Instead, preseason is effectively a time to evaluate those on the roster bubble. Those 5th-7th round draft picks, undrafted free agents, and those who were on the fringes of the 53 man roster the year before.

What does this mean for fantasy? Well, it will mean less and less every year as this trend continues. In the end, it will eventually end up that all pre seasons might tell us is the order of the depth chart. But it will not give us too much insight in terms of who is looking good or who is going to threaten starting jobs.

A lot of this is conjecture. I could be completely wrong. However, having seen teams get away with no preseason and survive, it seems less likely we will glean much if any useful information going forward. Except for whom the back-up Running Back is likely to be, should the starter go down.

5)   *The use of more Flex spots.*

In all honesty, if you are still playing in a league with one flex spot, and you hate it, this is now the time to force a change! 1 flex spot is unnecessary and reduces the skill level of the league. It also means you can start more players. Who is not up for playing more players in their line-ups!

Flex spots mean more creativity, more strategy, and believe it or not, more flexibility. Shocking I know! In a year of uncertainty, with more injuries and last minute lineup changes required than ever before, those flex spots made it easier to set a lineup.

Therefore, if you are in need of freshening up your league, add more flex spots. Every league should have a 2 minimum for flex spots. It makes the game more exciting, less predictable and means there many more different combinations to master and win with.

I cannot champion this enough. If you do not believe me that playing with an extra flex or two is more fun, try it for a year? What is the worst that can happen? You hated it and therefore you changed it back. The whole reason we play fantasy football is because we love playing with our favourite players. So why limit the amount we can play with. When instead, we can expand it and enjoy it even more.

Worried about your knowledge? Guess what, it will expand your knowledge of players. Red Zone is more fun when you are rooting for players like Josh Reynolds or Scotty Miller to come down with the ball in the End zone. It shows some love to more and more players. And allows you to expand your knowledge of NFL rosters. You will finally learn the WR3s on almost every team, as well as even a few of the backup TEs and RBs.

If 2020 has taught us anything, it is that we can all be doing a little bit more fun in our lives. So, spice it up with a flex spot or two. You will not be disappointed.

These are all things I can see changing the game of Fantasy Football forever. Some people and leagues already do some or all these things. And that is great. However, it is very much in the minority.

All leagues need a refresh as we head into 2021. And therefore, now is the perfect time to update. To react to what has happened and make changes. Did some of the rules and uncertainty make 2020 less fun for playing fantasy football for you? Then be at the forefront of change in your league and make some changes now.

These suggestions and probably changes for most leagues will not only make them fairer. They will make them more fun, for the most part. And really, when it comes to fantasy football, it should be exactly that. Fun.

If you are unsure of any of these changes, or you want to discuss them in more detail before you implement, then please do shoot me an email to 5yardrush@gmail.com. And if you experience resistance to change from the commissioner, show them this book. If that does not convince them, speak to league-mates and garner support that way. Remember, you are only trying to make your league more fun. Where is the harm in that?

CHAPTER 7

The Top 10 Mistakes Fantasy Players Make When Preparing for the New Season

Written by **Adam Murfet**

I have been wracking my brains around this chapter for a while. I posted this question to the other writers of 5 Yard Rush in our WhatsApp group (thanks chaps for all the insight, input, and support), to a varying degree of fantasy players with different skill levels and observing or pouring through around 200 previous drafts over the last 2 years.

This list is not exhaustive. However, these seem to be the most common trends amongst fantasy players of all skill levels based on research of over a couple hundred drafts and my experience of 20 plus years playing fantasy football.

And so, without further ado, here are the Top 10 mistakes made my fantasy players year after year.

1)   *Ranking fantasy players purely on last year's points total.*

I would say honestly that many players will look at the previous season leaders and use that as their number one piece of research. Because 1) It is easy to find and 2) It seems to be the most relevant as it is the most relevant data.

Let me dispel both of those myths. First, it is easy to find. But is it any easier than buying this book or looking at more informed current rankings based on new information by your favourite analysts? I do not think so.

Now, is it the most relevant data? No! Because circumstances have changed. Players have been signed, players have been let go, coaches have moved on. Each of the thirty-two teams will have changed since last season.

Last year's data is important. As is the previous three years' worth of data. But for it to be the only thing you rank on? That will lead to some of the biggest mistakes you can ever make in fantasy football. Why? Because you will be buying all these players at their ceiling. Because most players do this. But how many players truly repeat as a top player year after year? The answer is not a lot.

Looking at the last 5 years of historical data for half point PPR scoring, I looked at the top 6 QBs and TEs as well as the top 12 RBs and WRs over the past 5 years. Only 1 player out of the entire data set finished as a top finisher at their position in all five seasons. That was Tight End Travis Kelce.

Finishing 4 out of 5 was Tight End Zach Ertz, and Wide Receivers Davante Adams, Julio Jones, Michael Thomas, DeAndre Hopkins, Mike Evans, and Julio Jones.

There are some honourable mentions to QB Deshaun Watson who has been a top 6 QB the last 3 years after his rookie season, as well as Patrick Mahomes who has been top 6 2 of the 3 years, he has been a starter, with one injury plagued year in between. Also, Josh Allen has been in the top 6 for the two years since his rookie year.

I bring this up because it is incredibly difficult to sustain success. So, taking one year into isolation could really lead you to buying players at their ceiling. Therefore, look at historical data and price guys accordingly.

Also, circumstances and situations change. Head Coaches and coaching staffs leave, and new ones get appointed. Players get traded. It is very hard to survive and thrive through all the change. And 99% of players do not. There is that 1% of players who do. These guys are the elite, The best of the best.

You can find the data in the back of the book in the appendix.

2) *Drafting players with High Touchdown Numbers.*

This one is such a common mistake. Fantasy players look for Wide Receivers, Tight Ends, and Running Backs with a high number of Touchdowns last year.

Touchdowns are situational. They are almost random. They are difficult to predict and difficult to rely on. We see all the time players going from 8-10 Touchdowns to just 2-3 the following year. That is not to say the player is any worse than they were in the previous year. It is just the circumstance and situation has changed significantly. Injuries, a poor conversion rate in the Red zone, schedule, defensive scheme, game situations all prove to be huge factors in who gets the ball for Touchdowns. Therefore, chasing players with high Touchdown totals do not make a ton of sense.

What you should do, as a fantasy player, is search for those with a high number of targets, but a low number of Touchdowns. In 2019, Robert Woods had just 1 receiving Touchdown off over 120 targets. That number is extremely low. So low that it was bound to positively regress back to the mean. In 2020 he scored 6, which was the difference on him being a WR1 in 2020 when he was a high end WR2 in 2019. Robert Woods' ADP was the late 4th, early 5th in 2020, and he outperformed it in spades.

The Wide Receivers who are due the "Robert Woods Touchdown Bump" in 2021 if their targets remain relatively consistent are:

- Robby Anderson- 136 targets- 3 Touchdowns
- Terry McLaurin- 134 targets- 4 Touchdowns
- Cooper Kupp- 124 targets- 3 Touchdowns
- Jerry Jeudy- 113 targets- 3 Touchdowns

Inversely, players who will see their Touchdown numbers come down in 2021 are:

- Davante Adams- 18 Touchdowns
- Tyreek Hill- 15 Touchdowns
- Adam Thielen- 14 Touchdowns

Do not buy players at their absolute ceiling. They will disappoint you time and time again. Therefore, it is always best to buy players at the lowest point, on the way up, or players who are being undervalued by the market, for whatever reason.

This form of strategy will give you a bigger chance of success in 2021 and beyond. So please, stop chasing Touchdowns.

3) *Overlooking Consistency.*

One of my best friends in the Fantasy Football Industry is a guy called Bob Lung. We call him Mr. Consistency. That is because he writes the book, literally, every year. It is called the Consistency Guide and it is terrific. It is one of the tools I use most every year.

Truth be told, people overlook consistency. A lot of it comes down to chasing previous high levels of performance that cannot be obtained every year. However, I think people struggle to analyse performance on a regular basis.

In the appendix section of this book, and the 2020 version of the Fantasy Football Playbook, I have attached a consistency raw numbers guide. These data points tell you players in the top of their position, and how many MVP Games (top 5 points average scoring weeks) Solid games (average points total for positions 6-24 [18 for Tight Ends]) or Bust games (below the average 24th placed [18th placed for Tight Ends] score).

I want to know how people compiled their points. Were they steady and consistent? Or did they have a rollercoaster season. I am never interested in getting people who flash and score big just 2-3 times a game but bust over 50% of the time. Can you trust those people in your lineup week to week? I cannot.

However, most fantasy players will just focus on the total points. That will not help you if they go missing in a close week against an opponent and you lose by a few points. When you do your tiers, consistency should be part of the makeup. You need to dig deeper to see how the players made up their points.

Lucky for you, I have done most of the work for you. Just flip to the appendix and look for the consistency data. If you have bought this version, but did not buy last years, feel free to ask me for the data for 2020. I will share it with you.

Consistency should not just be a tiebreaker. It should go into your decision-making process and help you shape your tiers. It is much more worthwhile to take someone who has more solid games, but less MVP and less bust games than someone who only flashes a handful of times a year. To use an English football analogy, I would rather someone consistently get the shot on target from 25 yards and test the keeper, than someone who will put it in the top bins once or twice a year, but then send it skywards over the bar on every other attempt. View consistency the same way.

4)   *Players do not do enough prep.*

This is a strange one to read I bet. Because you have bought this book. You are probably a fantasy football obsessive. You devour podcasts, do mock drafts, play in a ton of leagues and live, eat, sleep, and breathe fantasy football.

I get it! I am one of those people also. Hence why I am writing another book about it. However, you will be surprised by the amount of people who just do not do any prep.

The typical player will start to think about their home league fantasy draft just a few weeks before. They probably do not bother listening to podcasts. Instead, they focus more on looking at last year's notes, looking at the league from last season, noting who the top performers were, and probably look at some form or magazine or make some printouts from an online draft kit.

They probably have not bothered to look at historical data. They probably have not bothered to do any mock drafts. These players probably do not even know who half the rookies are.

This is such a common mistake. Players who do not do a lot of prep rely on their knowledge, experience, and previous year's draft plans to carry them through. I have seen someone win a league by a long way, so decided to enact the exact same plan. Only, the landscape had changed, and it was not going to work.

These are the same owners who take a player in round one, lose them to injury, blame their losing season on that one injury, and do the exact same thing next year. We all probably know someone who does this year after year. These are the people that you need to exploit.

I can tell you are not one of those people. And that is because you are reading this book. You are looking to get an edge. You are one of the bright shining lights who is looking to win every year. You listen to podcasts, create tiers, pick up little hints and tricks and use it to improve.

Therefore, your mission, as someone who is working to win, is to find the people in your draft who are not clued up. If you can identify those that have not done the homework or prep, you can feed them some information and really put them in a bind. There is nothing better than working out where everyone is at the start of the draft in terms of their prep and knowledge and using this to your advantage. Find those that are holding on to their magazines or draft kits. Those who are scrambling because they expected to take Keenan Allen in the 5th round like last year, and he went in the third. Use their lack of prep to your advantage.

The one consistent trait for those who did not do enough prep is that they never ever blame their lack of prep as the reason they did not win. It will always be the injury to a player, or they had a harder schedule than everyone, or that they were unlucky every week as they came against a monster every week. This happens in most leagues. Guess what? The lack of prep was easily the biggest factor.

Think back to leagues you did not do well. Why didn't you do well? You listened to the podcasts, you read the books. Why did it go wrong? I am willing to bet, if you are honest with yourself, you probably over prepared and went into autopilot. Am I right?

5) Over preparing.

This one also happens a lot. And I know what you are thinking. How can I over prepare? Well, it's very simple. When you do too many drafts, and have read all the materials, you forget to do the other things that make you successful in a draft.

You end up building an unconscious bias of who to draft, because you have done so many drafts. You basically appear to draft on autopilot. You know where players come off the board, so you do not pay attention to what other players are doing? You end up drafting teams that are extremely like the other teams you drafted. You ended up drafting 7 teams and you got Ronald Jones on 6 of those 7, because he was there in the 5th round and you needed a Running Back.

You end up with similar Quarterbacks, similar Running Backs. You have Joe Mixon on 4 of your 7 teams. And then he goes down and that is your season.

It happens to everyone. You become too robotic you are barely thinking when you draft. This is over preparation. You need to take every single draft in isolation of all the other drafts you have done. You know the prices and roughly where people will go. However, that does not mean you should do the same thing every time. If it were that automatic, you would not need humans to play fantasy football.

By being present in every draft, you will naturally diversify your rosters. Because you will be trying to block other opponents. You will be looking at where the value falls. You will be taking calculated risks versus taking the same players all the time.

The preparation allows you to be comfortable for several different draft scenarios. You have been working and preparing for each draft. However, do not let your preparation turn into complacency. Because if you go into autopilot, or adopt draft fatigue, you will make critical errors which will yield to roster mistakes. This will mean that all the research and preparation will have been for nothing. As it would have been entirely counterproductive.

So, strike a balance. Do the preparation. Acquire the knowledge. However, be present in the draft so you can execute on your plan and put all your preparation to good use. Otherwise, you have lost more than those who did not prep. You lost time, and hope. And you do not want to be losing either.

6) Following what others are doing too much in the draft and forgetting your own plan.

This one is tied into the other two previously mentioned. It is all about balance. However, sometimes, we want to get one over a rival, or the champ. So, we anticipate their next move and "snipe" them, to try and put them on tilt. However, by doing this, you end up taking a player who does not really help you, who perhaps was not good value at the selection, and you missed out on a true value in the round.

I see this happen 2-5 times a draft on average. It is a bold strategy. However, it also blows a torpedo sized hole into your own roster construction. People always fear the champion repeating. They work on trying to torpedo their draft.

You need to focus on your own draft. You should watch what they are all doing. You should anticipate their moves. You can even "snipe" them if the value is right. However, do not go reaching to take a guy that is not going to help you. The most common reaches are RB3's and WR2's. This is where you can really get punished. QB2's when they are trying to get a QB1 is also common. Why take a player you do not need, just to spite another player, for very minimal gain. It is good to be prepared and good to watch what everyone is doing. Better than good in fact. However, if you spend too much time focused on other players' strategy and less on your own, it could come at your own detriment.

You need to be very careful. However, you can still play the game. There is nothing stopping you getting another league-mate taking the player you think the champ, or anyone is about to take. This is the best bit of drafts. Get others to do your bidding.

You can always stir the pot in the background. Tip other players' hands and get them to snipe said player for you. There are plenty of ways to be effective without torpedoing your own draft. So, make that your play going forward this season. Focus more on what is going on, use it to your own draft advantage, and help your fellow league-mates out whilst enacting your plan. Some people might disapprove when it all comes out (and trust me, it will come out). However, that is the game. We all play this game for the strategy, skill, and tactical side of it. However, we all play this game because we love to win. So, do not hurt your chances to win due to revenge or any other agenda. Let others do that for you.

7) Drafting on FOMO (Fear of Missing Out) instead of drafting on value.

This happens every year. The run on a position group happens. This means you quickly follow on the train instead of going in another direction due to Fear of Missing Out (FOMO). FOMO in drafts is real. You follow the pattern of the board. Your research goes out of the window and you completely forget about everything else you are doing. Because you are worried a certain position group is not going to get back to you. You therefore reach for a position group, such a Running Backs in round 3, because you get serious FOMO.

Every year, the positions that get overdraft are Running Backs in Round Three, and Tight Ends in the middle rounds. People start to see them flying off the board and therefore worry about missing out. That is when FOMO kicks in. The panic sets in and rational thought goes out of the window.

All the data in this book, with regards to consistency analysis, the value of positions per round, the Points Against Streaming metric, all tell you not to overdraft. We have done all the work for you and taken the research out of the equation for you. You just need to look at the data in this book, take a deep breath, and focus on your tiers and your plan.

Do not panic if there is a run on a position. This is always going to happen. It happens in every single fantasy football draft. Expect it, anticipate it, and get ahead of it. You have done the research and you are prepared for this to happen.

Now you look at the value of the players left in your pick slot. If a player of that position group is there, and it's good value, then pull the trigger. However, if, because of the run, and other people's FOMO, a Wide Receiver stands out as a screaming value, take the best player available and pull the trigger. It really is that simple. This FOMO is why Keenan Allen and Stefon Diggs fell even lower than they should have gone. They were marked down for ambiguous situations, which was fair. But they went even later than what was warranted due to these position runs. People's FOMO kicked into hyper drive, meaning people overpaid for mediocre talent.

Do not be that person. If the value is there to take a player that the position has had a run on, then fine. However, take a deep breath and see if there is a better value on the board. Work out the opportunity cost of zagging when everyone is zigging.

Do not be rushed into a decision. Also, do not worry about being different. Follow your research, follow your tiers. And, most importantly, follow the advice and data outlined in this book. If you do that, you will be in a greater position to win, and capitalise.

8)   *Fantasy players who do not create their own tiers.*

I have already touched on this one about being underprepared. However, this is a very specific point on this. People who use other expert tiers, like my friend Adam Rank's for example, are doing it wrong. It is right to consult these and take these into consideration. However, you need to create your own tiers. The reasons for this are twofold.

1)   Adam Rank is not in your league. Instead, he is offering a rankings and tiers perspective for all scoring and league formats. If your league has custom scoring or does something slightly different from normal, then Adam's tiers and ranks will not be as accurate. Because he is not a mind reader.

2)   Lots of people read Adam Rank's rankings and tiers. If you get spotted just following his list, they will work out what you are doing. Therefore, you will just end up giving the other players your draft strategy. They will know before you, what you are doing. You will be giving your league-mates the advantage.

Therefore, it is imperative that you do your own tiers. I have already talked about how to do this in this book. However, even if you are not great with spreadsheets and data, just at least combine a few experts' rankings and tiers. If you have multiple sources, and merge them all together, that will at least be better than just using one person. However, try and do your own where possible. You will benefit a lot more.

This does seem like a cop-out and like I am asking you to do some work. However, if you want to win, you need to put the work in. It is as simple as that. Besides, you want to win because you bought this book. Stocks and I have done a lot of the work for you. However, you will need to apply some of these methods, do some of your own work, and create your own plan to become successful. We are just here to offer advice, inside knowledge, and a blueprint for success. You will need to fill in the blank. Think of this book, and any fantasy football resource as your toolkit. However, you are the one that needs to use the tools to build your roster. No other fantasy expert will be in the draft room with you. Therefore, you are the one who needs to construct the plan.

We are here to help you succeed. However, it is your plan and therefore you are the one that should get the credit and the rewards at the end of the season when you are lifting the championship trophy. You are not going to put mine and Stocks' name on the trophy, are you? And nor should you. You did the work. We just assisted.

9)   Having too many "my guys".

This one is a personal bugbear of mine. Having a list of "my guys" is the number one sure fire way to overpay for players and leave you in real trouble at the end of your drafts. There is a typical draft saying that is "go get your guys!". At the end of the day, it's your game and your roster. If you want to do it, and you will have fun that way, then absolutely do it.

However, if you have grand designs about winning your league, sometimes you need to forget about your "guys". If you walk into a draft hell bent on getting 4 or 5 of your "guys" you will end up snookered, overpaying, and with an unbalanced roster. You need to stick to your tiers, follow your prep, and seek out value at each available opportunity.

Having said that, if you see a gap in the market and you think a player is undervalued based on Average Draft Position (ADP) and therefore you want to go one round earlier than ADP to ensure you get him, because he is in a tier that is higher than your other players, that is a different story.

I keep referring to Robert Woods from last year because he was pretty much one of my only "guys" alongside Keenan Allen and Brandin Cooks. These guys were criminally underrated by the market. Therefore, I did not mind moving them up in my tiers and rankings and taking them one round earlier than ADP to ensure I got them. That might have seemed like a reach to players around me. But on my board, in my tiers, they were still a value. And they still outperformed their draft position from where I took them. On all my rosters last year, Woods and Allen were my most common 4th/5th round combination in most drafts. Both were WR1's by the end of Week 16 in 0.5pt PPR. Therefore, I did not overpay, and I certainly did not reach. I went up to get them, but they were still, for me, terrific value. And that showed at the end of the season.

Therefore, you need to balance your tiers with value. But it is also your board. If you have Robby Anderson as your WR13 on your board, in your 4th or 5th tier, and he has got a 6th/7th round ADP and you want to take him in the 5th, who am I to judge. If, at the end of the season, you can analyse why you thought this, and take a long look in the mirror and be satisfied, then that is all that matters. The key thing to understand is why are they your "guys" and use that as your rationale as to where to draft them.

Most players pick them because they like them, or they heard their name on a podcast, or they like seeing them on Red zone. Nothing wrong with any of that. Just be careful overpaying for mediocre talent. As this will be what lets you down in December when you are on the outside of the playoffs looking in.

10)   Overvaluing Rookies.

This is another really common mistake that happens every single year. Players get extremely excited for Rookies coming into the NFL and expect them to be the next big thing immediately. However, it is very rarely the case. Justin Jefferson set all kinds of rookie records last year and turned in a WR1 performance for the ages in 2020. However, two things of note here. Firstly, he was not even in the top 4 of Rookie Wide Receivers drafted in 2020. And secondly, it does not happen that often, at any position. There is a slightly higher chance of a Rookie Running Back breaking into the top 12 of their position in their first season. However, in the last 5 years, a Rookie Running Back has managed to break into the top 12 a little under 12% of the time. That is still not an amazing hit rate.

However, when you look at other positions, it is even lower. At QB, the hit rate for a Rookie QB to be in the top 6 of the position is exactly 0%. Zero! At Wide Receiver is happens just 3% of the time and the same goes for Tight Ends, just 3% of the time for top 12. That number falls to less than 2% if you focus on just the top 6 Tight Ends.

Every fantasy football player is guilty of it. Everyone loves the shiny new toy. However, the truth of the matter is that it is rare a Rookie will make a significant impact in fantasy football. And, even when they do, it is rarely the player that we expect. Who would have predicted James Robinson and Philip Lindsey would have finished RB1's in their rookie year? No one! They were both undrafted Free Agents who ended up in phenomenal positions due to late roster moves. They absolutely deserve their success. But there were not players drafted with significant draft capital in fantasy football drafts.

Yet every year, the majority of fantasy football players want to invest significant value into rookies. In the odd scenario, like Jonathan Taylor in 2020, it will work. However, for every Jonathan Taylor, there are 5 or 6 examples where players were taken in a similar round and it did not work. D'Andre Swift, J.K Dobbins, Henry Ruggs III, Clyde Edwards-Helaire for example.

I am not saying fade all Rookies. You might find the diamond in the rough. However, I would just air on the side of caution, and do not overdraft them. If someone wants to reach for rookie talent, let them.

All this advice applies to redraft leagues. Of course, when you factor in Dynasty, this all changes and could not be further from the truth.

So, when you do your tiers this year, just keep in mind previous rookie success, and maybe slide the rookies down just a tier or two. Do not assume their college production will translate to the NFL immediately. Especially at Wide Receiver, Quarterback and Tight End. Let others make the mistakes.

CHAPTER 8

A Starter Guide to Dynasty Fantasy Football

Written by Adam Murfet

One format of fantasy football that has really taken off over the past four or five years is Dynasty Leagues.

One chapter on Dynasty fantasy football is probably not going to do the concept any real justice. However, I know many people are fascinated to try it, but perhaps do not know how it works, or why to play it. Therefore, this chapter is more for them.

If you have been playing Dynasty fantasy, or even Keeper leagues (this is where you keep a certain number of players year after year), this chapter is perhaps more of a skim over, with some more useful points on strategy coming towards the end of the chapter. What I am saying is, we will not be offended if you want to skip this section or just glance at it. This is geared at fantasy players with 0-3 years' experience.

What is a Dynasty League?

A Dynasty league is a slightly more realistic NFL experience for fantasy football. You have one draft at the start, in year one, and then all subsequent drafts in future years are just for rookie players coming into the NFL.

So, if you play in a 12 team, 16-man roster league which is standard, you will probably add some more bench spots to allow for stashing rookies/ young players. So, it would mean you might extend to somewhere between 20/22 men rosters. That way you can draft new players every year via the rookie drafts.

It also means your main draft becomes massively important. If you mess up there, it can take a long time to rebuild. You will have to go in with a clear plan of how to build your roster and it requires a bit more skill.

The idea of a league like this is to be more strategic. Only one team can win once a year. However, you can start to devise a win now strategy, a win in the medium term, or even the longer term. I will explain this when I go through the chapter. However, Dynasty fantasy football leagues tend to be more active, have more trades, and continue action well into the offseason.

Why Play Dynasty Fantasy Football?

Well, as I have just mentioned, it is more strategic and more active. Therefore, if you love fantasy football (and I am guessing you do if you have bought this book), then it is more fun.

The biggest barrier to entry for people is they do not know how to start, run, or play in a Dynasty league. By the end of this chapter, this will no longer be the case.

We all know the favourite part of a league is the draft. However, the second favourite thing about fantasy football is trades. They cause everyone to stop in their tracks, comment, and pass judgement. They are a talking point for days/weeks at a time.

Dynasty leagues means far more trades. Two major reasons why are because the league is not going to end in January, meaning people are either trying to win a title this season, or reload for next season. The other reason is you have more to trade than just players.

That is right! Just like the NFL, you can also trade your future draft picks. If you are on the cusp of a title this season, but you need one more key ingredient to get that title, you can trade away your first round pick next year for something this year. It is a great win/win trade as you get the chance to win your title now, and the other team can get a key piece to help them improve in the future. Trading picks means more trades happen in Dynasty leagues.

However, it is even better than that. There is nothing worse than falling to 2-8 and you are waiting for the season to end. Your team has injuries, and you are just treading water. However, you have some players who you are not too keen to keep next season as they are aging, but they are going off right now! You can trade those players and load up on either picks or players for next season.

This means you, standing at 2-8 can still be active in the league. Sure, you are not winning the trophy this year. But by working hard now, you can set yourself up to challenge and make the playoffs next year. You can start trade talks and work on getting some younger players and more picks to give you more chances to improve.

Therefore, Keeper leagues are starting to die out. They are the halfway house between redraft and dynasty. There are some great keepers out there (The British Fantasy Football League for example, is an exceptional Keeper League), but these types of leagues are the exception and not the rule.

The other reason to play Dynasty fantasy football is that you will start to learn so much more. If you have not been one for the NFL Draft, or not had a reason to get into it, you will start to pay more attention to it. If you have wanted to watch more college football but did not know how or why, dynasty leagues give you a great reason to get involved.

However, none of the above is a prerequisite to play in Dynasty leagues. Some people just like the idea of drafting a team and keeping it year after year. I am sure we have all drafted a team or had a championship team we never wanted to part ways with. Well, this is how you that heartbreak stops.

The idea is that you will learn more about players, depth charts, younger players, just by playing the game. It could be a rocky start. However, in Dynasty leagues, you always could change your fortunes. And you have many more options to do so than in a redraft league.

How do you Start a Dynasty League?

It is just as simple as starting a normal league. All sites have a Dynasty option when you start a new league, whether that's NFL.com, Sleeper, Yahoo, ESPN, and My Fantasy League etc... So, starting a league is not much different to starting your annual draft.

The only considerations you will need to make are the following:

1)   Add more bench spots for younger players/more strategy options (4-6 is a good number)

It opens the strategy of the game and rewards players for having deeper player pool knowledge.

2)   The use of a taxi squad for rookies.

This is therefore allowing you to draft rookies in the later round of rookie drafts who have little to no chance of starting Week One, or much in their Rookie season.

3)   Think about the number of rounds your Rookie Draft should be.

I would say if you had a taxi squad and a good bench size, 4-5 rounds are good. However, if you are all quite new, maybe start with 3 rounds.

4)   Decide when your Rookie Drafts should be held.

This seems silly to think about as most drafts take place in August. However, it is fun to do these much sooner, like in June or July, to allow for additional trading. I host almost all of mine in May, not long after the NFL draft.

5)   A rule to avoid deliberate tanking.

This is a contentious one. However, you have now given the league an incentive to lose on purpose. The number 1 pick! I would be creating some rules such as "setting a lineup to win every week", "No dropping studs onto your bench if they are fit to play", "no ignoring injuries and making sure free agents are claimed to cover roster holes where possible". I would also say that fantasy players trading all their best players for picks is perfectly acceptable for me, as they are trying to win in future years. If someone trades half their roster but collects a lot of 1st and 2nd round picks over the next couple of years, that is more than acceptable.

Some Strategy to get Started and Get Success Early.

This book is all about winning. Therefore, not giving you some tips on how to be successful would be silly. These strategy points apply to all levels of experience.

The Start-Up Draft.

Everything starts with the draft. You will hear Dynasty leagues refer to the main draft as a "Start-up draft". You will also find a lot of people will fire up these "start-up drafts" from February until July. Those who love fantasy football love to do it early, as they can start drafting almost immediately.

Obviously the later you do a star-up draft, the more information you will have. For example, if you do a start-up draft in February, you do not know where the free agent, out of contract players are going to land. Meaning you can overdraft players who might not have good value. However, you also might get an absolute steal on some players who find themselves in better positions.

One great example of each is if you spent a 4-6th round pick on Leonard Fournette last year in a Dynasty Start-up, you would have felt sick with his release in August and ending up with the Bucs. His numbers in the regular season certainly did not return where he was drafted.

However, if you took Stefan Diggs with an 8th-10th round pick (I got him in the 13th in a start-up last year), you were singing to the fantasy gods a song of praise and thanks. He turned out to be the absolute steal of most drafts last year. So, as I said, swings and roundabouts.

When it comes to a start-up, the tendency is to draft all the young players higher than normal redraft leagues. Also, real NFL draft capital matters. Therefore, if a real NFL team spent a first-round pick on a Wide Receiver, such as Denver did on Jerry Jeudy in 2020, then it will mean he will likely go much higher than someone like T.Y Hilton or Jarvis Landry.

This also means older players with a short time left in the NFL can be drafted for very little investment. Tom Brady, Julian Edelman, T.Y Hilton, Desean Jackson, Emmanuel Sanders, Julio Jones, will all be going between 3-10 rounds later due to their age and profile. It means they become almost risk free, and great additions if you want to make a short-term early charge.

The best thing in a start-up draft is to let the draft come to you. Do not go in with a "win now" or draft for the future strategy, as it could lead to you not getting the right value for players where you draft them. It is important to see how the board falls. Reaching for young players with little production history is the single quickest way to be stuck with a dud roster. The second quickest is to just draft a bunch of players based on last year's production who are aging. Again, they could get hurt or move and you will be stuck with a team of duds.

So, a blended approach is good. It is great to get some young rookie/sophomore talent on board. But you also need players who will produce now.

Also, after the elite few Running Backs come off the board, you will start to see more Wide Receivers come off the board than usual redraft leagues. It makes complete sense though. Because the average Running Back barely makes it past their Rookie contract with effective, starter numbers. Whilst Wide Receivers do not hit their prime until their age 27/28 year. It means Wide Receivers become more productive, in general, the older they get. Therefore, Wide Receivers have far more value in a Dynasty format than Running Backs, simply because they will be around longer.

It is also ok to take Quarterback slightly earlier, if they are an elite, young option. For example, if Patrick Mahomes is available in the third round, it is far more acceptable to take him there than in a redraft league. Because you just get this feeling that Mahomes will be a significant top 5 fantasy quarterback for the next 8-10 years. Therefore, you have your QB position sewn up for the immediate and long-term future.

Other things to consider in start-up drafts is not to reach for average Running Back talent. This pool of players tends to only help in the very short term and can be bench fodder for your team if you have too many of this type of player. Remember, you are stuck with these players unless you release them and claim new players from the Free Agency pool. Make sure you have plenty of cover, but do not go reaching for it.

The last thing in a start-up draft, if your league allows, is to try and trade up and down the board, based on your needs. If you have a tier of players to go after, but no one is standing out to you, put your pick "on the block" and try and either trade up later picks or acquire extra picks.

In the same vein, if there is a screaming value on the board, and it is worth trading up for, then make an offer and trade up. In a start-up draft this offseason, Keenan Allen was still on the board in the middle of the 6th round. Since I did not expect him to make it to me three picks later, I moved up the board. My trade for the 6.6 was the 7.4 and the 9.4 with me also getting the 13.4. The key to this was I still had my pick at 6.9, so it worked out well for me.

You can still use some or most redraft tactics in your drafts. It is different, but a lot of the principles remain the same. It is just the values that differ and require a little more knowledge on depth charts.

However, always remember this principle, you cannot win your league at the draft. But you can certainly lose it.

Trading rookie draft picks.

This is the real difference to most leagues. Most people do not know how to trade picks or what to offer. And truth be told, most experts do not either. What is a strange concept that you need to get your head around is your draft picks hold a different value at different times of the year?

Your rookie draft picks are worth a lot less during the regular season than they are a week before the rookie draft. Why? Because who knows what players will be in the draft come October, let alone what teams they will be playing on. But after the NFL draft, we start to have a real value on who these players are and the ones we want to target.

Lots of teams overpay or giveaway rookie picks in the regular season because at that point they hold little to no value. If you are selling your rookie picks, do not fall into this trap. If you are buying rookie picks, always try and get more as you are buying an unknown commodity.

You also need to remember that if you are trading a player to a contender, for picks, you are weakening what you are getting in return. How? Because by making them stronger now, you are potentially having them go further in the playoffs or winning it. Therefore, if you swap Stefon Diggs for a first and second in 2021 and a first in 2022, and the person you trade Diggs to is currently projected to be picking at the 1.08, if they win the league via the playoffs, they will be picking at the 1.12. That is a huge value difference. Therefore, you need to factor that in when acquiring picks. The 1.12 is nowhere near as valuable as the 1.08. To put this into context, the 2020 rookie draft Average Draft Position meant you were likely to get Clyde Edwards-Helaire or Justin Jefferson at the 1.08. At the 1.12 you were taking Henry Ruggs III or Laviska Shenault. That is a massive difference in the calibre of player you will get.

The argument that a first rounder is a first rounder is not true. You go from day 1 starting talent/elite talent down to picking someone at the end of the first round who might not be all that effective right away. If you are building for a rebound next year, the 1.12 is not going a long way to help you.

The way around this is to either get more picks so you can continue to trade and trade up from 1.12 to higher up in the first round, or to get players who can help you next year.

You will have players in your league that will go all in in a particular year, and therefore trade a lot of future picks to make it happen. If you identify someone like this, make sure you cash in. If this is you, make sure you get the pieces you need to win now, because you will not be improving too much next year.

Surprisingly, the best time to trade rookie draft picks is in the draft itself. For example, lots of teams will need Quarterback's this year as the Quarterback carousel is spinning faster than ever in the NFL. Therefore, if you do not need a Quarterback, and you are in the position where you could take Trevor Lawrence, you could probably trade that pick for a King's ransom.

I was in this exact position last year. I did need a Quarterback, but I was sceptical on Tua. I was on the clock and managed to get 2 additional first round picks and the first pick of the second round, to move back exactly 1 spot. Someone was all in on Tua Tagovailoa. I cashed in. I took Justin Herbert, CeeDee Lamb, Justin Jefferson and Ke'Shawn Vaughn with my pick and the extras. It looks like a masterstroke now, but at the time I took some heat for it.

Would I have got that deal before the draft? Absolutely not. So sometimes it pays to wait. However, a word of caution on that. If you wait too long, you might not have a buyer, this is where knowing your league-mates and their needs is essential before any rookie draft.

Back to trading rookie picks. I personally think the best value you can get is player plus pick deals. I think it gives you cover in-case the draft pick does not work out.

Just like the real NFL, you have to judge these players based off zero NFL production or stats. Therefore analysts, like myself and better professionals, will be wrong. I really liked Ke'Shawn Vaughn last year. He has barely done anything of significance in the NFL to date. Lots of people were lower on Justin Herbert and Justin Jefferson in their positions than what they have produced so far to date. There is a real risk with drafting rookies in a rookie draft. However, having more picks does mean you have more lottery tickets. And by that logic, you have a lot more chance to win big in the rookie draft.

However, being able to get players will also help you. I have seen fantasy players be successful for years without many if any rookie picks. And I have seen many fantasy players take a loser to a title within a year or two with great rookie drafts.

Do not Have a Five-Year Dynasty Plan.

Typically, most Dynasty leagues fold after three or four years. Especially if they have never met in person, are a random group of people, or if no money is involved.

There is nothing worse than building for the future, only for the league to fold before you get to see your master plan come to fruition.

Therefore, do not assume the league will still be in place five years from now. Do not use your start-up to draft all the young players who will take five years to get to their prime. Instead, make sure you have that blend of experience and youth.

If you are trading away assets now for future assets, make sure you get something that will help you the following season.

This seems short-signed, but something to consider. Obviously, if you are playing in the same league with people for 5/10/20 years and are only now just considering moving over to dynasty then the above might not be relevant.

However, if that is not the case, work on the assumption the league will fold in a few years. And if it does not then that's great news.

Trade in the Off-season.

The same reason why I would urge start-up leagues (although I play in them) do not start drafting in February, is the same reason why I would suggest you trade in the early offseason. Why? Because you can offload players who could decline the following season, by trading them at their peak ceiling. Or, if you happen to find out some good information, you can buy players cheaply.

If you are someone who keeps up to date with NFL news and can see where players could be going/ being traded, then you can get some very good prices on players.

When some fantasy owners were sweating on Jared Goff and does he start next year, I was acquiring him for draft picks 1 round below his worth, as I was following the news and believed he would be traded. As a result, Goff starts next year in Detroit and I do not have to worry too much if it is short term for the price, I paid for him.

The other aspect to this is that trading in the off-season is fun. It keeps the league alive all year around. It gives you a reason to stay in touch with everyone throughout the season. Remember, fantasy football is about fun and about keeping in touch with friends. Therefore, anything that helps keep the league alive throughout the year, is a great thing.

And, as I have said before, who does not love a trade to be part of or discuss.

The top 10 Tips to Succeed in Dynasty Leagues.

1)   Go get your guy.

Unlike redraft, this is a format where if you want a certain player, for whatever reason, you need to go up and get your guy. Because, if you miss out, you might never own him. So, if you are desperate to own Patrick Mahomes on your team, as he is your favourite player, why not spend a first-round pick on him to ensure you get him? This will not be popular with the fantasy football community on twitter. However, if he is your guy, and you do not want to miss out getting him, go draft him in round 1.

2)   Age matters but it is not the end all or be all.

Throughout this chapter, I have told you that age is important, and it will determine a player's value. However, it is only one way to measure a player. Personally, I would use it more of a tiebreaker between players than the overarching metric in which I am measuring their value. As I have also mentioned previously, the league might not be around forever. Therefore, if you rely on 22-year-old Wide Receivers to get to their prime, there might not be a league for them to be going off in their prime.

3)   Know the rules and scoring, inside and out.

This is something I preach in all strategy guides in any format. It is important, in every league, to fully understand the scoring and the rules. If there is premium scoring on Tight Ends, or a Superflex spot on the roster, this will change the way people draft, as well as the value of players. Read your rules and know your scoring.

4)   Picks are worth less than players, in a start-up draft or a rookie draft.

Picks are far easier to acquire than players. Therefore, if you love someone and want to get them, or there is a screaming value on the board, go and trade up to get that player. As I mentioned with Keenan Allen earlier in the chapter, I traded up to get the chance to draft him. If I were trying to trade for Keenan Allen, it would have cost me a lot more than 2 draft picks to get him.

5)   Trade during a start-up draft.

For the reasons above, it is much easier to get the players you want if you make the trade. However, it is also good for trading back. So many times, I get to a round and there is not a player I am dying to pick. If I have a tier of seven guys here and I can pick one of these guys in the next round, then drop down a round, put your pick on the block and get some extra pieces.

This is the difference between having a good draft, and a great draft.

6)   Know your League-mates.

I have talked about this principle a lot in this section of the book so far. However, in Dynasty leagues, this is more critical. The reason for this is that if they have a favourite team, or favourite players, you can extract maximum value from that person. For example, if your league mate has a signed Mike Evans jersey on his way, and he is available in the 4th or 5th round, you might be able to put your pick on the block to him and get more than if you were just offering it out on the market.

This also helps with anticipating what they might do from a draft perspective in advance, and all the other benefits that I have talked about already. You never know when that handy nugget of information you gleamed will come in handy.

7)   If your league has kickers and D/STs, do not worry about drafting them.

Seriously, do not worry about drafting them. In a redraft it rarely makes sense. In a Dynasty start-up, drafting these positions makes absolutely no sense. Defences are rarely good for multiple years in a row. Therefore, there is entirely no value in drafting either of these positions.

Instead, what you want to be doing for these picks is taking high upside guys. Whether that is rookies, who could flash that you can stash on your taxi squad, a handcuff to an elite Running Back option, or a young Wide Receiver 3 on the depth chart like Russell Gage of Atlanta where they might ship or trade Julio Jones due to cap issues.

If your option does not pan out by late August, you can always drop the for a Kicker or a D/ST and you have lost absolutely nothing. Remember, it is just having a couple of extra lottery tickets you are having at the end of your draft.

8)   Commit to the League.

There is nothing more annoying than seeing three or four people leave a Dynasty league after a year because they either joined too many leagues, or they just messed this one up so badly it is not going to be fun for them.

If you join a league, commit to it. I know we are all probably guilty of leaving leagues after a year or two. I certainly have done it. But if everyone commits to the league, and embraces point nine, then there should be no reason to leave. As I have stated before, the reason I have left Dynasty leagues is because they are not active enough and become redraft leagues with no redraft draft. These are the worst kinds of leagues to be part of. This leads me to point nine…

9)   Be Active.

This is not to say you need to reply to every message, or to post in the group every day. Far from it. But when things are going on in the league, just be present. Remember, fantasy football is supposed to be fun. If you are not being active, or joining in, then what is the point.

And listen I get it. After the pandemic and everything life has thrown at people over the last two years, saying "I'm busy right now" or "I need a couple weeks break" is fine to say. If you need to disappear for a bit, no one is going to hold it against you. However, just give people a heads up or let people know, so you do not get bombarded with trade offers you have no intention of replying to or even acknowledging.

Chat forums in the apps you host your leagues in are not the best for interaction. Try using a WhatsApp group, or a twitter group, or a Facebook group. My favourite league to play in right now uses a Facebook group to host everything in. My friend Peter invited me into the league and Joel, the Commissioner, welcomed me with open arms. When I saw there was a Facebook group that hosted the interaction, I questioned why! However, I now get it and I love it. It is all beautifully documented, all the history of the league. I am not a Facebook fan at all, but a closed Facebook Group to host the league is awesome, if done right.

10)   Have fun

Everything should be fun. If it is not, why are you doing it. Seriously though, if you are miserable in your league and you are ruining the enjoyment of everyone else in the league because you are not having fun, then probably best you break point eight and just leave. Do not end up being that person just because you are angry for losing in your playoffs, or you think the Commissioner upset you in some way. At the end of the day, it is not just your league. It is everyone's league. And the happiness of one does not trump the happiness of everyone in it. So please, do not be that person and either suck it up, let it go, or get out.

CHAPTER 9

A Starter Guide to
Auction Fantasy Football

Written by **Adam Murfet**

Auction leagues are becoming more and more rare in the fantasy football landscape. There are a couple of reasons for this. 1) People do not know where they can play in auction leagues as most platforms do not offer the ability to do Auction leagues. Two of the three leading platforms in the world NFL.com and Sleeper.app do not offer auction leagues. And 2) Most people do not understand it.

I am hoping that by the end of this chapter you will want to engage in Auction leagues. Why? Because they are fun, challenging, and you could own every single player. If you do not get them, that is on you.

What is an Auction League?

An Auction league is a league where the draft is not a draft of sorts, but it is an actual auction. Typical Auction leagues start with $200 starting fund for each owner. After that, you enter a live draft where an order is randomly generated.

Each owner will take it in turns to nominate a player to be bid on. This is a very strategic process as sometimes you do not want to nominate players you want, but instead put-up players who will cause others to spend their money.

You are unable, in a standard draft, to bid more than your available amount. You also cannot bid $200 on a player. This is because, at the end of the auction, you must have your roster filled. Therefore, the most you can bid on 1 player in a 16-man roster league is $185 (leaving $15 for the remaining 15 players to sign).

This format allows you to have an opportunity to sign any player. Therefore, if you do not get a player you wanted, you only have yourself to blame.

The live draft can take anywhere between 2-3 hours. Once you have filled your roster, you will not be able to bid on anymore players, even if you have any money. And, in most leagues, if you do not spend your money, you lose it at the end of the auction.

Typically, in a live auction, each player is only available to be bid on for about a minute (but this can be changed in the settings). It also is not an eBay scenario, where the last second bid is the winner. If you make a bid in the final seconds, the clock resets to 10-15 seconds for the rest of the owners to bid on and raise the price.

The final 30-40 players tend to go very quickly as there are less bidders and less money. Therefore, once nobody can bid the price up anymore, the player is automatically won by the winning bid. Eventually, when people are down to minimum money, the nominating player might end up winning the auction just by nominating. This only occurs on the final 10-15 players.

There are other formats for auction. My Fantasy League, for example, allow for a slow auction. This is where you can set a timer of hours or even a day, for a new bid to be outbid. I have been in auctions that have gone on for over a month. I have also been in several bespoke auction leagues. But the typical out of the box Auction league looks like the above.

Strategy for Auction Leagues

There is a lot of strategy that goes into being successful in auctions. It is a very difficult format to get the team you desire out of the auction. However, if you are savvy, smart, and patient, you can build a championship winning roster in the auction. Then it is supplementing and topping up with Waiver Wire adds and Free Agency.

Having said that, there are some things you can do that will allow you to walk away from the draft with a great starting roster.

1)   Do not overpay for stud players.

This is something people do often in an auction. They want to walk away from the auction with 1 or even 2 of the stud Running Backs. However, you need to make sure you have budget left for the other positions. You should refrain from spending more than $70 on a player like Christian McCaffrey and keep it closer to $60 for Kamara or Cook, in a $200 budget auction.

The same sort of thought process should be applied for Stud Wide Receivers such as Adams, Hill etc.

Before the season starts, I will publish on the website an auction guide price sheet. Try and stick to this where possible.

2)   Save money for the end of the Auction.

If you are patient, you are buying a lot of Wide Receiver 2's (Wide Receivers likely to finish between 13-24 overall in format) for cents on the dollar. If you become one of the last players to fill your roster, and you remain patient, you can snag some real bargains at the end of the auction. However, this requires discipline and patience. But, if you can do that, it will lead to some real success at the end of the Auction.

3)   Do not overspend on your bench players.

When it comes to your bench players, you should not be spending more than $1-$2 per bench player, unless it's late in the auction and you want to have more depth at RB and WR. However, in most cases, keep the bench players to just $1-$2 max.

4)   Setting the Market.

I mentioned saving money for the end of the auction. However, I have found in the last few years that the first 5 guys tend to be bought for round about what I have in my values cheat sheet that I have worked out beforehand. This "setting the market" means you can snag one of your top choices for market value. Once the early guys are gone, panic starts to set in. This means from minutes 30-1 hour 30 in the draft, players tend to be overpriced and over drafted. The dream scenario is to get 1-2 studs very early, set the market on these guys, and then let others run up the bidding on average/slightly above average talent and pay top dollar for them. Then you can swoop in at the end and make a ton of savings to even out the money you paid on your studs.

5)   Watch out for overpaying for Handcuffs.

This is so typical. Someone like Zeke Elliott will come off the board and then within 5-10 player nominations, Tony Pollard gets nominated. Suddenly, Pollard's price goes through the roof because people are gambling. Let them gamble and watch out for spending on these guys, as they are auction killers.

6) Avoiding getting into a bidding war.

The most common mistake in an auction draft is you get outbid by $1, so you outbid the other person by $1. "Hey, what's $2 more?" Unfortunately, $2 becomes $4 that becomes $6 that becomes $8 before you have even had a chance to think. This is how you end up getting into trouble and having below average talent on your roster. Prepare a sheet with your values and your budget and stick to it! If you are going to overpay, make sure you only bid over the price once, and by a dollar. No more, no less. You can make back a dollar in the auction. You cannot make back $8.

7) Set your tiers and do not overpay for "your guys".

This is a common theme across the 2020 Fantasy Football Playbook and this edition. Do not overpay for "your guys". Use your tiers to avoid overpaying. Why pay $45 for J.K Dobbins when you could potentially get David Montgomery for $27-$30 and you have them in the same tier? It does not make a lot of sense. If you have that wide a valuation on the players, you probably have not done your tiers right.

Going into a draft wanting to walk away with a certain player or two will lead you to overpay. That is the facts. So, do not walk into the draft with "your guys" and walk in with your tiers. This will allow you to build a winning roster as opposed to be top heavy on just one or two players. So many people burn through cash early they end up not being able to get anyone until the very end of the auction, meaning they miss out of the guys that will likely win them a championship.

8) Do not bid on players you do not want and do not drive up the price if you are unwilling to pay that price yourself.

The second most common mistake in Auction Drafts is that someone will feel a player is going too cheap, so they run up the bidding to make people pay a fair market price, only to then be stuck spending money on a player they did not need or want.

This happens in every single draft I have ever been in. I have seen people bid up on QBs and TE's when they already spent at the position, and then they overspend themselves. It is a bonehead move that means you end up scoring an own goal. By trying to get someone to spend more money, you have therefore ended up paying through the nose for a mistake.

The easiest way to avoid this is to only bid if you would be happy to win the bid at that price. If you raise the bid on someone like Curtis Samuel to $4 but you already have 4 Wide Receivers, and you win him for that, when he is a $7-$10 valuation on your board, then you have done well and you have added a piece you will probably use. Putting a bid of $15 in on DeShawn Watson when you already got Mahomes for $27 is a big own goal, as you can only start 1 Quarterback. So, tying that money up on your bench is going to cost you big time on the board.

Let other people run up the bidding or let someone get a steal. Someone getting a steal does not cost you money. Artificially bidding someone up and winning the auction at that price is a serious own goal.

9) Keep a note of every team's roster and budget.

Some platforms like ESPN make this quite easy. However, I am old school and I use a pen and paper. I write down all the roster and budgets remaining. That means, when it comes to nominations, you can be extremely strategic, and you are able to put in nominations and bids to keep the costs down on guys you are targeting.

For example, if you are targeting an RB3, and you see that everyone either has a RB3 or does not have the money to compete for one, then it is a good time to nominate a target and go for them. If you have a tier of 3-4 guys this is even better, as you have 3 or 4 attempts to get a guy under market price, for a position of need. This should really help you stretch your budget even further and grab a couple more bargains later.

At the end of the day, you want to walk away from the draft with a core of 10-12 players you can build a championship team around. This allows you some fluidity in Free Agency and Waivers, as well as ensuring you do not feel obligated to spending loads of money on bench players that might have little to no impact on your roster.

So, track those rosters, track those dollars, and find the perfect time to strike your bargains to build the best team that you can in the auction.

10) Take a Kicker/DST Mid-Draft.

Yes, that is right, I am advocating you to take these positions in the peak hour where everyone is overpaying for players. You should not spend more than $1 on a kicker and $1 on a D/ST. Therefore, if you nominate these during the peak hour, 2 things will happen. You will either: 1) Get the Kicker/DST of your choice when there is more choice, very early. Or 2) someone outbids you and they end up spending $1-3 more on the position then they should. It is the literal win/win scenario for you. Because either an opponent has overspent, or you get your top Kicker and D/ST choice when others are flapping around and overpaying for WR3/RB3 talent.

It also means you can get late WR's for a dollar or two at the end of the auction when those who only have $1 left for a few bench players or Kickers and D/STs cannot over bid. It leads to you zagging when everyone zigs, getting a tiny positional advantage and not overspending.

This strategy really leaves you in control of the Auction and not the other way around.

I really love Auction drafts. It has so many levels of strategy that allow you to really think about what you want to do/how you want to attack it. Every single Auction Draft is different. Which means you can do all the prep that you want for it. However, if you do none, you will come unstuck very quickly.

Your preparation and plans might fall away very early. And that happens a lot. But if you remain fluid at all costs. However, if you do not have a cheat-sheet and some room for notes, then you are in real trouble. Make sure you are the one setting the market, getting deals late and not running up the prices. Let others do the dirty work for you. You can just sit back, relax, and have a lot of fun.

Remember, this is a format not a lot of people play. So, you can just have fun with it. Try different things and just have fun. A live Auction Draft is probably one of the most fun drafts you can do. Put it on your bucket list as something to try and do before you stop playing this wonderful game of Fantasy Football.

If you want to do an Auction League, but do not have the players, then reach out to us here @5yardrush on twitter and we will either connect you to other players who are interested in doing a league. Or we will run a listener league. We are going to do one book league that will be an Auction League. So, if you are reading this and want to try it, then drop us a message and we will sign you up to it. It should be a lot of fun and hopefully I will convert a lot of you to playing Auction Leagues in the future.

CHAPTER 10

A Starter Guide to Franchise Flex Frenzy Fantasy Football

Written by Adam Murfet

I was invited to try this format by my friend Jon Helmkamp last year. And I absolutely fell in love with the format immediately. It is crazy.

However, the reason I am writing about it is I genuinely believe this format will take off. I believe once people know about it, know how to run it, and understand it, it is something that could go mainstream in about four- or five-years' time.

The reason I believe this is because it is so interesting, fascinating, strategic, and fun. There are many different paths to victory, as well as many ways you can approach both your draft and your roster construction.

Certain aspects of this league will certainly take off before others. Because of the nature of it. However, I wanted to add a chapter to this book about it because I absolutely love it and I implore you all to try it in at least one of your leagues in 2021. I will also be running a book league version of this format in 2021, so make sure you get in touch with me, and I will add you to the list. If the demand is high, I will even do two leagues.

What is a Franchise Flex Frenzy League?

A Franchise Flex Frenzy league is a league that consists of two drafts. Before the first draft, you set a draft order. Then, during the first draft, you end up drafting up to 5 franchises, over 5 rounds, where you can have players from that team on, on your roster. All 32 franchises in the NFL have two copies each of them, and the draft is five rounds. You are allowed to draft both copies of the same franchise, but then that also means you will have less franchises to draft from. However, it also means you will not have competition for those players, and therefore you will not need to spend high draft picks on those players.

For example, if you took both copies of the Tampa Bay Buccaneers franchise, you will not need to spend any of your first 10 or 12 picks on Tampa Bay players, as no one else can draft them.

However, if you are competing with another fantasy owner over a franchise, then you need to compete over players.

Then, when the 5 found frenzy draft has been completed, you will then draft your roster. The draft order is the reverse order of the franchise draft.

What makes this format very different is that you are not drafting any defined positions on your roster, with the exception of Quarterback. The starting lineup is:

QB

9 Flex Spots

1 Super Flex Spot

Optional: DST and Kicker

8 Bench spots

So, it becomes less about drafting specific players and more about BPA. But you also have to consider who you are competing for players with. This leads to a lot of strategy upon strategy.

You can play this as either a redraft format or a dynasty format. If it is dynasty, then you probably need to add somewhere between 3-4 extra bench spots.

When it comes to Waivers and Free Agency, I would recommend Daily Waivers with Free Agent Acquisition Budget (FAAB). A $100 budget is the best amount to use for this. This will allow direct bidding between the two copies.

Also, if a player gets released or traded, and is signed by another team, you have 1 week to trade that player from your roster, or drop them, if they did not sign with another team that you control. This makes the Dynasty aspect even more challenging. Because you will need to take contracts and impending Free Agents into consideration. Otherwise, you will be in big trouble in year two.

How to host and play this format?

You can play this format on any platform. I hosted two of these Franchise Flex Frenzy leagues on Sleeper.app last year.

I would recommend you host the Franchise Draft on a Google Sheet and then pin it to the league chat. Then you allow people to draft the 5 round Franchise Draft on there. Once that is complete, you can ask all league owners to change their team name to the franchises they drafted.

One of my examples from last year was LAR>TB>TEN>PIT>DAL as my team name. That way, it is very easy for people in Sleeper to see who has control of what franchises.

Then, when it comes to the roster, just remember to use Flex spots, so it will take some construction. I recommend PPR however you can use any scoring format you choose.

Takeaways from Year One

Some of the things I have learned after playing this format or a year are as follows:

1)   The Draft Board will look weird

Below are the first 36 players that came off the board in my dynasty Franchise Flex Frenzy league, which I won. I will not list the franchises; I will just list the names.

- Saquon Barkley

- Christian McCaffrey

- Lamar Jackson

- Kyler Murray

- Davante Adams

- Michael Thomas

- Dalvin Cook

- Ezekiel Elliott
- DeAndre Hopkins
- Patrick Mahomes
- Clyde Edwards-Helaire
- Dak Prescott
- Tyreek Hill
- Joe Burrow
- Chris Godwin
- Travis Kelce
- Derrick Henry
- Deshaun Watson
- Alvin Kamara
- Jonathan Taylor
- George Kittle
- Calvin Ridley
- Josh Allen
- Julio Jones
- Matt Ryan
- Kenny Golladay
- Josh Jacobs
- Kenyan Drake
- Aaron Rodgers
- JuJu Smith-Schuster
- Joe Mixon
- Mike Evans
- Drew Brees
- D.J Moore
- Nick Chubb

- Amari Cooper

Notable late round picks:

- David Montgomery 13.1

- Daniel Jones 14.2

- Darius Slayton 15.1

- Carson Wentz 19.5

- Zach Ertz 17.5

- Miles Sanders 20.8

- Terry McLaurin 15.9

- Noah Fant 17.12

That is an example of how crazy a Franchise Flex Frenzy gets. ADP and traditional drafting guides go out of the window. You are drafting from a very restricted pool of maybe 50 players. So, you need to rank those players and take your guys. There is no such thing as value or reaching for your guy as the pool is extremely shallow. You need to take your guys when you can and be prepared to lose a lot of your guys.

2) Locking up both copies of a Franchise do give you a distinct advantage… but not a huge amount.

The desire when picking near the turn is to pass on a top franchise in exchange of having more chance of locking up an entire franchise. There is merit in this strategy. However, I saw data from 4 of these leagues, and in no cases, did a team that locked up an entire franchise win the league. It is an extremely small sample size so do not put too much stock into this. However, it is something to consider. At the end of the day, as with the draft, the franchises should be taken as best available. Because, whilst you might get both shares of Washington or Philadelphia, you might benefit more of getting a share of Dallas or Tennessee or New York Giants. Especially if you end up getting the first pick from that share and can lock up Dak Prescott or Derrick Henry or Saquon Barkley.

The benefit of stacking a franchise is you can leave those picks to the end and be aggressive on the other three franchises you have. A lot will depend on which franchise you have both shares of, and what franchises you got in your other spots. At the end of the day, if you go with the best franchise and best player available, whilst also monitoring who is likely to get back to you and who will not get back to you, then you will be in good shape in your draft.

3) If drafting towards the end of the first round of the Franchise Draft, look to see what player you will guarantee.

If you are sitting in the 10th, 11[th,] or 12th spot in the Franchise draft then you know you will probably secure a stud player. If 1 copy of Kansas City, Green Bay, Buffalo Bills have come off the board, and the other one is still there, selecting this franchise is your way of securing an effective 1.01. In this format, there is 3, maybe 4 1.01's depending on how the franchises are selected. Therefore, you can secure a top copy.

The same way that if you think Christian McCaffrey is the 1.01, if you are sitting in the 1.12 spot in the Franchise draft, you can draft McCaffrey there and lock him in as the 1.01. You need to use these draft spots as an advantage here. Ideally you either want to secure the second copy of a team here, or the first copy but being the 1.01.

Again, this is why there is so much strategy in this format. You just need to be watching every pick and what people are doing. It is very easy to trip over your own feet by over-thinking decisions. However, if you are able to make good selections, you can walk away with an excellent, and a deep roster.

There is a lot more strategy and nuance to this format. It is crazy, it is fun, and the draft process will blow your mind. I highly recommend this format. I hope you are able to get in at least one league with this format this season. I know you, and your friends will really enjoy it if and when you get a chance to enact this.

And, as I mentioned previously, if you do want to play in our book version of this format, then please do drop us an email, or DM to our twitter @5yardrush and I will make sure you are on the list to join us in 2021 in this format.

If you are looking to set this up, and you do have some questions, then please do email us or get in touch. I will be on hand to answer any questions and help you get this setup. I do hope you enjoy playing this format.

CHAPTER 11

The Value of Each Round of a Fantasy Football Draft

Written by **Adam Murfet**

The Value of Each Round of a Fantasy Football Draft.

If you read last year's Fantasy Football Playbook, you will be aware of this section. Of all the positive feedback we got last season for the book, this was the section we got the most feedback on.

It is amazing to break down the value of drafts by round and look at the history of the position. When I say history, I focus on the last three years for this exercise.

The 2019 and 2018 data were available in last year's book. However, I have added the data from 2020 into this and then also seeing how that has changed things from last year.

It is worth noting, that there are not 12 players in every round. I have taken players with their pure ADP value, to ensure a more accurate representation of players, as opposed to rounding up players and putting players into a position that did not reflect their true ADP. I therefore used their true, raw ADP data.

How Did We Work This Out?

I took the ADPs off of both FantasyAlarm.com and Fantasy Football Calculator for 0.5 PPR as a nice balance for the exercise. I then worked out the fantasy points scored that season using the totals for weeks 1-16 (again, most leagues do not play in week 17 so why count the data) and took an average points per game per position in each round. This then, allows you to see how you should construct your team, based on a points per game average. This gives you a view as to how likely a pick with an ADP in that round is likely to bust.

Now, just a few things to explain here. I have only done Running Backs and Wide Receivers for rounds 1-10. Quarterbacks and Tight Ends I have done rounds 1-12. In some rounds, there will be a gap as no players were selected. Also, some of the data will be just one data point. I will highlight this as I go along, and you can also see in the charts appendix.

I have taken the ADP of the last two years and averaged the points together from each year to flatten out some of the variances and add more data.

Lastly, from rounds 2-12, I will add an additional column, a points per round difference explaining the drop, or gain from waiting a round. I will also write the difference from last year's combined data and this years'.

This is a guide for drafts. You should still have a fluid strategy. However, if you have tiers of players, this could be used as a tiebreaker. If you have not been making the playoffs in leagues for a while, try this in one league, see if it works for you. One final note, this is a one QB league in 0.5 PPR format. You can make some small adjustments accordingly for PPR, but it will not make monumental changes.

Round 1

Position	2020-2018 PPG Average	2018-2019 Points Per Game	Difference
QB	N/A	N/A	N/A
RB	16.95	16.44	+0.51
WR	15.73	15.79	-0.06
TE	13.46**	13.46**	N/A

** Just Travis Kelce was selected in 2019 and no one was in the first round in 2018 at Tight End. Therefore, this is Kelce's points per game average in 2019

The points gap between Round 1 Running Backs and Round 1 Wide Receivers grew even further in 2020, despite the injuries. That tells you that zero RB is still not the strategy to adopt to build the most successful team in 2021.

It will not shock me, or anyone that the first 5-6 picks in 2021 (with the exception of Superflex/Tight End premium leagues) will be Running Backs. These players have an elite advantage over the rest of the field due to elite production, as well as position scarcity. You will not find a bigger advantage over the rest of the field, then taking one of the top 5 Running Backs in the draft. And that include taking Travis Kelce over the rest of the Tight End field. Therefore, you need to consider taking an elite Running Back round 1, because the drop off, as you see through the rest of this, is still significant.

Round 2

Position	2020-2018 PPG Average	2018-2019 Points Per Game	Difference	Difference from Previous Round
QB	23.99*	N/A	+23.99	+23.99
RB	14.52	14.74	-0.22	-2.43
WR	14.73	14.69	+0.04	-1.00
TE	11.93**	8.69**	+3.24	-1.53

* Lamar Jackson and Patrick Mahomes were taken with second round ADP. As they are the only QBs to be taken in the second round in the last 3 years, they set the market for this data set.
* No TE was taken in the 2ⁿᵈ round in 2019. This data set includes only Travis Kelce and George Kittle in 2020 and Rob Gronkowski in 2018.

In the first significant change from last year's data, we see that Wide Receivers outperformed Running Backs in this round. It is ever so close, with just 0.19PPG in it. However, the 2019-2018 data had Running Backs take the edge. This meant strategically, going Running Back/Running Back, depending on where you were in the draft, yielded the best results. The shift in 2020 meant that Wide Receivers in Round 2 outscored Running Backs in Round 2 by 0.71 PPG.

A couple of learning points from this are as follows:

1)   Wide Receivers were just much deeper in round 2 than Running Back. And this made sense given three quarters of the first round happened to be Running Backs, whilst only a quarter at most seemed to be Wide Receivers. So of course, the WR4 reckons to be better than the RB10 and so on.

2)   Running Backs were still selected in the second round at a ratio of around 2:1, meaning there was a wider scope of data for them to fail. Whilst more data points give you a more solid average it does also cap upside. The round 2 Wide Receivers were Tyreek Hill, DeAndre Hopkins, Chris Godwin, and Julio Jones. That elevated their floor massively.

3)   The drop off at Running Back is real. Running Backs dropped by almost 2.5 PPG from round 1 to round 2. That is a massive drop, considering we are still in an elite portion of the draft. It is not like we are in the later rounds. We are still selecting the top 24 players in the draft.

It is worth exploring, if the trends remain the same in 2021, moving away from a Running Back/Running Back approach and look more towards a Running Back/Wide Receiver Start. Let us see what round 3 brings.

One thing of note is the two Quarterbacks being selected here in the second round. This is the earliest Quarterbacks have been selected in the last five year. Despite the popular "Late Round Quarterback" approach, fantasy managers tried to gain an edge and select these two Quarterbacks extremely early. In truth, the plan backfired with Mahomes finishing as the QB4 and Jackson the QB10. Jackson's numbers from his historic 2019 proved not to be sustainable, whilst Mahomes showed great leadership on the field to take his team to their second consecutive Super Bowl. However, that did not contribute to elite production in the fantasy points column.

I am still adamant that there is no advantage to be gained taking a Quarterback that early. And so far, that is still proving to be the case. So, ignore Quarterback in round two and move on.

Round 3

Position	2020-2018 PPG Average	2018-2019 Points Per Game	Difference	Difference from Previous Round
QB	21.15*	21.15*	0	-2.84
RB	10.89***	11.10	-0.21	-3.63
WR	12.80	13.06	-0.26	-1.93
TE	13.89**	13.89	0	+1.96

*This data includes Aaron Rodgers in 2018 and Patrick Mahomes in 2019. No QBs were selected in the 3rd round in 2020.

** No Tight Ends were selected in the 3rd round in 2020.
*** Only Todd Gurley had a 3rd round ADP in 2020, which skews the data down significantly.

There were no Quarterbacks or Tight Ends selected in the third round in 2020. Therefore, when I wrote about the Tight Ends and Quarterbacks here in 2020, I mentioned you cannot invest in Quarterbacks and Tight Ends here.

I have changed my mind slightly on Tight End. If Kelce is still on the board here (which he will not be) then he is extremely good value. If Kelce, who is producing WR1 numbers in the Tight End slot, is still on the board in round two, then I would have no problem with you taking him there. I still have too much concern over the rest of the field, however. Therefore, I would fade Tight End if Kelce were gone until the double-digit rounds.

Quarterback still is not providing value. No Quarterbacks were taken in round 3 in 2020, meaning that except for Jackson and Mahomes, no Quarterbacks were taken on average for the first 55 picks in the draft. That is how it should be, including Mahomes and Jackson. There is no value, as this data set is continuing to show, to take anything other than Wide Receiver or Running Backs in the first 55 picks, with the exception of Travis Kelce, who is an elite Wide Receiver in another position. If someone else selects a position outside of Wide Receiver or Running Back (Or Travis Kelce) in the first fifty picks, plus, then you have to see that as value sliding to you down the board. Let others make the mistakes. Do not fall into the trap.

Looking at the Running Backs and Wide Receivers, we can see a decrease in both positions. The Running Back drop is huge. However, it is only based on one player, which is Todd Gurley, who was taken as the RB15 off the board. The rest seems natural. The further we go in this draft, the more the talent drops off. Right? However, it is worth monitoring the rate of decline in each of the positions, in order for us to discover where we are more likely to hit on players and prospects, simply by looking at it on a per round basis.

Rounds 4-6

Round 4

Position	2020-2018 PPG Average	2018-2019 Points Per Game	Difference	Difference from Previous Round
QB	N/A	N/A	N/A	N/A
RB	11.81	12.13	-0.33	+0.92
WR	11.89	11.16	+0.73	-0.91
TE	10.93*	14.62**	-3.69	-2.96

* Zach Ertz and Mark Andrews contributed to this average in 2020
**Only Zach Ertz 2018 stats contribute to this figure

Round 5

Position	2020-2018 PPG Average	2018-2019 Points Per Game	Difference	Difference from Previous Round
QB	22.56	20.47	+2.09	+1.41
RB	9.25	9.02	+0.23	-2.56
WR	10.47	9.96	-0.51	-1.43
TE	10.36*	8.78	+1.58	-0.57

* Only Darren Waller was taken in the 5th round in 2020, based on ADP.

Round 6

Position	2020-2018 PPG Average	2018-2019 Points Per Game	Difference	Difference from Previous Round
QB	20.30	18.72	+1.58	-2.26
RB	10.96	10.82	+0.14	+1.71
WR	11.53	11.35	+0.18	+1.06
TE	6.33*	6.33	0	-4.03

*No Tight Ends were selected in Round 6 in 2020 based on ADP

Lots to unpack here in the start if the middle rounds. Let us start at Quarterback. This is where the movement from Late Round Quarterback to Mid-Round is starting to play its part. In round 5, you had Dak Prescott, and Kyler Murray taken here in 2020. In round 6, Russell Wilson and Deshaun Watson. These look sure fire top 6 QBs going forward and will give you an advantage to the position. The 2020 PPG average for round 5 was the highest data point by almost 3 points per game. With the exception of Josh Allen, whose ADP will rise to this 5th round/6th round range in 2021, and Aaron Rodgers, who will do the same and is in line for some serious regression, you have all the top QB performers here in this tier.

I am of the belief that you need to walk away from the draft with an elite QB. So now, more than ever, it is important to grab a QB here. And the data is backing that up.

We have now seen the fall of RB points slow down. This means this is the range to get a solid RB3. There is not a huge difference between a Running Back in round 6, and a Running Back in round 3, if you can find who is being criminally undervalued.

Last year, players with round 6 ADP were Cam Akers and David Montgomery and D'Andre Swift. Two rookies who were effective, and a Running Back who was heavily faded after a terrible end to 2019. All these players will see a rise this year. And that means some players will fall down as a result. Have a look at our rankings to see who a value in rounds could be 5/6 for you.

As for Wide Receivers, the PPG numbers were highly consistent. That is because there is so much depth at the position. You are likely to find a WR1 in these rounds, or very productive WR2's. This yields to consistent production and knowing you will get a consistent performer in this section of the draft.

Again, be on the hunt for value. Stefon Diggs, Keenan Allen, Calvin Ridley, Terry McLaurin were all criminally under-valued last year. There are some bargains to be had in this section of the draft for Wide Receiver, so be on the lookout.

As for Tight End, there is nothing in this data that suggests you should consider a Tight End here. The only Tight End that helped the position in 2020 is Darren Waller. Only three Tight Ends were taken between Rounds 4-6 in 2020. They were Zach Ertz, Mark Andrews, and Darren Waller. Only Waller returned his ADP, just! The others were busts. As a result, I can comfortably predict now that Darren Waller will be over-drafted in 2021. You are best to adopt the approach of draft Travis Kelce or fade the position in 2021, based on Value.

Rounds 7-10

Round 7

Position	2020-2018 PPG Average	2018-2019 Points Per Game	Difference	Difference from Previous Round
QB	17.31*	17.31	0	-2.99
RB	10.50	11.05	-0.55	-0.46
WR	10.53	10.29	+0.24	-1.00
TE	8.38	8.99	-0.61	+2.05

* No Quarterbacks were drafted in the 7th round 2020.

Round 8

Position	2020-2018 PPG Average	2018-2019 Points Per Game	Difference	Difference from Previous Round
QB	20.12	19.25	+0.87	+2.81
RB	9.48	9.61	-0.13	-1.02
WR	9.25	8.98	+0.27	-1.28
TE	6.84	6.13	+0.71	-1.54

Round 9

Position	2020-2018 PPG Average	2018-2019 Points Per Game	Difference	Difference from Previous Round
QB	16.63	15.48	+1.15	-3.49
RB	5.46	5.25	+0.21	-4.02
WR	9.64	9.13	+0.51	+0.39
TE	9.23	9.95	-0.72	+2.39

Round 10

Position	2020-2018 PPG Average	2018-2019 Points Per Game	Difference	Difference from Previous Round
QB	22.13	23.06	-0.83	+5.50
RB	7.68	8.78	-1.10	+2.22
WR	8.64	8.21	+0.43	-1.01
TE	6.98	7.10	-0.12	-2.25

Rounds seven and eight once again lean the way of Running Backs and Wide Receivers. The depth is wearing out here. For Running Backs, after this range you are basically picking committee backs or handcuffs. Therefore, this is another reason why you need to get Running Backs early on your roster. We saw this in the 2020 version of the Fantasy Football Playbook and it still rings true this year

For Wide Receivers, it is a similar story. There is a safe floor of relatively productive WR3s with potential WR2 upside in this group. You can continue to hammer the position in the draft here and accrue depth

The data above suggests that Tight End is not a good selection here until round 9. I think you could either target round 9 or wait until round 11. The third option is to stream. As you will see in the Points Against Streaming section, streaming Tight Ends is not only a viable option, but one that can yield a ton of success. Therefore, this year, as mentioned a couple of times, I am promoting the late Tight End approach. Tight End is not the position to invest significant draft capital unless you are drafting Travis Kelce early.

As for the Quarterbacks, we are starting to see a seismic shift in the way we approach the position. For years, including last year, it was advantageous to draft Quarterbacks late. However, with consistency at the top of the position, that matches the talent of the top Quarterbacks in the league, it is becoming very clear that there is a big tier gap between the top 5-6 Quarterbacks in the league and the rest of the other QBs. Therefore, it is advantageous you select a Quarterback in rounds 5 or 6, as I have mentioned previously in the book.

With fresh data comes fresh perspectives and new applications. We, as fantasy players, owe it to ourselves to adopt, adapt and improve in an ever-changing landscape. As the league continues to grow and evolve, as well as the skills of the players, we as fantasy players, if we want to continue to be successful, also need to continue to evolve.

Therefore, what was right a year ago, may not be the right approach now. And that, for me, is certainly the case when it comes to Quarterbacks.

As you can see in the data here, as well as in the appendix especially, you can see that the game is shifting towards a mid-round Quarterback approach being the most optimal.

The Perfect 10 Rounds of a Fantasy Football Draft.

Based on all the data I have compiled; I have explored what the perfect draft would look like. I have also worked out what it will be on a points per game basis so you can see that by drafting well in the first 10 rounds, what it could look like from a points perspective for your team.

If we are to take the standard 1QB, 2RB, 3WR, 1TE, 1 Flex (should have more really yet one remains the standard) (forget Kickers and D/STs at this point) for this exercise, this is what your team will average on a points per game Basis:

Position	Points Per Game
QB	22.56 (Round 5)
RB	16.95 (Round 1)
RB	14.52 (Round 2)
WR	12.80 (Round 3)
WR	11.89 (Round 4)
WR	11.56 (Round 6)
TE	9.23 (Round 9)
FLEX	WR- 10.53 (Round 7)
TOTAL	110.04

You will notice this is down a point from last year. This mostly contributes to taking a Quarterback in round 5 as opposed to round 11 (where we were relying on finding a Lamar Jackson). As the data is telling us, finding that high floor, high ceiling Quarterback is proving to be much harder to find in the 10-12th rounds. Therefore, we need to protect the value and take Quarterback higher. So, whilst it does lead to you taking a one-point reduction over last year, these are all floor plays, with the view of being able to exceed 120 points in a 0.5pt PPR league week to week.

Compiling data from public leagues dating back to 2007, a score of 120 points will win you about 80% of your games. This in turn will yield 10 wins and therefore 1st place in your regular season.

Therefore, as long as you can get ten PPG out of your Kicker and D/ST (scoring 100 points with your Kicker and 100 with your D/ST will yield 12.5 PPG) you should break through that 120-point barrier most weeks.

Again, most people will have many different draft strategies entering a draft. I will always keep this in my back pocket as a blueprint to success. When I look at most of my teams in leagues that won last year, my teams looked a lot like the above.

However, it is not a rigid structure. Having tiers and projections are extremely important. You do not want to miss out on values or big targets you think will break out.

The real reason for this exercise, other than to prove the concepts in our strategy section, is so you can see what you are potentially giving up in order to take a Tight End or Quarterback too early. It is important to understand what you are potentially giving up executing your strategy.

Please check out the charts section in the appendix to go through the raw data and view all the players who contributed. I have also done round 11 and 12 Quarterbacks and Tight Ends for you to compare. Do not forget, you can always reach out to me with any questions.

CHAPTER 12

PAS Points Against Streaming

*Written by **Adam Murfet***

2020 Streaming Review.

To understand the art of streaming, I need to share with you the results of my 'I Streamed a Stream' model for 2020. I learned a lot from the process, and I have managed to glean some interesting results out of it that I am going to share with you.

With this being the 3rd year, I have consciously dedicated column inches to streaming, who the best plays are every week, and the results of streaming, I have learned a great deal.

I will make constant references to the 2020 Fantasy Football Playbook. That is because I broke down a lot of the strategy and streaming concepts in there and not a lot of the strategy has changed from 2020 to 2021. And the results of the stream model continue to show that.

I would strongly recommend you buy a copy of the 2020 Fantasy Football Playbook (QR Code is in the back of this book) in order to really get the best of this section of the book. If you bought the 2020 Fantasy Football Playbook, then please do find it, open it up, refresh yourself of the concepts mentioned in there, and then read this. I think by doing this, you will get a great deal out of the following forty pages or so.

You can also find the entire PAS metrics in the appendix at the back of the book for quick reference also. These are very useful cheat sheets for your fantasy drafts. And, as always, feel free to reach out to me via email or via Twitter @Murf_NFL. If you want the excel spreadsheets, then also please get in touch and I am happy to send them.

Overall Results.

All points are 0.5pt PPR as that was the popular choice for this experiment. Below is how I finished streaming players owned 30% or below on ESPN.com prior to waivers of the week they were picked:

Quarterback – 302.34 points. Overall rank: 12th

Running Back – 205.9 points. Overall rank: 9th

Wide Receiver – 159.8 points. Overall rank: 31st

Tight End – 154.0 points. Overall rank: 3rd

Kicker - 126 points. Overall rank: 13th

D/ST - 123 points. Overall rank: 7th

There are some standout results here. Due to all the injuries in 2020, I was able to stream a RB1 performance. I also chipped in with a very strong Tight End performance, in what was a weak year for the position, whilst also chipping in with D/ST1, QB1 finishes.

I had a poor year from a kickers perspective. I started very behind and whilst I made a strong run towards the end, a poor showing from Joey Slye in Week Seventeen cost me a K1 spot. I am relatively pleased to have streamed the WR31 given how deep the position is owned. It is a solid WR3 performance.

What does this mean?

Over the course of the coming pages, I am going to break down each position and what it means. There is a ton of data and learnings from this. However, from a top-level perspective, the first lessons to gleam here are positions of scarcity. Picking from a pool of 30% owned players every week, to finish with top eight performances in four of the six positions shows that these positions were not all that hard to replace week on week, whilst being effective

Quarterbacks.

If you bought this book in 2020, you would have read that last year I streamed the QB2 overall. So, to fall down to 12 this year is a disappointment. However, there is some learning from this and reasons for this result.

The first is there was a lot less volatility at the position in 2020. With the exception of Dak Prescott, the majority of the Quarterbacks barely missed any time. Mahomes was rested for a game, but other than that, the top performances seemed to play week in, week out in 2020. That was not the case in 2019. There was also a lot less Quarterback benching in 2020, meaning it was easier to predict outcomes and harder to stream top tier Quarterbacks unlike last year.

Secondly, due to COVID, more Quarterbacks were owned, meaning less were available to stream. According to ESPN data, 23 Quarterbacks were owned by more than 50% of players by the end of the season. This made it an extremely short pool to stream from every week as it thinned out towards the end of the season. Typically, this number would be closer to 16 or 17 in most seasons. However, with the fear of last-minute rescheduling or cancellation, most teams rostered two Quarterbacks and some even rostered three Quarterbacks. Due to the scarcity in the streaming pool, you had less advantageous outcomes available to you. This made streaming the position harder. Will this be corrected to the mean in 2021? It is hard to say right now. However, the merit of keeping a second Quarterback on the roster might be something more players adopt moving forward.

Lastly, Quarterbacks mostly finished where we expected. Ok, maybe no one expected Josh Allen/Aaron Rodgers/Kyler Murray 1-2-3, however, most expected them to finish in the top 6/7 Quarterbacks. With the exception of the performance of Justin Herbert, nobody was truly shocked with the performance of the top Quarterbacks. Whilst at the other end of the scale, only Daniel Jones and Carson Wentz truly disappointed from where they were expected to finish from a fantasy position. Without that diversity, it becomes harder to find a way up the streaming charts.

Wide Receivers and Running Backs.

The biggest surprise in 2020 was streaming a RB1 performance. To stream the RB9 overall meant a lot of things had to go wrong at the position. And boy, did it get ugly. Christian McCaffrey, Saquon Barkley and Joe Mixon suffered significant injuries to themselves, Ezekiel Elliott had his Quarterback suffer a season ending injury that affected his performance, Nick Chubb, Austin Ekeler, Chris Carson, Miles Sanders all missed significant time, Leonard Fournette was cut right before the start of the season. There was so much volatility at the position. And it was because of this, that my stream model, as well as many fantasy players globally, were able to exploit this to our advantage and bring in players such as Mike Davis and James Robinson to help us out significantly. Also, even moving, and utilising scat back players such as Nyheim Hines and J.D McKissic.

If you listened to me on the podcast, or in this book last year, you would have invested in lots of Running Backs. Someone like David Montgomery, Jonathan Taylor or Antonio Gibson might have been the 3ʳᵈ Running Back you drafted. If you did, you are welcome. Those guys were the next man up on rosters. And, as a result, they helped you advance to the playoffs. This is why I continue to tell people to invest in Running Backs and Wide Receivers. It is a scarce position. This season is an outlier, a fluke. However, if you still invested, you were probably in a great place still when you lost a big weapon. Or you were in an even better place to profit by flipping your backup Running Back for an absolute song and building a Championship roster

As for Wide Receivers, this proved, for the second year in a row, to be the hardest position to stream. Because all the solid, consistent producers are owned. When you stream Wide Receivers, it becomes streaky. You can have a 20pt week one week, and then a 1.5pt week the next. It really is feast or famine sometimes for Wide Receiver streaming.

Once again, this is why I would advise you to load up on Wide Receivers. It is the same principle as with the Wide Receivers. You have more chances hitting from your bench, than you do from the Waiver Wire. Unless there is a significant injury.

Of the top 24 Wide Receivers, only two were drafted outside the top 50 Wide Receivers. They were Robby Anderson, drafted as Wide Receiver 57, and Chase Claypool, drafted as Wide Receiver 84. These were the two success stories off the Waiver Wire last year, as well as some good Russell Gage weeks when Julio went down. Other than that, it was spits and starts. So, make sure you continue to hammer the position.

What is coming up over the next Pages?

I will start off with Quarterback, before following up with Running Back, Wide Receiver, Tight End, Kicker and ending with D/ST. There will also be some additional analysis based on some of the end of season totals for the position. However, what came out of this process is the Points Against Streaming (PAS) metric that I will touch upon next.

Points Against Streaming (PAS) Metric.

Based on the data I have accumulated by streaming every week, I decided to create a new metric in 2019. This will be to analyse all 2020 players and how they did above my streaming model. It does not make sense to use the optimal stream option as nothing is perfect and people will not pick the best stream option every week for 16 weeks. As such, I have decided to build this metric based off my stream rollercoaster week on week. I have worked out how to analyse each player, based on the games they played and broken down how they performed against their stream counterparts.

What is the reason for this?

The answer is truly two-fold:

1) It highlights position scarcity and how many players will finish above the streaming average. This also takes into account injury so players who finished below the stream model's point total might end up over the PAS threshold line as their average per game will be higher. This is useful to know and truly understand position scarcity.

2) To help in drafts by giving you visibility about who to draft and when. I will eventually do a draft board based on PAS (minus Kickers and D/STs) and see how that mirrors a mock draft and ADP data. Ultimately, if I can provide you more data that will allow you to make a decision based on a tiebreaker, then it will only help right?

I hope this metric will become useful and it is something I will take into account during my drafts over the summer.

Understanding the Points Against Streaming (PAS) Metric.

To explain the PAS metric, it is simply collating the stream picks I made for 0.5pt PPR last season and also setting an aggregate score against each position. I would then compare that against the players who played in that position. This happens by taking into account the number of games they played (above six), to work out who had a positive PAS and who had a negative PAS. This metric should be looked at to identify potential players you want to draft. It will identify consistency, draft value, help you make tiers and important drafting decisions. However, the biggest thing it will do is weed out poor performers.

In short, it is a metric to be used amongst other data you collate and use (or you just use everything I present here in the Fantasy Football Playbook Appendix), to help you.

I have covered a lot already and will also be going into more depth. PAS is another piece of information to arm yourselves with prior to the draft. PAS demonstrates position scarcity, or lack of it in this case. PAS will also start to define tiers for you.

Lastly, PAS will also tell you about the potential strength of replacements on the Waiver Wire. Therefore, if you are trying to finalise a draft strategy, look at the PAS scores of players to help you decide how many of each position you need pre-draft. This is just a guide, that I hope helps you to make better decisions in the draft.

Streaming Quarterbacks

This time last year, I was writing about the turmoil at the position with a number of key names getting injured, as well as Andrew Luck retiring. In 2020, it was almost a complete reversal of fortunes. Dak Prescott was injured in Week Six, and Joe Burrow after Week Eight. However, that was the extent of the significant injuries at the position in 2020. Therefore, what we saw was almost the complete opposite to what we saw in 2019, complete predictability.

Despite COVID-19, despite games being postponed or threatened to be called off, very few Quarterbacks missed significant time in 2020. However, fantasy players took more caution than ever. A record number of Quarterbacks were owned in 1QB leagues in terms of the 50% threshold of ownership. You needed your second QB, in case you could not start your primary one on Sunday due to positive COVID tests by one of the teams in the game, or an entire room got ruled out (see Denver and the Kendell Hinton week for example).

This made streaming Quarterbacks much harder. Because so many were owned. Therefore, it was slim pickings for many weeks. As you will see below, a number of Quarterbacks managed to beat the stream on a PAS metric basis. I did, however, stream the QB12 on the year. This, if you can do consistently, will allow you the flexibility to take some extra flyers in your draft that could hit.

Quarterbacks Who Finished with A Positive Points Against Streaming Value.

These are the Quarterbacks who finished with a positive Points Against Streaming value against my 2020 Streaming performance:

Rank	Name	Total Points	Games Played	PPG Average	PAS
1	Patrick Mahomes	374.4	15	24.96	7.18
2	Josh Allen	395.56	16	24.72	6.94
3	Aaron Rodgers	382.76	16	23.92	6.14
4	Kyler Murray	378.74	16	23.67	5.89
5	Deshaun Watson	369.32	16	23.08	5.30
6	Russell Wilson	359.78	16	22.49	4.71
7	Justin Herbert	332.84	15	22.19	4.41
8	Lamar Jackson	332.78	15	22.19	4.41
9	Ryan Tannehill	343.86	16	21.49	3.71
10	Tom Brady	337.92	16	21.12	3.34
11	Kirk Cousins	306.2	16	19.14	1.36
12	Ben Roethlisberger	267.22	15	17.81	0.03
13	Gardner Minshew II	160.16	9	17.80	0.02

As you can see from the graphic above, there were thirteen Quarterbacks who finished with a positive PAS score in 2020. Ten of them beat the stream by over three points per game, and five by over five points a game. That works out to be scoring 22% more points a week, if they scored five points over, which is a lot. This also did not take into account Dak Prescott, as he did not play the minimum number of games to qualify for this exercise, yet he was on a record pace.

What Does That Tell Us for Quarterbacks?

Interestingly, it tells us that the position has rebounded from the floor it was five or so years ago. Five years ago, it is fair to say that the talent of NFL Quarterbacks was on a very wide scale. Therefore, you had 2-4 elite Quarterbacks (for fantasy football anyways) and then after that, everyone was kind of the same. You had no significant tier distinctions between QB6 and QB16. That is why streaming a Quarterback gave smart players an edge.

However, in the last five years, there has been heavy recruitment of Quarterbacks from colleges in the NFL. They have gotten past their rookie years and are now shining in the NFL. Patrick Mahomes, Deshawn Watson, Josh Allen, Lamar Jackson, Justin Herbert, Joe Burrow, Dak Prescott, are all Quarterbacks that are thriving in the NFL. And the previously good ones, Aaron Rodgers, Tom Brady, Russell Wilson have risen to the challenge and are now competing with these guys year in year out.

Quarterbacks are just better now. And they will continue to get better. When you add significant talent to a position, depth occurs. However, what also occurs more is talent tiers. What used to be smart twelve months ago, and drafting a Quarterback late, has now changed into "taking an elite Quarterback in the middle rounds is the most optimal strategy". As you have seen, getting an extra 22% more points a week from a position is significant. That is the difference between the playoffs and the toilet bowl, depending on the rest of your roster.

How high do I need to draft Quarterbacks?

This is a massive question and one I feel I have answered a few times in the book already. For me, as I documented last year in the Fantasy Football Playbook, there was absolutely no advantage to draft Mahomes in the second or third rounds in 2020. We saw last year that drafting Mahomes and Jackson in those ranges burned you. Mahomes, not as much, but you certainly did not get value for your draft selection. Twelve months on, nothing has changed.

What has changed based on last year is the number of elite Quarterbacks now and the impact they make. You can see here in the PAS modelling, that getting one of those elite options gives you a distinct advantage at the position. The ADP, at time of writing for most of these options, is between the 5th and 6th round. You can advocate for one QB over another, but I think the tier gap for the elite four or five options outside of Mahomes (who will go in the 3rd round probably in your drafts) and Rodgers (who has some Touchdown efficiency regression that needs to be considered and therefore someone who would sit behind Allen, Prescott, Watson, Wilson, and Jackson in a separate tier with Herbert) is fairly small. For me, walking away with one of those five QBs is a must in order to be successful in 2021. However, not if their ADP shoots up into the 3/4th round. Rodgers and Herbert are your safety net that IF you miss the run on these Quarterbacks, you can still get someone productive and not pay a significant penalty. However, miss out on them, and you have given up a significant advantage to opponents in your league.

Giving up a significant advantage at the position that scores the most points most week means you have to draft extremely well to overcome it. It is not impossible. It just makes it more difficult.

One thing I have not mentioned is that Mahomes was top of the PAS metric due to playing one game less. This is very true that had he played in the final week, he probably would have been the QB1 overall. However, the Points Per Game gap to the next tier is not significant enough to warrant the extra investment. If you have already read the chapter about the perfect draft by round, you will see that the drop off for Running Backs and Wide Receivers in this block of rounds 2-5 is severe, and far outweighs the minor benefit of having Mahomes.

The strategy I advocate highly for 2021 1QB leagues is grabbing a Quarterback in that 5-6th round range and grabbing one of Allen, Prescott, Watson, Wilson, and Jackson at the time of writing. If they have been injured or something else has happened, then of course, it will need to be revisited.

All the data in 2021 points to drafting one of these 5QBs being the most optimal when it comes to lineup construction in 2021.

What Else Does the PAS Data Show for Quarterbacks?

Below is a list of all the Quarterbacks and how they performed against my streaming model:

14	Matt Ryan	280.44	16	17.53	-0.25
15	Drew Brees	209.48	12	17.46	-0.32
16	Joe Burrow	173.72	10	17.37	-0.41
17	Cam Newton	259.98	15	17.33	-0.45
18	Ryan Fitzpatrick	153.24	9	17.03	-0.75
19	Derek Carr	272.12	16	17.01	-0.77
20	Carson Wentz	198.4	12	16.53	-1.25
21	Matthew Stafford	260.56	16	16.29	-1.50
22	Teddy Bridgewater	241.22	15	16.08	-1.70
23	Jared Goff	239.98	15	16.00	-1.78
24	Baker Mayfield	248.12	16	15.51	-2.27

25	Mitchell Trubisky	153.7	10	15.37	-2.41
26	Philip Rivers	239.96	16	15.00	-2.78
27	Drew Lock	181.32	13	13.95	-3.83
28	Tua Tagovailoa	135.46	10	13.55	-4.23
29	Daniel Jones	180.02	14	12.86	-4.92
30	Andy Dalton	136.36	11	12.40	-5.38
31	Nick Mullens	116.28	10	11.63	-6.15
32	Nick Foles	104.18	9	11.58	-6.20
33	Sam Darnold	134.02	12	11.17	-6.61
34	Taysom Hill	152.62	16	9.54	-8.24
35	Alex Smith	71.58	8	8.95	-8.83
36	Jalen Hurts	108.94	15	7.26	-10.52

So, what is it telling us? Well, here are some quick takeaways:

- When QB play is relatively healthy and stable (fewer injuries and fewer disruptions), then it becomes easier to predict who is going to be fantasy relevant, at least in the top tier, versus those that are not. Let us look at the top 8 players in the PAS Metric and view their ADP in 2020 by aggregating between Yahoo, CBS, MFL and Fantrax, using Fantasy Pros as the lead source for this.

1. **Patrick Mahomes- ADP QB1**
2. **Josh Allen- ADP QB9**
3. **Aaron Rodgers- ADP QB12**
4. **Kyler Murray- ADP QB6**
5. **Deshaun Watson- ADP QB5**
6. **Russell Wilson- ADP QB4**
7. **Justin Herbert- ADP QB36**
8. **Lamar Jackson- ADP QB2**

There are no bizarre shocks here with the exception of Justin Herbert. And guess what, Rookies are hard to evaluate. Herbert did not start Week One, had no easy path to the job early doors, and it took a freak accident for him to start. However, when he got his chance, he silenced all the doubters on his way to Offensive Rookie of the Year honours.

The three ADP players missing from the top right based on their projections are Dak Prescott, who suffered a season ending injury very early into the season, when he was performing at the overall QB1 in fantasy football and was projected to have a record-breaking year. Drew Brees was the QB7 in ADP who also missed significant time due to injury. The last one was Tom Brady, who was QB8 in ADP and he finished up in 10th in PAS.

Fantasy analysts and players were better this year than ever before at predicting the outcomes of top fantasy Quarterbacks. Because there was a lot more stability at the position. Should stability continue, (and how can you project otherwise) then you can look at that second tier of QBs behind Mahomes and be aggressive. They have safe floors and a ton of upside. Rather than gambling on finding the high QB upside late, go after the QBs who will deliver you the performance you expect and project.

Running Back Streaming.

The Running Back position in 2020 might be the single greatest achievement for the PAS metric and my streaming model. I was able to stream an RB1 in 2020 despite this being the most difficult position to project in recent years when it comes to Waiver Wire success.

According to the same ADP sources, via Fantasy Pros, who aggregate CBS, MFL, and Fantrax ADP data, 59 Running Backs were drafted inside the top 200 picks in drafts in 2019. That says I was working with, in theory, less than 30 Running Backs from the pool to amass a RB1 score, starting from RB60 and down.

Now, I say in theory as Running Backs get dropped, rosters change, and ownership numbers change significantly.

To stream a RB1 in any year is nigh on impossible. Yet, I managed to do it. How? And what does this mean for the position going forward.

The Challenges of 2020 for Running Backs.

2020 will always be an outlier year for Running Backs. Yes, it is easily the most punishing position, with significant injuries that will happen to players. However, so many significant things happened that absolutely turned the position on its head. I will capture them all here chronologically below:

- **Leonard Fournette Cut/Ryquell Armstead gets COVID-** literally days before the season, yet after almost all fantasy drafts, the Jags basically cut their 1st Round Running Back, and placed his backup on IR (he was never to return in 2020). This meant there was a competition for a role days before the season very few could have predicted. Enter James Robinson, who made the job his own. His overall ADP average was 332. If you snagged him on Waivers or Free Agency, he probably won you a league, or at least got you to the playoffs. These things just do not happen.
- **Christian McCaffrey getting injured, would only play once after Week 2 all season-** Losing the 1.01 in drafts is a massive blow to those who drafted him. This is not unprecedented, however. Saquon Barkley had this happen to him 12 months previously, as well as David Johnson in 2017. These things can and will happen at the Running Back position. Perhaps though, what was not expected, was Mike Davis finishing as a top 15 Running Back. And let us call it right, he ran out of steam. He

was on pace to finish inside the top 10 until a late season dip in performance hurt his numbers. Although, he popped up with a nice week in Week Sixteen to help owners win a championship. Yes, replacements doing well for a few games can and will happen. 2 Waiver Wire/ Free Agents having the impact Robinson and Davis had over the course of a season, extremely rare.

- **Saquon Barkley getting injured**- Second significant injury in successive years for Barkley and the 1.02 would end up missing nearly 3/4ers of the season. Meaning the 1.02 in drafts went down not long after the 1.01.
- **Dak Prescott out for the season/Zeke suffering as a result-** Through the first 5 weeks of 2020, when Dak Prescott was on record pace, Zeke was the RB3 in all formats. He was holding his draft position and was performing at a high level. People forget that, based on what happened the rest of the season, when the Red Rifle Andy Dalton took over. But this massively impacted Zeke. Simply put, the offense did not work as well under Dalton as it did under Dak. Zeke was basically lost as a result. In 0.5pt PPR from weeks 6-17, Zeke was the RB25 (He was the RB24 in full point PPR). Nobody suffered more than Zeke when Dak was ruled out for the season, meaning the 1.03 in drafts became virtually anonymous.
- **Joe Mixon getting injured, out for the season-** Another 1st round Running Back, Joe Mixon, also fell to the injury curse that was spread on Running Backs in 2020. After getting injured during a game, he was forced to miss the final 10 games of the season. After a slow start with his new QB in weeks 1 and 2, Joe Mixon was the RB4 in all formats in weeks 3-6 before his injury. He was on course to potentially excel his high ADP and return value. However, with the injury that was not to be.
- **Nick Chubb Injured, missing ¼ of the season-** To make matters worse, another 1st round Running Back, Nick Chubb, missed a quarter of the season due to injury. This made the 5th 1st round Running Back out of 9 that was severely impacted by injury, either directly or indirectly. That is a huge number that is not sustainable and will arguably regress in 2021.

As a result of all these actions, the position was in a bit of flux. And the savvy players were there to take advantage. My stream model highlighted high upside plays that paid off, until they were owned too much. That, mixed with bye week covers, allowed me to stream a top nine finish at the position.

What does this mean?

In truth, it was, as far as I am concerned, an outlier. You cannot predict that much chaos in a year to happen. There will always be opportunities to stream in certain weeks and take advantage of some of the injuries/ heavy schedules and rotations. However, it is unlikely we will see the kind of carnage we saw at the Running Back position in 2020 again.

However, what I will say is that the position is still something you can stream, if smart. There are, as a result of the injuries and talent, less and less "bell-cow" Running Backs in the NFL. Teams are opting more for 1a and 1b concepts, like the Buccaneers and the Ravens, so as to preserve tread on the tyres of Running Backs as they progress deeper into the season/playoffs. You also have more and more teams deploying catching backs such as the Colts and the Bears. These will limit the touches of the number one Running Back and therefore cap their upside.

Because of this, you can stream these "scat" backs and secondary backs. If you hit, you will have productive weeks. However, you will need to be clever with matchups and when to utilise the stream.

With all that being said, here are the 22 Running Backs that beat the stream. Even though I was the RB9 on the season, my stream model benefits from not having a bye, hence the discrepancy.

RBS 1-22- The Ones Who Beat the Stream.

Rank	Name	Total 0.5 PPR Points	Games Played	PPG Average	PAS
1	Dalvin Cook	315.8	14	22.56	10.50
2	Alvin Kamara	336.3	15	22.42	10.36
3	Derrick Henry	323.6	16	20.23	8.17
4	Aaron Jones	235.4	14	16.81	4.75
5	Nick Chubb	199.7	12	16.64	4.58
6	James Robinson	225.9	14	16.14	4.08
7	David Montgomery	237.8	15	15.85	3.79
8	Jonathan Taylor	234.8	15	15.65	3.59
9	Myles Gaskin	143.7	10	14.37	2.31
10	Josh Jacobs	214.8	15	14.32	2.26
11	Chris Carson	169.3	12	14.11	2.05
12	Austin Ekeler	138.3	10	13.83	1.77
13	David Johnson	163	12	13.58	1.52
14	Ezekiel Elliott	197.7	15	13.18	1.12
15	Antonio Gibson	184.2	14	13.16	1.10
16	Miles Sanders	156.4	12	13.03	0.97
17	D'Andre Swift	166.8	13	12.83	0.77

18	Kareem Hunt	199.5	16	12.47	0.41
19	Jeff Wilson Jr.	135.8	11	12.35	0.29
20	Ronald Jones II	172.3	14	12.31	0.25
21	Melvin Gordon III	182.4	15	12.16	0.10
22	Clyde Edwards-Helaire	158	13	12.15	0.09

To start my deep dive into 2020, I need to understand the whole landscape. Here are the 22 Running Backs that had a positive PAS (Points Above Streaming) score. Now, I know I have lost some of you here, because I just told you I had the 33rd best Running Back yet 46 beat the model. The difference is not all of the above played every game. Therefore, their average points per game is higher, their total points are lower.

What is clearly demonstrated from the above is the appearance of tiers. They allow you to help break up the data to clearly define groups. Of those who beat the model, the apparent tiers from 2020 are as follows:

TIER 1
- Dalvin Cook
- Alvin Kamara

TIER 2
- Derrick Henry

TIER 3
- Aaron Jones
- Nick Chubb
- James Robinson

TIER 4
- David Montgomery
- Jonathan Taylor

TIER 5
- Myles Gaskin
- Josh Jacobs
- Chris Carson
- Austin Eckler
- David Johnson

TIER 6
- Ezekiel Elliott
- Antonio Gibson
- Miles Sanders

TIER 7
- D'Andre Swift
- Kareem Hunt
- Jeff Wilson Jr.
- Ronald Jones Jr.
- Melvin Gordon III
- Clyde Edwards- Helaire

When it comes to analysing these tiers, we need to measure their consistency, changes in situation in 2021, and also all the returning Running Backs, to break down who can rise in tiers, who can slide in tiers, and work out where to slot in the injured backs.

It goes without saying that Christian McCaffrey and Saquon Barkley will be in that first tier in 2021 if they are injury free and ready to go. And the ADP will show that. But how do you rank the others?

Well I have laid out the facts and cases for players throughout this book, as well as also giving you a top 60 player breakdown. However, part of fantasy football is developing your own process. Everyone at 5 Yard Rush wants to arm you with the information to make better fantasy decisions, without making them for you.

I have laid the case I think Zeke could and should be in a higher tier and given their situations in 2021, it is easy to move Josh Jacobs and David Johnson down. Whilst you can also easily elevate Antonio Gibson and Melvin Gordon III.

Teams Without A Top 24 Running Back.

I wrote about this in last year's book, so I wanted to give you an update. I talked about the offenses that did not have a top 24 Running Back in 2019, and it might be an idea to fade these players. Those teams were Chicago, Tampa Bay, Houston, San Francisco, Kansas City, Washington, Detroit, and Miami

Let us look at each of these teams. Chicago, Houston, and Miami I can group together. Their Running Back rooms got extremely thin in the season, to where there was really only one featured back. Chicago got the ball moving with David Montgomery. He benefited from an easy schedule down the stretch, but he has shown resilience and proved he can be fantasy relevant. As for David Johnson and Myles Gaskin, they got the majority of the work in 2020. I do not expect this to be the case in 2021. Houston really muddled the backfield with adding Mark Ingram and Philip Lindsay. It does not look like there is a clear winner in that backfield. As for Miami, I doubt Gaskin is given the chance to repeat. I think they will either draft a back or bring in a committee back. Last year, Miami brought in Howard, Breida, Gaskin and Ahmed. If you followed the advice set out in 2019, you would have swerved to miss Breida and Howard and saved a draft pick. Save another one and fade Gaskin.

Now, let us look at Kansas City, Washington, and Detroit. All three invested in Running Backs very high in the draft. And they used them, for the most part, to good effect. Key piece of advice here. If a team did not have a top 24 Running Back in 2020, they are a good bet to invest in the position high in the draft, as long as they do not have other needs. I will get to those needs in a second. These rookies all hit, to a degree, and produced a top 24 season.

That leaves Tampa Bay and San Francisco. Ronald Jones broke into the top 24, despite yielding carries to Leonard Fournette, who was signed in the offseason. It is unlikely he will be an RB1 in 2021, but the path to RB2 territory remains the same. So, I need to take the L there.

And San Francisco with Mostert was a fade depending on price. Whilst Jeff Wilson returned a top 22 PAS metric score, he did not play enough to warrant a top 24 finish. San Francisco and Kansas City, as I stated last year, are not as hot places for Running Backs as you would hope. Edwards- Helaire the 1st round Rookie, was the RB22 on the season and fell well below his ADP. I would expect these lessons to be learned in 2021.

So, which teams did not have a top 24 Running Back in 2021? These teams are the ones we could either see investment in the draft or look to fade when it comes to our Running Back search. They are Atlanta, New England, Cincinnati (However they lost Mixon, so if Mixon is a go in 2021 as we expect, they will have their top 24 RB), Pittsburgh, San Francisco, New

York Giants (Again, with Barkley we expect this to not be the case), New York Jets, Buffalo Bills, Los Angeles Rams (however, with Cam Akers this could and should change in 2021), and the Los Angeles Chargers (again, they lost Austin Ekeler for over half a season, and therefore probably have a top 24 RB in their ranks).

That means all eyes are on Atlanta, New England, Pittsburgh, San Francisco, the Jets, and Buffalo for the drafting of a top Running Back. Otherwise, these are fading situations. I would also add Tampa as a Running Back situation to fade. Especially if Fournette performs at the level he did in the playoffs, they could split the backs more evenly.

Other Takeaways

Other things to take away from this is that in realistic terms, anything outside of the RB2 and upwards range is completely random. Once you take the top 24 guys, positions 25-60 are purely luck based. This probably is not what you want to hear, let me explain.

The players in tiers 6-7 were all separated on a points per game basis of anywhere from fractions of a point to the biggest gap of 1.12 points per game. Across a Fantasy Football season, assuming everyone is fit and healthy, this equates to roughly 40 points. So that is nine players, including my stream model as a player, split from anything as little as 0.16 points in a season to as much as 16.5 points. Given the average player, who starts a game and gets 15 touches of the ball accrues on average 11 PPR points, one injury, one big play, one coaches decision can change a Running Back finishing RB30 and RB24. The difference between RB24 and RB30 last year was 10.1 PPR Points. Now, I am not advocating streaming Running Backs as a strategy. Far from it, the above proves that it is just random/ who is fittest who ends RB25 and who ends RB40. Therefore, the only way to have a better chance is to draft more players at that position. Which is why we do it. If there was a better way, we would draft four Running Backs maximum, but we do not. That is because we know that it does not work.

So, What's the Point?

I know I just said streaming is not a winning strategy, but it can give you an advantage over just general stashing. It requires patience and reading our Waiver Wire picks each week. If you have one RB spot that you just stream week to week, taking the best dart throw of that week, you should achieve a top 36 Running Back.

Streaming diversifies your chances of hitting from outside the top 24 Running Back and effectively gives you more chances to get lucky. Instead of having your static three or four Running Backs on your bench, you can add one new body every week. It is just widening your odds, based on ongoing situation changes, match-ups and with new, up to date, and better data. That is the whole point of PAS. It is to find those players who make a difference game by game vs the stream. As well as to highlight potential draft targets, it should also be used for streaming targets also.

The Rest

So, what about the remaining Running Backs? Well, this is how they finished:

23	Kenyan Drake	179.7	15	11.98	-0.08
24	Mike Davis	177	15	11.80	-0.26
25	Raheem Mostert	91.7	8	11.46	-0.60
26	James Conner	147.1	13	11.32	-0.74
27	J.K. Dobbins	159.5	15	10.63	-1.43
28	Nyheim Hines	161.7	16	10.11	-1.95
29	Todd Gurley II	150.7	15	10.05	-2.01
30	Rex Burkhead	95.1	10	9.51	-2.55
31	J.D. McKissic	151.4	16	9.46	-2.60
32	Damien Harris	88.8	10	8.88	-3.18
33	Chase Edmonds	141.5	16	8.84	-3.22
34	Leonard Fournette	114	13	8.77	-3.29
35	Giovani Bernard	134.6	16	8.41	-3.65
36	Wayne Gallman	126.1	15	8.41	-3.65
37	Latavius Murray	124.7	15	8.31	-3.75
38	Darrell Henderson Jr.	122.3	15	8.15	-3.91
39	Sony Michel	71.8	9	7.98	-4.08
40	Jamaal Williams	111.6	14	7.97	-4.09
41	Devin Singletary	124.6	16	7.79	-4.27
42	Gus Edwards	123.7	16	7.73	-4.33
43	Carlos Hyde	76.9	10	7.69	-4.37

44	Cam Akers	96.3	13	7.41	-4.65
45	Adrian Peterson	118.5	16	7.41	-4.65
46	Zack Moss	94.6	13	7.28	-4.78
47	Kalen Ballage	79.4	11	7.22	-4.84
48	Jerick McKinnon	109.7	16	6.86	-5.20
49	Tony Pollard	106.7	16	6.67	-5.39
50	James White	92.1	14	6.58	-5.48
51	Duke Johnson	70.4	11	6.40	-5.66
52	Justin Jackson	55.8	9	6.20	-5.86
53	Alexander Mattison	80.4	13	6.18	-5.88
54	Frank Gore	92.2	15	6.15	-5.91
55	Malcolm Brown	97.6	16	6.10	-5.96
56	Le'Veon Bell	66.6	11	6.05	-6.01
57	Phillip Lindsay	62.5	11	5.68	-6.38
58	Boston Scott	83.1	16	5.19	-6.87
59	Brian Hill	82.9	16	5.18	-6.88
60	Joshua Kelley	69.7	14	4.98	-7.08
61	Devontae Booker	77.2	16	4.83	-7.24
62	La'Mical Perine	47	10	4.70	-7.36
63	Mark Ingram II	49.9	11	4.54	-7.52
64	Kyle Juszczyk	72.1	16	4.51	-7.55
65	Benny Snell Jr.	69.9	16	4.37	-7.69

66	**Alfred Morris**	**39.2**	**9**	**4.36**	-7.70
67	**Ty Johnson**	**55.3**	**13**	**4.25**	-7.81
68	**Josh Adams**	**33.6**	**8**	**4.20**	-7.86
69	**Chris Thompson**	**32.6**	**8**	**4.08**	-7.99
70	**DeeJay Dallas**	**48.4**	**12**	**4.03**	-8.03
71	**Kerryon Johnson**	**62.3**	**16**	**3.89**	-8.17
72	**Samaje Perine**	**60.2**	**16**	**3.76**	-8.30
73	**Jordan Wilkins**	**55.3**	**15**	**3.69**	-8.37
74	**A.J. Dillon**	**39.3**	**11**	**3.57**	-8.49
75	**Darrel Williams**	**45.5**	**13**	**3.50**	-8.56
76	**Ito Smith**	**48.8**	**14**	**3.49**	-8.57
77	**Peyton Barber**	**53**	**16**	**3.31**	-8.75
78	**Jalen Richard**	**41.6**	**13**	**3.20**	-8.86
79	**Matt Breida**	**37.5**	**12**	**3.13**	-8.94
80	**Dion Lewis**	**47.7**	**16**	**2.98**	-9.08
81	**Jeremy McNichols**	**37.9**	**16**	**2.37**	-9.69
82	**Royce Freeman**	**31.1**	**16**	**1.94**	-10.12

Wide Receiver Streaming.

This continues to be the hardest position to stream optimally out of all the six positions. Because no matter how well you think you can do, because the Wide Receiver options are so deep, and there is so much talent, it is almost impossible to make a significant dent whilst streaming.

Having said that, it is still highly important you stream the position and invest in Wide Receivers both in the draft and through the Waiver Wire. According to Fantasy Pros ADP data that they gather from Yahoo and Fantrax, 67 Wide Receivers were drafted in the first 200 picks in 2020. So, to be consistently streaming the Wide Receiver 30/31 means I am outperforming the rest of the pool by 36 or so positions. That is a huge advantage. Not to mention, some of the players I streamed, such as Justin Jefferson, who was dropped heavily in the first few weeks, Chase Claypool who went undrafted, Brandon Aiyuk, who was dropped after the injury to Jimmy Garoppolo, and Tee Higgins, were all players I would have hung on to on my team. These four, with two or three existing Wide Receivers would have been a deadly WR corps to have on the roster.

That is why streaming and being active on the Waiver Wire, allows you to find these players, give yourself more lottery tickets, and allows you to hit more than other players who wait for the Waiver Wire to come to them.

Streaming forces you to be extremely active on the Waiver Wire. Most of my teams rack up 50+ transactions off of the Waiver Wire in a given season. Because eventually, I will find someone who will stick and add value.

The other positive about streaming Wide Receivers, is that you will probably keep two slots on your roster that you will use for just streaming. Maybe more. So, there are no agonising drop decisions. It is dropping someone who did not pan out for a streaming option based on a good match-up one week, so you throw them back to the pool and grab someone else.

If you start to get into the habit of picking these players up off the Waiver Wire every week, and being active, you will find that not only will you be streaming above the average position and possibly streaming a flex starter across the season. But you will also find a gem and find someone like Justin Jefferson who ended up returning WR4 numbers in 0.5pt PPR in weeks 9 thru 17 last season. It just makes perfect sense. So, make sure you give it a whirl next season.

Also, please revisit this corresponding strategy section in the 2020 Fantasy Football Playbook.

Who Outperformed the Streaming Model In 2020?

So, who did outperform the streaming model in 2020? Well as mentioned previously, I created the PAS metric to look at players who stream in a positive outcome vs my model. And this metric takes into account the number of games a Wide Receiver played. However, for what it is worth, my streaming Wide Receivers finished 1.1 points higher than Chris Godwin did in 2020. And his ADP was second round, 20th overall.

So, without further ado, here are the Wide Receivers who beat my streaming model in 2020 and ended up with a positive PAS score:

WR'S The Ones Who Beat the Stream.

Rank	Name	Total 0.5 PPR Points	Games Played	Total PPG	PAS
1	Davante Adams	300.9	14	21.49	12.09
2	Tyreek Hill	285.4	15	19.03	9.63
3	Stefon Diggs	265.1	16	16.57	7.17
4	Calvin Ridley	236.5	15	15.77	6.37
5	Will Fuller V	162.4	11	14.76	5.36
6	A.J. Brown	206.5	14	14.75	5.35
7	Adam Thielen	217	15	14.47	5.07
8	DeAndre Hopkins	230.3	16	14.39	4.99
9	Justin Jefferson	230.2	16	14.39	4.99
10	D.K. Metcalf	229.8	16	14.36	4.96
11	Keenan Allen	195.1	14	13.94	4.54
12	Tyler Lockett	215.4	16	13.46	4.06
13	Julio Jones	120.6	9	13.40	4.00
14	Mike Evans	213.6	16	13.35	3.95
15	Allen Robinson II	211.9	16	13.24	3.84
16	Chris Godwin	158.5	12	13.21	3.81
17	Brandon Aiyuk	154.5	12	12.88	3.48
18	Brandin Cooks	191.5	15	12.77	3.37
19	Robert Woods	200.1	16	12.51	3.11

20	Terry McLaurin	180.3	15	12.02	2.62
21	Amari Cooper	190.8	16	11.93	2.53
22	D.J. Moore	178.5	15	11.90	2.50
23	Jamison Crowder	142.52	12	11.88	2.48
24	Marvin Jones Jr.	189.8	16	11.86	2.46
25	Diontae Johnson	177.8	15	11.85	2.45
26	Antonio Brown	94.6	8	11.83	2.43
27	JuJu Smith-Schuster	185.6	16	11.60	2.20
28	Curtis Samuel	173.6	15	11.57	2.17
29	Chase Claypool	183.9	16	11.49	2.09
30	Corey Davis	158.9	14	11.35	1.95
31	Cole Beasley	166.5	15	11.10	1.70
32	Robby Anderson	176.6	16	11.04	1.64
33	CeeDee Lamb	174.7	16	10.92	1.52
34	Cooper Kupp	162.7	15	10.85	1.45
35	Sterling Shepard	129.5	12	10.79	1.39
36	Tyler Boyd	153.14	15	10.21	0.81
37	Jarvis Landry	151.96	15	10.13	0.73
38	Nelson Agholor	161.6	16	10.10	0.70
39	Tee Higgins	161.1	16	10.07	0.67
40	D.J. Chark Jr.	127.1	13	9.78	0.38
41	DeVante Parker	134.8	14	9.63	0.23

42	Marquise Brown	154	16	9.63	0.23
43	Emmanuel Sanders	134.3	14	9.59	0.19

Now in a similar style to Running Backs as I outlined in the Running Backs section, in order to improve, I need to understand the landscape and the tiers, and the tiers really do present themselves in a very clear way here.

TIER 1
- Davante Adams

TIER 2
- Tyreek Hill

TIER 3
- Stefon Diggs
- Calvin Ridley

TIER 4
- Will Fuller V
- A.J. Brown
- Adam Thielen
- DeAndre Hopkins
- Justin Jefferson
- D.K. Metcalf

TIER 5
- Keenan Allen
- Tyler Lockett
- Julio Jones
- Mike Evans
- Allen Robinson
- Chris Godwin

TIER 6
- Brandon Aiyuk
- Brandin Cooks
- Robert Woods

TIER 7
- Terry McLaurin
- Amari Cooper
- D.J. Moore
- Jamison Crowder
- Marvin Jones Jr.
- Dionte Johnson
- Antonio Brown

TIER 8
- Juju Smith-Schuster
- Curtis Samuel
- Chase Claypool
- Corey Davis

TIER 9
- Cole Beasley
- Robby Anderson
- CeeDee Lamb
- Cooper Kupp
- Sterling Shephard

TIER 10
- Tyler Boyd
- Jarvis Landry
- Nelson Agholor
- Tee Higgins
- D.J. Chark
- Devante Parker
- Marquise Brown
- Emmanuel Sanders

What I find interesting with these tiers, is the calibre of Wide Receiver my streaming model matches up to. All of these Wide Receivers in Tier 10 failed to have even a one Point per Game advantage over my streaming model.

In fact, when looking at these tiers, I draw the conclusion that it is more important than ever to take Running Backs earlier, as the position is scarcer. Wide Receiver, with another loaded draft class about to enter the NFL, has never ever been this deep. There is absolutely no doubt that the NFL is a passing league, based on the calibre and talent of the Wide Receivers in the league.

Position Scarcity for Wide Receiver.

What do I mean by that? Well, it is pretty simple. Only one Wide Receiver beat my streaming model by double digits in 2020, Davante Adams. Another one, Tyreek Hill, beat it by 9.63 points per game, whilst Stefon Diggs had a 7.17-point advantage over my stream model every week.

It shows that the difference makers are exactly that. It is important to have elite Wide Receivers, as they will be the difference between you winning a week and not. In the appendix, you will find the Wide Receiver Consistency charts. There, you will see that the majority of the Wide Receivers bust against my consistency chart metric (scoring in the top 24 of the position) over 50% of the time.

Therefore, finding those elite difference makers is important. However, you need to combine this with getting elite numbers at the Running Back balance. I would argue drafting 5,6 or 7 this year is more advantageous than ever, as that is the only way I can see you getting two elite Running Backs and an elite Wide Receiver. Being able to get a Cook, Kamara, Henry, Elliott, following that up with an Ekeler, Aaron Jones or Cam Akers, and then getting Michael Thomas, Mike Evans, or A.J Brown are massively going to help your chances in building a championship roster. I am not sure how you manage to do that in other draft positions right now if the ADP is roughly correct.

What this demonstrates, is that Wide Receiver is a less scarce position. It is still a highly important position to draft. However, there are far less game changing Wide Receivers, and far more safe Wide Receivers who will not lose you weeks, than there are Running Backs. And that is despite the fact that there are more Wide Receivers available to draft than any other position in Fantasy Football.

Other Takeaways

To demonstrate this, it is important to look at the patterns in the data. The Wide Receiver tiers are far more bunched, with some tiers being separated by less than a Point per Game. This truly highlights that although the position is less scarce, it is still just as hard to find difference makers.

All the Wide Receivers appear to be much of a muchness. Yes, situations will change in 2021. However, with those changes comes the opportunity for some to arrow up, like Terry McLaurin, Brandon Aiyuk and Robert Woods. And those who will arrow down like Jamison Crowder, Marvin Jones Jr and Will Fuller V/

However, there seems to be less and less Wide Receivers who really make the difference. That could lead to a change in strategy, and perhaps an advantage to you, over others in 2021. What if, for example, you took advantage of good offenses, in good matchups vs bad defences? By picking up the Wide Receive two or even three in a good offense, against a bad defence, could yield huge results.

I emphasised this point in 2020 and the same can be said in 2021. Therefore, it is important you are utilising the streaming principle, in order to give you the greatest chance of success in 2021.

What's Next?

Well with all things in Fantasy Football, the next step is to try it. Try this strategy in a redraft league, or one of the 5 Yard Rush Listener Leagues this year. There will be plenty of opportunities to try and gain an advantage by streaming more. Plus, raiding the Waiver Wire and robbing your friends and league-mates of targets is so much fun.

This chapter has really taught me a lot and I hope you find it useful as well.

WR The Rest of The Wide Receivers.

Without further ado, here was how the rest of the Wide Receiver class of 2020 got on vs my streaming model against PAS.

44	Laviska Shenault Jr.	128.1	14	9.15	-0.25
45	T.Y. Hilton	136.2	15	9.08	-0.32
46	Russell Gage	145.06	16	9.07	-0.33
47	Tim Patrick	135.7	15	9.05	-0.35
48	Michael Gallup	143.8	16	8.99	-0.41
49	John Brown	80.3	9	8.92	-0.48
50	Keke Coutee	70.5	8	8.81	-0.59
51	Christian Kirk	122.4	14	8.74	-0.66
52	Mike Williams	129.7	15	8.65	-0.75
53	Jerry Jeudy	131.6	16	8.23	-1.18

54	**Preston Williams**	65.8	8	8.23	-1.18
55	**Allen Lazard**	81.3	10	8.13	-1.27
56	**Randall Cobb**	81.1	10	8.11	-1.29
57	**Jakobi Meyers**	113.02	14	8.07	-1.33
58	**Rashard Higgins**	102.4	13	7.88	-1.52
59	**Keelan Cole Sr.**	121.9	16	7.62	-1.78
60	**Darnell Mooney**	121.6	16	7.60	-1.80
61	**Marquez Valdes-Scantling**	120.8	16	7.55	-1.85
62	**Gabriel Davis**	119.4	16	7.46	-1.94
63	**Travis Fulgham**	96.9	13	7.45	-1.95
64	**Darius Slayton**	116	16	7.25	-2.15
65	**Zach Pascal**	114.9	16	7.18	-2.22
66	**Kendrick Bourne**	105.2	15	7.01	-2.39
67	**Breshad Perriman**	84.1	12	7.01	-2.39
68	**Sammy Watkins**	68.9	10	6.89	-2.51
69	**Greg Ward**	106.6	16	6.66	-2.74
70	**Hunter Renfrow**	103.6	16	6.48	-2.93
71	**Mecole Hardman**	101.6	16	6.35	-3.05
72	**David Moore**	101.3	16	6.33	-3.07
73	**Tre'Quan Smith**	86.1	14	6.15	-3.25
74	**Josh Reynolds**	98.3	16	6.14	-3.26
75	**Michael Pittman Jr.**	78.9	13	6.07	-3.33

76	Willie Snead IV	77.7	13	5.98	-3.42
77	Jalen Reagor	65.7	11	5.97	-3.43
78	Danny Amendola	83.4	14	5.96	-3.44
79	Tyron Johnson	69.5	12	5.79	-3.61
80	K.J. Hamler	75.1	13	5.78	-3.62
81	Golden Tate	69.02	12	5.75	-3.65
82	Damiere Byrd	91.4	16	5.71	-3.69
83	Larry Fitzgerald	73.9	13	5.68	-3.72
84	A.J. Green	87.8	16	5.49	-3.91
85	Henry Ruggs III	71.1	13	5.47	-3.93
86	Denzel Mims	49.2	9	5.47	-3.93
87	Scotty Miller	86	16	5.38	-4.03
88	Demarcus Robinson	85.1	16	5.32	-4.08
89	Richie James Jr.	52.9	10	5.29	-4.11
90	James Washington	84.2	16	5.26	-4.14
91	Anthony Miller	84.2	16	5.26	-4.14
92	Jalen Guyton	83.1	16	5.19	-4.21
93	Chris Conley	77.1	15	5.14	-4.26
94	Braxton Berrios	78.8	16	4.93	-4.48
95	Isaiah McKenzie	78.58	16	4.91	-4.49
96	Jakeem Grant Sr.	63.3	14	4.52	-4.88
97	Cam Sims	70.2	16	4.39	-5.01

98	Quintez Cephus	56.9	13	4.38	-5.02
99	Donovan Peoples-Jones	51.4	12	4.28	-5.12
100	Marvin Hall	51.3	12	4.28	-5.13
101	N'Keal Harry	57.4	14	4.10	-5.30
102	Miles Boykin	60.1	16	3.76	-5.64
103	Collin Johnson	50.2	14	3.59	-5.81
104	Cordarrelle Patterson	52.9	16	3.31	-6.09
105	DaeSean Hamilton	50.8	16	3.18	-6.23

Streaming a Tight End.

One of the most polarising views I have is my lack of belief that you need to invest significant draft resources into the position. In last year's edition, I wrote in great detail about the penalties you will pay for investing in the position early. These views were never more poignant that in 2020, when the Tight End position basically fell off a cliff.

I might have been wrong about Travis Kelce, however. One revision to this strategy in 2021 is if you want to invest in Kelce early, there is strong statistical sense to do so. If you can get Kelce in the second round, or tail end of the first, the pick looks safer than it has ever been.

However, I stressed last year that investing in the middle range Tight End will get you into a lot of trouble. And in 2020, it absolutely did. The only two Tight Ends that returned any value on their ADP were Travis Kelce and Darren Waller. Kittle, Andrews, Ertz, Higbee, Engram, Gronkowski, Henry, Cook, and Hooper were all drafted inside the first 100 picks.

This strategy continues to be a loser in Fantasy Football. I outlined the case last year, so please refer to this chapter in the 2020 version for the proof of my reasoning.

However, the real proof is the results below. In 2020, I was able to stream the TE3 overall. However, most damning for the position is that only 4 Tight Ends averaged over 10 points per game in 0.5pt PPR. The position really fell off a cliff in 2020. And whilst it might rebound slightly in 2021, there is not enough needed to invest high in a Tight End, unless you draft Travis Kelce, who is essentially a WR1 in his own right.

Review of The Tight Ends That Beat the Stream.

In 2020, despite me finishing with the TE3, five Tight Ends finished above my streaming model. Here are the five Tight Ends that scored above my Tight End stream on a points per game basis:

Rank	Name	Total 0.5 PPR PPG	Games Played	Total PPG	PAS
1	Travis Kelce	260.26	15	17.35	8.29
2	Darren Waller	225.1	16	14.07	5.01
3	George Kittle	101.1	8	12.64	3.58
4	Mark Andrews	141.1	14	10.08	1.02
5	Robert Tonyan	150.6	16	9.41	0.35

This list shows you real volatility of the Tight End Position. There is no real consistency in the position outside of Kelce and maybe Darren Waller at a push.

Draft Strategy for Tight Ends.

"What all of the above tells you is this: The Tight End position is volatile! There is almost no stability, no depth, and no guarantee for success". This is a direct quote from the 2020 book, and I have left it in as it is truer than it was twelve months ago. There is absolutely no need to invest in such a volatile position with valuable draft capital. Rounds 1-9 are for you to be taking the best value you can for the spine and core of your team.

Other than drafting Travis Kelce, there is absolutely no value in drafting a Tight End in the first eight or nine rounds of a fantasy draft. It would be more beneficial to walk away with four Running Backs, four Wide Receivers and one Quarterback in those first nine rounds. This is the value of drafting, as outlined in the previous chapter. Therefore, investing in the middle round Tight End is throwing away points from your lineup.

There is some case for Darren Waller. However, with the Raiders adding a Receiving Running Back to the roster, it should impact Waller's targets. If he sees just a 10% reduction in targets, his value falls by three or maybe even four rounds. You are buying Darren Waller at his absolute ceiling right now. You are not buying any value on him. You are just assuming all the risk, as personally, I think he struggles to repeat his 2020 performance.

Therefore, you need to re-read the chapter from last year's Fantasy Football Playbook from the PAS section, adopt a Kelce or late Tight End approach, and be ready to stream the position. Because streaming Tight End will yield you a good enough performance at the position to where you are only yielding points to a handful of Tight Ends.

Only 2 Tight Ends played more than half a season and beat my streaming model by more than 1.1 points on a weekly basis. Therefore, in teams where I did not draft a Tight End in the first 10 rounds, which was a significant amount, I had a huge advantage over the rest of the league, as I was able to hoover up all that Wide Receiver value in the middle rounds, drafting a ton of Keenan Allen, Brandin Cooks and Stefon Diggs, on my way to a near 80% playoff appearance record across all my leagues.

Look at the data from last year's book and look at the results in this year's book as a result. I am sure the Tight Ends will rebound. However, I think it will be at least 2-3 years before we will have to adopt and adapt the Kelce or Tight End late strategy in order to remain successful.

Tight End's- The Tight Ends Who Have a Negative PAS Against the Stream Model.

Here are the Tight Ends who finished behind the stream model:

6	T.J. Hockenson	141.8	16	8.86	-0.20
7	Mike Gesicki	132.8	15	8.85	-0.21
8	Logan Thomas	140.62	16	8.79	-0.27
9	Dallas Goedert	93.4	11	8.49	-0.57
10	Hunter Henry	115.3	14	8.24	-0.82
11	Jonnu Smith	119.7	15	7.98	-1.08
12	Rob Gronkowski	126.8	16	7.93	-1.14
13	Noah Fant	118.3	15	7.89	-1.17
14	Eric Ebron	113.8	15	7.59	-1.47
15	Hayden Hurst	121.1	16	7.57	-1.49
16	Jimmy Graham	118.6	16	7.41	-1.65
17	Jared Cook	108.9	15	7.26	-1.80
18	Dalton Schultz	115	16	7.19	-1.87

19	Tyler Higbee	106.2	15	7.08	-1.98
20	Austin Hooper	90.5	13	6.96	-2.10
21	Evan Engram	109.5	16	6.84	-2.22
22	Irv Smith Jr.	83.5	13	6.42	-2.64
23	Jordan Reed	60.1	10	6.01	-3.05
24	Zach Ertz	59.5	11	5.41	-3.65
25	Trey Burton	69.3	13	5.33	-3.73
26	Dan Arnold	81.3	16	5.08	-3.98
27	Jordan Akins	65.2	13	5.02	-4.04
28	Dawson Knox	54.8	12	4.57	-4.49
29	Gerald Everett	72.4	16	4.53	-4.54
30	Mo Alie-Cox	64.9	15	4.33	-4.73
31	Tyler Eifert	64.9	15	4.33	-4.73
32	Kyle Rudolph	51.4	12	4.28	-4.78
33	Richard Rodgers	58.5	14	4.18	-4.88
34	Darren Fells	65.7	16	4.11	-4.95
35	Anthony Firkser	64.2	16	4.01	-5.05
36	Greg Olsen	41.9	11	3.81	-5.25
37	Jack Doyle	52.6	14	3.76	-5.30
38	Drew Sample	58.9	16	3.68	-5.38
39	Chris Herndon	58.2	16	3.64	-5.42
40	Tyler Kroft	35.9	10	3.59	-5.47

41	Cameron Brate	54.2	16	3.39	-5.67
42	Nick Boyle	30.3	9	3.37	-5.69
43	Jacob Hollister	53.4	16	3.34	-5.72
44	Harrison Bryant	49.8	15	3.32	-5.74
45	David Njoku	42.8	13	3.29	-5.77
46	Will Dissly	49.1	16	3.07	-5.99
47	Durham Smythe	45.8	15	3.05	-6.01
48	Cole Kmet	48	16	3.00	-6.06
49	Donald Parham Jr.	38.9	13	2.99	-6.07
50	Pharaoh Brown	35.3	13	2.72	-6.34
51	James O'Shaughnessy	40.2	15	2.68	-6.38
52	Ross Dwelley	40	16	2.50	-6.56
53	Adam Shaheen	39	16	2.44	-6.62
54	Marcedes Lewis	33.7	15	2.25	-6.81
55	Tyler Conklin	34.9	16	2.18	-6.88
56	Adam Trautman	30.6	15	2.04	-7.02
57	Ryan Izzo	24.4	12	2.03	-7.03
58	Jesse James	31.9	16	1.99	-7.07
59	Ian Thomas	30.5	16	1.91	-7.15
60	Foster Moreau	29.5	16	1.84	-7.22
61	Jason Witten	25.4	16	1.59	-7.47

I think there are a few players who could break into the top five next year. Logan Thomas has a new Quarterback in Ryan Fitzpatrick who has a history of making Tight Ends relevant for fantasy football. And Zach Ertz can find a new home in 2021, and revisit some of the glory years, whilst his replacement Dallas Goedert can thrive without having to share targets if he is healthy. Also, maybe Noah Fant will have a new QB throwing him the ball, whilst Jared Cook hooks up with Rookie phenom Justin Herbert in L.A.

There is a chance the position rebounds a tad in 2021. However, do not get sucked in to overpaying for a position that does not make too much difference to the box score in 2021.

Streaming Kickers.

Kickers is not a fan's favourite position. In the 2020 Fantasy Football Playbook, I outlined how flat the position is. The 2020 numbers do also fall into that same trends that we have seen for the past five or six years between an average gap between the K1 and the K12 being between 2.5-2.7 points. As a result, not much has really changed from the strategy I wrote around 12 months ago.

However, I had an extremely bad year streaming kicker. There were some weather affected games that hurt my streaming kicker, as well as some unusually high Waiver Wire activity on kickers. I can only assume either more people were streaming Kickers in 2020, and that affected the outcome, that more kickers were being owned due to COVID, or that I just generally sucked at picking Kickers. Truth be told, it is probably a combination of all three.

I started extremely badly with my streaming Kickers and it left me with too much of a hole to climb. Having said that, I still did not yield too much of an advantage to those who lead the way in kicking in 2020.

However, having said that, folks who went to go and get Justin Tucker and Harrison Butker in 2020 drafts, were left sorely underwhelmed by their performances. Both players had 11th round ADP and they failed to make the top five at the position, and therefore only beat my stream model by around a point per game or less. This is why drafting kickers should not be your priority, or something you need to do. Because the only kickers that beat my stream by more than 1.5 points per game, were either undrafted, or drafted in the last round. Therefore, my strategy worked as I got an advantage over players who drafted kickers before the 16th round.

Simple advice for kickers in 2021. If you have to draft a kicker, and really you should not need to, make sure you do not take one before the last round. You are just giving points away.

Streaming Kickers- Who Beat the Stream Model?

Below are the 19 Kickers who beat the streaming model in 2020:

Rank	Name	Total Points	Games Played	PPG Average	PAS
1	Younghoe Koo	160	15	10.67	3.26

2	**Jason Sanders**	**160**	**16**	**10.00**	**2.59**
3	**Daniel Carlson**	**152**	**16**	**9.50**	**2.09**
4	**Tyler Bass**	**149**	**16**	**9.31**	**1.90**
5	**Greg Zuerlein**	**141**	**16**	**8.81**	**1.40**
6	**Rodrigo Blankenship**	**141**	**16**	**8.81**	**1.40**
7	**Ryan Succop**	**138**	**16**	**8.63**	**1.22**
8	**Brandon McManus**	**128**	**15**	**8.53**	**1.12**
9	**Justin Tucker**	**136**	**16**	**8.50**	**1.09**
10	**Harrison Butker**	**131**	**16**	**8.19**	**0.78**
11	**Cairo Santos**	**130**	**16**	**8.13**	**0.72**
12	**Wil Lutz**	**128**	**16**	**8.00**	**0.59**
13	**Ka'imi Fairbairn**	**126**	**16**	**7.88**	**0.47**
14	**Jason Myers**	**125**	**16**	**7.81**	**0.40**
15	**Graham Gano**	**124**	**16**	**7.75**	**0.34**
16	**Randy Bullock**	**93**	**12**	**7.75**	**0.34**
17	**Joey Slye**	**122**	**16**	**7.63**	**0.22**
18	**Stephen Gostkowski**	**114**	**15**	**7.60**	**0.19**
19	**Zane Gonzalez**	**90**	**12**	**7.50**	**0.09**

What are the Takeaways?

There is really only one. If you drafted a kicker before the 16th round, you lost ground on the others and did not get any value on your draft choice. Therefore, if you do nothing else in 2021, do not draft a kicker before round 16. However, please try and refrain from drafting one, unless your draft is literally the weekend before the NFL season.

The Kickers Who Failed to Beat the Stream.

These are the 12 Kickers that were regular starters in the NFL who failed to beat the stream. Worth noting the Jacksonville Jaguars had multiple kickers in 2020, and therefore do not have a kicker on this list:

20	Mason Crosby	115	16	7.19	-0.22
21	Dustin Hopkins	115	16	7.19	-0.22
22	Chris Boswell	93	13	7.15	-0.26
23	Matt Prater	113	16	7.06	-0.35
24	Nick Folk	112	16	7.00	-0.41
25	Michael Badgley	112	16	7.00	-0.41
26	Cody Parkey	100	15	6.67	-0.74
27	Samuel Sloman	53	8	6.63	-0.79
28	Robbie Gould	97	15	6.47	-0.94
29	Sam Ficken	53	9	5.89	-1.52
30	Dan Bailey	86	16	5.38	-2.04
31	Jake Elliott	70	16	4.38	-3.04

Streaming D/STs.

In 2019 I streamed the DST7 overall. In 2020 I streamed the… DST7 overall. What changed? Not much. It was very similar to all other D/ST seasons, with the exception of there not being one huge leading D/ST scoring team. As a result, there was a much closer gap at the top than normal.

However, almost everything worked out to be rather similar. In the 2020 book I talked about the strategies around D/ST and hopefully you bought that. Not only for the data, but also for the strategy. I also broke down previous D/ST performances. The truth is, there is just not much of a gap in D/STs and there is no advantage drafting one before the 15th round of drafts, if at all. All the strategy you need to stream D/STs is in the 2020 book. In essence, the strategy around what is optimal for D/STs has not changed an inch from 2020 to 2021.

The D/STS that Beat the Stream Model.

Below are the nine teams that beat the stream model:

Rank	Name	Points Week 1-17 Total	Total PPG	PAS
1	**Indianapolis Colts**	151	9.44	2.20
2	**Pittsburgh Steelers**	150	9.38	2.14
3	**Los Angeles Rams**	149	9.31	2.07
4	**Baltimore Ravens**	143	8.94	1.70
5	**Miami Dolphins**	139	8.69	1.45
6	**Washington Football Team**	127	7.94	0.70
7	**New Orleans Saints**	122	7.63	0.39
8	**Buffalo Bills**	118	7.38	0.14
9	**Tampa Bay Buccaneers**	117	7.31	0.07

Now, even though I finished at the D/ST7, there were nine teams that beat me. That is due to the way I worked out the PAS. Effectively, my stream model, alongside the Buccaneers and the Bills, were split by just two points across the season.

What was different to last year was simply no one blew the stream model out of the water. Just three teams beat the stream by more than two points per game and just five by more than one point per game. It goes to show that match-up streaming by unowned D/STs is a viable strategy if you want to grab a late round flyer in the draft instead. However, I would advocate taking a late round D/ST over a kicker personally.

Also, this kind of stability and uniformity is why some fantasy managers get rid of the position all together. They do not feel it offers enough skill. I would challenge this slightly and say if you are savvy, there is an advantage to be made. However, it could be considerable work to gain that minor advantage/

How Did the Rest of the D/STS Compare Against the Stream?

Here is the performance of the rest of the D/STs vs my stream model:

10	Kansas City Chiefs	110	6.88	-0.37
11	Arizona Cardinals	107	6.69	-0.55
12	New England Patriots	104	6.50	-0.74
13	Philadelphia Eagles	103	6.44	-0.80
13	Seattle Seahawks	103	6.44	-0.80
15	New York Giants	103	6.44	-0.80
16	Carolina Panthers	97	6.06	-1.18
17	Cleveland Browns	94	5.88	-1.37
17	Green Bay Packers	94	5.88	-1.37
19	Chicago Bears	90	5.63	-1.62
20	San Francisco 49ers	88	5.50	-1.74
21	Dallas Cowboys	78	4.88	-2.37
22	Denver Broncos	74	4.63	-2.62
23	Los Angeles Chargers	72	4.50	-2.74
23	Atlanta Falcons	72	4.50	-2.74
25	Tennessee Titans	70	4.38	-2.87
26	New York Jets	65	4.06	-3.18
27	Minnesota Vikings	57	3.56	-3.68
28	Jacksonville Jaguars	52	3.25	-3.99
29	Houston Texans	48	3.00	-4.24
30	Cincinnati Bengals	45	2.81	-4.43

31	**Las Vegas Raiders**	39	2.44	-4.80
32	**Detroit Lions**	27	1.69	-5.55

Last year 11 D/STs finished within a point either side of the stream model. This season, that number is 10. So again, it shows remarkable consistency amongst the D/ST position. As I have already mentioned, there are three viable strategies when it comes to D/STs. Feel free to check them out in the 2020 Fantasy Football Playbook.

What Now?

If you can build your roster right and have a decent roster that you constructed during your draft, then streaming the right players and pieces, at the right time is key. This should improve your chances of winning considerably.

If you ever want to run some questions by me on this, you are more than welcome to. You can contact me on Twitter @Murf_NFL, or you can email me at agmurfet85@gmail.com. Let me know how it is working for you. If you are happy with the results of your draft by using PAS and the strategies outlined throughout all the streaming parts and chapters, let me know.

CHAPTER 13

The Top 101 Fantasy Football Players in 2021

Written by *Adam Murfet*

I have been hard at work with two different committees of people who have been extremely helpful in putting together a consistent mock draft panel. It is a result of this panel that we now have the top 101 players likely to be drafted in the first 9 rounds of fantasy drafts.

The format for these mock drafts is a 1QB PPR. Since this will reflect the majority of drafts conducted by players, this is the format we chose. You can check the Superflex Strategy Guide in the 2020 Fantasy Football Playbook that will offer guidance as to how to draft in that format. There will also be some further guidance in the future on 5yardrush.co.uk with regards to Superflex.

For the ADP of the mock drafts, the two mock draft committees drafted in the same slots and they completed mock drafts in January, February, March, and April. There is also a 5 Yard Rush staff mock in January that was also added to the data.

The idea of this is to be ahead of the curve by having player insights in near real time from some of the best fantasy players on the planet and how Free Agency, Rookies pre-NFL draft and Rookies post NFL Draft change the board.

As part of buying this book, you will receive up to date copies of the mock draft data via a downloadable sheet and portal that will be updated once a month. The data is also in the back of this book, which is correct up until time of printing.

A massive thank you to those who have been part of the committees. I have left a special thank you for you in the back of the book.

In the meantime, enjoy our top 101 player breakdowns and use this as another tool to get ready for your leagues in 2021.

Christian McCaffrey

RB

Pros

- Elite production; huge volume and rarely leaves the field
- Elusive and as involved in the passing game as the running game

Cons

- Recovering from injury
- Will be working with a new QB

Summary

Christian McCaffrey will likely be the consensus 1.01 in fantasy football in all scoring formats for 1QB. He finished as the RB53 despite not even completing 3 games. Rarely leaves the field and is involved in every possession. The only concern is his injury and how he has recovered prior to pre-season. Should he be fully fit, there is no doubt that Christian McCaffrey is a league winner and can end up scoring points similar to the top QBs or maybe even more.

2020 Fantasy pts total 0.5 PPR	81.8
2020 Position Rank	53
2020 Total snap % played from games played	77
Round projection from mock drafts	1
2021 Projected fantasy pts total 0.5 PPR	323.8
2021 Projected position rank	1

Carolina Panthers

Derrick Henry

RB

Pros

- Huge rushing volume
- Rushing champion 2 years in a row
- plenty of goalline work with little competition. Huge rushing volume

Cons

- Doesn't catch many passes which moves him down in PPR scoring

Summary

The 2 time reigning Rushing champion continues to defy the odds of being fantasy relevant without catching a ton of passes. To get over 2000 yards rushing in a season is an amazing achievement and unlikely to be matched by anyone currently playing in the next few years. He doesn't have a path to being the overall RB1, however his path to being a top 5 RB is easier to route and easy to pencil in. Feel good taking him in the top 5 in your drafts in 2021.

2020 Fantasy pts total 0.5 PPR	323.6
2020 Position Rank	2
2020 Total snap % played from games played	65
Round projection from mock drafts	1
2021 Projected fantasy pts total 0.5 PPR	296.2
2021 Projected position rank	3

Tennessee Titans

Saquon Barkley

RB

Pros
- Incredible YPC numbers;
- Essential in the passing game
- Enormous volume

Cons
- 2 seasons in a row interrupted by injury

Summary
Barkley has put enough on tape to show that, similar to McCaffrey, he will be involved and instrumental in both the running and receiving games. However, 2 years in a row he has had his season cut short to injury. Having missed so much time in the last 2 seasons does make him a risk. However, if he plays 17 games in 2021, he will easily finish in the top 3 at the Running Back position.

2020 Fantasy pts total 0.5 PPR	12.4
2020 Position Rank	119
2020 Total snap % played from games played	50
Round projection from mock drafts	1
2021 Projected fantasy pts total 0.5 PPR	280.6
2021 Projected position rank	4

New York Giants

Dalvin Cook

RB

Pros
- Overcome significant injury concerns in his first years in the NFL to play 14+ games in last 2 seasons
- In a run first offense that also uses their Running Backs as heavy targets and receivers

Cons
- Despite being more durable, he does seem to miss time in fantasy playoffs

Summary
Dalvin Cook has been a huge success for fantasy owners over the last two years. He puts up consistent week winning production and the Vikings want to continue to use him as a weapon. It is doubtful Cook will play 17 games in a season, and the adding of an extra game does mean there is more opportunity for him to break records. However, the fact he has missed the fantasy playoffs the last few years is something to keep an eye on.

2020 Fantasy pts total 0.5 PPR	315.8
2020 Position Rank	3
2020 Total snap % played from games played	70
Round projection from mock drafts	1
2021 Projected fantasy pts total 0.5 PPR	270.6
2021 Projected position rank	5

Minnesota Vikings

Alvin Kamara

RB

New Orleans Saints

Pros
- Consistent performnces over the last 4 years in fantasy football
- Used a lot in the passing games; always a high producer of Touchdowns

Cons
- Change of QB is a worry. If Taysom Hill starts, we have seen Kamara's production fall through the floor.

Summary
If Brees was coming back in 2021, off the back of Kamara finishing as the RB1 in 2020, he would easily be a top 3 Running Back. However, with some down weeks midseason with Taysom Hill under centre, there is some concern that Kamara's ceiling is capped. There is no guarantee that Hill will be the QB in 2021. However, with that uncertainty, with the numbers on record, there is some hesitancy as to what Kamara will be in 2021. If you roll the dice, you could win big with Kamara in 2021

2020 Fantasy pts total 0.5 PPR	336.3
2020 Position Rank	1
2020 Total snap % played from games played	65
Round projection from mock drafts	1
2021 Projected fantasy pts total 0.5 PPR	297.8
2021 Projected position rank	2

Ezekiel Elliott

RB

Dallas Cowboys

Pros
- Great history of production in fantasy football
- Great hands and racks up receptions in the passing game

Cons
- Production drops off if Dak isn't under centre;
- Can have goal-line touches vultured by Tony Pollard

Summary
Coming off a down year, Elliott will be looking to rebound with Prescott back under centre. We saw a number of fumbles and drops last year which is un-characteristic. I expect 2021 to be a rebound year for Zeke and think he is a value pick if he falls outside of the top 5 picks in the draft. However, don't expect double digit touchdowns from Zeke, as the Cowboys will look to use Pollard more.

2020 Fantasy pts total 0.5 PPR	197.7
2020 Position Rank	11
2020 Total snap % played from games played	72
Round projection from mock drafts	1
2021 Projected fantasy pts total 0.5 PPR	264.9
2021 Projected position rank	6

Jonathan Taylor

RB

Pros
- Unbelievably natural runner between the tackles
- Strong running style that makes him difficult to bring down
- Highly durable back

Cons
- Has a productive receiving back who will take touches away for competition
- Not been trusted with top tier, elite volume
- Handling issues with drops and fumbles part of his profile

Summary
2020 showed just how good Taylor is. However, he has becomes the most hyped player in fantasy football as a result. If you want Taylor, you will have to draft him higher than his worth. There is concern he will not get enough touches to return a top 5/6 Running Back performance. Not to mention the Colts have brought back Marlon Mack. We know Frank Reich is a firm believer of rotating work to protect the lead back, as he comes from the Doug Pederson. Whilst Taylor is a fantastic talent, and one of the best pure runners in the NFL, be weary of overpaying due to a favourable end of 2020 schedule.

2020 Fantasy pts total 0.5 PPR	234.8
2020 Position Rank	6
2020 Total snap % played from games played	50
Round projection from mock drafts	1
2021 Projected fantasy pts total 0.5 PPR	219.8
2021 Projected position rank	12

Indianapolis Colts

Nick Chubb

RB

Pros
- One of the best 2 or 3 pure runners in the NFL
- Highly productive runner between the tackles
- Huge Touchdown producer

Cons
- Will lose touches to Kareem Hunt, including touches in the receiving game

Summary
Chubb has shown how productive he is with carries and touches in the NFL and fantasy football. However, due to him having Kareem Hunt to share work with, his upside is capped. There is a path to low end RB1 production that is relatively safe. However, with Hunt lurking around, Chubb's ceiling is much lower than if he had the backfield to himself.

2020 Fantasy pts total 0.5 PPR	199.7
2020 Position Rank	9
2020 Total snap % played from games played	49
Round projection from mock drafts	1
2021 Projected fantasy pts total 0.5 PPR	245.7
2021 Projected position rank	9

Cleveland Browns

Davante Adams

WR

Pros
- Great catch radius; 4 WR1 performances in the last 5 years
- Very little competition for targets in the offense

Cons
- Some injury concerns having missed time in each of the last three season

Summary
Adams will most likely be the 2021 WR1 and it's hard to see why not. Highly productive Wide Receiver in a high powered passing offense. Whilst he might see a slight regression in Touchdowns in 2021, he will still be right up there as the top performing Wide Receiver in 2021, provided he can play the majority of his seventeen games this season.

2020 Fantasy pts total 0.5 PPR	300.9
2020 Position Rank	1
2020 Total snap % played from games played	84
Round projection from mock drafts	1
2021 Projected fantasy pts total 0.5 PPR	269.6
2021 Projected position rank	1

Green Bay Packers

Tyreek Hill

WR

Pros
- Fastest Wide Receiver in the NFL
- Incredibly take it to the house production
- Lead receiver in the leading offense in the NFL

Cons
- Has had off the field issues in the past
- Competes for touches with Travis Kelce

Summary
Hill is nicknamed the Cheetah for good reason. His rapid speed allows him to take plays to the house. In a highly productive offense, Hill is one of the two primary reads. Arguably has the safest floor of any Wide Receiver and is remarkably consistent. Well worth a 1st round pick. There is no doubt that if Hill is on the field for 17 games this season, he can challenge for the overall WR1 spot alongside Adams.

2020 Fantasy pts total 0.5 PPR	285.4
2020 Position Rank	2
2020 Total snap % played from games played	85
Round projection from mock drafts	1
2021 Projected fantasy pts total 0.5 PPR	268.2
2021 Projected position rank	2

Kansas City Chiefs

Travis Kelce

TE

Pros
- Leading Tight End in fantasy football in 4 of the last 5 seasons (and 1 second place)
- Will give you a massive positional advantage
- One of the 2 leading targets in the leading offense in the NFL

Cons
- Taking a Tight End round 1 means passing on a Wide Receiver or Running Back, meaning roster construction will be more challenging

Summary
The other part of the 1-2 Kansas City punch is Travis Kelce. Incredibly safe production for a fantasy production that produces anything but. Kelce's stock continues to rise and it will be highly unlikely he will be anything other than TE1 in 2021. He will give you a significant advantage at the Tight End position, especially as he is a top 5 WR in his own right.

2020 Fantasy pts total 0.5 PPR	260.3
2020 Position Rank	1
2020 Total snap % played from games played	86
Round projection from mock drafts	1
2021 Projected fantasy pts total 0.5 PPR	251.1
2021 Projected position rank	1

Kansas City Chiefs

Josh Jacobs

RB

Pros
- 1st round draft selection in 2019
- Shown consistent volume carrying the ball

Cons
- Inconsistent
- Now has fresh competition in Kenyan Drake for touches; not had many receiving targets in the backfield

Summary
Jacobs divided opinion prior to Drake joining the team. Now this backfield confuses people. I fully expect Jacobs to fall out of the second round, and maybe even the 3rd on ADP in drafts by the summer. Jacobs is inconsistent, will have a new offensive line in 2021 and new competition. It is hard to see how he finishes any higher than a mid RB2 in 2021.

2020 Fantasy pts total 0.5 PPR	214.8
2020 Position Rank	81
2020 Total snap % played from games played	61
Round projection from mock drafts	2
2021 Projected fantasy pts total 0.5 PPR	179.4
2021 Projected position rank	21

Las Vegas Raiders

Clyde Edwards-Helaire

RB

Pros
- 1st round draft selection in 2020
- Size, speed and breakout metrics all point towards an above average Running Back

Cons
- Was very poor in the red zone in 2020,
- Failed to shine despite the lack of serious competition in 2020
- In a pass first offense

Summary
CEH was one of the most over-drafted players in 2020. The hype train took off, left the station and left him on the platform on his tod. He didn't look ready in 2020. However, with a year under his belt, with an offseason and pre-season and even less competition for touches in 2021, perhaps CEH can breakout in 2021 and show why the Chiefs spent a first round pick on him.

2020 Fantasy pts total 0.5 PPR	158.0
2020 Position Rank	22
2020 Total snap % played from games played	581
Round projection from mock drafts	2
2021 Projected fantasy pts total 0.5 PPR	184.6
2021 Projected position rank	20

Kansas City Chiefs

D'Andre Swift

RB

Pros
- High second round draft selection in 2020
- Size, speed and breakout metrics show an above average Running Back
- Was productive in a shared backfield in 2020 and beat out the competition

Cons
- The entire offense for the Lions is different in 2020 with the exception of Hockinson
- Could be on a bottom 5 offense in 2021

Summary
The entire Lions situation is different in 2021. They have a new HC, new OC, new QB, potentially 3 new WRs and maybe some support Running Backs. However with no Adrian Pederson, it should mean Swift won't be as handcuffed like he was early in the season. However, the major issue for swift will be that the Lions project to be a bottom 5 offense in the NFL right now, which means they might find themselves behind in a lot of games in 2021, and reduce the passing down situations Swift will be in. Swift projects to be a high risk, potentially high reward player in 2021

2020 Fantasy pts total 0.5 PPR	166.8
2020 Position Rank	18
2020 Total snap % played from games played	48
Round projection from mock drafts	2
2021 Projected fantasy pts total 0.5 PPR	212.2
2021 Projected position rank	14

Detroit Lions

DeAndre Hopkins

WR

Pros
- Arguably the best hands in the NFL
- Year 2 in a high powered NFL offense
- 4 WR1 performances in the last 5 years

Cons
- Needs a better WR2 to take some of the coverage away from him

Summary

DeAndre Hopkins was excellent in his first year at the Cardinals. No Preseason or offseason and he returns a WR5 overall season. A former 99 Wide Receiver on Madden, Hopkins is consistently a top 12 WR. He is a very safe pick that could also have extremely high upside also. It is incredibly rare to come into a new team and report at the same high level. It just shows how good Hopkins really is. He should improve in 2021.

2020 Fantasy pts total 0.5 PPR	230.3
2020 Position Rank	5
2020 Total snap % played from games played	92
Round projection from mock drafts	2
2021 Projected fantasy pts total 0.5 PPR	237.4
2021 Projected position rank	5

Arizona Cardinals

Stefon Diggs

WR

Pros
- Lead receiver in a high powered offense with a leading NFL QB
- Coming into year 2 in the offense to likely to increase numbers in year 2

Cons
- Can go missing in games and bust on occasion

Summary

The trade that sent Diggs to Buffalo was one mentioned more for the capital traded, than for the calibre of what Diggs would bring to the Bills. The Bills became contenders immediately, whilst having the most productive year of his career. Criminally under-rated last year, that will not be the case in 2021. Can Diggs elevate his game further in 2021? I wouldn't bet against it.

2020 Fantasy pts total 0.5 PPR	265.1
2020 Position Rank	3
2020 Total snap % played from games played	89
Round projection from mock drafts	2
2021 Projected fantasy pts total 0.5 PPR	249.2
2021 Projected position rank	3

Buffalo Bills

James Robinson

RB

Pros
- Elusive
- Strong and reliable
- Very consistent

Cons
- Went Undrafted in 2020 NFL Draft
- Now faces some competition from Carlos Hyde
- Will be in a new system in 2021

Summary
You could argue that James Robinson was the feel good fantasy story of 2020. However, he will be less of a surprise in 2021. How good will the Jags be in 2021? That remains to be seen. Will Hyde or another Running Back impact Robinson? Perhaps? But enough to stop him being an RB1? Maybe not. As a result, there is some risk right now in Robinson's stock. However, by summer, if there is little competition to Robinson other than Hyde, you can feel confident in Robinson in 2021.

2020 Fantasy pts total 0.5 PPR	225.9
2020 Position Rank	7
2020 Total snap % played from games played	69
Round projection from mock drafts	2
2021 Projected fantasy pts total 0.5 PPR	138.2
2021 Projected position rank	37

Jacksonville Jaguars

Austin Ekeler

RB

Pros
- Highly productive receiving back
- Very productive Running Back who has won out over serious competition in the past

Cons
- Coming back from injury
- Will he get the goal-line work?

Summary
Ekeler has always been a productive Running Back and was rewarded with a lucrative but not outrageous contract in 2020. However, the concerns around Ekeler is how healthy will he be in September, and will second year Joshua Kelly take away any of the goal-line touches? It remains to be seen. However, I think Ekeler is one of the safer second round picks and I have no doubt some might select him in the back end of the first.

2020 Fantasy pts total 0.5 PPR	138.3
2020 Position Rank	29
2020 Total snap % played from games played	58
Round projection from mock drafts	2
2021 Projected fantasy pts total 0.5 PPR	251.5
2021 Projected position rank	8

Los Angeles Chargers

Aaron Jones

RB

Pros
- Scored more Touchdowns than any other Running Back in the last 2 seasons
- Less competition now Williams has left

Cons
- Protected by coaches and therefore has limited snap count

Summary
Aaron Jones is coming off a RB5 season, yet his Touchdown production dropped from '19 to '20. He has no Jamaal Williams to take touches from him. However, will we really see Jones be on the field for more than 60% of snaps? I'm not sure. So as a result, his path to being an RB1 is clear. However I doubt he will be in that elite tier of Running Backs due to his lack of snaps.

2020 Fantasy pts total 0.5 PPR	235.4
2020 Position Rank	5
2020 Total snap % played from games played	60
Round projection from mock drafts	2
2021 Projected fantasy pts total 0.5 PPR	242.4
2021 Projected position rank	10

Green Bay Packers

D.K Metcalf

WR

Pros
- Produced elite multiple game winning weeks in 2020
- Incredible catch radius and physical receiver

Cons
- Splits targets with Lockett
- In a run first offense
- Has a new Offense Coordinator in 2021 that could change the landscape

Summary
D.K Metcalf's stock continues to rise at an alarming rate. There are some great reasons for it. A top 10 WR in 2020, with some truly great game winning weeks. However, the real concern with Metcalf is the price. Based on the 5 Yard Rush Mock draft data, there is a full 3 round difference between Metcalf and Lockett. There is not 3 rounds of value difference between them. They had near identical numbers in 2020 and I would expect something similar in 2021. Beware the price and the changes in scheme in 2021.

2020 Fantasy pts total 0.5 PPR	229.8
2020 Position Rank	7
2020 Total snap % played from games played	91
Round projection from mock drafts	2
2021 Projected fantasy pts total 0.5 PPR	225.3
2021 Projected position rank	8

Seattle Seahawks

Cam Akers

RB

Pros
- Great production metrics in college and second round selection in NFL Draft in 2020
- Seems to have won the lead job in L.A towards the end of 2020

Cons
- Very thin production profile in 2020
- L.A Rams scheme has kept fantasy players guessing over the past three seasons

Summary
Cam Akers is getting more and more hype as the offseason continues. He had a fantastic last 3 games with the Rams. However, as we continue to track the changes in LA, it is hard to believe that they truly commit to Akers in 2021. Fantasy players have fallen for this in 2020 with Akers and Henderson, and in 2019 with Todd Gurley. I expect both backs to be productive, but perhaps they cannibalise each others upside? That is a potential outcome.

2020 Fantasy pts total 0.5 PPR	96.3
2020 Position Rank	43
2020 Total snap % played from games played	35
Round projection from mock drafts	2
2021 Projected fantasy pts total 0.5 PPR	189.4
2021 Projected position rank	18

Los Angeles Rams

David Montgomery

RB

Pros
- Finished the season strong and was the RB2 in all scoring formats from Week 11 onwards
- Very little wide receiver depth meaning will have consistent volume

Cons
- With no Tarik Cohen, had more opportunity than ever before in 2020. Expect that to go down in 2021
- Bears offense projects to be a bottom 5 offense in 2021

Summary
David Montgomery broke out in 2021. However, there are question marks still remaining about how good he is against good teams. He punishes bad teams, but struggled against top 12 teams in 2020. The path to being an RB1 will muddled slightly with regards to Tarik Cohen being available in the passing game. However, Montgomery has proved he is not as bad as his 2019 campaign made him out to be. Having said that, I don't think his 2020 campaign is a true reflection of his stock in fantasy football either.

2020 Fantasy pts total 0.5 PPR	237.8
2020 Position Rank	4
2020 Total snap % played from games played	74
Round projection from mock drafts	3
2021 Projected fantasy pts total 0.5 PPR	199.7
2021 Projected position rank	16

Chicago Bears

Calvin Ridley

WR

Pros

- Prolific Touchdown scorer
- Shines most as a WR2 in an offense, which he is likely to be in 2021
- Red Zone threat
- No real competition for targets behind him.

Cons

- Inconsistent when required to play the alpha WR role and struggles in double coverage
- Learning from a new OC in 2021

Summary

Ridley has shown he knows where the pay dirt is and how to find it regularly. He has 26 Touchdowns in just 3 seasons in the NFL and last year he had a career high 143 targets and 90 receptions. These will decrease considerably unless Julio Jones misses significant time yet again in 2021. He projects to finish over 1000 yards despite having a reduced workload and looks set to challenge his 2020 Touchdown total of 9 yet again in 2021. Ridley is still a solid option and the third round seems the right place to grab him.

2020 Fantasy pts total 0.5 PPR	236.5
2020 Position Rank	4
2020 Total snap % played from games played	78
Round projection from mock drafts	3
2021 Projected fantasy pts total 0.5 PPR	198.6
2021 Projected position rank	18

Atlanta Falcons

Mike Evans

WR

Pros

- 7 consecutive seasons with 1,000 yards in his first 7 seasons (an NFL Record) Consistent Red Zone threat
- 4 WR1 finishes in his last 5 seasons

Cons

- Will be sharing the load with Chris Godwin and potentially others
- Will have weeks where he busts very badly
- Ceiling is the bottom end of WR1 not the top

Summary

Mike Evans continues to put up Hall of Fame numbers in his career and he is coming off a Super Bowl winning season. He was instrumental in the success, leading the team in receiving yards and Touchdowns. However, he will have weeks where he will score very few points. That is the issue with being on a team with so many weapons. However, if he remains healthy, nobody would doubt him making it 8 seasons from 8 with 1,000 receiving yards. If he can get 10 Touchdowns then he is great value here.

2020 Fantasy pts total 0.5 PPR	213.6
2020 Position Rank	10
2020 Total snap % played from games played	80
Round projection from mock drafts	3
2021 Projected fantasy pts total 0.5 PPR	212.9
2021 Projected position rank	10

Tampa Bay Buccaneers

Patrick Mahomes

QB

Pros
- Arm talent mixed with scheme and weapons means he will always be a high QB producer for fantasy football
- Can guarantee he will be top 5 in yards and touchdowns in 2021

Cons
- ADP, can you risk taking a QB this high and missing out on values at other positions

Summary
If you want Mahomes, you will need to select him in the third round in almost any draft. There is hardly any chance he slides lower. As has been mentioned already, is the value really there to take Mahomes this high? He has the safest floor of any QB in fantasy football and the highest ceiling. However, in three years in fantasy football, he only has 1 overall QB1 finish.

2020 Fantasy pts total 0.5 PPR	380.4
2020 Position Rank	4
2020 Total snap % played from games played	98
Round projection from mock drafts	3
2021 Projected fantasy pts total 0.5 PPR	391.78
2021 Projected position rank	2

Kansas City Chiefs

J.K. Dobbins

RB

Pros
- 2nd round draft selection in 2020
- Great combine metrics set him up for success in 2021
- Less competition now Mark Ingram II has left the team

Cons
- Lamar Jackson will cap the upside of Dobbins
- Baltimore yet to show they are ready to commit a bell-cow workload to Dobbins
- Edwards will be a factor for touches in 2021

Summary
Dobbins came out of a very strong class of Running Backs and has more than held his own so far. However, we have yet to see truly elite fantasy production from him. The issue with the system he is in is can you see him climbing much higher than he finished last season. I certainly think he will outperform RB21 in 2021 as he will have more work early. But vastly outperform this to break the top 12? I am not as confident on that.

2020 Fantasy pts total 0.5 PPR	159.5
2020 Position Rank	21
2020 Total snap % played from games played	47
Round projection from mock drafts	3
2021 Projected fantasy pts total 0.5 PPR	172.6
2021 Projected position rank	24

Baltimore Ravens

Michael Thomas

WR

Pros

Finished as a WR1 in 4 of the last 5 seasons, including being the overall WR1 in 2019 with a record breaking season

very little competition for targets in 2021

Cons

Uncertainty at the QB position and who will start in 2021

Coming back from a significant injury

character concerns started to show in 2020 with reported fighting in training

Summary

There is no doubt that Michael Thomas, when fit, with the volume he can be fed, is going to compete for the WR1 overall spot. However, there is significant doubts starting to creep in due to who could be throwing him the ball in 2021. If it is Winston, that will alleviate the concerns quite considerably. If it is Hill, he could find it hard to get the targets to break into the top 12 of Wide Receivers. He is an intriguing buy low prospect right now due to the uncertainty and I have no doubt his stock will rise considerably if Winston gets the nod to start Week One. 3rd round would be a massive steal, or a slight overpay, depending on who is throwing the ball to him.

2020 Fantasy pts total 0.5 PPR	63.9
2020 Position Rank	98
2020 Total snap % played from games played	73
Round projection from mock drafts	3
2021 Projected fantasy pts total 0.5 PPR	235.9
2021 Projected position rank	6

New Orleans Saints

A.J Brown

WR

Pros

- Great chemistry with his QB
- 1st round draft selection in 2019
- Very little competition for targets heading into 2021

Cons

- Run first offense will handicap true ceiling potential. Will struggle to break 120 targets again in 2021 as only has a career high 106 so far for his career.

Summary

A.J Brown has been phenemonial in his first two seasons in the NFL. His athletic profile, 19 touchdowns in 2 years and breaking the 1,000 yard mark both years shows how good he is. His only draw back is it is likely he will continue to be constricted to less volume than he deserves purely down to the system he is in.

2020 Fantasy pts total 0.5 PPR	212.5
2020 Position Rank	11
2020 Total snap % played from games played	81
Round projection from mock drafts	3
2021 Projected fantasy pts total 0.5 PPR	241.8
2021 Projected position rank	4

Tennessee Titans

Joe Mixon

RB

Pros
- Finally looks like he will be on a high powered offense in 2021
- Was the RB4 in weeks 3-6 last year prior to getting injured

Cons
- Returning back from injury
- Failed to reach 10 Touchdowns in any season so far in his career
- Just 1 RB1 season in his career (9th in 0.5pt PPR in 2018)

Summary
Joe Mixon might be one of the hardest players to project. We have always loved the talent and what he can bring. However, he has failed to do it frequently enough, when fantasy players have needed him. Admittedly, he has played on some terrible Bengals teams over the past couple of years. However, I feel this is a pivotal season for Mixon as if he failed to deliver again, there might be no meaningful path back to him being a true three down back in the NFL again.

2020 Fantasy pts total 0.5 PPR	89.1
2020 Position Rank	49
2020 Total snap % played from games played	65
Round projection from mock drafts	3
2021 Projected fantasy pts total 0.5 PPR	220.6
2021 Projected position rank	11

Cincinnati Bengals

Chris Godwin

WR

Pros
- Playing on the Franchise Tag, meaning he is playing for a new contract next year
- Efficient TD scorer
- Likely to be target leader on team in high passing offense

Cons
- Played hurt last year and might not do that again when on the franchise tag
- Won't be the first look in the Redzone too often and more likely 3rd read

Summary
The 2019 Pro Bowler might have realised a dream in winning a Super Bowl in Tampa last season. However, it wasn't all sunshine and roses for the 3rd year receiver. Having had a Pro Bowl year in 2019, you could say 2020 was a down year, as he missed 4 games, as well as playing hurt. This year is a huge year for Godwin. And with a lot of show in order to get life-changing money in 2022, he will need to have a year much more like his 2019 numbers than his 2020 numbers.

2020 Fantasy pts total 0.5 PPR	158.5
2020 Position Rank	32
2020 Total snap % played from games played	85
Round projection from mock drafts	3
2021 Projected fantasy pts total 0.5 PPR	191.6
2021 Projected position rank	21

Tampa Bay Buccaneers

George Kittle

TE

San Francisco 49ers

Pros
- Former all time receiving leader for a TE in a single season
- Likely to get an Quarterback upgrade in 2021
- Little competition for targets over the middle

Cons
- Injury plagued 2019 and 2020 seasons
- Will likely be playing with a new QB in 2021

Summary
George Kittle is going to cause Tight End fans to have kittens in drafts. On the one hand, having a consistent producer of fantasy points in a position that lacks any real consistency outside of 2 or 3 guys means you gain a significant advantage. However, on the other side you have a player that has struggled with injuries, having missed eight games in 2020 and was struggling with fitness in the post season in 2019. If he is injury free, there is some value here. However, can you see a path to Kittle playing 17 games in 2020?

2020 Fantasy pts total 0.5 PPR	101.1
2020 Position Rank	19
2020 Total snap % played from games played	83
Round projection from mock drafts	3
2021 Projected fantasy pts total 0.5 PPR	199.5
2021 Projected position rank	2

Antonio Gibson

RB

Washington Football Team

Pros
- Highly versatile
- Heavily involved in the passing game
- Seen a significant upgrade at QB this offseason having played for 4 different QBs in 2020

Cons
- Will likely cede some touches in the passing game

Summary
Gibson came out of nowhere for a lot of fantasy players in 2020. However, if you bought low on Gibson, it paid off for you in a big way. Gibson should see an increased workload in 2021, will be part of a better offense, have a better Quarterback to work with, and could potentially break out to be a top 5 Running Back in 2021. He was an RB1 despite playing for a team that finished with a 7-9 record and played with 4 different QBs. With stability and an increase in offense, it looks likely we will see a significant breakout. Grab him as your RB2 and he could return huge numbers.

2020 Fantasy pts total 0.5 PPR	184.2
2020 Position Rank	12
2020 Total snap % played from games played	43
Round projection from mock drafts	3
2021 Projected fantasy pts total 0.5 PPR	251.9
2021 Projected position rank	7

Keenan Allen

WR

Pros

- Great rapport built with QB
- Little competition for targets
- 4 WR1 finishes in the last 4 years

Cons

- Never been a prolific Touchdown scorer

Summary

Keenan Allen was a fade for many players last year due to uncertainty at the position. However, after Herbert started extremely early, the two got on a same page very quickly. As a result, Allen's 100 Receptions and big play ability helped Herbert to Offensive Rookie of the Year honours. Allen has never had more than 8 Touchdowns in his career and failed to hit the 1,000 yard mark despite having 100 receptions. These are areas that would need some improvement if Allen is to crack the top 5 for Wide Receivers in 2021.

2020 Fantasy pts total 0.5 PPR	195.1
2020 Position Rank	14
2020 Total snap % played from games played	83
Round projection from mock drafts	3
2021 Projected fantasy pts total 0.5 PPR	230.6
2021 Projected position rank	7

Los Angeles Chargers

Justin Jefferson

WR

Pros

- 1st Round NFL Draft Selection in 2020
- All time leading Rookie Wide Receiver season in yards
- Little competition for targets

Cons

- Plays on a run first offense

Summary

Justin Jefferson showed how elite he can be with a rookie season for the ages. After not getting many targets in the opening four weeks, he then took off like a bullet train on the way to a very impressive WR1 season, finishing 6th in fantasy points for Wide Receivers. The only question mark around Jefferson is... can he do it again in 2021?

2020 Fantasy pts total 0.5 PPR	230.2
2020 Position Rank	6
2020 Total snap % played from games played	82
Round projection from mock drafts	3
2021 Projected fantasy pts total 0.5 PPR	210.1
2021 Projected position rank	13

Minnesota Vikings

Chris Carson

RB

Pros
- Re-signed by Seattle despite hitting Free Agency
- Should be in a more run friendly scheme in 2021

Cons
- Injury plagued seasons in 2019 and 2020
- Has fumbling issues that has cost him his starting role in the past

Summary
Carson is someone who most fantasy players will be happy that he is still in Seattle. It gives him the best chance to succeed. However, he will need to have safer hands and have more durability in order to build on a solid, if slightly unspectacular 2020.

2020 Fantasy pts total 0.5 PPR	163.9
2020 Position Rank	17
2020 Total snap % played from games played	50
Round projection from mock drafts	3
2021 Projected fantasy pts total 0.5 PPR	198.7
2021 Projected position rank	17

Seattle Seahawks

Miles Sanders

RB

Pros
- Dynamic running style
- Over 5 yards per attempt in 2020
- Should have less competition now Pederson has left

Cons
- Low Touchdown numbers;
- Will see less work due to nature of Jalen Hurts

Summary
Sanders was overdrafted last year after flashing a heavy workload at the end of '19 when the Eagles had their backup QB ready to line-up at WR to run decoy routes as a last resort. Injury struck Sanders in 2020 but showed his effectiveness running the ball, averaging 5.3 YPC in 2020. However, with Hurts rushing at the rate he does, it is hard to see a RB1 ceiling for Sanders in 2021, despite finally getting out from under the rug of RBBC fan Doug Pederson.

2020 Fantasy pts total 0.5 PPR	156.4
2020 Position Rank	23
2020 Total snap % played from games played	71
Round projection from mock drafts	3
2021 Projected fantasy pts total 0.5 PPR	218.2
2021 Projected position rank	13

Philadelphia Eagles

Darren Waller

TE

Pros
- TE2 in 2020 and TE3 in 2019
- Consistent over 1,100 yard and 115 targets in both '19 and '20
- Became teams number 1 Redzone threat in 2020

Cons
- Vegas have changed their O-Line
- Maybe more competition from the backfield due to addition of Drake

Summary
The Raiders will look highly different in 2021, with wholesale changes at the O-Line position and potentially the Wide Receiver position, whilst also adding Drake to the backfield. In truth, only Jon Gruden knows what they are going to do in 2021 right now. And whilst Waller has produced significantly in 2019 and 2020, can we trust all things will remain the same for him in 2021?

2020 Fantasy pts total 0.5 PPR	225.1
2020 Position Rank	2
2020 Total snap % played from games played	91
Round projection from mock drafts	3
2021 Projected fantasy pts total 0.5 PPR	197.1
2021 Projected position rank	1

Las Vegas Raiders

Adam Thielen

WR

Pros
- A WR1 in 3 of the last 4 years
- Never dipped below 12 YPR as a pro
- Little competition for targets

Cons
- In line for Touchdown regression in 2021 as will be righting for Redzone targets with Jefferson
- Entering age 31 season means risk for injury increases

Summary
Thielen has been a staple for strong Fantasy Receiver corps over the last 5 years. Has had struggles with injures in 2019. However has only missed 1 NFL game in all his other seasons, and that was due to COVID protocols. With Jefferson the new kid on the block, it is likely Thielen will cede his Alpha status to him in 2021. However, with very little completion behind him, there will still be plenty for him to feast on.

2020 Fantasy pts total 0.5 PPR	217
2020 Position Rank	8
2020 Total snap % played from games played	91
Round projection from mock drafts	4
2021 Projected fantasy pts total 0.5 PPR	212
2021 Projected position rank	11

Minnesota Vikings

Kenny Golladay

WR

Pros
- Extremely big Yards per attempt numbers in his career, averaging over 15 in each of his last 3 seasons
- Likely to get more targets in 2021 on a new team

Cons
- Being on a new team means a learning curve and an early dip in production, coming off a significant injury in 2020
- Failed to score more than 5 TDs in 3 of his last 4 seasons

Summary
Golladay divides a lot of opinions due to the high praise he drew coming out of college. He had a good year in 2018 and an excellent year in 2019, before only playing 5 games in 2020. Now he lands in a new team, in a new offense and with a QB who has struggled in his first two years. He could help Daniel Jones take the next step, or he could drown with him. There is risk involved selecting Golladay, but significant reward if it all comes together.

2020 Fantasy pts total 0.5 PPR	55.8
2020 Position Rank	103
2020 Total snap % played from games played	69
Round projection from mock drafts	4
2021 Projected fantasy pts total 0.5 PPR	171.6
2021 Projected position rank	33

New York Giants

Terry McLaurin

WR

Pros
- Topped over 1,100 yards despite having 4 different QBs throw to him in 2020
- Will get more consistent QB play in 2021

Cons
- Low Touchdown numbers
- Will draw more coverage due to lack of receiving threat on the team

Summary
McLaurin put up more than impressive numbers in 2020 whilst playing under one of the worst QB situations in living memory. He will continue to get better and having a more stable QB situation, whilst also some receiving help will help him increase his numbers even further. More likely to improve in 2021 than to regress.

2020 Fantasy pts total 0.5 PPR	180.3
2020 Position Rank	21
2020 Total snap % played from games played	93
Round projection from mock drafts	4
2021 Projected fantasy pts total 0.5 PPR	210.9
2021 Projected position rank	12

Washington Football Team

Allen Robinson

WR

Pros

- Once again put up WR1 numbers despite being attached to a terrible QB situation; entering the prime age of his career
- Amassed over 150 targets in each of his last 2 seasons

Cons

- Will still have to deal with sub par Quarterback play more than likely

Summary

Allen Robinson's career numbers have been nothing more than exceptional, considering he has spent almost his entire career catching balls from Blake Bortles and Mitchell Trubisky, both backups in the NFL now. With no real receiving competition, Robinson will use this Franchise Tag year to bolster his numbers further and put himself in the shop window for a team needing an elite receiving option in 2022. Expect Robinson to produce in another difficult situation once again where few would thrive bar him,

2020 Fantasy pts total 0.5 PPR	211.9
2020 Position Rank	12
2020 Total snap % played from games played	85
Round projection from mock drafts	4
2021 Projected fantasy pts total 0.5 PPR	204.4
2021 Projected position rank	15

Chicago Bears

D.J Moore

WR

Pros

- 1st round draft choice in 2018
- Topped 1,175 yards in each of his last 2 years
- Has a great Offensive Coordinator who will scheme him open

Cons

- Low Touchdown numbers, never scored more than 4 in a year
- Low catch percentage in his career so far

Summary

D.J Moore has put up some very good receiving numbers whilst struggling to truly break out. Moore has struggled with consistency whilst the Panthers have been in turmoil over the last 2-3 years. With Darnold the new signal caller in Carolina, this is more of an arrow sideways as opposed to an arrow up situation for Moore.

2020 Fantasy pts total 0.5 PPR	178.5
2020 Position Rank	22
2020 Total snap % played from games played	87
Round projection from mock drafts	4
2021 Projected fantasy pts total 0.5 PPR	192.3
2021 Projected position rank	20

Carolina Panthers

Julio Jones

WR

Pros
- A WR1 in 4 of the past 5 years
- Had a Hall of Fame Career to Date
- Still the #1 Receiver on his team

Cons
- Age and injuries starting to catch up with him
- How many more good years does he have left?

Summary
Julio Jones has had an incredible career up until this point. However, Jones is about to enter his 11th year in the NFL. How many more good and productive years does he have left. Was 2020 the start of the decline, or is he going to show fantasy players he still has 1/2 good years left in him yet.

2020 Fantasy pts total 0.5 PPR	120.6
2020 Position Rank	53
2020 Total snap % played from games played	72
Round projection from mock drafts	4
2021 Projected fantasy pts total 0.5 PPR	184.9
2021 Projected position rank	26

Atlanta Falcons

CeeDee Lamb

WR

Pros
- 1st round draft selection in 2020
- Prominent Wide Receiver in one of the NFL's top 5 offenses
- Elite college production and breakout metrics

Cons
- There is a lot of mouths to feed in Dallas, how many Targets will Lamb get

Summary
CeeDee Lamb came out of the blocks early in 2020. His production was halted slightly when Dak Prescott was done for the season. However, he was able to still record a WR2 season despite all this. Expect Lamb to hit more heights in a Dallas offense that is ready to fly out of the blocks. If they are anywhere close to where they were at the start of 2020, 2021 could be a career year for Lamb with the sky being the limit.

2020 Fantasy pts total 0.5 PPR	180.7
2020 Position Rank	20
2020 Total snap % played from games played	63
Round projection from mock drafts	4
2021 Projected fantasy pts total 0.5 PPR	205.0
2021 Projected position rank	14

Dallas Cowboys

Najee Harris

RB

Pros
- Played agasint the highest standard of competition in College.
- Do it all Running Back who could be the best pass catcher at the position in this class.
- Tough, Explosive competitor who has the want to lead by example.

Cons
- Hurdles too much!
- Has only been the lead Back for one year
- Occasionally runs tall and doesn't lower his pads when engaging in contact.

Summary
Harris has a huge upside that see him as our number one Running Back prospect in this year's Class. He can do it all and is as deadly when catching the ball as he is when rushing with it. He is a bulldozer of a Running Back and can straight up hit a guy in the mouth and drive him backwards with his explosive power.

2020 Fantasy pts total 0.5 PPR	N/A
2020 Position Rank	N/A
2020 Total snap % played from games played	N/A
Round projection from mock drafts	4
2021 Projected fantasy pts total 0.5 PPR	201.1
2021 Projected position rank	15

Pittsburgh Steelers

Amari Cooper

WR

Pros
- Arguably the #1 Wide Receiver in one of the NFL's top 5 offenses
- Has great chemistry with his QB

Cons
- A lot of mouths to feed in Dallas
- Can bust at an alarmly high rate some weeks which gives him more of a boom or bust profile

Summary
Cooper has been a force to reckon with in Dallas. However, despite a WR1 season in 2019, he struggle when Dak Prescott went down in 2020. He still returned a WR2 season, but with the emergence of new star Wide Receiver CeeDee Lamb, will Cooper still be the primary read in the offense as the season goes on? His chances of being a WR1 in 2020 depend on it still being so.

2020 Fantasy pts total 0.5 PPR	190.8
2020 Position Rank	16
2020 Total snap % played from games played	82
Round projection from mock drafts	4
2021 Projected fantasy pts total 0.5 PPR	184.6
2021 Projected position rank	27

Dallas Cowboys

Ronald Jones

RB

Pros
- Home Run ability shown in college and also with a 98 yard touchdown last year

Cons
- Will be battling for carries with at least 1 if not 2 other backs
- Not going to get a lot of 3rd down work whilst also splitting carries

Summary

Ronald Jones was told he would be the lead back in 2020 and for the most part he was. However, he has yet to show that he can handle a full workload and it is unlikely he is going to get a full workload in 2021. Fournette re-signed with the team after an impressive playoff and Super Bowl run, whilst there will also be more competition for Jones. Jones can be effective on a reduced workload. However it is unlikely he will break into the top 16 RBs in 2021 unless there is significant injuries to other at the position.

2020 Fantasy pts total 0.5 PPR	172.3
2020 Position Rank	16
2020 Total snap % played from games played	48
Round projection from mock drafts	5
2021 Projected fantasy pts total 0.5 PPR	161.7
2021 Projected position rank	29

Tampa Bay Buccaneers

Cooper Kupp

WR

Pros
- Previous top 6 WR in 2019
- Slot receiver so will get a lot of targets
- Used a lot in the Redzone previously
- QB upgrade in 2021

Cons
- Lost touches to Woods in 2020 and that could continue in 2021 with Stafford's style of play
- Could lose more touches to the TE and RB positions

Summary

Kupp had a tough 2020 that saw him fall outside the top 24 Wide Receivers. As a slot receiver, his game relies on a high volume of receptions and constant redzone work. Kupp should still see a high volume of targets in 2021, but there are questions how he will be used in the redzone. Low usage down there again in 2021 will keep Kupp as a WR3. Better usage will see him return to the WR2 fold.

2020 Fantasy pts total 0.5 PPR	162.7
2020 Position Rank	27
2020 Total snap % played from games played	80
Round projection from mock drafts	5
2021 Projected fantasy pts total 0.5 PPR	176.1
2021 Projected position rank	29

Los Angeles Rams

Josh Allen

QB

Pros
- QB1 in 2020
- Rushing threat with over 420 yards and 8 Touchdowns Rushing in each of his 3 years in the NFL
- Passed for a career high 4,544 yards in 2020

Cons
- Can be a little inaccurate and erratic
- Can make mistakes leading to him to bust on occasion

Summary
Josh Allen came of age in 2020 and if he plays to a similar standard in 2021, he will be in the MVP conversation. This duel threat QB who is as much a danger with his legs as he is with his arm, looks nailed on to get close to 500 yards on the ground again, whilst also getting 8 rushing touchdowns again in 2021. Remember in some formats, those extra points for rushing Touchdowns could be the difference between winning or losing one week. He could easily repeat as the QB1 in 2021

2020 Fantasy pts total 0.5 PPR	405.06
2020 Position Rank	1
2020 Total snap % played from games played	95
Round projection from mock drafts	5
2021 Projected fantasy pts total 0.5 PPR	398.9
2021 Projected position rank	1

Buffalo Bills

Lamar Jackson

QB

Pros
- QB1 in 2019 with record setting year
- Back to back 1,000 yard rushing seasons as a QB
- 7 rushing TDs in each of his last 2 seasons

Cons
- Low volume passer, failing to pass for 3,150 yards in a season so far
- Requires high TD efficiency to be a top 5 QB

Summary
2019-2020 saw 2 very different Lamar Jackson's. Both seasons he was consistent on the ground. However, teams in 2020 knew how to contain him in the redzone, making it harder for him to walk away with Touchdowns. Last year he dropped 10 touchdowns on his 2019 total and added 3 more INTs. Jackson needs to be closer to 35 passing Touchdowns if he is to be a top 3 Quarterback for fantasy football in 2021.

2020 Fantasy pts total 0.5 PPR	341.78
2020 Position Rank	10
2020 Total snap % played from games played	94
Round projection from mock drafts	5
2021 Projected fantasy pts total 0.5 PPR	350.58
2021 Projected position rank	5

Baltimore Ravens

Mark Andrews

TE

Baltimore Ravens

Pros
- A Top 5 TE in 2019 and 2020
- Main Redzone receiving threat for the team

Cons
- His production is tied to how Jackson performs and requires volume from him. Could see some competition from a new WR

Summary
Mark Andrews has had two solid albeit unspectacular years at Tight End. Andrews is a safe floor, low ceiling Tight End play. Whilst he might give you some consistency at the position, it is doubtful he will return 5th round ADP. Don't feel the need to reach here for him

2020 Fantasy pts total 0.5 PPR	141.1
2020 Position Rank	5
2020 Total snap % played from games played	65
Round projection from mock drafts	5
2021 Projected fantasy pts total 0.5 PPR	164.9
2021 Projected position rank	4

JuJu Smith-Schuster

WR

Pittsburgh Steelers

Pros
- A WR1 in 2018
- Versatile Wide Receiver who can line up in the slot or outside
- In a high powered passing offense

Cons
- A lot of mouths to feed in Pittsburgh
- Has not been anywhere close to his 2018 form over the last 2 years

Summary
JuJu is coming off a WR2 year that was remarkably unremarkable. He was surprising the highest scorer of the 3 steelers Wide Receivers in PPR formats. However, you could have thrown a blanket over JuJu, Johnson and Claypool in 2020. Expect the same again in 2021. The Steelers only signed JuJu to a 1 year deal in Free Agency, and there was not a huge market for him, which is showing the NFLs reluctance to commit long term to the former Pro Bowler.

2020 Fantasy pts total 0.5 PPR	185.6
2020 Position Rank	18
2020 Total snap % played from games played	84
Round projection from mock drafts	5
2021 Projected fantasy pts total 0.5 PPR	160.7
2021 Projected position rank	38

Robert Woods

WR

Pros
- Was the top producer on his team in 2020
- Has received an upgrade at QB who is more likely to target him with deep shots
- Coming off 3 years with at least 129 targets in each season

Cons
- Always seems to underperform in the Touchdown column

Summary
Robert Woods is going into his third offseason in a row where he has been criminally underrated. A fringe WR1 player in each of the last 3 years, he sees a significant upgrade at WR and some competition go away in Josh Reynolds. Woods looks nailed on for another top 15 WR finish in 2021.

2020 Fantasy pts total 0.5 PPR	200.1
2020 Position Rank	13
2020 Total snap % played from games played	89
Round projection from mock drafts	5
2021 Projected fantasy pts total 0.5 PPR	215.1
2021 Projected position rank	9

Los Angeles Rams

Melvin Gordon

RB

Pros
- Solid Touchdown producer with scoring 9 TD as a minimum in each of his last 5 season
- Likely to be in line for more touches now Lindsay is off the team in 2021

Cons
- Legal issue hangs over him that could potentially see him miss time
- Failed to amass 250 touches in each of his last 3 season

Summary
Melvin Gordon didn't seem to excite anyone when he went to Denver. However, he had a sneaky productive season as he amassed over 1,100 yards from scrimmage last year and 10 Touchdowns. If he can get over 250 touches, which is possible with less competition, he could be on the fringe of the RB1 conversation come December. However, what will help Gordon most is an upgrade at QB.

2020 Fantasy pts total 0.5 PPR	184.2
2020 Position Rank	13
2020 Total snap % played from games played	62
Round projection from mock drafts	5
2021 Projected fantasy pts total 0.5 PPR	159.2
2021 Projected position rank	31

Denver Broncos

Diontae Johnson

WR

Pros
- Took a step forward in his second year in the NFL last season to return a WR2 season
- In a high powered passing offense

Cons
- A lot of mouths to feed in Pittsburgh, Juju coming back added competition he didn't need in 2021

Summary

Dionte Johnson has made some excellent showreel plays in the NFL and has dealt with less than ideal QB play in each of his first 2 seasons. Ben will be returning in 2021, as is JuJu. With that many mouths to feed and a QB whose big arms days are probably behind him, it is likely that the ceiling for Johnson in 2021 is similar to what he produced in 2020. A solid, mid-range WR2 season is on the cards for Johnson.

2020 Fantasy pts total 0.5 PPR	177.8
2020 Position Rank	23
2020 Total snap % played from games played	71
Round projection from mock drafts	5
2021 Projected fantasy pts total 0.5 PPR	197.8
2021 Projected position rank	17

Pittsburgh Steelers

Kareem Hunt

RB

Pros
- One of the best Pass-catching backs in the NFL
- On a team that is committed to using him a significant amount

Cons
- Won't get many of the carries on the ground as they will go to Nick Chubb
- High performance last year was due to Chubb missing 25% of the season which you can't bank on

Summary

If you took Kareem Hunt in the 5-7th round range in ADP last year you hit big on the way to him being a RB1 in 2020. However, if Chubb plays 17 games in 2021, Hunt will be more of a RB2 play with upside, than a RB1 play. Bake regression into his 2020 numbers before you consider taking him. But for the late 5th/6th round spot, he is probably as good as it gets if you need a starting/flex Running Back here

2020 Fantasy pts total 0.5 PPR	199.5
2020 Position Rank	10
2020 Total snap % played from games played	51
Round projection from mock drafts	5
2021 Projected fantasy pts total 0.5 PPR	174
2021 Projected position rank	23

Cleveland Brown

Raheem Mostert

RB

Pros

Paid as the lead back in a high powered offense (If everyone can remain healthy)
Shown flashes of game winning week ability

Cons

Looked a little lost last year and struggled with injuries after assuming lead back status in 2020
Will have competition at the position

Summary

We have yet to see Mostert do it over 16/17 games in the NFL as a lead back, and that remains a concern. Mostert's best season is 151 touches, which will struggle to get him to finish higher than low end RB2. At the moment he is top of the tree in San Francisco. However, how long will that last before the reigns get handed over to Jeff Wilson Jr. or someone else. The good news for Mostert is Jerick McKinnon and Tevin Coleman have left the team, vacating 146 touches from 2020. Right now the assumption is Mostert will get the lions share of that.

2020 Fantasy pts total 0.5 PPR	91.7
2020 Position Rank	48
2020 Total snap % played from games played	42
Round projection from mock drafts	5
2021 Projected fantasy pts total 0.5 PPR	157.0
2021 Projected position rank	33

San Francisco 49ers

Travis Etienne

RB

Pros

- Game splitting pace and acceleration. Any play can go the distance
- Has been ACC offensive player of the year twice
- Runs very tough and has superb vision

Cons

- Isn't a proven pass blocker yet
- Has some receptions but might not be a bell cow as a three down back

Summary

Travis Etienne has been Clemson's stalwart in the backfield for the last four years. Owns the ACC rushing touchdown record and has proven himself on the biggest stage of them all. Has game breaking speed and will shred all levels of the Defence if given the chance to do so. Can he prove he can be a competent pass catching Running Back? We will see.

2020 Fantasy pts total 0.5 PPR	N/A
2020 Position Rank	N/A
2020 Total snap % played from games played	N/A
Round projection from mock drafts	5
2021 Projected fantasy pts total 0.5 PPR	171.7
2021 Projected position rank	25

Jacksonville Jaguars

Tyler Lockett

WR

Pros
- A WR1 in 2020
- Great connection with his QB

Cons
- A move to a more run focused offense in 2021 caps Lockett's upside
- Competition with Metcalf for who will get the most targets on this team

Summary
Lockett is coming off the best season of his career, and was paid as a consequence. Has always produced good numbers on limited targets. If he slips to the 6th round in drafts this summer he is good value. There is not 3.5 rounds + difference between Metcalf and Lockett in season-long in 2021.

2020 Fantasy pts total 0.5 PPR	215.4
2020 Position Rank	19
2020 Total snap % played from games played	889
Round projection from mock drafts	6
2021 Projected fantasy pts total 0.5 PPR	185.8
2021 Projected position rank	24

Seattle Seahawks

D.J Chark

WR

Pros
A WR2 in 2019
Averaging over 13 yards per reception in his career

Cons
- Suffered with inconsistent QB play in 2020
- With a new QB, New Coach, New OC, there is uncertainty what is in store for Chark in 2021

Summary
D.J Chark was a player who struggled with some injuries, as well with who was throwing him the ball in 2020. He did break through the 1,000 yard mark as a receiver in 2019. However, with all the changes afoot in Jacksonville, is it likely we see 2019 D.J Chark, 2020 D.J Chark or something in the middle?

2020 Fantasy pts total 0.5 PPR	127.1
2020 Position Rank	49
2020 Total snap % played from games played	83
Round projection from mock drafts	6
2021 Projected fantasy pts total 0.5 PPR	185.7
2021 Projected position rank	25

Jacksonville Jaguars

Deshaun Watson

QB

Pros
- A Top 6 QB in the last 3 years
- Doesn't need elite weapons so still be highly effective, as shown in 2020

Cons
- Legal issues ongoing could mean Watson missing time in 2021, with everything on the table to missing a whole year, to a portion, to a couple, to none

Summary
There is uncertainty at the time of writing what is going to happen to Watson in 2021. He is facing extremely serious civil and criminal charges. If you aren't sure of the outlook, given how the commissioner has used the Commissioners Exemption list in the past, you will have to assume he will spend part of the 2021 season on that list, and therefore the best advice might be to not select him. As for how long, who knows. Hopefully when you hit draft season, and conduct your drafts, you will have more idea as to what is likely to happen.

2020 Fantasy pts total 0.5 PPR	376.32
2020 Position Rank	5
2020 Total snap % played from games played	100
Round projection from mock drafts	6
2021 Projected fantasy pts total 0.5 PPR	230.94
2021 Projected position rank	31

Houston Texans

Kyler Murray

QB

Pros
- QB1 until week 17 last season and finished as QB2
- High rushing floor makes him a cheat code similar to Allen and Jackson

Cons
- Still growing as a passer in the league and has a tendency to make mistakes

Summary
Kyler Murray took Arizona to within 1 win of the playoffs in 2020 and took a massive leap forward in his sophomore season. He has high performance at the position with a very safe floor. Barring an injury in the first quarter of the last game of the season, he would have ended up as the QB1. With hopefully more weapons in a pass friendly team, mixed with his grea rushing ability, Murray will be looking to go one better in 2021.

2020 Fantasy pts total 0.5 PPR	390.74
2020 Position Rank	2
2020 Total snap % played from games played	97
Round projection from mock drafts	6
2021 Projected fantasy pts total 0.5 PPR	378.66
2021 Projected position rank	3

Arizona Cardinals

Courtland Sutton

WR

Pros
- A WR2 in 2019 and the leading receiver on his team
- Should see an increase in QB play in 2021

Cons
- Played less than 1 game in 2020 due to injury

Summary

Sutton's 2020 season didn't even get off the ground, being injured Week One. He missed the rest of the 2020 season and will look to be ready for OTA's in 2021. He has great talent and showed in 2019 that when given the chance, and his number is called, he can make plays. However, how much will Jeudy and the 2 Tight Ends impact Sutton as he looks to rebound from 2020 and have a career year?

2020 Fantasy pts total 0.5 PPR	8.1
2020 Position Rank	180
2020 Total snap % played from games played	40
Round projection from mock drafts	6
2021 Projected fantasy pts total 0.5 PPR	172.7
2021 Projected position rank	31

Denver Broncos

Odell Beckham Jr.

WR

Pros
- Been a former WR1 in the past
- Has the ability to make highly skilful plays few Wide Receivers can make

Cons
- A series of injuries has meant he has only finished as a WR2 once since 2017, with no WR1 finishes
- In a run first offense

Summary

I don't think most people would have expected to be able to get OBJ in the 6th round of drafts. And maybe come draft season, he might not fall this far again. However, he is in this position on merit. Despite only being 28, he has suffered from not meeting his exceptionally high standards. In 2016 he was the WR4, and since then he has finishes of WR16, WR26, WR83, and WR85. Not all of this can be blamed on injuries. In 2019, he played every game. He just struggled to get on the same page with QB Baker Mayfield. Being a run first offense doesn't help either. Could it be the days of OBJ being a WR1 are over?

2020 Fantasy pts total 0.5 PPR	75.3
2020 Position Rank	85
2020 Total snap % played from games played	70
Round projection from mock drafts	6
2021 Projected fantasy pts total 0.5 PPR	186.4
2021 Projected position rank	23

Cleveland Browns

Brandon Aiyuk

WR

Pros

A 1st round Draft selection in 2020

Will see an upgrade at QB in 2021

Cons

- Finished as a WR3 due to injury/poor QB play
- Had less than 100 targets last year

Summary

Aiyuk is someone who is very interesting coming into 2021 draft season. He did reasonably well despite catching balls from backup QBs for most of the season. He also missed a few games himself. With an upgrade at QB, there is no reason not to believe Aiyuk can take a massive step forward in 2021.

2020 Fantasy pts total 0.5 PPR	154.5
2020 Position Rank	33
2020 Total snap % played from games played	86
Round projection from mock drafts	6
2021 Projected fantasy pts total 0.5 PPR	191.3
2021 Projected position rank	22

San Francisco 49ers

Brandin Cooks

WR

Pros

- Topped 1,000 receiving yards in 5 of the last 6 years
- Leading receiving option on his team
- Very little competition for targets

Cons

- Uncertainty over who will throw him the ball in 2021, which could lead to an extremely wide range of outcomes

Summary

A WR2 last time out, Cooks has no Will Fuller to contend with in 2021. The issue for him however, is he might not have Deshaun Watson throwing him the ball in 2021 due to his legal issues. If it is Tyrod Taylor at QB in 2021 for Houston, Cooks' range of outcomes goes down from being a WR2 with upside to a WR3 being his ceiling. There is risk baked in here with the uncertainty.

2020 Fantasy pts total 0.5 PPR	191.5
2020 Position Rank	15
2020 Total snap % played from games played	87
Round projection from mock drafts	6
2021 Projected fantasy pts total 0.5 PPR	199.1
2021 Projected position rank	16

Houston Texans

Tee Higgins

WR

Pros
- Picked 33rd Overall in 2020
- Tied to a highly productive QB
- Will have room to grow in 2021

Cons
- How fit and ready is Joe Burrow going to be for Week One. That is the question?

Summary
Higgins is another one in this range of Wide Receivers, like Brandon Aiyuk, who has the potentially to really break out in his sophomore year. It will all depend on how healthy Joe Burrow is and if they can avoid drafting someone like Jamarr Chase in the NFL Draft.

2020 Fantasy pts total 0.5 PPR	161.1
2020 Position Rank	30
2020 Total snap % played from games played	75
Round projection from mock drafts	6
2021 Projected fantasy pts total 0.5 PPR	168.8
2021 Projected position rank	34

Cincinnati Bengals

Dak Prescott

QB

Pros
- Was on record setting QB pace thru 5 games in 2020
- Previously a top 6 QB on 2 occasion
- QB on one of the NFL's 5 best offenses

Cons
- Returning from a severe injury, how long will it take to be ready?

Summary
Dak Prescott has been impressive in his time in the NFL. But never more impressive than he was at the start of 2020. He was the QB1 and on course to shatter a ton of QB records before an injury curtailed his season. As a result, and fresh off the back of a newly minted contract, he is ready to take the league by storm again, with his massive array of weapons. If he is ready by OTA's then its going to be wheels up for Dak.

2020 Fantasy pts total 0.5 PPR	138.64
2020 Position Rank	32
2020 Total snap % played from games played	92
Round projection from mock drafts	6
2021 Projected fantasy pts total 0.5 PPR	362.94
2021 Projected position rank	4

Dallas Cowboys

Tyler Boyd

WR

Pros
- Extremely consistent WR who averages over 11 yards per reception
- Showed upside with an improvement at QB for the first half of 2020

Cons
- More of a #2 WR and as a result his ceiling is capped

Summary
Boyd has always done the job he is asked to do. However, he is not seen as an alpha receiver by his team, or by the NFL. As a result, he is going to be limited to between 100-110 targets. He is going to need to haul in over 70% of those to be in the WR2 conversation in 2021. It's possible, but also watch out for who the Bengals draft at 5?

2020 Fantasy pts total 0.5 PPR	153.1
2020 Position Rank	35
2020 Total snap % played from games played	74
Round projection from mock drafts	6
2021 Projected fantasy pts total 0.5 PPR	151.1
2021 Projected position rank	42

Cincinnati Bengals

Russell Wilson

QB

Pros
- Been a top 6 QB in 3 of the last 5 years
- Shown what he can do when he is allowed to let rip

Cons
- Led all QBs in INTs in the Redzone in 2020
- The new OC might not be willing to let Russ cook as much

Summary
Russell Wilson has proven time and time again what an exceptional QB he is in the NFL. And, for the most part, those numbers corralate into fantasy. As the QB who is the latest of the big 7, he is the line of demarcation between consist great performance and starting to gamble at the position. Taking him as the QB6/QB7 off the board in this range is absolutely fine and will represent a decent return in 2021.

2020 Fantasy pts total 0.5 PPR	372.78
2020 Position Rank	6
2020 Total snap % played from games played	98
Round projection from mock drafts	6
2021 Projected fantasy pts total 0.5 PPR	348.54
2021 Projected position rank	6

Seattle Seahawks

A.J Dillon

RB

Pros
- Drafted in the 2nd round in 2020

Cons
- Stuck behind Aaron Jones
- Doubtful he is going to be as relevant as people are hoping in 2021

Summary

A.J Dillon, at one point, looked like he was going to be the lead back in Green Bay. However, when Aaron Jones re-signed with the team, those dreams were shattered. His ADP will be all over the place. In reality, he will have a role, and will be the chief handcuff to own in fantasy football. However, the 6th round is just too early for a player who is going to struggle to be a RB2 in 2021.

2020 Fantasy pts total 0.5 PPR	39.3
2020 Position Rank	80
2020 Total snap % played from games played	16
Round projection from mock drafts	6
2021 Projected fantasy pts total 0.5 PPR	103
2021 Projected position rank	49

Green Bay Packers

David Johnson

RB

Pros
- Former Number 1 Overall RB in 2016 in fantasy football, also a RB1 in 2018
- Lead back on his team that could get more work if Watson isn't playing

Cons
- Injuries are a concern
- It is a crowded backfield with the additions of Ingram and Lindsey there. He will need to earn every touch this season

Summary

David Johnson came into the NFL like a train. And under Arians, he looked like the real deal. The RB1 in 2016, he was injured week 1 in 2017 and did not return for the season. He has struggled since. However, he was consistent last year in Houston with RB2 production on a consistent basis. However, he faces a lot more competition in 2021. Will he struggle to maintain the lead back status in Houston in 2021?

2020 Fantasy pts total 0.5 PPR	163
2020 Position Rank	19
2020 Total snap % played from games played	74
Round projection from mock drafts	6
2021 Projected fantasy pts total 0.5 PPR	171.6
2021 Projected position rank	26

Houston Texans

Ja'Marr Chase

WR

Pros
- Aggressive and physical – wins catches consistently because of these traits
- Superb route running
- Plays from every position across the line

Cons
- Can be lazy when run blocking
- If he isn't involved in the play he almost doesn't try sometimes

Summary
Ja'Marr Chase is heads and shoulders clear of everyone else in this draft class and the only reason the gap has apparently closed is due to his 2020 opt out. He has a great combination of size/speed/physicality which makes him a nightmare for Defences to cover. Whilst he doesn't have breakaway speed he can convert when catching over the top due to his ability to bully Defenders off the ball.

2020 Fantasy pts total 0.5 PPR	N/A
2020 Position Rank	N/A
2020 Total snap % played from games played	N/A
Round projection from mock drafts	6
2021 Projected fantasy pts total 0.5 PPR	166.2
2021 Projected position rank	35

Cincinatti Bengals

Justin Herbert

QB

Pros
- Reigning NFL Offensive Rookie of the Year
- Set a ton of Rookie QB records
- Has weapons to continue in a positive way in 2021

Cons
- Expectations will be higher, how will he cope?
- Need additional weapons as has lost Hunter Henry and Mike Williams

Summary
Justin Herbert seemed to shock a lot of the fantasy community with his electric arm and strong performances in 2020. However, he is here to stay. He has Keenan Allen back. However, he has a new coach and a new OC. Can Herbert keep it up in 2021?

2020 Fantasy pts total 0.5 PPR	342.84
2020 Position Rank	9
2020 Total snap % played from games played	99
Round projection from mock drafts	7
2021 Projected fantasy pts total 0.5 PPR	326.18
2021 Projected position rank	9

Los Angeles Chargers

Aaron Rodgers

QB

Pros
- Reigning NFL MVP
- Proved he doesn't need tons of weapons to put up extremely good numbers
- 3 top 6 QB finishes in the past 5 years

Cons
- Number 1 in TD efficiency in 2020, this will regress significantly in 2021
- Contract dispute could cause distractions

Summary
Rodgers doesn't have the rushing floor others above him have. He also has contract disputes about his future that lead many to question if 2021 is his last year in Green Bay. Having said that, the reigning MVP had an elite year in 2020 and will have everyone back in 2021. Expect the efficiency they scored Touchdowns to regress slightly in 2021 as it will be neigh on impossible to maintain. He should be a lock for a QB1 finish. However he should probably finish closer to 12th than 1st.

2020 Fantasy pts total 0.5 PPR	~~387.26~~
2020 Position Rank	3
2020 Total snap % played from games played	98
Round projection from mock drafts	7
2021 Projected fantasy pts total 0.5 PPR	340.44
2021 Projected position rank	7

Green Bay Packers

DeVante Parker

WR

Pros
- A WR1 in 2019

Cons
- Will see more competition for targets in 2021
- Only had 1 productive year as a WR

Summary
Parker was a player that, despite being taken in the first round in 2015, has failed to live up to expectations. When everyone was ready to forget about Parker, he flashed his talent in a WR1 (7th WR Overall in 0.5pt PPR) season in 2019. In 2020 he struggled a little with injuries, and with getting on the same page with Franchise QB Tua Tagovailoa. Expect enhanced competition for Parker in 2021 and, as a result, he could find it difficult to break into the top 24 WRs.

2020 Fantasy pts total 0.5 PPR	134.8
2020 Position Rank	42
2020 Total snap % played from games played	78
Round projection from mock drafts	7
2021 Projected fantasy pts total 0.5 PPR	142.9
2021 Projected position rank	51

Miami Dolphins

Deebo Samuel

WR

Pros
- 2nd round draft selection in 2019

Cons
- Lost lead receiver status to Aiyuk in 2020
- Coming off a significant injury in 2020

Summary
Deebo Samuel was someone we expected to take a leap in 2020. However, with injuries to himself, Jimmy G his QB, plus the drafting and emergence of Brandon Aiyuk, it just didn't happen. And as a result, it looks like Samuel, despite an upgrade at QB, is a risk of being a low ceiling player in 2021? Are we likely to see more out of Samuel than a fringe WR2/WR3 performance in 2021? Possible but unlikely.

2020 Fantasy pts total 0.5 PPR	64.2
2020 Position Rank	97
2020 Total snap % played from games played	62
Round projection from mock drafts	7
2021 Projected fantasy pts total 0.5 PPR	176.0
2021 Projected position rank	30

San Francisco 49ers

Chase Claypool

WR

Pros
- Getting significant targets on a pass first offense
- A WR2 in 2020

Cons
- Lots of mouths to feed in Pittsburgh
- Tied to a QB who is struggling to get the ball down the field

Summary
Claypool was another rookie WR that took the league by storm in 2020. He made huge plays and had no problem finding the end zone. He finished as a WR2 with his other 2 Steelers receivers. Since everyone is back for 2021, this caps the upside significantly, as does Ben's arm and having one of the lower Air Yards per Attempt in the NFL. Claypool is worth owning, but his ceiling isn't much more than what he achieved in 2021

2020 Fantasy pts total 0.5 PPR	183.9
2020 Position Rank	19
2020 Total snap % played from games played	63
Round projection from mock drafts	7
2021 Projected fantasy pts total 0.5 PPR	194.8
2021 Projected position rank	19

Pittsburgh Steelers

Marquise Brown

WR

Pros
- 1st Round Draft selection in 2019

Cons
- Struggling to use his speed as a differentiator
- Will have additional competition for targets in 2021
- QB is unlikely to throw a high number of passes or yards in 2021

Summary
We have been waiting for the real "Hollywood" Brown for 2 years. It's fair to say that Hollywood Brown should be renamed "straight to DVD" Brown for fantasy purposes. He's not consistent enough to rely on in fantasy football. It's not all down to him. His QB is unlikely to throw for 3,500 yard this year. However, considering he didn't have competition for targets in each of his first 2 years, and now it is likely he will, I can't see the ceiling be any higher than a WR3 spot for Brown

2020 Fantasy pts total 0.5 PPR	154
2020 Position Rank	34
2020 Total snap % played from games played	78
Round projection from mock drafts	7
2021 Projected fantasy pts total 0.5 PPR	123.4
2021 Projected position rank	60

Baltimore Ravens

Jarvis Landry

WR

Pros
- Averaging 1,000 yards a season in the last 6 seasons

Cons
- 2020 was his worst season in the last 6
- Was productive but has a very low ceiling

Summary
Stable fantasy asset who has shown consistency over the past six seasons. Landry isn't an exciting player to own in fantasy, and is a borderline starting option. However, he is going to produce decent numbers for a rotational/bye week/flex play option most weeks. He carries upside if OBJ fails to play 17 games, which is more than just possible.

2020 Fantasy pts total 0.5 PPR	152
2020 Position Rank	36
2020 Total snap % played from games played	71
Round projection from mock drafts	7
2021 Projected fantasy pts total 0.5 PPR	161.02
2021 Projected position rank	37

Cleveland Browns

Leonard Fournette

RB

Pros
- Former 1st round draft selection
- Averaged over 100 scrimmage yards a game in the 2020 postseason

Cons
- Had less than 100 carries in the regular season in 2020
- Will be splitting time with 1 or maybe even 2 backs

Summary
Lombardi Lenny as he is now affectionally known did virtually nothing in the regular season and was on the verge of asking the Buccaneers to release him. However, when Ronald Jones got COVID-19 and injuries, it all changed. In the NFL playoffs he looked like a back reborn. The issue with Fournette is can he do this more frequently in 2021? He has a lot of competition and he won't be the lead ball carrier. However, if his playoff form returns, there is no way he isn't getting the ball. He is a low risk, high reward at this stage of the draft, but if you can get him latter than the late 7ths, even better.

2020 Fantasy pts total 0.5 PPR	114
2020 Position Rank	38
2020 Total snap % played from games played	43
Round projection from mock drafts	7
2021 Projected fantasy pts total 0.5 PPR	158.1
2021 Projected position rank	=31

Tampa Bay Buccaneers

DeVonta Smith

WR

Pros
- Has proven he can be the Alpha in the WR room
- Superb hands and route running
- Can make any play a big one

Cons
- Smaller in stature than perhaps we like to see

Summary
DeVonta Smith has proven everything he needs to do to be considered a top tier Wide Receiver. He was the Heismann winner and Wideouts just don't win that award. He broke records for his touchdown receptions in 2020 and made Corners look like they were playing Peewee football.

2020 Fantasy pts total 0.5 PPR	N/A
2020 Position Rank	N/A
2020 Total snap % played from games played	N/A
Round projection from mock drafts	7
2021 Projected fantasy pts total 0.5 PPR	172
2021 Projected position rank	32

Philadelphia Eagles

James Conner

RB

Pros
- A RB1 in 2018

Cons
- Was RB26 last year despite playing 13 games

Summary
James Conner has signed for Arizona. However, he will be competing with Chase Edmonds for touches in the backfield. Conner and Edmonds will fight to be the lead back. However, perhaps expect them to be more of a 1a/1b situation. Conner's ceiling is a low end RB2 right now.

2020 Fantasy pts total 0.5 PPR	147.1
2020 Position Rank	26
2020 Total snap % played from games played	63
Round projection from mock drafts	8
2021 Projected fantasy pts total 0.5 PPR	161.8
2021 Projected position rank	28

Arizona Cardinals

Zack Moss

RB

Pros
- Currently set to be the lead back on his team
- Will get some receiving work

Cons
- Less then 500 Rushing Yards in rookie year
- Josh Allen will vulture a lot of Touchdowns by the goal-line
- Could see more competition come in 2021

Summary
Moss failed to get the majority of the work nor did he make a significant impact in terms of fantasy football. As a result, it wouldn't shock me if this RBBC becomes even more complicated. Will require injuries or dominate on his limited touches in order to really return value in 2021

2020 Fantasy pts total 0.5 PPR	94.6
2020 Position Rank	45
2020 Total snap % played from games played	45
Round projection from mock drafts	8
2021 Projected fantasy pts total 0.5 PPR	106.5
2021 Projected position rank	45

Buffalo Bills

Henry Ruggs III

WR

Pros
- 1st round draft selection in 2020
- Unique speed

Cons
- Failed to break the top 80 at the position
- Will struggle with a QB not known for his strong vertical game

Summary
Ruggs, despite being the 1st Wide Receiver selected, really couldn't have had a worse 2020 season. At the end of the day, it's hard to see Ruggs consistently perform enough in this offense to be a top 24 Wide Receiver. However, he is the profile of player who could have huge weeks off very few plays. Extremely boom or bust.

2020 Fantasy pts total 0.5 PPR	71.1
2020 Position Rank	89
2020 Total snap % played from games played	66
Round projection from mock drafts	8
2021 Projected fantasy pts total 0.5 PPR	108.2
2021 Projected position rank	70

Las Vegas Raiders

Jerry Jeudy

WR

Pros
- A 1st round draft selection in 2020
- Will potentially see an upgrade at QB in 2021

Cons
- Struggled to get acclimated in his natural role due to injuries to Sutton as well as no preseason or OTA's

Summary
Jeudy is actually in a great situation in 2021, especially if he gets an upgrade at QB. He was a stud in college, he has all the right breakout metrics, and he is on a good offense with weapons. Jeudy will need some time, but he could be expected to be one of the biggest improvers in 2021

2020 Fantasy pts total 0.5 PPR	131.6
2020 Position Rank	44
2020 Total snap % played from games played	75
Round projection from mock drafts	8
2021 Projected fantasy pts total 0.5 PPR	161.6
2021 Projected position rank	36

Denver Broncos

Robby Anderson

WR

Pros
- A WR2 season in 2020
- A potential upgrade at QB in 2021 with Sam Darnold

Cons
- Just 3 TDs off 95 receptions
- Not great numbers put up with Darnold in the past in New York

Summary

Anderson had a breakout year in 2020 and returned a WR2 performance and put up almost 1,100 receiving yards on a team that struggled for wins. The move to bring Darnold in is both a positive and negative for Anderson. They have played together for 3 seasons before, so will have some rapport. However, they hard proved to be a dynamic duo when they worked together in the past. Was it the New York system or are they really just not a good match?

2020 Fantasy pts total 0.5 PPR	176.7
2020 Position Rank	24
2020 Total snap % played from games played	78
Round projection from mock drafts	8
2021 Projected fantasy pts total 0.5 PPR	182.5
2021 Projected position rank	28

Carolina Panthers

Damien Harris

RB

Pros
- One of the best college profiles seen on such limited workload
- Great with his hands

Cons
- Has failed to carve out a significant role on his team
- Just 2 career NFL Touchdowns
- Not on a productive Fantasy offense

Summary

Harris has yet to do anything as a fantasy player in the NFL, failing to finish above RB50. His rookie injury was essentially a write-off due to injury. He struggled to command significant carries over Burkhead and Michel in 2020 and I doubt he will be able to earn many more touches in 2021

2020 Fantasy pts total 0.5 PPR	88.8
2020 Position Rank	50
2020 Total snap % played from games played	41
Round projection from mock drafts	8
2021 Projected fantasy pts total 0.5 PPR	115.8
2021 Projected position rank	43

New England Patriots

Michael Gallup

WR

Pros
- On a top 5 NFL offense
- A WR2 in 2019

Cons
- Plenty of competition for targets which can lead him to be the odd man out

Summary

Gallup has been reasonably productive in his career in the NFL to date. He can put up yards and can be a decent add in this range, given the offense he is on. However, don't expect Gallup to have a high ceiling. He has starter flex appeal with upside should Cooper or Lamb miss time in 2021

2020 Fantasy pts total 0.5 PPR	143.8
2020 Position Rank	38
2020 Total snap % played from games played	87
Round projection from mock drafts	8
2021 Projected fantasy pts total 0.5 PPR	155.1
2021 Projected position rank	40

Dallas Cowboys

T.J Hockenson

TE

Pros
- A 1st round selection in the NFL Draft in 2019
- Finished at a top 5 TE in 2020

Cons
- Despite being a high scoring Tight End, is his ceiling better than other players in this range from a flex perspective?

Summary

Hockenson is yet to truly break-out and could see an increase in production with Goff under centre in Detroit. However, there is still the question that perhaps the limited ceiling you might get from a Tight End here won't give you enough of an advantage over the remaining Tight Ends that you could be passing on better options. He could however return ADP on a late 8th/9th round ADP as the Lions don't have tons of established weapons in the offense.

2020 Fantasy pts total 0.5 PPR	141.8
2020 Position Rank	4
2020 Total snap % played from games played	74
Round projection from mock drafts	8
2021 Projected fantasy pts total 0.5 PPR	138.8
2021 Projected position rank	6

Detroit Lions

Chase Edmonds

RB

Pros
- Currently the lead back on the roster
- Took Away a significant amount of touches from Drake in 2020

Cons
- Has only started 4 games in the NFL in 3 years
- Has yet to amass 1,000 rushing yards

Summary
4 starts in the NFL in 3 seasons for Edmonds. You are only taking him here if you believe Edmonds will either be the lead back in Arizona, or, at the very least, the 1b. However; despite the appeal; this is nothing but a pure gamble. Having said that, how many more Running Backs left in the draft at this stage have a path to the type of ceiling Edmonds has if he gets the bulk of the work?

2020 Fantasy pts total 0.5 PPR	141.5
2020 Position Rank	28
2020 Total snap % played from games played	46
Round projection from mock drafts	8
2021 Projected fantasy pts total 0.5 PPR	185.3
2021 Projected position rank	19

Arizona Cardinals

Marvin Jones Jr.

WR

Pros
- A WR1 and 2 WR2 finishes in the last 4 seasons

Cons
- Changing teams and now paired with a Rookie QB. Could be more unpredictable in 2021

Summary
Jones Jr. Has been a steal in this sort of range for the last 3 or 4 years in fantasy football. The veteran has benefited massively from injuries to others, which elevated him to receive more targets than maybe projected. However, in 2021, he finds himself in a new offense, with a rookie QB. His range of outcomes could be anywhere from a WR2-WR5 or lower. There will be an adjustment period for him so be cautious. But at this stage of the draft, he's worth consideration

2020 Fantasy pts total 0.5 PPR	189.8
2020 Position Rank	17
2020 Total snap % played from games played	90
Round projection from mock drafts	9
2021 Projected fantasy pts total 0.5 PPR	145.6
2021 Projected position rank	48

Jacksonville Jaguars

Laviska Shenault

WR

Pros
- Will see an upgrade at QB in 2021
- Will get an offseason and OTA's this year

Cons
- Despite being highly touted, Shenault struggled to be a significant fantasy producer in 2020
- More mouths to feed in 2021 in this Jags offense could spell trouble

Summary

Shenault flashed at times in 2020 to show he has the size, speed and skill to be successful in the NFL. However, with a new offensive system, a new rookie QB, and new competition in the shape of Jones Jr. This is going to be make or break for Shenault in the NFL. Will he sink or will he swim?

2020 Fantasy pts total 0.5 PPR	128.1
2020 Position Rank	47
2020 Total snap % played from games played	64
Round projection from mock drafts	9
2021 Projected fantasy pts total 0.5 PPR	160.7
2021 Projected position rank	39

Jacksonville Jaguars

Zach Ertz

TE

Pros
- Top 3 Tight End 2017 + 2018
- Top 5 Tight End in 2019

Cons
- Injuries/contract dispute proved to be a huge distraction as Ertz was a non-factor in 2020

Summary

Ertz has been an elite fantasy option in the past, but there is a huge amount of uncertainty for him this year. He is up for trade, and despite rumours a trade was close, at time of writing, he is still an Eagle. He will need to be traded for him to have a chance of being fantasy relevant in 2021. However, if he lands in the right spot, he could be a screaming value here.

2020 Fantasy pts total 0.5 PPR	59.5
2020 Position Rank	32
2020 Total snap % played from games played	81
Round projection from mock drafts	9
2021 Projected fantasy pts total 0.5 PPR	87.9
2021 Projected position rank	26

Philadelphia Eagles

Jamison Crowder

WR

Pros
- Let the Jets in receptions in each of the last 2 seasons

Cons
- Despite all those targets, WR3 was the best season he produced
- More competition this year in a new offensive scheme

Summary

Crowder has been a solid late round Wide Receiver option over the past few years. He has been very valuable, especially in PPR leagues. However, with Darnold and Gase leaving town in 2021, the ceiling for Crowder is certainly lower. Nevertheless, he is still a solid pick in the 9th round here if available. Just don't be picking him for upside.

2020 Fantasy pts total 0.5 PPR	142.5
2020 Position Rank	39
2020 Total snap % played from games played	79
Round projection from mock drafts	9
2021 Projected fantasy pts total 0.5 PPR	112.6
2021 Projected position rank	67

New York Jets

Nyheim Hines

RB

Pros

RB2 in 2020

Cons
- Not a starter and unlikely to be one unless there is an injury to Taylor

Summary

Hines is a scat back who is unlikely to start any games in 2021. Having said that, he was a RB2 in 2020 on just 36% of the snaps, meaning he was highly productive when he was on the field. Hines can easily benefit from the extra game in 2021. He will need to be weary of Mack returning to the team in 2021 also.

2020 Fantasy pts total 0.5 PPR	161.7
2020 Position Rank	20
2020 Total snap % played from games played	36
Round projection from mock drafts	9
2021 Projected fantasy pts total 0.5 PPR	152
2021 Projected position rank	34

Indianapolis Colts

Devin Singletary

RB

Pros
- Averaged over 5 yards a carry in 2019

Cons
- Just 4 career touchdowns and failed to reach 200 touches in a season
- Unlikely to get as much work this season as he had last season

Summary
There is no significant ceiling for Singletary unless he is the only back getting touches. If that's the case, due to no Touchdown upside it is unlikely he would ever be anything other than a RB2. Others should be considered here before Singletary.

2020 Fantasy pts total 0.5 PPR	124.6
2020 Position Rank	34
2020 Total snap % played from games played	57
Round projection from mock drafts	9
2021 Projected fantasy pts total 0.5 PPR	106.0
2021 Projected position rank	47

Buffalo Bills

Corey Davis

WR

Pros
- Former 1st round draft selection
- Coming off the best year of his career

Cons
- Signing to a new team who have yet to produce a WR2 or better in the last 4 seasons

Summary
The Jets have invested heavily in the offseason in Davis. Davis is coming off his best season of his career. A former first round pick, it was about time he showed what he could do. However, his career trajectory reminds me of another former first round pick; Davante Parker. It's a gamble and hoping the Jets are a relevant offense in 2021. But maybe a gamble worth taking in this range?

2020 Fantasy pts total 0.5 PPR	158.9
2020 Position Rank	31
2020 Total snap % played from games played	77
Round projection from mock drafts	9
2021 Projected fantasy pts total 0.5 PPR	149.5
2021 Projected position rank	45

New York Jets

Curtis Samuel

WR

Pros
- On a new team but reuniting with an offensive system he knows and his old Head Coach
- Not huge competition for targets

Cons
- Yet to have a top 24 season at the position
- Could argue his most productive season was not in the system he is about to go into

Summary

Few players have had the hype profile on Twitter that Curtis Samuel has had. A darling of Matt Harmon's "Perception Reception" a few years ago. However, I'm not sure this offensive scheme is the best fit for Samuel and for fantasy football fans. I expect to see more of his 2018/2019 numbers than an upward trajectory from his 2020 numbers. Draft with caution.

2020 Fantasy pts total 0.5 PPR	173.6
2020 Position Rank	25
2020 Total snap % played from games played	68
Round projection from mock drafts	9
2021 Projected fantasy pts total 0.5 PPR	150.8
2021 Projected position rank	43

Washington Football Team

Christian Kirk

WR

Pros
- Second round pick in 2018

Cons
- Should concede targets to A.J. Green
- Could see a replacement overtake him on the depth chart

Summary

Kirk has disappointed fantasy owners over the last couple of years. However, none more so than in 2019. This pass friendly offense was supposed to yield positive results for Kirk. Despite playing 14 games in 2020, and playing on 77% of snaps, Kirk failed to break 700 yards receiving and failed to see 70 targets. If more competition gets drafted, it's fair to say that Kirk's stock could be worthless. Other Wide Receivers are fancied here in this range.

2020 Fantasy pts total 0.5 PPR	122.4
2020 Position Rank	50
2020 Total snap % played from games played	77
Round projection from mock drafts	9
2021 Projected fantasy pts total 0.5 PPR	81.1
2021 Projected position rank	81

Arizona Cardinals

Mike Davis

RB

Pros
- Made the most of his opportunity last season by putting together a RB2 season

Cons
- Never had a starting Running Back Job in the NFL before last season
- Really faded away in the second half of the season

Summary
Davis was productive stepping in for Christian McCaffrey. However, he did run out of gas towards the end of the season. He does remain in the NFC South in 2021. However, he goes to Atlanta. Right now, Davis is the top of the depth chart right now in Atlanta. They might draft a back or sign another back. Regardless, he should still be productive with a ceiling of RB2 but a floor of RB4.

2020 Fantasy pts total 0.5 PPR	177
2020 Position Rank	15
2020 Total snap % played from games played	60
Round projection from mock drafts	9
2021 Projected fantasy pts total 0.5 PPR	168.1
2021 Projected position rank	27

Atlanta Falcons

CHAPTER 14

Rankings

Written by **Chris Mitchell & Adam Murfet**

Quarterbacks

Rank	Stocks		Murf	
	Player	Points	Player	Points
1	Kyler Murray	379.88	Josh Allen	398.90
2	Josh Allen	376.66	Patrick Mahomes	391.78
3	Patrick Mahomes	354.33	Kyler Murray	378.66
4	Lamar Jackson	352.36	Dak Prescott	362.94
5	Russell Wilson	330.13	Lamar Jackson	350.58
6	Tom Brady	324.14	Russell Wilson	348.54
7	Ben Roethlisberger	298.45	Aaron Rodgers	340.44
8	Taysom Hill	295.78	Tom Brady	339.66
9	Kirk Cousins	292.59	Justin Herbert	326.18
10	DeShaun Watson	292.04	Jalen Hurts	320.92
11	Aaron Rodgers	292.01	Ryan Tannehill	320.18
12	Dak Prescott	289.67	Trey Lance	317.04
13	Ryan Tannehill	288.59	Trevor Lawrence	309.76
14	Joe Burrow	280.68	Joe Burrow	304.56
15	Matt Stafford	279.13	Ryan Fitzpatrick	298.72
16	Justin Herbert	277.78	Trevor Lawrence	293.18
17	Sam Darnold	276.12	Kirk Cousins	288.70
18	Trevor Lawrence	273.72	Matt Ryan	287.64
19	Baker Mayfield	272.09	Matthew Stafford	283.14
20	Jalen Hurts	266.64	Daniel Jones	283.02
21	Matt Ryan	266.4	Derek Carr	282.76
22	Derek Carr	257.77	Ben Roethlisberger	282.26
23	Cam Newton	257.51	Jameis Winston	272.88
24	Zach Wilson	257.49	Baker Mayfield	270.26
25	Jimmy Garopollo	251.66	Jared Goff	263.74
26	Andy Dalton	250	Tua Tagovailoa	260.94
27	Daniel Jones	249.55	Carson Wentz	255.74
28	Jared Goff	249.07	Justin Fields	255.52
29	Tua Tagovailoa	241.03	Zach Wilson	247.98
30	Ryan Fitzpatrick	236.91	Sam Darnold	238.94
31	Drew Lock	236.82	Deshaun Watson	230.94
32	Carson Wentz	229.41	Drew Lock	200.94

Stocks Running Backs

Rank	Standard	Standard Points	Half Point PPR	Half Point PPR Points	PPR	PPR Points
1	Christian McCaffrey	297.71	Christian McCaffrey	342.75	Christian McCaffrey	387.8
2	Derrick Henry	287.31	Alvin Kamara	282.24	Alvin Kamara	319.56
3	Dalvin Cook	248.26	Derrick Henry	294.99	Derrick Henry	302.68
4	Alvin Kamara	244.93	Dalvin Cook	269.68	Dalvin Cook	291.11
5	Nick Chubb	239.85	Austin Ekeler	245.21	Austin Ekeler	280.06
6	Aaron Jones	221.29	Chris Carson	242.34	Chris Carson	263.94
7	Chris Carson	220.74	Aaron Jones	240.06	Aaron Jones	258.83
8	J.K. Dobbins	211.37	Nick Chubb	249.11	Nick Chubb	258.36
9	Austin Ekeler	210.36	D'Andre Swift	222.03	D'Andre Swift	250.83
10	Cam Akers	205.21	Ezekiel Elliot	222.09	Ezekiel Elliot	250.59
11	Saquon Barkley	194.63	Cam Akers	226.66	Cam Akers	248.11
2	Ezekiel Elliot	193.59	Saquon Barkley	220.9	Saquon Barkley	247.17
13	D'Andre Swift	193.23	J.K. Dobbins	222.25	J.K. Dobbins	233.12
14	Najee Harris	182.34	Najee Harris	200.34	Najee Harris	218.34
15	Jonathan Taylor	180.89	Kenyan Drake	198.19	Kenyan Drake	217.84
16	Mike Davis	180.22	Mike Davis	198.72	Mike Davis	217.22
17	Kenyan Drake	178.53	Jonathan Taylor	197.69	Jonathan Taylor	214.49
18	Josh Jacobs	170.6	Joe Mixon	180.87	Joe Mixon	199.98
19	Antonio Gibson	167.65	Josh Jacobs	183.73	Josh Jacobs	196.85
20	Joe Mixon	161.76	Antonio Gibson	180.68	Antonio Gibson	193.72
21	Clyde Edwards-Helaire	156.49	Travis Ettiene	169.92	Travis Ettiene	192.02
22	Zack Moss	154.32	Clyde Edwards-Helaire	173.24	Clyde Edwards-Helaire	189.99
23	Kareem Hunt	151.04	David Johnson	166.54	David Johnson	186.18
24	Melvin Gordon	150.27	Kareem Hunt	166.95	Kareem Hunt	182.86
25	Miles Sanders	148.8	Zack Moss	167.93	Zack Moss	181.55
26	Travis Ettiene	147.82	Melvin Gordon	164.52	Melvin Gordon	178.77
27	David Johnson	146.91	Myles Gaskin	158.2	Myles Gaskin	176.77
28	David Montgomery	139.82	Miles Sanders	159.6	Miles Sanders	170.4
29	Myles Gaskin	139.64	Chase Edmonds	142.66	Chase Edmonds	164.98

30	James Conner	132	Leonard Fournette	142.28	Leonard Fournette	163.08
31	Raheem Mostert	129	Kenneth Gainwell	137.64	Kenneth Gainwell	161.5
32	Leonard Fournette	121.48	James Conner	143.2	James Conner	154.4
33	Chase Edmonds	120.34	David Montgomery	146.19	David Montgomery	152.57
34	Ronald Jones	119.51	Raheem Mostert	139.78	Raheem Mostert	150.56
35	Kenneth Gainwell	113.77	Joshua Kelley	124.24	Joshua Kelley	139.11
36	Gus Edwards	112.91	James Robinson	122.61	James Robinson	136.61

Murfs Running Backs

Rank	Standard	Standard Points	Half Point PPR	Half Point PPR Points	PPR	PPR Points
1	Derrick Henry	283.20	Christian McCaffrey	323.80	Christian McCaffrey	369.80
2	Christian McCaffrey	277.80	Alvin Kamara	297.80	Alvin Kamara	338.30
3	Alvin Kamara	257.30	Derrick Henry	296.20	Saquon Barkley	310.60
4	Saquon Barkley	250.60	Saquon Barkley	280.60	Derrick Henry	309.20
5	Dalvin Cook	250.60	Dalvin Cook	270.60	Ezekiel Elliott	291.90
6	Ezekiel Elliott	237.90	Ezekiel Elliott	264.90	Dalvin Cook	290.60
7	Nick Chubb	230.20	Antonio Gibson	251.90	Austin Ekeler	289.00
8	Antonio Gibson	228.90	Austin Ekeler	251.50	Antonio Gibson	274.90
9	Austin Ekeler	214.00	Nick Chubb	245.70	Aaron Jones	271.40
10	Aaron Jones	213.40	Aaron Jones	242.40	Nick Chubb	261.20
11	Jonathan Taylor	201.80	Joe Mixon	220.60	Joe Mixon	243.60
12	Joe Mixon	197.60	Jonathan Taylor	219.80	Miles Sanders	239.70
13	Miles Sanders	196.70	Miles Sanders	218.20	Jonathan Taylor	237.80
14	D'Andre Swift	187.20	D'Andre Swift	212.20	D'Andre Swift	237.20
15	David Montgomery	181.20	Najee Harris	201.10	Najee Harris	226.10
16	Chris Carson	179.20	David Montgomery	199.70	David Montgomery	218.20
17	Najee Harris	176.10	Chris Carson	198.70	Chris Carson	218.20
18	Cam Akers	169.90	Cam Akers	189.40	Chase Edmonds	212.80
19	Josh Jacobs	166.40	Chase Edmonds	185.30	Cam Akers	208.90

20	Clyde Edwards-Helaire	161.10	Clyde Edwards-Helaire	184.60	Clyde Edwards-Helaire	208.10
21	J.K. Dobbins	159.60	Josh Jacobs	179.40	Travis Etienne	201.20
22	Chase Edmonds	157.80	Myles Gaskin	174.70	Myles Gaskin	195.70
23	David Johnson	156.10	Kareem Hunt	174.00	Kareem Hunt	194.00
24	Kareem Hunt	154.00	J.K. Dobbins	172.60	Josh Jacobs	192.40
25	Myles Gaskin	153.70	Travis Etienne	171.70	David Johnson	187.10
26	Mike Davis	152.10	David Johnson	171.60	J.K. Dobbins	185.60
27	Ronald Jones	147.20	Mike Davis	168.10	Mike Davis	184.10
28	Javonte Williams	145.60	James Conner	161.80	Leonard Fournette	183.10
29	James Conner	144.80	Ronald Jones	161.70	Nyheim Hines	182.50
30	Melvin Gordon	144.20	Melvin Gordon	159.20	J.D. McKissic	179.70
31	Raheem Mostert	143.00	Javonte Williams	158.10	James Conner	178.80
32	Travis Etienne	142.20	Leonard Fournette	158.10	Ronald Jones	176.20
33	Leonard Fournette	133.10	Raheem Mostert	157.00	Melvin Gordon	174.20
34	Michael Carter	133.00	Nyheim Hines	152.00	Raheem Mostert	171.00
35	Nyheim Hines	121.50	Michael Carter	149.50	Javonte Williams	170.60
36	Kenyan Drake	118.60	Kenyan Drake	144.10	Kenyan Drake	169.60

Stocks Wide Receivers

Rank	Standard	Standard Points	Half Point PPR	Half Point PPR Points	PPR	PPR Points
1	Tyreek Hill	206.63	DeAndre Hopkins	268.69	DeAndre Hopkins	333.81
2	A.J. Brown	206.24	Michael Thomas	254.22	Michael Thomas	314.17
3	Justin Jefferson	203.67	Justin Jefferson	249.87	Stefon Diggs	298.59
4	DeAndre Hopkins	203.57	Tyreek Hill	248.49	Justin Jefferson	296.07
5	Michael Thomas	194.28	A.J. Brown	244.96	Davante Adams	292.09
6	Stefon Diggs	187.71	Stefon Diggs	243.15	Tyreek Hill	290.35
7	Davante Adams	184.99	Davante Adams	238.54	A.J. Brown	283.68
8	D.K. Metcalf	181.36	Amari Cooper	223.05	Amari Cooper	274.18

9	Allen Robinson	173.49	Allen Robinson	222.38	Allen Robinson	271.28
10	DJ Moore	173.18	D.K. Metcalf	217.63	DJ Moore	256.93
11	Amari Cooper	171.91	DJ Moore	215.05	Brandin Cooks	254.2
12	Brandin Cooks	167.23	Brandin Cooks	210.71	D.K. Metcalf	253.9
13	Robert Woods	165.38	Robert Woods	207.19	Keenan Allen	253.5
14	Courtland Sutton	160.97	Keenan Allen	205.7	Robert Woods	249
15	Chase Claypool	158.78	Marvin Jones Jnr	201.39	Marvin Jones Jnr	246.93
16	Terry McLaurin	158.23	Terry McLaurin	199.83	JuJu Smith Schuster	245.67
17	Keenan Allen	158	Tyler Lockett	199.78	Tyler Lockett	241.86
18	Tyler Lockett	157.71	JuJu Smith Schuster	198.76	Terry McLaurin	241.42
19	Mike Evans	157.71	Courtland Sutton	197.27	Courtland Sutton	233.57
20	Marvin Jones Jnr	155.85	Chase Claypool	192.42	Cooper Kupp	233.39
21	JuJu Smith Schuster	151.85	Cooper Kupp	190.31	CeeDee Lamb	230.88
22	Brandon Aiyuk	147.56	Mike Evans	189.64	Diontae Johnson	229.63
23	Cooper Kupp	147.23	CeeDee Lamb	188.86	Chase Claypool	226.05
24	Adam Thielen	147.22	Brandon Aiyuk	183.96	JaMarr Chase	225.72
25	CeeDee Lamb	146.84	Diontae Johnson	183.71	Mike Evans	221.57
26	JaMarr Chase	141.4	JaMarr Chase	183.56	Brandon Aiyuk	220.36
27	Kenny Golladay	140.26	Adam Thielen	182.92	Adam Thielen	218.62
28	Calvin Ridley	139.41	Calvin Ridley	175.76	Calvin Ridley	212.11
29	Diontae Johnson	137.8	Julio Jones	172.62	Julio Jones	209.92
30	Julio Jones	135.33	Kenny Golladay	171.14	Tee Higgins	206.92
31	Tee Higgins	133.14	Tee Higgins	170.03	Kenny Golladay	202.01
32	Elijha Moore	129.81	Elijha Moore	165.35	Elijha Moore	200.88
33	Robby Anderson	126.91	Robby Anderson	160.89	Robby Anderson	194.88
34	Chris Godwin	126.28	Odell Beckham Jnr.	153.66	Odell Beckham Jnr.	184.27
35	Odell Beckham Jnr.	123.06	Chris Godwin	153.58	Chris Godwin	180.88

36	T.Y. Hilton	117.98	T.Y. Hilton	147.69	T.Y. Hilton	177.39

Murfs Wide Receivers

Rank	Standard	Standard Points	Half Point PPR	Half Point PPR Points	PPR	PPR Points
1	Tyreek Hill	218.20	Davante Adams	269.60	Davante Adams	327.10
2	Davante Adams	212.10	Tyreek Hill	268.20	Tyreek Hill	318.20
3	A.J. Brown	193.80	Stefon Diggs	249.20	Stefon Diggs	305.70
4	Stefon Diggs	192.70	A.J. Brown	241.80	A.J. Brown	289.80
5	D.K. Metcalf	183.30	DeAndre Hopkins	237.40	DeAndre Hopkins	294.90
6	DeAndre Hopkins	179.90	Michael Thomas	235.90	Michael Thomas	292.40
7	Michael Thomas	179.40	Keenan Allen	230.60	Keenan Allen	289.10
8	Mike Evans	172.90	D.K. Metcalf	225.30	D.K. Metcalf	267.30
9	Keenan Allen	172.10	Robert Woods	215.10	Robert Woods	263.10
10	Adam Thielen	170.50	Mike Evans	212.90	Mike Evans	252.90
11	Robert Woods	167.10	Adam Thielen	212.00	Adam Thielen	253.50
12	Justin Jefferson	166.10	Terry McLaurin	210.90	Terry McLaurin	257.40
13	Terry McLaurin	164.40	Justin Jefferson	210.10	Justin Jefferson	254.10
14	CeeDee Lamb	162.50	CeeDee Lamb	205.00	CeeDee Lamb	247.50
15	Brandin Cooks	158.10	Allen Robinson	204.40	Allen Robinson	253.90
16	Calvin Ridley	157.60	Brandin Cooks	199.10	Brandin Cooks	240.10
17	Chase Claypool	156.80	Diontae Johnson	198.70	Diontae Johnson	248.20
18	Allen Robinson	154.90	Calvin Ridley	198.60	Calvin Ridley	239.60
19	D.J. Moore	154.80	Chase Claypool	194.80	Chase Claypool	232.80
20	Brandon Aiyuk	153.80	D.J. Moore	192.30	D.J. Moore	229.80
21	Chris Godwin	149.60	Chris Godwin	191.60	Chris Godwin	233.60
22	Diontae Johnson	149.20	Brandon Aiyuk	191.30	Brandon Aiyuk	228.80
23	Odell Beckham Jr.	148.90	Odell Beckham Jr.	186.40	Odell Beckham Jr.	223.90

Rank	Standard		Half Point PPR		PPR	
24	D.J. Chark	145.20	Tyler Lockett	185.80	D.J. Chark	226.20
25	Julio Jones	144.40	D.J. Chark	185.70	Tyler Lockett	228.30
26	Tyler Lockett	143.30	Julio Jones	184.90	Julio Jones	225.40
27	Amari Cooper	139.10	Amari Cooper	184.60	Amari Cooper	230.10
28	Courtland Sutton	137.70	Robby Anderson	182.50	Robby Anderson	227.50
29	Robby Anderson	137.50	Cooper Kupp	176.10	Cooper Kupp	222.60
30	DeVonta Smith	137.50	Deebo Samuel	176.00	Deebo Samuel	215.00
31	Kenny Golladay	137.10	Courtland Sutton	172.70	Courtland Sutton	207.70
32	Deebo Samuel	137.00	DeVonta Smith	172.00	DeVonta Smith	206.50
33	Cooper Kupp	129.60	Kenny Golladay	171.60	Kenny Golladay	206.10
34	Tee Higgins	128.80	Tee Higgins	168.80	Tee Higgins	208.80
35	Ja'Marr Chase	127.70	Ja'Marr Chase	166.20	Ja'Marr Chase	204.70
36	Jarvis Landry	125.52	Jerry Jeudy	161.60	Jerry Jeudy	198.10

Stocks Tight Ends

Rank	Standard	Standard Points	Half Point PPR	Half Point PPR Points	PPR	PPR Points
1	Darren Waller	189.56	Darren Waller	245.73	Darren Waller	301.9
2	Travis Kelce	179.84	Travis Kelce	230.1	Travis Kelce	280.37
3	George Kittle	169.41	George Kittle	215.91	George Kittle	262.41
4	T.J. Hockenson	147.4	T.J. Hockenson	193.23	T.J. Hockenson	239.06
5	Mark Andrews	136.6	Mark Andrews	168.48	Mark Andrews	200.35
6	Jonnu Smith	110.24	Noah Fant	144.02	Noah Fant	178.31
7	Noah Fant	109.73	Jonnu Smith	143.39	Jonnu Smith	176.55
8	Jared Cook	96.46	Jared Cook	119.53	Hunter Henry	148.24
9	Hunter Henry	89.08	Hunter Henry	118.66	Dallas Goedert	148.04
10	Dallas Goedert	88.12	Dallas Goedert	118.08	Irv Smith Jnr.	144.96
11	Irv Smith Jnr.	85.66	Irv Smith Jnr.	115.31	Jared Cook	142.61
12	Tyler Higbee	85.41	Jack Doyle	110.12	Logan Thomas	138.24
13	Jack Doyle	83.05	Tyler Higbee	109.5	Jack Doyle	137.18

Rank	Standard	Standard Points	Half Point PPR	Half Point PPR Points	PPR	PPR Points
14	Brevin Jordan	79.48	Logan Thomas	108.34	Austin Hooper	134.78
15	Austin Hooper	78.83	Austin Hooper	106.81	Tyler Higbee	133.59
16	Kyle Pitts	78.78	Brevin Jordan	99.12	Mike Gesicki	122.95
17	Logan Thomas	78.44	Mike Gesicki	98.46	Evan Engram	122.09
18	Rob Gronkowski	77.08	Evan Engram	97.65	Brevin Jordan	118.75
19	Gerald Everett	74.92	Gerald Everett	96.73	Gerald Everett	118.54
20	Mike Gesicki	73.96	Kyle Pitts	96.03	Anthony Firkser	118.15
21	Evan Engram	73.22	Anthony Firkser	95.18	Kyle Pitts	113.28
22	Anthony Firkser	72.21	Rob Gronkowski	94.78	Rob Gronkowski	112.48
23	Cole Kmet	67.07	Cole Kmet	88.38	Cole Kmet	109.68
24	Pat Freiermuth	66.77	Pat Freiermuth	85.97	Zach Ertz	106.8
25	Robert Tonyan	65.73	Robert Tonyan	85.23	Pat Freiermuth	105.17
26	Blake Jarwin	63.95	Zach Ertz	84.38	Robert Tonyan	104.73
27	Adam Trautman	63.25	Blake Jarwin	84.28	Blake Jarwin	104.61
28	Zach Ertz	61.95	Adam Trautman	83.09	Adam Trautman	102.94
29	O.J. Howard	57.24	O.J. Howard	71.88	Harrison Bryant	88.21
30	Harrison Bryant	52.93	Harrison Bryant	70.57	C.J. Uzomah	87.1
31	C.J. Uzomah	52.55	C.J. Uzomah	69.83	O.J. Howard	86.52
32	Chris Herndon	47.33	Chris Herndon	65.54	Chris Herndon	83.76
33	Dan Arnold	46.93	Cameron Brate	60.6	Cameron Brate	77.48
34	Dalton Schultz	44.06	Dan Arnold	57.97	Hunter Long	71.52
35	Cameron Brate	43.73	Dalton Schultz	57.49	Dalton Schultz	70.93
36	Hunter Long	43.05	Hunter Long	57.29	Dan Arnold	69.02

Murfs Tight Ends

Rank	Standard	Standard Points	Half Point PPR	Half Point PPR Points	PPR	PPR Points
1	Travis Kelce	198.10	Travis Kelce	251.10	Travis Kelce	304.10

2	George Kittle	153.50	George Kittle	199.50	George Kittle	245.50
3	Darren Waller	149.10	Darren Waller	197.10	Darren Waller	245.10
4	Mark Andrews	131.90	Mark Andrews	164.90	Mark Andrews	197.90
5	Logan Thomas	112.90	Logan Thomas	147.90	Logan Thomas	182.90
6	Dallas Goedert	110.60	Dallas Goedert	145.60	Dallas Goedert	180.60
7	T.J. Hockenson	104.80	T.J. Hockenson	138.80	T.J. Hockenson	172.80
8	Rob Gronkowski	102.10	Noah Fant	130.60	Noah Fant	163.10
9	Noah Fant	98.10	Robert Tonyan	125.40	Robert Tonyan	152.90
10	Robert Tonyan	97.90	Rob Gronkowski	124.60	Rob Gronkowski	147.10
11	Kyle Pitts	88.80	Kyle Pitts	117.30	Kyle Pitts	145.80
12	Eric Ebron	88.10	Eric Ebron	116.10	Eric Ebron	144.10
13	Jonnu Smith	85.40	Jonnu Smith	111.40	Jonnu Smith	137.40
14	Jared Cook	85.00	Austin Hooper	110.30	Austin Hooper	136.80
15	Mike Gesicki	84.10	Mike Gesicki	108.60	Mike Gesicki	133.10
16	Austin Hooper	83.80	Jared Cook	107.00	Jared Cook	129.00
17	O.J. Howard	80.00	Tyler Higbee	104.40	Tyler Higbee	129.40
18	Tyler Higbee	79.40	Blake Jarwin	104.20	Blake Jarwin	129.20
19	Blake Jarwin	79.20	O.J. Howard	101.50	O.J. Howard	123.00
20	Jordan Akins	76.90	Irv Smith Jr.	101.50	Irv Smith Jr.	126.50
21	Irv Smith Jr.	76.50	Cole Kmet	99.70	Cole Kmet	124.70
22	Cole Kmet	74.70	Jordan Akins	97.90	Jordan Akins	118.90
23	Hunter Henry	74.10	Hunter Henry	97.10	Hunter Henry	120.10
24	Anthony Firkser	72.70	Evan Engram	95.20	Evan Engram	122.20
25	Evan Engram	68.20	Anthony Firkser	95.20	Anthony Firkser	117.70
26	Zach Ertz	66.90	Zach Ertz	87.90	Zach Ertz	108.90
27	Adam Trautman	66.10	Adam Trautman	86.10	Adam Trautman	106.10
28	Dawson Knox	62.10	Chris Herndon	81.10	Chris Herndon	102.10
29	Chris Herndon	60.10	Dawson Knox	80.60	Dawson Knox	99.10
30	Gerald Everett	58.10	C.J. Uzomah	77.80	C.J. Uzomah	97.80
31	C.J. Uzomah	57.80	Gerald Everett	75.60	Gerald Everett	93.10

32	Mo Alie-Cox	54.20	Jack Doyle	71.80	Jack Doyle	89.80
33	Jack Doyle	53.80	Mo Alie-Cox	69.70	Mo Alie-Cox	85.20
34	Will Dissly	52.10	Will Dissly	67.60	Will Dissly	83.10
35	Dan Arnold	52.00	Dan Arnold	67.50	Dan Arnold	83.00
36	Kyle Rudolph	48.90	Kyle Rudolph	65.40	Kyle Rudolph	81.90

Your updated 2021 Rankings

CHAPTER 15

Rookie Portfolios

Written by *Chris Mitchell*

Year two of the Playbook! Who would have thought it? Not even after the success of last year was I sure we would have written another. Yet here we are, words on paper, thoughts jotted down in my illegible handwriting and finally painstakingly deciphered into the following pages. Much has changed since last year. Before we dive into what and how this year's Portfolio has evolved, I want to share with you the why and how I have come to my conclusions about the incoming Rookies.

Right out the gate, I need to see some information down and draw a line in the proverbial sand. At no point have I ever claimed to be a scout or evaluator nor have I written down anything I don't understand. I haven't blown smoke around or added mirrors in so that the information that follows tries to be something it isn't.

Every pencilled down antidote and observation is what I've seen. It is my analysis of the player as I've watched his tape and drawn from the tape what I've noticed and either liked or not liked. I will not pick up on many things and as a Monday morning Quarterback it is easy for me to sit here and say what someone does well or what he does not do. I try and watch the great players of our times and then compare incoming rookies to what I've seen the greats do. How does a guy run into a gap in zone coverage? How does a Wide Receiver launch off the line of scrimmage. Does he do well at breaking free of man coverage when pressed at the line or does he have a suddenness to the way he stops and changes direction when given some cushion from the Defensive Back in order to create separation that way. Can he arm fight? Does he adjust well when in the air to catch the Football? Can he hold off a Defender without pushing and getting flagged? These are all questions on just one position.

As I've sat down to look at players, watching their tape wasn't enough for me. I wanted to look into their past, what they had achieved at not only College but also at High School. How they represented themselves and what they have done for the cause. Was there anything either good or bad hiding in the past that might affect how I look upon a player. Does he have a past DUI charge that might not have surfaced or has he been exemplary in School or helped out at Charity work? These things all lend them sleeves to me and how I evaluate a player. After all, if I'm going to Draft you to my Fantasy Football Roster I want to know what washing [powder you use and how many single socks you own.

Sure a player might be superb at running into gaps, throwing a pinpoint pass deep downfield or even being superb at high pointing a catch. At a glance, all these things are great but are there other things that have helped or indeed in some cases hindered a player's on-field performance? Digging not just into their tape but also their history has given me a much better understanding of who they are and what they can do for the NFL teams who have added these guys to their rosters.

After all, it's the players landing spots that matter for Fantasy Football right? It is the skills they bring to each team that will ultimately determine if they make it onto YOUR Fantasy rosters come Rookie Drafts and later Keeper and Redraft Leagues.

I wanted to know about the players so that I was ready for my Drafts when they come. If there's a name on the board I want to know who he is and what he offers my Fantasy Team. This isn't an NFL Draft guide showing you what each player does well and doesn't. The time for those has passed as this is released after the Draft has taken place. This Rookie Portfolio is my personal thoughts and learnings on all the players I could cover between the inception of the 2021 Playbook and as close to the print date as I could possibly squeeze too. As said, I'm not a scout nor do I have an in-depth knowledge of what's required to run on the inside or outside of a Zone Concept. What I do have though is a passion for learning about the incoming Rookies and the love of turning their history and skills into a story for you to enjoy.

These are my thoughts and I hope they help you to build a better understanding of not just what they can do as a player in the NFL but who they are as a person and what they have achieved in their short careers so far. Whilst they have been short careers we all know the NFL stands for Not For Long so the way we are seeing players declare after less years playing in College doesn't surprise me. They want to get into the League with tread left on the rubber and earn the big money as fast as possible. I know I would!

So how did I come to my rankings and my conclusions? Well in my head and with the help of my good friend and 5 Yard family member Tom, I've tried to come up with a ranking system that works for me and my thought process. In reality, it was much harder to convey my thoughts into a spreadsheet and graphs and come up with a numerical list via translation. So I ended up sticking a pin in that and hoping to have it done for the 2022 Playbook. What I did was initially get a list of each position off of several of the sites I trust the most. Once I had players' names down I then started to watch tape on each guy. I scribbled down on each player what I saw and my thoughts. Each player was allowed the same amount of paper and each position had an individual colour (Sorry Hunter, Daddy stole loads of your colouring sheets).

Then once I had covered a position I got down to ordering them. I started looking into their history and past and then once I was done I put their sheet of coloured paper into a column. The first guy obviously went to number one and then as I progressed I slipped players in above or below other players who I thought were better or worse. It's that simple. It's a list of who I like above those I don't. I wish there was a grading system and I had rhyme and reason but up to this point I don't. But hey, we all value players differently and that's what makes trading in Fantasy Football so much fun.

Ok that is enough rambling from me, the Rookies await. I hope you enjoy the stories ahead of you and learn about the players as you go. These are all my findings and research into the players we will hopefully one day use as the pillars of our Fantasy teams.

Let us know @5yardrush on all socials your thoughts on the incoming Rookie class and if there is anyone missing from the lists ahead of you.

Stocks

CHAPTER 16

Quarterbacks

Written by *Chris Mitchell*

Trevor Lawrence

Clemson | QB | 6'6" | 220 lbs

In the last few years, the #1 overall pick has been a Quarterback. The difference with the #1 pick this year is we 100% knew who it was going to be. Before Baker Mayfield was drafted by the Browns in 2018, Sam Darnold was slated to go first overall. In 2019 Kyler Murray wasn't sure if he would actually play Football over Baseball and we also weren't sure if The Cardinals would actually move on from Josh Rosen. 2020 saw Joe Burrow drafted by The Bengals. However, coming out Burrow only had one season of elite production at LSU so we couldn't be sure how he would translate to the NFL. It turns out he is a stud. What differs this year is Lawrence has years of production at Clemson against good competition, he's played in Championship games and has won on the biggest stage. Not only that but he was the top High School prospect in his recruiting class and was sought after by almost all the top Colleges. There is much chatter amongst NFL scouts and Draft Twitter that Lawrence could be the best prospect out of College in the last 20 years. Better than Andrew Luck if you believe some people. So does he have everything we're after? Let's run down the hill and dig in!

As a Freshman he replaced Kelly Bryant as the starting Quarterback in his first season at Death Valley and had an immediate impact. Lawrence showed the deep ball accuracy and vision he has previously been admired for in High School but at an even higher standard. Clemson went 15-0 Lawrence's first season brushing aside Pitt in the ACC Championship game 42-10, Notre Dame in the Cotton Bowl 30-3 and finally a whooping of Alabama 44-16 in the College Football Championship. What a year for the Freshman! He finished the campaign throwing for 3,280 yards from 295 completions, a completion percentage of 65.2%, 30 touchdowns and just four interceptions. He also added 177 yards and one touchdown off 60 rushing attempts. The ground game is where T Law really explodes as a Sophomore.

2019 saw Lawrence and The Clemson Tigers get to the pinnacle of the College game again. They went undefeated throughout the season again putting the heat on all that stood before them. During the regular season The Tigers were only pushed once, in week five against North Carolina. Big Trev was running out of things to show the world he could do, and pundits had exhausted their armories of superlatives about the guy. This was until he engineered a late 4th quarter comeback against the Ohio State Buckeyes in the Fiesta Bowl to help the Tigers get to the promised land. Ultimately they got annihilated by the best College team we have ever seen in the 2019 LSU Tigers and Joe Burrow. Trevor finished his Sophomore year passing for 3,665 yards off 268 completions for a completion percentage of 65.8%, 36 touchdowns and eight interceptions. He was dynamic on the ground rushing 103 times for 563 yards and nine touchdowns. The comeback against The Buckeyes truly showed what Lawrence can offer when in a clutch situation. He stood call in the pocket when needed and then let rip when his reads got open. Not only that but he clocked over 100 rushing yards in that game showing he can be a dual threat Quarterback at an elite level when needed.

2020 saw Lawrence miss two weeks of the season after contracting COVID-19. He was unable to play against Boston College and then Notre Dame. However, that wouldn't derail his push for the Heisman Trophy or another College Football Championship, although he would tell you otherwise in a later interview after declaring for the NFL Draft. He came close in both making the Semi-finals of the College Football Playoffs and the last four of the Heisman Trophy voting eventually finishing second to Alabama Wide Receiver DeVonta Smith. Ultimately Lawrence finished the season with 231 completions for 3,153 yards, 24 touchdowns and five interceptions in just 10 games. He also added 203 yards and eight touchdowns on the ground off 68 carries. In a year where we weren't sure if we would see Sunshine at all that's some going, finishing with a career best 315 yards per game.

Watching tape on Lawrence really is a treat. I haven't mentioned any games specifically because whenever you watch him it's mostly highlight reel stuff. He truly is a lethal passer of the football. It all starts with his calmness in the pocket and his awareness of the incoming defenders. This enables him to stay on his toes and allows him to plant his feet when needed. He processes the field at lightning speed and will move off his first read if the throw isn't on. His long levers let him throw the ball into the tightest of windows and almost always consistently away from the defenders allowing only his receivers to make a play at the ball. Along with Zach Wilson his deep ball is phenomenal. His ball placement is on a dime and on a trajectory that helps him keep turnovers down to a minimum. This ability to stretch the field will mean more time in the pocket as the defense can't cram men into the pocket as they need to be aware of the deep ball. This also opens avenues up for Laurence to scramble for yardage or for the Running Back to be a viable weapon. As mentioned Lawrence is an effective runner of the ball and his size also means he can bang it home in short yardage situations. Just another weapon in his extremely deep arsenal. A truly dreamy sitch for NFL scouts and teams alike. He really could be the best since Payton Manning.

NFL Landing spot

This one is easy. Lawrence joins The Jaguars as the day one starter. Not only that but they brought in his stable mate Travis Ettiene too on day one. Having each other will be a huge thing for these former Tigers and Lawrence has now been given the keys to the Duval.

Justin Fields

Ohio State | QB | 6'3" | 223 lbs

In Justin Fields a team will be getting a Deshaun Watson comparison Quarterback, in size and speed at least. Some scouts say Fields is a thicker set version of Watson with additional burst. Watson is fast but Fields has a great initial burst when taking off from the pocket which is one of his best attributes. Fields was one of the top recruits in the nation coming out of school and the battle between himself and Lawrence started on national signing day when they both declared their schools. Fields chose Georgia as his commit however he was destined to sit behind Jake Fromm in his freshman year in 2018. As Fromms' backup, Fields completed 27-39 passes for 328 yards and four touchdowns. Fields showed the SEC what he could do on the ground too with 266 yards off 42 carries and four scores. The crowning game for the Freshman's first year was the game against Massachusetts. He made five of his eight throws for 121 yards and two touchdowns through the air and ran seven times for 100 yards and a score. Not bad for a backup hey!

When it was apparent that Georgia was going to keep rolling with Fromm, Fields decided it was time to leave and applied to enter the transfer portal. Ohio State were locked straight in to an aggravated Justin Fields opportunity and Fields then transferred to The Buckeyes to become the starter with a departed Dwyne Haskins now in the NFL. Justin Fields took to life in the Big Ten like a duck to water and was instantly on the tip of everyone's tongues in tailgate parties and bar stools across the country. Fields lit up the gridiron for The Buckeyes in his Sophomore year becoming one of the country's best players in 2019. Fields and Ohio State went all the way to the College Football Playoffs when they came up against Clemson. Fields was to throw two of his three interceptions of the season in this game and the Tigers would end up winning the Fiesta Bowl 29-23. Fields had a season of two halves rushing and passing. After week nine Fields never found the end zone again on the ground. After week nine Fields threw for 299 yards or more in four of the five games. This truly showcased what Fields was capable of doing and also highlighted what he needed to work on going into the 2020 season, a season Fields was likely to declare for the NFL in.

2020 and COVID-19 really seemed to cause trouble at times for Justin Fields. Not Corona itself per say but the after effects of will they won't they play and limited practice. With the Big Ten season not starting till the 24th of October, Ohio State would only be playing a six game regular season. Some people were concerned that this may hurt the players' Draft stock however with The Buckeyes being in the Playoffs they played eight games and Fields and Co had enough tape to not affect their value in my opinion. Justin Fields' first three games of the season were a trio of explosive dominating appearances as Nebraska, Penn State and Rutgers were all put to the sword. Fields threw for 318 yards and four scores against Penn State and then followed it up with a five touchdown, 314 yard demolition of Rutgers. In the first of these three games Fields only attempted 21 passes as Nebraska was gashed by Ohio State's run game. Fields did score a rushing touchdown in this game however and threw for two more. Then the first of two anomaly games for Fields in the 2020 season, Indiana rallied after being 35-7 down to chase Ohio State back to eventually lose 35-42. Fields threw three interceptions in this game, two touchdowns and 300 yards. So not a horrific display but it was the Indianna pass rush that caused Fields serious issues. Fields was at times panicked in the pocket and was too wary of the defenders blitzing that he made poor throws and was picked off. He was able to rally in the next game against Michigan State rushing for 104 yards and two scores. Then game two of the oddities. In a low scoring win for The Buckeyes, Fields had a 44% completion percentage and threw two picks. Again Trey Sermon and the run game were how Ohio State won. It was the College Playoff Semi-Final against Clemson where Fields showed what he is made of. The Buckeyes decimated Clemson winning 49-28. Fields finished the game with 385 yards, six touchdowns and one interception. He showed all the attributes of a franchise Quarterback at the next level. Unfortunately, for Fields and the Buckeyes, they would lose in the Natty to Bama, leaving Fields with season ending numbers of 1,521 yards with 15 touchdowns, five interceptions and five rushing scores as well.

Justin Fields has shown superb ball placement and anticipation as a starter for Ohio State. He has great accuracy and isn't afraid to go deep if needs be. On short or long passes he throws a tight spiral which makes the balls easier to catch and often locates his receivers early and this allows him to place the ball where only receivers can get them. Fields not only has a bazooka that he maybe trusts too much but he also exhibits the ability to feather passes into the breadbasket and over defenders if needs be. One slight on Fields passing game is that it is too often looking for the hero ball and disregards the shorter safer passes even if they are open. This can mean that when he panics during a blitz he throws the ball up rather than use the short yardage guys, these hasty passes have led to many of his interceptions. Saying that however Fields typically does a good job of protecting the football and not throwing many interceptions. As stated as a runner he is solid and is electric out of the pocket. He needs to work on his blitz pickup to be considered elite but can work on that with greater coaching in the NFL. NFL teams will blitz Fields all day long until he shows he can cope with it.

NFL Landing spot

Fields joins The Bears who have stated that 'Andy Dalton is the starter'. Whilst this might be true for now expect Fields to see some playing time if Dalton starts to struggle. He could do with a year to learn the game so this works perfectly for him.

Trey Lance

North Dakota State | QB | 6'4" | 226 lbs

North Dakota State! I know right? Apart from Carson Wentz and Easton Stick, I can't think of another player drafted from NDSU other than Lance's Left Tackle Dillon Radunz, who was drafted this year. The small school has destroyed FCS competition over the past decade and Lance's last full year was astonishing. He used his considerable skill set to take the Bisons all the way to the FCS championship game and then beat James Madison 28-20. What made the 2019 season so special was the fact Lance threw 28 touchdowns and ZERO interceptions. That wasn't a double shift key typo error right there. He threw no interceptions through the whole year. That in itself is a feat which I've never seen and probably never will again.

There will be obvious comparisons to Wentz seeing as they went to the same school. From the tape I've watched I think Lance is a more complete Quarterback than Wentz was at this stage of his collegiate career. Where Wentz has one up on Lance is the time he spent under centre as a starter at NDSU. Wentz started two of his four seasons. Lance has started just one. But what a season it was! Lance completed 192 of his 287 passes for 2,786 yards. He threw 28 touchdowns and zero interceptions. He also carried the ball 169 times for an earth-shattering 1,100 yards and 14 touchdowns. It's this aspect of his game which leads me to believe he is a better prospect for today's NFL than Carson Wentz was. Whilst Wentz was a top half of the draft prospect, he had some issues with reads and accuracy on the middle of the field passes. These are the things we are now seeing leech into his game for the Eagles.

Whilst Lance has only had one year as a starter, he has shown the full range of skills needed to become a top tier talent at the next level. In recent years the skills that NFL coaches seem to be drawn towards are size, running ability, arm strength, poise and big-play potential. Lance has a deadly combination of superior readability and passer accuracy. As a passer Lance has all the throws in his arsenal. He isn't afraid to zip fastballs towards the sidelines into tight windows on his receivers back shoulder away from defenders. That was quite a sentence about his passing, but Lance does have that kind of ability. Lance also showcases good deep ball accuracy and can air out a deep pass to enable his receivers to locate and latch onto the ball.

As a young Quarterback, Lance's pocket presence and poise are mature above his years. We sometimes see young players crumble under pressure and panic when faced with a pass rusher in their face. Lance showcases a tremendous ability to anticipate pressure on the pocket and either make a quick decision to dump the ball off or escape the pocket and put his wheels to work. Lance has tremendous skills as a dual-threat Quarterback and is electric when he takes off. He can run through defenders and gain extra yardage. This, however, is a double-edged sword. Lance takes way to many hits and most of these are full force and square on. He needs to learn how to slide to prolong his lifespan as a runner.

Where Lance will also need to improve is the way he tricks defenders with his eyes. He needs to manipulate the field better with his eyes rather than let the defenders know where he is looking and processing his reads. Once Lance lands on an NFL team the strength and conditioning coaches will help him to increase his endurance as a player. On occasion, he has missed passes late in games due to fatigue. This could also be because he runs the ball so much. As he matures, he should fill his NFL pads and become a better athlete. That's not to say he isn't athletic just at the next level it is bigger, faster and stronger and I believe Lance can grow into a top-level talent for an NFL franchise.

The NFL hasn't been kind to one year starters in the college game. In recent memory, we have seen Dwain Haskins and Mitch Trubisky hugely struggle at the next level. The best thing for Lance would be to land on a team where he sits for a year and then explodes onto the scene. Seems to have done ok for a fella called Patrick Mahomes and the Kansas City Chiefs. Joking aside I do see Lance as a starter in the NFL. He needs more reps for sure, and it's a huge shame we didn't get the chance to see him face top opposition at the start of the 2020 season. NDSU we're scheduled to have Oregon and Lance would have had his hands full facing the vaunted Ducks defence. That would have given us a great look at how he coped with a top grade defence. In no way am I degrading the FCS Defences but they just aren't up to the standards of a team like Oregon. We did manage to see Lance once in 2020. He faced off in a single game against Central Arkansas. It was in this game we saw a rusty Lance throw his first interception. He finished the game with a stat line of 15/30 for 149 yards, two touchdowns and one interception. He also ran for 143 yards and two touchdowns off of 15 rushing attempts. Once more he showcased his talents on the ground and through the air on the way to another win. To see Lance throw an INT was good as it almost became a joke that he didn't throw them. This game was a rusty game for Lance, and it must have felt good to get out there one last time before declaring for the NFL Draft.

NFL Landing Spot

The 49ers moved up for a Quarterback and we didn't know who they wanted and the fact they chose Lance shows us what a talent he could possibly be in the NFL. surely we now see Jimmy G stay for one more year in San Fran to teach the highly exciting prospect? Only time will tell but in that Offence Lance has all the tools to be elite in the coming years.

Zach Wilson

BYU | QB | 6'3" | 210 lbs

2020 sensation Zach Wilson has wowed us in a way we didn't think possible from an independent program nestled in the small town of Provo, Utah. Starting their campaign as the last game on the Week one slate, on labour day, the Cougars torpedoed Navy 55-3. Wilson started the season with a good but not mesmerising 13 completions for 232 yards, two touchdowns and an interception. BYU ran all over Navy and Wilson helped when needed through the air. At this point, Wilson wasn't on the radar of many and went largely unnoticed. What was evident though was the firepower BYU had and how they dispatched a Navy team that was meant to be a defence that would make life hard for teams who ran the ball 'like BYU'. It transpired that Navy hadn't practised tackling before the first game of the season and it showed. Everyone said it wouldn't happen again the following week for BYU, and the 55 points were an anomaly, not we're they wrong.

It wasn't until Week four that we would see the Wilson led Cougars in action again. Wilson threw for 392 yards and two touchdowns whilst running for minus nine yards and two touchdowns. A pair of ten plus yard sacks accounted for the minus yards Wilson finished up with on the ground. BYU annihilated Troy 48-7. Wilson and crew were now garnering some attention but there were still many who were on the "it's nothing special" train. Week five saw Wilson go full ham against Louisiana Tech. BYU won 45-14 and Wilson finished with 325 yards and two touchdowns through the air and 43 yards and three touchdowns on the ground. Zachary Wilson was now a name on many peoples lips. Although people were still saying that the strength of schedule was padding Wilson and BYU's numbers. It was becoming apparent that BYU we're no joke and Wilson was a threat through the air and on the ground but more importantly, he was showcasing himself as an elite leader of the team.

BYU suddenly found themselves a ranked team in the college rankings and got to 9th at one point. They had good wins against Houston and Boise State. It was at this point I messaged Tom to say that "BYU went mad again". He replied with "Wilson is getting so much hype". We finished this exchange with me saying " He's ballin 'out". Wilson and BYU kept winning until they took on a game against a ranked opponent with just two days notice. They lost a close one to Coastal Carolina which would be their only loss of the season in which they would go on to win the Boca Raton Bowl against a fancied UCF team. Through the season Wilson has shown the ability to not only lead a team but also that he has one hell of an arm, good pocket presence and the ability to scramble and pick up yardage and get into the paint. All things we look for in the modern Quarterback.

Wilson finished the 2020 season with 3,698 yards, a pass completion rate of 73.1%, 32 touchdowns and just three interceptions. He also added 10 more touchdowns on the ground and racked up 254 yards in the process. It should be noted that the Cougars Offensive Line is one of the best in the country at this point and Wilson was sacked just 11 times. However,

I don't think the lack of competition argument holds true here as not only are the people he is playing against not NFL calibre but neither are his teammates. Wilson elevated all those around him in my opinion and was supported by a great run game in Tyler Allgeier.

Whilst 2020 was a shot out of a cannon kind of year, Wilson didn't have the same kind of seasons in 2019 and 2018. In 2019 he picked up a hand injury and only played eight games, throwing for 2108 yards, a completion percentage of 62.7%, 11 touchdowns and seven interceptions, whilst only adding one touchdown on the ground. 2018 again saw him injured with a shoulder injury and again he only managed eight games. Through these eight games, he threw for 1,261 yards, had a completion percentage of 62.2%, managed just eight touchdowns and threw three interceptions. He did, however, run for 198 yards and two touchdowns on the ground. It should be noted that both injuries were on his throwing arm so his combine medical will be interesting to hear about and see if any NFL teams pick up on anything regarding these injuries.

When watching Wilson, it was always edge of the seat stuff and not often in a bad way. His footwork is tremendous, and he is always bouncing looking for a target to fire to or scramble away when needed. He plants his feet well when starting his throwing motion and is always looking upfield which I really like. Talking of his throwing motion, it's fast, short, sharp and from the decision to throw to the throw itself, the time is minimal. Not only is the throwing motion fast but it is also clean. His ball has great zip when released and shows on his deep ball. For me, he is possibly the most accurate deep ball passer in this class in contention with only Trevor Lawrence. He can float a ball in when needed or thread the ball into a tight window if required using that zip. One of the things I like best about Wilson is his ability to improvise in any situation and the main part of this is his ability to escape the pocket and pass on the run. It's one thing to escape and run for yardage. It's another to be able to be as accurate when passing the ball on the run as he is. As far as the needed swag for being an NFL Quarterback goes, Wilson took TWO of the Cheerleaders to his Prom. I'll just leave that there. Any time, any place.

NFL Landing Spot

The New York Jets have added more than just Wilson on the offensive side of the ball giving the young stud all the tools to succeed. Can he make the step up in competition?

Mac Jones

Alabama | QB | 6'3" | 214 lbs

Here we are again Rush Nation with another player who has had a superb 2020 but nothing else to really back it up on except a few good games standing in for an injured Tua in 2019. Mac Jones in 2020 was superb. He carved up good defences and was on point for most of the year. Like most prospects that come out of The Crimson Tides war machine production line, Mac has benefitted from playing with an elite cast of characters around him and increased exposure to the world through the lens of the media. This is no knock on Jones however as before this last season he wasn't the starting Quarterback so when he was given his chance he ran with it to great applom.

As a freshman Jones sat behind Tua and Jalen Hurts in the Bama Quarterback room. It's of little surprise to see that Jones barely took to the field in 2018. Jones completed five of his 13 passes for 123 yards and one touchdown. That touchdown was a 94 yard pass to Jaylen Waddle who went the length of the field to score. Apart from that one long score Jones never really had an impact in any other game in 2018.

With Hurts leaving Bama for The Sooners after not making a big enough dent into Tua's grasp on the starting job, Jones was thrust into the back-up role. Being the back-up for Bama is actually not the worst job in the world due to the way they win games. The Crimson Tide often roll over their opponents and pull their starters from the game in the late third early fourth quarter as the game is already won. Jones benefited from this process and found himself more used than ever before. In weeks two and three Mac threw for over fifty yards in each game in relief of Tua. Week four was one to forget for Jones in a blowout win against Southern Mississippi. Jones completed two of his three passes for 25 yards and an interception. After a 70 yard appearance in week six jones was thrown into the starting lineup against Arkansas in week seven as Tua left the game with an injury after just six completed passes. Jones made the most of his chance and looked good throwing as he finished the game with 18 completions for 235 yards and three touchdowns. Again in week nine Tua left early after picking up an ankle injury that would end his season, Jones was in the spotlight and played well. He finished week nine with 10 completions for 275 yards and three touchdowns. In a brutal last quarter loss to Auburn in week 10 jones through two interceptions, he did however, throw for 335 yards and four touchdowns off of 26 completions. Then in the final game of the season in the Citrus Bowl, Bama brushed Michigan aside 35-16 with Jones making 16 of his 25 passes for 327 yards and three touchdowns. Standing in for Tua obviously sat well with Jones as he became somebody we now knew and he had done well enough to gain the starting job for 2020, a season he knew would be his one shot at playing well with new recruit Bryce Hall waiting for his chance to show the world why he was one of the highest recruited Quarterbacks in the 2020 recruiting cycle. Jones would make the most of 2020. Jones blew the doors off Florida, Texas A&M, Ole Miss, Tennessee, LSU, Mississippi State, Notre Dame and Ohio State on the biggest stage in 2020. Making a good Georgia defense look average, Jones threw for over 400 yards to get the Crimson Tide a huge win in a game that some experts had Georgia -3 against the spread. Jones threw for 400+ yards against Texas A&M, Mississippi, Georgia, Florida and Ohio State.

He also threw four touchdowns against Texas A&M, Georgia, Mississippi State, Louisiana State and Notre Dame. He bettered that three times with five touchdown games against Auburn, Florida and Ohio State. Mac Jones played lights out on the biggest stage in the National Championship game finishing that performance with 36 completions for 465 yards and five touchdowns in a 52-24 whitewash of one of the best teams in College Football Ohio State. Mac Jones ended his one year as starter for Alabama throwing for 4,500 yards, 41 touchdowns, four interceptions and a completion percentage of 77.4%. Jones did his draft stock no harm at all. Oh, he had two career rushing touchdowns over the three years at Bama. Not exactly a rushing danger is our boy Mac.

When you watch Mac Jones play it is obvious that he is a pocket passer, using his accuracy and composure to slice defences apart with short quick passes to his Wide Receivers and letting his completions turn into big yards through YAC. Jones doesn't exude the musculin definition we are used to seeing of late in Draft prospects. Jones just looks like a normal guy under centre and that isn't a slight. Just an observation. He is a slightly underrated deep passer but struggles occasionally. Where he makes up for a small lack of arm power on his deep balls is his anticipation on his passes. He throws into tight windows really well and will often release the ball before his Receiver is into the finish of his route. Jones knew where his guys would be and would let the ball fly early knowing his target would be where he needed to be at the point of the catch. Being a pocket passer means he has the traits needed to do well at this in the NFL, he has good observation of incoming pass rushers and his movement in the pocket is good also. He controls the pocket well with good foot movement. Not being a runner or having a cannon arm may harm Jones' chances of being great at the next level so he will need some help from the supporting cast around him.

NFL Landing Spot

The New England Patriots get another averagely built white dude to win them another six rings! I jest but Jones has the skills possibly to get them there if he plays like he did in 2020 for Bama. He will sit behind Cam until the wheels fall off!

Kyle Trask

Florida | QB | 6'5" | 240 lbs

Oh what could have been for Kyle Trask had he not suffered an injury in practice in his Freshman year. In a freak moment in practice Trask took a hit from Jabari Zuniga that ended his Freshman season and with it any hopes of surpassing Feleipe Franks as starter for Murfs beloved Gators. Trask had Franks in his sights early doors but after the injury it wouldn't be until week 3 of his Sophomore year that Trask would eventually take over from Franks who wasn't playing well. After taking the reins however, Trask wasn't planning on letting go and played well as the starter for Florida. Trask is a big dude and is as pure of a pocket passer that there is in this class with some NFL Scouts coming out and saying that Trask is a better pure passer than Justin Fields is. High praise indeed but there is something in those swampy waters when you watch Trask play.

As I mentioned as a Freshman in 2018, he only played three games. Week one he made all three of his throws and rushed for a goal line touchdown. In week two he again was perfect on his throw making his sole attempt for 14 yards. Trask saw what was comparatively much more action in week three against Missouri. With Franks completing just 40.9% of his attempted throws and not throwing a touchdown, Trask was sent in off the bench. He made 10 of his 18 pass attempts for 126 yards and a touchdown. Lady luck was to intervene, however, and Trask would be injured as mentioned before and that would put the brakes on his Freshman year. Trask finished 2018 making 14 of his 22 passes for 162 yards and one touchdown.

2019 saw Trask back fighting fit and ready to try again to usurp Franks once more. This year would be different though as Franks was playing poorly and Trask was up for the challenge. With the Gators trailing Kentucky and Franks playing averagely at best with one touchdown and one interception Trask was given the green light to take to the field. He engineered a comeback from 21-10 down to eventually win 29-21. Although Trask wouldn't throw for a touchdown, he kept the rock safe and rushed for a two yard touchdown to take the lead 22-21. The Kyle Trask era had just begun in Florida. From week three onwards as the starter Trask threw two or more touchdowns in every game except the last game of the season in The Orange Bowl against Virginia. Trask would only throw one touchdown here but rush for another and The Gators would go on to win 36-28. In his Sophomore year Trask put on a clinic in how to be an accurate passer from the pocket and showed he can also offer a run option at the goalline as he finished the year with four rushing touchdowns. Kyle Trask led The Gators to a Bowl victory, a season record of 11-2 and threw for 2941 yards, 25 touchdowns with seven interceptions. We weren't to know just how electric Kyle would be in 2020 and with the emergence of his BFF Kyle Pitts added to that mix, the Kyles would light up the SEC. 2020 would see Trask put together an excellent season, dominating Kentucky, Vanderbilt, Ole Miss, South Carolina, Tennessee and Arkansas, plus also putting Florida on his back and helping to see a win over Georgia in which he threw for almost 500 yards. He also put in a head turning performance against Alabama in the SEC Championship, throwing for over 400 yards and three touchdowns and he also ran one in. Trask's lone bad game of 2020 was against Oklahoma in the Cotton Bowl, but he was playing without his top-three receivers and star tight end.

Trask started the season as he meant to go on with an absolute demolition of Mississippi as mentioned. Trask threw six touchdowns and amassed 416 yards in a stunning performance with Kyle Pitts. Pitts caught eight passes for 170 yards and four touchdowns. The world was on notice of The Swamp Monsters. It wouldn't be until week 10 that Trask would dip below the touchdown mark of three or less when he would throw two touchdowns and two interceptions against Louisiana State. In 'the world's largest cocktail party' Trask was at his ultimate best. In a game where Georgia was favourites, The Gators came to play ball and Trask ended up throwing for 474 yards, four touchdowns and interception against a very good Georgia Bulldogs defence. Against Bama as mentioned Trask was again superb against what many had called a generational defence. In the end though it wouldn't be enough and Bama would go on to get the win.

As I've said Trask is an elite short to middle range passer of the ball and whilst he has a big build its not his legs that help generate the power in his throws and this is evident on some of his deep balls. They can slow down and begin to drop out the sky. This can lead to Wide Receivers being under thrown and also presents opportunity for picks with faster safeties in the NFL. That being said Trask has superb ball placement on short to middle of the field passes, he has good precision on fast and lofted passes and also shows good anticipation on passes to the outside and also has elite field vision which helps him to protect the football mostly on short and middle of the field passes. His footwork in the pocket is top level but it's this footwork that also lets him down when he needs to get off script and start to make his own decisions. Whilst his decision making is good on plays he knows what's going on he doesn't process off script fast enough to make plays happen with enough regularity.

NFL Landing Spot

Trask gets to sit behind the GOAT in Tom Brady and learn the skills needed to succeed in Tampa whilst staying in state. Dream landing spot for The Gators finest QB in recent years. Can Brady teach Trask to be good enough? Time will tell!

Jamie Newman

Wake Forest/Georgia | QB | 6'4" | 230 lbs

For a man who spent 75% of his Collegiate career at Wake Forest to then transfer to Georgia but then opt out of the 2020 season because of CoronaVirus, it felt only right that both his teams should be mentioned in his bio title. Considering he never played a competitive snap for The Bulldogs it's almost a knock on The Demon Deacons to actually include Georgia on his resume. After he transferred there was meant to be a Quarterback battle for starters bragging rights between Newman and Stetson Bennet. It was much hyped and anticipated as the young gun was going up against Newman and his athleticism, in reality though it petered out faster than a scent on the breeze as Newman opted out and declared for the NFL Draft. Before we get into his past i would just like to point out that his father may have the greatest name on the big blue marble, Willie Bigelow Jr, what a name! Ok so back to Football, Newman is a nightmare for opposing Defences because of his athleticism and how Wake schemed for him. It would have been superb to see how he performed in Georgia but alas we only have his time at Wake Forest to go off and man it's some fun tape. That being said there actually isn't that much of it due to Redshirting and some injuries. Now let's get to his past and his time at Wake Forest.

Newman played in one game in 2017 before Redshirting and it was against Presbyterian where the Demon Deacons rolled them over 51-7. I say he played one game, he played just four snaps. He was actually out-snapped by Denver Broncos Quarterback (Wide Receiver actually) Kendall Hinton eight to four snaps. Newman threw four passes, completed two of them and was intercepted on another. After this game Newman Redshirted.

2018 was the year that Newman would take over from Sam Hartman as the starting Quarterback for Wake Forest after Hartman suffered a season ending broken leg against Syracuse. Newman wouldn't see any action until week four of the season against Notre Dame in which he would throw an interception. He did however score on the ground showcasing just how dangerous he is as a runner as he carried the ball eight times for 73 yards. In his first start as Quarterback against North Carolina State Newman completed 22 passes for 297 yards and three touchdowns whilst also rushing 13 times for 44 yards. The following week against Pitt, Newman would throw two interceptions in a loss but would bounce right back in the next game against Duke with a 177 yard, four touchdown game through the air and he would also run for 50 yards on the ground. Against Memphis though he really showed what a danger he is on the ground. He ran 23 times for 93 yards and three rushing scores! He would wind up being the first Demon Deacon to start his first career game on the road at a ranked opponent and produce a victory. His end of season numbers read 84/141, a pass percentage of 59.6%, 1,083 yards, nine touchdowns and four interceptions. He also ran 64 times for 247 yards and four touchdowns.

Now a fully fledged starter in 2019, Newman exploded out of the blocks in weeks one and two and had three touchdowns in both games. In week one he threw for 401 yards and three scores as I said but he also ran for a score and totaled 36 yards on the ground. Then in week three he completed 14 pass attempts for 214 yards, one touchdown and one interception. He also ran the ball 19 times for 78 yards and two scores. Against Elon in week four he shredded the Defence completing 27 passes for 351 yards and five touchdowns. Then against North Carolina State in week seven, Newman had a career performance in my opinion. He threw for 287 yards and three touchdowns whilst adding another 30 yards and two scores on the ground. Newman showed that he can place the ball on a dime and also how to escape the pocket when it was collapsing and scramble for first downs. He abused the Defense in the red zone by targeting Jack Freudenthal their big Tight End with regularity. Newman found Freudenthal three times inside the five yard line and all three completions went for touchdowns. Against Clemson two weeks later was a very different story for Newman however. He had a shocker as Dabo and company made his life a nightmare in a 52-3 whopping. Newman completed just six of his 14 pass attempts and threw two interceptions. He was also kept in check on the ground as he ran for just 19 yards. In the next game though he rebounded well as he threw for 284 yards and a score while rushing 29 times and racking up 144 yards and another touchdown on the ground. He would finish his Sophomore year making 60.9% of his throws, 2,868 passing yards and a 26/11 touchdown to interception ratio. He also carried the ball 180 times for 574 yards and six touchdowns as a runner.

Newman is a developmental Quarterback but has all the skills needed to be a serviceable backup or low end starter in the NFL. He needs to work on a few things in order to be given the reins. Imagine Jalen Hurts if you will, I see Newman in this vein. An incredible athlete who can carve teams up on the ground. He needs to work on his passing anticipation as he can get off target when asked to find a guy when not in rhythm. He also needs to show he can increase his poise when in the pocket as he can look to escape too fast before he needs to and then breaking the play down for his teammates who are still on their routes. This leads to them not being able to lend a block for the escaping Newman. Wake Forest schemed Newman into play superbly by offering a wide set field and allowing lanes to open for him. Increasing his passing repertoire will allow him to be less readable for Defences.

NFL Landing Spot

Jamie Newman finds himself backing up Jalen Hurts at The Eagles and is very similar in play style to Hurts which helps the team as a whole.

Kellen Mond

Texas A&M | QB | 6'3" | 217 lbs

Kellen Mond is one of the most productive Quarterbacks in SEC history and if you haven't watched much of The Aggies then his achievements could well have gone over your head, as they did mine if I'm honest. With that being said I had to ask the crew what they thought of Mond as a prospect and they didn't disappoint in their replies. What was consistent though was that they all thought that even with all of his positives and amazing plays he was too erratic and inconsistent to make it as a starter in the NFL. With all the info from the 5 Yard Family, I decided to open up his history and throw on some tape. Mond is crazy fun and infuriating to watch at the same time. Mond is one of only three Quarterbacks in the SEC to throw for over 9,000+ passing yards and 1,500 rushing yards, the other two? Dak Prescott and Tim Tebow, elite company right there so surely I am missing something and Mond has all the traits needed to make it? Mond entered his recruiting class as the top rated dual-threat Quarterback in his class and was graded as a five star recruit by ESPN and 24/7 Sports.

Mond was thrust into action in the first game of his Freshman year after Nick Starkel left with an injury. Mond then started the next five games as Starkel worked his way back to fitness. His game of the year came in his second week as the starter against Louisiana where he made 21 of his 34 pass attempts, racked up 301 passing yards and three touchdowns whilst adding four yards and a score on the ground. The following week he showed he can be effective as a runner as he racked up 109 rushing yards against Arkansas. He would end his Freshman season with 117 completions, a completion percentage of 51.5%, eight touchdowns and six interceptions. He also ran the ball 89 times for 340 yards and three touchdowns.

In just his second game as starter Clemson rolled into town and Mond had the game of his life in a 26-28 loss. Mond threw for a season-high 430 yards from 23-of-40 attempts with three touchdowns. He threw for 330 yards in the second half vs. Clemson, the most ever by an Aggie quarterback in school history but he couldn't quite get them over the line. He then ran for 98 yards and touchdown against Alabhama whilst throwing another touchdown but also having a two interception game. It would be his week 12 demolition of Louisiana State that would see him elevate his game to another level. He scored on the ground after having 20 rushing attempts but it was his razor like passing game that was the highlight. He threw for 287 yards off 23 completions and six touchdowns. He would end the year completing 238 passes for 3,107 yards, 24 touchdowns and nine interceptions whilst also rushing for 474 yards off of 149 attempts and scoring seven times.

2019 was meant to be a better year for Mond but he regressed slightly in most metrics. He only managed to throw 20 touchdowns and nine of those came in three games. Whilst his pass completion rate improved slightly, his total yards and yards-per-attempt fell a small amount. A cool start from his 2019 season was that he led all SEC QBs throwing and rushing for a touchdown in the same game. He had done it 14 times in his career up until the end of the 2019 season.

Mond made up for the down year in 2019 with a superb 10 games in 2020. The only loss on the season came to eventual Natty winners Alabama in week two and whilst the Aggies got trounced, Mond still managed to throw for 318 yards and three touchdowns against the best Defence in College. He wouldn't be Mond however, if he didn't throw a pick and Bama duly accepted one from Mond on their way to scoring 52 points. In the week three win over Florida, Mond threw for 338 yards and three scores. He then lit up South Carolina in week six when he threw for 224 yards and four touchdowns whilst adding another score on the ground. In the week nine win over Tennessee he was hyper efficient in an unlike Kellen Mond kind of game where he completed 26 of his 32 pass attempts for 281 yards and a touchdown. However, one of his sox incompletions did get intercepted in a rare Mond moment in the win. He also added another touchdown on the ground in that game. He would have a season ending stat line that read 188 completions, 2,282 yards, 19 touchdowns and just three interceptions. He also ran the ball 74 times for 294 yards and four scores.

Over the course of his four years at Texas A&M, he has become the all-time program record holder for career passing touchdowns (71), passing yards (9,429), completions (785), attempts (1,332) and total offense (11,001). Even after all this and how productive he has been, I'm now in the camp that unless he finds a coach who can transform this wild beast into a tamed talent he will be a backup in the League. He has too many moments where you question what he is doing. Guys like this get swallowed up by the NFL and spat out to either be a backup forever, play in the XFL/CFL or in the new FCF league. Mond has all the skills but has all the worry too. He has good arm strength and can thread the needle but he can also miss a guy wide open and throw to someone else on the rare occasion. He has also taken way to many hits for my liking so may be worn down already.

NFL Landing Spot

Mond lands in Minnesota and gets to sit behind one of the good guys in Kirk Cousins. A superb landing spot for Mond to hone his craft and possibly be the successor to Cousins when The Vikings decide to move on from Captain Kirk.

CHAPTER 17

Running Backs

Written by **Chris Mitchell**

Najee Harris

Alabama | RB | 5'10" | 200lbs

It's been a real battle to get here and start writing about Running Backs. I wanted the first player I wrote about to be my consensus #1 Running Back and Harris has convinced me he is the dawg. Size, strength, patience, vision and burst are all apparent in abundance when watching tape. Notice as I didn't say highlights but tape, most plays he takes part in could be considered highlight reel stuff he's that exciting. Running behind the Bama line makes his job easier and we've seen in the past how Alabama prospects have gone on to have very successful NFL careers. Harris, in my eyes, is no different. For what I look for in a running back coming out, he has every measurement I want. He is perhaps a little tall for the quintessential Running Back but that helps him in the passing game be a guy who can win in contested catches on wheel routes and corner routes from near the goal line. A true three-down back. Another reason his height doesn't bother me is the fact he is so thick his centre of gravity is lower than it would be if he was built like a seagull. His lower body is solid and keeps him trucking when he needs to, whilst keeping his overall weight balanced through contact. Not being 6' 2" doesn't worry me at all, in fact, I appreciate it when a Running Back in Fantasy Football almost always needs to be utilised in the passing game to be relevant as an RB1.

Harris played all four of his eligible years and found the end zone three times in his Freshman year in 2017. He only carried the ball 60 times as he was behind Damien Harris, Bo Scarborough and Josh Jacobs on the depth chart. 2018 rolled around and Harris found himself further up the pecking order as Bo was drafted by The Cowboys in the Seventh Round of the 2018 NFL Draft. This is where Harris really started to make a stamp on The Crimson Tides backfield committee. While Damien Harris and Jacobs were garnering all the hype for the upcoming Draft, Najee went about his business racking up 117 carries for 783 yards and four touchdowns. He had three fewer carries than Josh Jacobs did that year. While Jacobs and D.Harris were there, Najee wasn't used in the passing game. However, with the drafting of Damien Harris to The Patriots in the third round and Josh Jacobs at #26 overall to The Raiders in 2019, Najee Harris became the top dog at Alabama. The Crimson Tide have historically used a RBBC, but in 2018 Harris had 113 more carries than the next man up (Brian Robinson Jr who had 96 carries). Harris finished the 2019 campaign with 209 rushing attempts for 1,224 yards and 13 touchdowns with a rushing average of 5.9 yards per carry. It was in the passing game where Harris matured. He went from having a total of ten receptions in the previous two years to having 27 in 2019. 27 receptions for a Bama Running back is a lot. Before 2019 you have to go back to 2015 when Kenyan Drake had 29 receptions. However, this number could have been elevated slightly as a little known Running Back called Derrick Henry had 395 carries that year! Not only did Harris have 27 receptions in 2019, but he was also the main ball carrier, thus showing his ability to be a three-down back. He turned those 27 receptions into 304 yards and seven touchdowns, giving him 1,528 all-purpose yards and 20 touchdowns.

Between all the uncertainty and worry of the 2020 College season, Harris had his best year yet, winning the Natty with Bama and having an elite season. Harris nearly broke the hypersonic line of a 2,000 yard season. Najee had 1891 all-purpose yards and 30 touchdowns,251 rushing attempts accrued 1,466 yards and 26 touchdowns. He also caught 43 passes for the remaining 425 yards and four touchdowns. Harris had 79 rushing yards and two touchdowns and 79 receiving yards and another touchdown in the National Championship game truly showcasing his ability to be a three down Bell Cow in the NFL.

When you watch Harris during a game or on some tape via highlights or scouting profiles, it's evident he has the top-level ability that is needed at the NFL level. He and Etienne are very different Running Backs in the way they play and their body types. For me, another reason why Najee is my top guy this year in the Running Back class is how he plays and what he offers as a true power back. He is built evenly across his six' two" frame and his powerful legs let him continue to gain yardage after a tackle or to help move the pile in goal-line situations. He has a tremendous burst and speed initially to exploit gaps opened up by his linemen or to cut to the outside in a race to the sideline. What he does lack is that top-level speed in a long-distance run but his change of gear from his explosive first step to get into the backfield means he does make big plays for good yardage. It's just the long runs where he will get caught by NFL defenders before making it to the paint. His patience and vision are superb, and he uses it well coupled with his speed to attack gaps that his line will open before they have fully opened, allowing him to be in the secondary faster. Harris also showed a huge leap in 2020 in pass protection, showing a good knowledge of blitz packages and where to look for defenders breaking through the line. This was extremely evident on tape and helped keep Mac Jones upright. As I mentioned, his hands are solid and coupled with his height, Harris can be dangerous when he runs a route and gets into space. Those dump off yards will be great for Fantasy.

NFL landing spot

Harris walks right in as the RB1 in Pittsburgh and becomes an immediate Fantasy starter week one. Should see a better Offensive line in 2021 meaning Harris should feast.

Travis Etienne

Clemson | RB | 5'10" | 200lbs

Size. That is why Travis Etienne isn't my top back in this year's Draft class. He's a little too small for what I like in my Bell Cow Running Back. It was super close as I've said on the podcast and many others will have Etienne as the #1. That's fine by me; we all have our quirks and preferences. It was even a close call between Etienne and Javonte Williams for the number two spot but after all is said and done, Etienne has the games against the top opponents that made him my second guy. He has the pass-catching prowess that makes a three-down Running Back at the next level, but has he maxed out his frame already? Will he be able to bang it in on the goal line? Only time will tell but a little more height and weight would have seen him top the pile this year. What Etienne does have in abundance is speed and quickness. He is a pocket-rocket Back, and he exploded out of High School for The Tigers. In his first year, Etienne showed great speed and burst through the 13 games he played. He totalled 766 yards off of 107 attempts, good for 7.2 yards per carry (YPC) and 13 touchdowns. He only caught five receptions for 57 yards. He wasn't utilised in the passing game at all in 2017.

2018 saw Trevor Lawrence join The Tigers and Etienne benefited hugely from the big man under centre. As mentioned in the Lawrence profile, he makes the Running Back a greater weapon and Etienne sure showed us he can be a weapon. On the way to The Tigers winning the National Championship, Etienne racked up 1,658 yards with 24 touchdowns and averaged 8.1 yards per carry. He also caught 12 passes for 78 yards and two trips into the paint. Whilst 12 catches aren't anything to write home about it was a huge uptake for him from 2017. Etienne showed electric speed and vision in the Championship winning year and put NFL scouts on notice with 24 touchdowns on the ground. At this point however, it has to be noted that the ACC competition isn't as good as the SEC and whilst The Tigers have faced the very best in the Playoffs, Etienne will find the bigger and stronger defenders harder work in the NFL.

Here we go. Now the biggest issue, bar his size for me rears its ugly head in the form of ball security.You gotta hold onto the rock if you're going to be a top Running Back. It's an absolute must and we've seen players benched and abandoned in the big leagues for not being able to keep their mitts on the ball. For some reason in 2019 Travis Etienne started to have fumble issues. He fumbled the ball twice once against Georgia Tech and then again against North Carolina. The North Carolina game was especially a rough one for Etienne as he didn't pick up blitzes at all and only managed 61 yards on the ground. He did have a touchdown to save his day, however. There is no doubt Etienne has a nose for the end zone and has the talent to make regular trips into the paint. It's his long play ability that he regularly turns into six points, not his short-yardage power. 2019 was overall a fairly good year for Travis, and he ended the year with an average of 8.2 yards per carry. 1,500 yards with 17 touchdowns plus he took 29 receptions for 298 yards and turned them into two touchdowns.

2020 saw the passing game become a huge weapon for Etienne. He had obviously worked hard in the offseason on becoming a competent pass catcher and a weapon as a receiver. Not only had he worked on the catching and route running, but it was clear he had spent time with Lawrence developing chemistry. Etienne was indeed a huge part of the pass game for The Tigers catching 41 passes for 512 yards and two touchdowns. A couple more receiving touchdowns would have been nice but the outlet yardage will have NFL teams salivating at his capabilities. In the 12 games Etienne played in 2020, he carried the ball 168 times for 914 yards and scored 14 touchdowns. Once again proving himself as an integral piece of The Tigers offence, however, the fumble monster would once again rear its ugly head. Etienne fumbled four times in the 12 games last season losing three of them. They all came in four weeks too, almost like the yips in golf when standing over a putt. This would worry me as a coach in the NFL.

Travis Etienne has the speed of a cheetah. Pure and simple his speed, agility and vision mean if he gets into the secondary he's gone. He uses fantastic anticipation to get into a lane that is opening and burst into the gap. He also uses his hips well when attacking space so that he isn't square to tacklers, meaning he is more elusive than perhaps he comes across to defenders. His speed also means if a defender is coming from the wrong angle Etienne will simply run away from them. He also shows good patience behind the line, allowing running lanes to open, then using his elite speed to bust off huge plays. I may have done him a disservice when talking about his size as the 2020 season saw him improve his balance after contact, allowing him to add a few yards after contact but the bigger defenders in the NFL will possibly stop that happening at the next level. Etienne won't run over defenders, that isn't his game. What he will do is run around them or cause people to take wrong angles due to them misjudging his speed. Pairing him with a hammer back in the NFL may prolong his life in the big leagues. Allowing Etienne to use his pass catching ability and speed will be his biggest weapons after the Draft.

NFL Landing Spot

Currently slated as the pass catching Running Back behind James Robbinson, expect Ettiene to breakout in the second half of the season as his talent shines through.

Javonte Williams

North Carolina | RB | 5'10" | 220lbs

Football IQ and footwork. Those are the two main traits that come to mind when you sit down and watch the Tarheel prospect. Williams has exquisite footwork and vision that allow him to burst off big plays. He is the kind of student athlete that coaches love to teach. In his three years at North Carolina, Williams has improved his game year on year to the point that he was, for me, pushing Ettiene for the number two spot in my rankings. Williams has, over the last three years, displayed all the traits of a three down starting Running Back in the NFL and in 2020 it all came together for an explosive season, in which he shared the backfield with Michael Carter. Imagine the damage this battering ram of a Running Back could do if he was the only cow in that field. Year on year improved production points to me that he is indeed a fast learner but not only that; he has the willingness and passion to learn about the game. How many times do we see wasted talent in the NFL because the player isn't bothered about playing Football? Williams doesn't strike me as the kind of player who will neglect his learning and rookie duties.

As a Freshman Williams was a bench warmer and sat behind Antonio Williams, Michael Carter and Jordon Brown. Williams only had six carries in the first three weeks of the season, two per week having a game high 15 yards in week three. He would then go four weeks without a single carry and in week eight, Williams carried the ball four times for 17 yards but found the end zone for the first time as a College player. The Tarheels had lost eight straight when Western Carolina came to play and Williams found himself a role for the first time that season. Whether North Carolina wanted to see what they had in Williams or if it was a pure rotation strategy after losing eight straight, Williams blew up. 17 carries for 93 yards and three touchdowns on the ground along with two receptions for 38 yards announced Javonte Willimas to the ACC and those keen College Football watchers. In the final game of the season, Williams was again the lead ball carrier for NC and turned 16 carries into 83 yards and a touchdown. 2018 saw Williams finish with 43 carries for 224 yards and five touchdowns, just over five yards per rush (5.2) and eight receptions for 58 yards.

'Step up Sophomore' as my boy Pittsy would say. Williams took a more prominent role heading into the 2019 season, as Antonio Williams and Brown were no longer on the roster. It would be the two-headed monster we now know of Williams and Carter. Carter would end the season with 11 more carries than Williams but overall it would be a timeshare. Williams improved every stat line from his Freshman year and proved a valuable asset on the pass game for Sam Howell averaging 10.4 yards per reception over the season. Williams started his second year with his first over 100 yard rushing games, turning 18 carries into 102 yards. In week five The Tarheels took on Clemson and Williams had an impressive outing considering NC got beaten 21-20 in a super tight affair. Williams had ten carries but found the end zone and accrued 49 yards. The following week North Carolina took on Georgia

Tech, and Williams had a huge game turning 20 carries into 144 yards and a touchdown. In the final regular game of the season Williams only carried the ball nine times for 58 yards but found pay dirt twice. He also had three receptions for 42 yards and a touchdown, his first and only of the season. Williams would finish his Sophomore season with 166 carries for 933 yards, 5.6 a carry, five touchdowns, 17 receptions for 176 yards and one touchdown.

In a shortened 2020 season, Williams made a huge case as to why he should be considered one of the best running backs in the class and a high Fantasy Football draft pick. There was only one game in his Senior season where Williams had less than double digit carries, a 49-9 blowout of Western Carolina in which he only carried the ball three times yet still found the end zone with a three yard run. If you want to see what Williams is all about, look up his game tape from the Miami game. He turned 23 carries into 236 yards and three touchdowns. There is one specific play that the college guys mentioned in their top 100 breakdown where Williams shows an impressive first cut to beat the man off the edge and bounce outside, lowers his pad and strikes a DB backwards and finishes him with a stiff arm, drops a nasty spin move on the incoming Safety to gain more yards. The vision and forward thinking Williams shows in this play is outrageous. Williams ended 2020 with 157 carries for 1,140 yards and 19 touchdowns. He also caught 25 passes for 305 yards and three touchdowns. The full package.

Williams is superb in pass protection and uses his size and ability to see the play develop to protect his Quarterback, a huge tick for NFL scouts. Williams isn't a small back and whilst this isn't a problem it can make him easier to tackle. Where Williams nullifies this somewhat is in his elite footwork. He keeps his feet high and moving when entering the tackle so that he isn't easy to wrap up. He often gains extra yardage through this ability to make players miss and the way he levels pads means he is able to take on bigger lineman when pushing for extra yards and not being brought down for a loss. Williams is also a superb catcher of the ball and will be a great asset for short dump off passes where he can use his size and bruising running style to break off big plays. Williams has the potential to be a three down back in the NFL if he gets the opportunity to do so.

NFL Landing Spot

Williams joins the high powered Broncos Offence and will run alongside Gordon for this year. He will play most of the pass catching role and breakout next year. Love this pick!

Jermar Jefferson

Oregon State | RB | 5'10" | 217lbs

If this book was classed as NSFW then I would go on an excited expletive-ridden rant about Jefferson here, however, it's for all kids, big and little, so I'll keep it clean. Good God almighty is Jefferson explosive, I mean seriously fast out of the blocks. When you watch his highlights, he goes from the snap to lightspeed faster than anyone I've seen this year. It's almost as if he has a NOS button that his coaches press as soon as the play starts and it's this explosion which leads him to bounce right of Defenders in a forward motion that means his yards after contact are absurd. Now don't hear what I'm not saying Rush Nation, Jefferson isn't just a bulldozer that just runs uphill. His shot out of a cannon approach to being a Running Back is also joined by a serious cut step and a shifty hip slant that makes his change of direction lethal. This lethality, coupled with the TNT explosiveness out of the backfield means his contact with Defenders is often at speed and his balance keeps him moving forward and helps to keep him upright resulting in extra yardage and often a lot of them. Breathe Stocks, breathe! Ok ok, I'm chilled now, sorry that was a lot but you can tell how excited I am about JJ right here. Only playing three years for The Beavers, Jefferson has loads of tread left on the tyres and this is a huge bonus for me. Now, exciting plays get me all hot under the collar so I could be looking through rose tinted glasses, but I'm in love with what I've seen on tape thus far.

2018 and Jefferson's Freshman year was one hell of a start for any Running Back in their Collegiate career. It only took Jefferson two games to make a mark for The Beavs. In his second outing of the season, he went bananas against Utah State. He carried the ball 22 times for 238 yards and four touchdowns, four! Welcome to the PAC-12 son! The 238 yards against Utah State was the fourth-best in OSU history. With the OSU record for rushing yards in a single game falling so close, Jefferson decided in week five to break it against Arizona State. He had 31 carries, two touchdowns and 254 yards, the second-best single-game total in OSU history. Then in the following week against Washington State, he had 25 carries for 138 yards and four touchdowns, yes, another four touchdown game. Easy money for Jermar, this Running Back business. In his Freshman year he would have seven games over 100 yards and finish the season with 239 rushing attempts, 1,380 yards and 12 touchdowns on the ground with a further 25 receptions and 147 receiving yards. This explosive Freshman season would set the Oregon State true Freshman rushing record with 1,380 yards and is the only player in program history with two 'four touchdown games'.

As a Sophomore Jefferson regressed a little for The Beavers as he only played in nine games and only six of these were as a starter. In week two he ran 31 times for 189 yards and one touchdown. Then in week five against Arizona, he had 22 carries for 105 yards and three scores. His performance of the year came in a game against Washington State where he carried the ball 21 times for 132 yards and two touchdowns but also caught three passes for 52 yards and another two touchdowns. His final game of the year was in a good performance against a strong Oregon Ducks Defence, when he carried the ball 20 times for 142 carries for 685 yards and eight touchdowns whilst catching nine receptions for 85 yards and two touchdowns through the air. Whilst it wasn't the year he would have been hoping for after his blow up Freshman year, Jefferson was still productive at Oregon State, averaging a decent 4.8 yards per carry. Onward towards 2020, my man.

In a limited six game season, Jefferson set out to make a mark on the PAC-12 and boy did he. Five of his six games went over the 100 yard mark and one was over the 200 yard mark. He never carried the ball less than 18 times and was always a threat to get into the end zone. His 21 carries for 120 yards and three scores in week one against Washington State were electric, where he also had five receptions for another 50 yards. He followed this up with a 23 carry, 133 yard one touchdown performance against Washington. He nearly got 200 yards in week three against California and then would get over this hump in week four against Oregon in The Rivalry Game. He would go on to set the Rivalry rushing record of 226 yards off of 29 carries with two touchdowns added in for good measure. His 82 yard first quarter run would be the longest of his Beavers career. His six game stat total read, 133 rushing attempts, 858 yards and seven scores and nine receptions for 67 yards.

Whilst Jefferson hasn't been prolific in the receiving game, he has shown enough for me to suggest he can do it in the NFL. It will require him to take extra reps in practice and for him to muscle into that area on the team, but he has the skills to do it which adds to his three down abilities. As a Running Back, Jefferson has proven that he can constantly be productive throughout his career and his 2020 game against The Ducks showed that he can do it against a solid Defense when given the opportunity. As I mentioned, he is lightning fast and accelerates into the open back field faster than most Defenders can run. He uses superior vision to limit tackling angles taken on him which leads to extra yards too. He isn't afraid to lower the pads and engage in contact, using his good contact balance to bounce around the play and get free from the contact. He needs to work on his route tree and passing game usage but his vision and speed means he can be dangerous when used as a pass catcher.

NFL Landing Spot

Jefferson finds himself in a battle for a roster spot amongst The Detroit Lions Running Back room in which given the chance he backs up Swift and be part of the rotation.

Jaret Patterson

Buffalo | RB | 5'9" | 195lbs

We all saw it, the historic game against Kent State. If you haven't seen the highlights or even the box score I command you to put this book down and hit up Youtube, damn it! Watched it? Right, now we're all up to speed with the enigmatic Mr Patterson let's get down to business. So you've seen the highlights now? If not why not? I'm literally not going to stop telling you to until you have! Ok now we can go. It wasn't just the historic game against Kent State in 2020 that Patterson was equaling records. It took him just five games to smash through the 1,000 yard mark and that equalled the FBS record for fastest time to do it. Granted, the Kent State game helped him immensely in getting to 1,000 yards but he also equaled the single game touchdown record in that game too, with a mind boggling eight touchdowns. Let that just sink in for a minute. Cam Newton only threw for eight all year for The Patriots in 2020, Patterson destroyed The Golden Flashes for the same amount in less than 60 minutes as he was dragged with time still to go. It wasn't just his Junior season that was impressive, however. Patterson has been prolific his entire career for The Bulls, improving year on year and had 2020 been a full season I have no doubt his numbers would have been better than the year before. I mean jeez, he even had 558 all-purpose yards in a single game in High School, Patterson can do it all.

Patterson started life as a Bull fast. Not super sonic fast but to the tune of 34 yards and a score off of nine carries. Ok so maybe at a slow canter, rather than fast but he found the end zone and that was to be a recurring theme throughout his entire career in Buffalo. His first 100 yard game came in week four where he rushed for 104 yards from 14 carries and scored two touchdowns. He would have another two 100 yard games with his second being his best game of the year. Patterson rushed 18 times for 187 yards and two scores against Kent State. He would finish his Freshman year averaging a touchdown a game and setting Freshman records for both rushing yards and touchdowns. His final year numbers were 183 carries, 1,013 yards and 14 touchdowns adding 62 yards from seven receptions. The best, however, was yet to come.

As a Sophomore, Patterson was truly dynamic for The Bulls and finished the season averaging over 30 carries a game over his last five weeks for Buffalo. Eight of his 13 games went for over 100 yards and again he averaged over a touchdown a game over the course of the season. Patterson was now the lead Running Back and putting the MAC on notice. If you want to see him at his glorious best, go and watch him in weeks 11 and 12. In week 11 Patterson scored five times, four on the ground and once in the receiving game. He put up 192 yards from 32 carries and those aforementioned five scores. He also had three catches for 35 yards as he single handedly tried to eradicate the City of Toledo from existence. He gave Bowling Green State PTSD the following week as he racked up a godly 298 yards off of 26 carries and six touchdowns. Yep just six, low by his standards. Patterson would finish

2019 having the best season in School history as a Running Back, setting School records for rushing yards and touchdowns and was named Bowl MVP in the win against Charlotte. His end of year numbers read 312 carries, 1,799 yards and 19 touchdowns. He also caught 13 passes for 209 yards and a touchdown.

I'm sad and ashamed to admit this, but without his historic game in 2020 I wouldn't even have heard of Patterson until doing these writeups. He truly is a treat of a Running Back. In 2020 the MAC played just six games, but Patterson only needed five games to equal many FBS records and if he had more I think we would be looking at him in a very different light right now. I'm going to start with his season numbers, so you can see how impressive he was before his week five madness. He ran the ball 141 times, gained 1072 and scored 19 rushing touchdowns. From six games that is BANANAS. Patterson is truly underrated and we are all doing him a disservice. In week four he carried the ball 31 times for 301 yards and four touchdowns, causing hemorrhages all over the Bowling Green State field. The Bills returned home and then Patterson became a national headline as he rushed for 409 yards and eight scores off of 36 carries. He may well have broken both the single game rushing yardage, and touchdown records had he not been pulled from the game. Patterson was elite in 2020, and it's a crying shame I didn't see more of him live as he is hugely exciting to watch.

As a prospect, Patterson offers it all, albeit in a small frame. Having said that, his size isn't really an issue due to his elite footwork and stepping ability. Patterson's legs almost never stop stepping and this constant ground attack means he can gain extra yards when dragged into a pile and allows him to break free of would-be tacklers as they can't get a good grasp on his lower half. Fairly frequently Patterson is able to slide out of Defenders grasps and hot foot it for more yards. His shorter height than some other Running Backs in this class mean he also has a lower centre of gravity and when combined with his grasping the baby ball holding means he is a very secure runner of the Football. He doesn't have a breakneck burst and that can cause him to be caught by ensuing Defenders, but occasionally his good vision allows him to stretch tackling angles and gain extra yards. He hasn't caught the ball much in his career but had really safe hands and can be used all over the field. Look for this role to expand at the next level.

NFL Landing Spot

Patterson can make an impact behind Antonio Gibson as the pass catching change of pace guy from day one in my opinion.

Kenny Gainwell

Memphis | RB | 5'11" | 191lbs

Now here, Rush Nation, is an intriguing prospect and as bustable as they come. Yet Gainwell has exhibited all the hallmarks I want to see from my Running Back. What Kenny Gainwell has shown on tape for me is enough for him to be the lead back but not only that, he has in my eyes, shown enough to be considered the ONLY Running Back on his team at some point in his career. He has to unlock the potential we have seen and could do with hitting the power rack and adding some thickness to his frame and some power through the hips but he has everything I want in my Stud Running Back. That sounds as if he should be higher right? I hear you ask, Stocks why at four if he has everything you want? Well, he has only played one full season and he Redshirted his first year after just four games. This confused me as I thought a Redshirt year was your first year in College, I was however mistaken and I'll explain why. Firstly, you need to know what a Redshirt actually is. For those of you who already know, you can skip to the next paragraph. This description of the meaning of Redshirt is taken from Wikipedia as it is far more eloquent than I could have written it:

"Redshirt, in United States college athletics, is a delay or suspension of an athlete's participation to lengthen their period of eligibility. Typically, a student's athletic eligibility in a given sport is four seasons, aligning with the four years of academic classes typically required to earn a bachelor's degree at an American college or university. However, in a Redshirt year, student athletes may attend classes at the college or university, practice with an athletic team, and "suit up" (wear a team uniform) for play – but they may compete in only a limited number of games)".

I didn't think it was possible to play at all as a Redshirt, however, it turns out the NCAA changed the ruling on Redshirting and to allow players to play in up to four games per year without losing a season of eligibility. Gainwell chose to major in Criminal Justice so perhaps wanted the extra year in School to study. However, after just two years at Memphis, he declared for the NFL Draft. What shocked me most about Gainwell's history is that he played Quarterback in High School. He has only played one full season as a Running Back, yet to me looks like the real deal. As a Quarterback he was obviously a dual threat and actually ran for more yards than he did pass (4,730 rush/3,682 pass), had 24 100-yard rushing games, and 75 rushing touchdowns compared to 32 touchdown passes. So it's no surprise to see him run so well after converting to this position. As a Tiger in his first year before Redshirting, he played in four games and as I've said, he had just four rushing attempts for 91 yards and a touchdown and six receptions for 52 yards.

After becoming the lead back for The Tigers in 2019 after an injury to Patrick Taylor Jr in week one, Gainwell never had under 14 rushing attempts in any game. He also featured well in the pass game and utilised his touches in that area very well. He started all 14 games for Memphis and eventually went on to finish the season, leading all FBS (the most competitive subdivision of NCAA Division I) Freshman in all-purpose yardage. After finding his feet in weeks one and two he would bust off six consecutive 100-yard rushing performances, the most for any Freshman in Memphis history, all with Antonio Gibson on the field, and we've seen what he can do in the NFL. Although Gibson was used more as a receiver than a Running Back, Gainwell would finish as the third receiver in receiving yards on the team. Half of his games in 2019 would see him go over the 100 yard rushing mark and as mentioned six of these came in a row and the last was in a win against South Florida. His standout game on the ground came in week five against Louisiana-Monroe, where he had 14 rushing attempts for 209 yards and two scores. It would be his week seven performance against Tulane where we would see what Gainwell could do with his hands in the receiving game. He had 18 rushing attempts for 104 yards and a touchdown but it was his 203 yards off nine receptions and two touchdowns that really caught people's attention. This performance of 100 rushing yards and 200 receiving yards was the first in the FBS since 1997, showing what he can really do when thrown the ball but while also being used in the ground game. Finally, his season high game for touchdowns was the following week in the week eight clash against Tulsa, where he carried the ball 24 times for 149 yards and three touchdowns. He became the third player in School history to go over the 2,000 yard mark for all-purpose yards following DeAngelo Williams who did it three times in 2003, 2004, 2005 and Darrel Henderson who did it once in 2018. Gainwell would end 2019 with 231 rushing attempts, 1,459 yards and 13 touchdowns on the ground and 51 receptions, 610 yards and three touchdowns through the air.

As I've mentioned, for me, Gainwell needs to add some mass in order to deal with the bigger bodies in the NFL and by adding this muscle will see him add functional strength as a byproduct which will help him have more drive through piles but also help in staying on his feet through contact and allow him to break more tackles. He exhibits superb vision, probably down to him playing Quarterback and also for his slightly smaller build shows good but not elite power when hitting gaps and Defenders. We all know that to be a three-down Running Back in the NFL you have to be able to catch the ball and Gainwell does it with ease. He is a hands catcher that allows him to focus on the play and not the catch and his use in the pass game will be invaluable to his success in the NFL.

NFL Landing Spot

Poor Kenny G! As one of the woak Fantasy guys hoping for big things for Gainwell, joining Miles Sanders hurts his stock unless he can usurp Sanders and take on all the carries.

Trey Sermon

Ohio State | RB | 6'0" | 213lbs

Ah, the transfer portal strikes a dagger to the heart of Oklahoma and ends up benefiting The Buckeyes. In all honesty, it was a perfect move for Sermon to make. At Oklahoma he would have been part of a committee of Running Backs, and Ohio State needed a stud as JK Dobbins had just left for the NFL. If Sermon had stayed at The Sooners he may well have been behind Oklahoma's Running Back, Rhamondre Stevenson in the pecking order and we wouldn't have seen what he could do leading a backfield. Sure, he had to deal with Master Teague but he was given the bigger workload and showed he can be effective when given the chance. His 2020 season was fantastic, and he stepped up against major competition, his skillset shone through. Whilst he is no JK Dobbins, he exhibits most of what we like to see from our Running Backs in the NFL and I think he can be a decent rock carrier at the next level if given time to mature into the role. In what was Sermons backfield in his first two years for the Sooners, he was fantastic, yet his road to the NFL took a bump in his Junior year. So what happened? Why did he elect to transfer to The Buckeyes? Let's dig in and find out what went wrong in Oklahoma. After all, as a High School Senior, Sermon weighed 214 pounds, stood nearly six foot one and was almost NFL size ready then and there.

Fresh outta High School Sermon was ready to rumble for The Sooners, as a Freshman in 2017 and saw action straight away. He played in all 14 games and was second to Rodney Anderson in carries. In his first year Sermon saw his carry count bounce around and had games where he had just two or three carries but then had games where he would carry the ball 17, 18 or even 20 times. When he was given the ball more than a couple of times he made hay whilst the sun shone and had a good yards per carry. Finishing the year, he would have an average of 6.1 yards per carry and against Baylor in week four he would have his only over 100 yard rushing game. He carried the ball 12 times, gained 148 yards and scored twice. The next two weeks saw him go over 100 all-purpose yards as he was used in the passing game and scored against Iowa State through the air. As a Freshman Sermon would finish the year with 121 carries, 744 yards and five touchdowns whilst also having 16 receptions, 139 yards and two touchdowns through the air.

2018 saw Sermon lead the team in Rushing attempts and become the dude in the backfield. He had four games over the 100 yard mark although he wasn't used as much as a receiver, logging less catches than in 2017. His big game came against Texas Tech, where he logged 26 carries for 206 yards and three touchdowns. Sermon would follow up that superb outing the very next week with 16 carries, 124 yards and two more scores in the game against Oklahoma State. As a Sophomore Sermon looked great as the lead back and finished his year with 164 carries, 947 yards and 13 touchdowns. He only caught 12 passes for 181 yards and never found paydirt. Things were looking good for Sermon heading into 2019.

BUMP. There's that derailment I was talking about. Jalen Hurts was by far and away the lead ball carrier for The Sooners and Kennedy Brooks somehow niggled his way up the pecking order bumping Sermon down the order. 10 games into Sermon's season he suffered a leg injury that would see his season ended right there. Sermon only carried the ball 54 times as a Junior for 385 yards and just four touchdowns. With Sermon looking for more involvement, he entered the transfer portal and Ohio State offered him a place. He didn't need to be the bell cow, he just wanted to be guaranteed touches. 2020 was a good year for Sermon as I've mentioned. While The Buckeyes only played 10 games, Sermon was effective in the six games he managed to put together for Ohio State. It took him a while to get up to speed and against Michigan State he really let the stabilisers off. He turned 10 carries into 112 yards and a score. Then in the following week he had 29 carries against Northwestern which he turned into 331 yards and two scores. Against the much heralded Clemson defence, he carried the ball a whopping 31 times and totaled 193 yards and another touchdown. Sermon would end his season with 116 carries, 870 yards and four touchdowns. He also wasn't highly used by The Buckeyes in the pass game and only caught 12 passes for 95 yards.

As a prospect heading into the NFL, I love how Sermon doesn't have much wear on his tyres and a good injury history baring the leg injury in 2019 and his SC Joint dislocation in the Natty. The dislocation wasn't bad though and he was ready for his pro day. He has many translatable tools that will flourish in the NFL, and I think he exhibits good hands in the passing game but hasn't been given much of a chance in that regard by The Sooners or Ohio State. We all know that Running Backs need to be three down guys to take the hold of a backfield at the next level and given time, Sermon can add catches to his skill set. As a runner he is patient behind the line and attacks gaps as they are opening. He is super tough and plays with veracity when running but also shows good balance when taking hits and protects the ball very well when running or being tackled. Sermon isn't a breakaway athlete and won't take many balls to the house, but as a pounder he can do it all. He has shown he can do it against the best Defences too which I love to see from my Running Backs.

NFL Landing Spot

Sermon joins the 49ers and we all know how good the Niners utalise their Running Backs. Sermon will join the committee of Running Backs but has the skills to rise to the top of the pile.

Michael Carter - North Carolina

North Carolina | RB | 5'8" | 202lbs

I know what you are thinking! Another North Carolina Running Back. How can they lose two great weapons from that backfield? The Tar Heels loss is the NFL's gain as after Williams, Michael Carter is a solid NFL prospect in his own right. While I have Javonte Williams at three, Carter was the stablemate and in his own right half of the devastating duo that North Carolina had. The smaller of the pairing, Carter is a perfect receiving back. He isn't just that though, Carter can hit the line and crush through a gap given his burst and vision. Playing all four years at NC, he started well and although he wasn't the lead back in his Freshman year, he produced to a level that made him stand out. So with that being said, let's take a peek into the first of his four years.

2017 saw the Freshman Carter thrust into action straight away. In his first game for North Carolina, Carter rushed for 94 yards off of 11 rushing attempts and scored twice. What an introduction to College Football, Mr Carter. It shouldn't have been a surprise, though, as he was named USA Today Florida Offensive Player of the Year when playing in High School. Carter would score again in week two even though his yards per attempt were poor. Then in week three he scored twice more to take his tally to five scores in three games. He tallied 68 yards off of 14 attempts and as mentioned those two scores against Old Dominion. It was week seven that proved to be his best for The Tar Heels; Carter carried the ball 13 times for 157 yards and another two scores against Virginia. His best week as a Receiver came in the last game of the year where he caught four passes for 51 yards and a score. He would finish his Freshman year with 97 rushing attempts, 559 yards and a team high eight scores.

As a Sophomore in 2018, Carter was joined by Williams and the two of them battled it out to be the second back to Antonio Williams. Carter turned out to be the winner, but he didn't see as much action as he did as a Freshman. Carter would only play in nine games for The Tar Heels and would only find the end zone twice in the season. His down tick was perhaps due to Williams taking some snaps, but as a runner Carter was effective without hitting paydirt. He finished the year with a rushing average of 7.1 yards per attempt. His stat line read 84 carries for 597 and just two scores. As a runner Carter was productive and he showed out for NC.

2019 saw Carter take the reins of the backfield along with his buddy Williams backing him up. The pair of them tore it up; both nearly going over 1,000 yards on the ground. Carter led the team with a career high 177 carries with an YPC (yards per carry) of 5.7. The Tar Heels didn't really get into the end zone on the ground much, but Carter managed to find paydirt three times. He achieved over 100 yards just once, and that was in week 11 against Mercer. He garnered 159 yards off nine carries and scored twice. He would finish his junior year with 177 carries, 1,003 yards and three scores. Carter caught 21 passes for 154 yards and scored twice.

Carter's best year was in 2020 as again he went over 1,000 yards and this time found the end zone with much more regularity. He had four games over 100 yards. Of those four one was over 200 yards and one was over 300 yards! His first was in week two where he rushed for 16 times for 121 yards. Week three against Virginia Tech saw him get 214 yards off 17 carries and score twice. In week 10, Carter dropped a hatrick of touchdowns against Western Carolina off just eight carries. Then he went full ham against Miami. He carried the ball 24 times and racked up a whopping 308 yards and two scores. He averaged 12.8 yards per carry in the final game of his College career. As a Senior, Carter finished his year with 156 carries, 1,245 yards and nine scores. He also caught 25 balls for 267 yards and scored twice, showing he can act as a catching back and not just a runner.

The 2020 Carter/Williams show in North Carolina was the perfect showing for what Carter can offer in the NFL. He is the perfect balance of runner and catcher without being built like a banger and can smash through the line time after time. His smaller frame than Williams means he has to act smarter when running as he would get caught up in tackles and closed gaps. Where he makes up for being smaller is in his patience and vision. His decision making skills are elite and this split second thinking makes him very elusive when being tackled or when making Defenders miss due to a poor angle into the tackle. This was super apparent in one play in 2020 against Syracuse. NC ran a jet sweep bluff and handed the ball off to Carter. The Left Tackle drops back, taking an Edge Rusher with him and opens a lane for Carter to explode through. Carter's speed and ability to get to the outside fast means the Linebacker is coming from the wrong angle and the Cornerback is chasing him from an inside field position allowing Carter to finally be pushed out of bounds for a 53 yard gain. A bonus of his smaller size and elite decision making skills is it makes him lower to the ground and so harder to tackle and to grab. This means he can break out of tackles and gain extra yardage. Carter could do with adding some extra weight if he wants a longer career in the NFL, but he doesn't want to lose any speed if he does.

NFL Landing Spot

Carter becomes The Jets day one starter I think and has immediate upside with Wilson running the show. As Long as the Offensive line can hold up Carter could be Fantasy gold.

Kylin Hill

Mississippi State | RB | 5'11" | 210lbs

Kylin Hill is a man who has principles and morals and isn't afraid to fight for them. In 2020 after the Black Lives Matter movement gained traction, Hill garnered National News headlines when he threatened to hold out of the season, essentially a boycott of the season if the State of Mississippi did not change their State flag. The flag of Mississippi had a symbol of the Confederacy on it. Ultimately, the State of Mississippi voted to change their flag and Hill suited up for the Bulldogs. As a High School prospect, Hill was ranked number six in his recruiting class by 247 Sports and was ranked a four-star prospect by ESPN. Hill is one of our very own Tom's favourite prospects at Running Back this year and it's easy to see why when you watch his tape. Playing all four years for The Bulldogs, Hill has had less usage than other four year players due to not being the starter straight away and opting out of 2020 after just three games over COVID-19 concerns. Let's get down to the nitty gritty and dig into his past.

As a Freshman, Hill played in all 13 games for The Bulldogs and was used moderately in the first two weeks. He had 62 yards in both games and rushed nine and 10 times respectively. It was in his 10 carry, 62 yard performance in week two that he would find the end zone for the first time at Mississippi State. He then had a few down weeks in which he had between two and eight carries and never found the end zone. In the week 12 loss to Mississippi however, Hill would get the workload. He had 13 carries for 82 yards and a touchdown. Hill's final season stats would read 78 carries for 393 yards and two scores. Strangely for the Hill we think of today, he only had four receptions over his entire Freshman year, totaling just 38 yards. Hill's usage in the passing game was yet to be seen or his abilities were yet to be discovered.

As a Sophomore, Hill would see more work and greater results in the running and passing game. In his first game of the season, he would carry the ball just nine times for 50 yards and a score but also have one reception for 52 yards and another touchdown. Then in week two versus Kansas State, Hill blew up. He had 17 rushing attempts and turned them into 211 yards and two scores. He again had only one reception but found paydirt again on a 16 yard catch. He would go over the 100 yard mark twice more in the season; once against Auburn, where had a monster 23 rushing attempts for 126 yards in a game where The Bulldogs got ahead early and were just grinding the clock. The other game was in a win over rivals Mississippi in week 10, when he turned 17 carries into 108 yards and a score. He would be second on the team in rushing yards behind the Quarterback and would be second on the team in receptions when the curtain closed on The Bulldogs's season. Hill missed two games in his Sophomore year due to a lower leg injury but still managed to finish the season with 117 carries, 734 yards and four touchdowns. He also had 22 receptions for 176 yards and another four touchdowns, expanding his role as a pass catcher for the Dawgs.

Junior year rolls around and Hill again improves as a Running Back and as a Receiver. He would become the lead rushing option for Mississippi State and would end up leading the team in rushing attempts, yards and touchdowns come the year's end. Eight of his 13 games would be over the 100 yard mark in rushing yards, and one of these would be over the 200 yard mark. He was the only SEC Running Back to average over 100 yards per game over the season which is some feat regardless of Division. His first four games of the season were all over 100 yards with the best performance being in week four against Kentucky. He carried the ball 26 times and rushed for 120 yards and three scores. A close second would be his week one game against Louisiana where he had 27 carries, 197 yards and one touchdown. A strong outing in week eight against a good Texas A&M Defence saw him rack up 21 carries for 150 yards and a score in a loss. The following week would be his best week of the season in a game against Arkansas. Hill totaled 234 yards rushing off 21 attempts and found the end zone three times. He would finish his year with 242 rushing attempts, 1,350 yards and 10 touchdowns. He also had 180 receiving yards of 18 receptions and just one score. A big-time year for The Bulldogs lead Back.

After all the stress of the boycott in 2020, Hill had a bit of a nothing year for his draft stock. As a Running Back Hill offered virtually nothing, just 15 attempts through three games. As a pass catcher he was elite, however, in week one he caught eight passes for 158 yards and a score. In his final game for Mississippi State, he caught 15 passes for 79 yards. He would finish the year with 295 all-purpose yards through three games. After being suspended for a locker room incident he would then opt out of the season and declare for the NFL Draft. I love Hill's tape and highlight reels. He is a strong shifty Running Back that has incredible second level speed which means that once he is free in space he's gone! He has top level contact balance and it's this trait which will give him the edge at the next level. He has a natural style when running and never looks like he is hurrying or trying to make something happen. He can be lined up anywhere on the field so has a three down starter look to his game and can be molded into a weapon in the NFL given some time to adjust. His abilities to bounce off tackles and use his speed to burst through gaps or off Defenders mean he is a dangerous weapon as a Running Back and his excellent pass catching skills mean he is a threat in the pass game too.

NFL Landing Spot

Hill lands in place of Jamaal Williams on a Packers roster that didn't need a Running Back. Hill can act as the pass catcher if given a fair shake.

Khalil Herbert

Virginia Tech | RB | 5'09" | 204lbs

Go Hokies! For those of you that don't know it, I'm a VT fan. The jerseys, helmets and stadium are cool, and their field intro is one of, if not the best in College Football. Come at me Penn State fans! Ok so I've stolen the intro for Khalil Herbert, unfair of me I know, he in his own right is a headline setter. Herbert has played Football in College for five seasons, four at Kansas and his last at Virginia Tech. After Majoring for four years at Kansas in Business, he enrolled in Graduate courses at VT and the rest they say is history. As a Freshman in 2016, Khalil only played in eight games for The Jayhawks and in just three of those he was a listed starter. In his eight games he tallied 44 carries, 189 yards and three scores. Without a shadow of a doubt, his best game of his Freshman year came in the loss to Memphis where he logged six carries for 74 yards and a score but also caught three passes for 39 yards. Herbert found himself fighting for snaps in the backfield committee and ended the year third on the list of rushing attempts.

As a Sophomore, Herbert was used much more in the running game. If you go and look at his first two weeks in 2017, you could be mistaken for thinking he was going to languish down on the depth charts forever. That however, was about to change as in week three he was given the bulk of the work and took full advantage of it. Against Ohio he logged 19 carries for 137 yards and two touchdowns. He also caught two passes for 18 yards. In week four his big game happened. Herbert was given all the ball and proceeded to carry the ball 36 times in the loss to West Virginia. He turned those 36 touches into 291 yards and two scores. He also chipped in with one five yard carry! So close Khalil, so close. Those would be his only two games that went over the 100 yard mark and after his week four explosion he was backed off carry wise and never saw over 13 carries after that breakout performance. He would finish his Sophomore year with 120 carries, 663 yards and four touchdowns which came in back to back games. He also only caught eight passes on the year for 38 yards.

2018 was pretty much a carbon copy of his previous year for The Jayhawks as he logged 113 carries for 499 yards and five touchdowns while catching nine passes for 39 yards. He never once went over 100 yards however, and had a two game high of 21 carries. It was tough sledding for Herbert in Kansas and there was to be a change in 2019. After playing just four games as a Senior, he left the team and finished the year with 384 yards off 43 attempts with two touchdowns.

Herbert joined The Hokies as a Grad Transfer and as soon as he adorned his pads with the glorious burgundy of Virginia Tech, he was dynamic and productive. In his week one outing he rushed with a good average (17.3 YPA), caught two receptions for 46 yards and even had two kick returns for 45 yards. He carried the ball six times for 104 yards and a touchdown. In his week two fixture against Duke he carried the ball 20 times, racked up 208 yards and scored twice. He returned three kick returns for 150 yards adding a new facet to his game. In his next two games he went over 100 yards in both and scored three touchdowns over this two game span, one of these was a receiving score against Boston College, his first career receiving touchdown. Then again in week six he went over 100 yards against Louisville as he logged 21 carries for 147 yards and one touchdown. Strangely in week seven he only logged one play and that was at kick returner where he returned one ball for 12 yards. In the final game of the season, Herbert once again went over the coveted 100 yard mark. This was in the final game of the Commonwealth Clash, a tournament across all sports when Virginia and VT played each other. Against The Cavaliers, Herbert had 20 rushing attempts for 162 yards and a touchdown, ending his Collegiate career with a score against his new School's most bitter rivals. Perfect. He would end his year totalling 155 carries, 1,183 yards and eight touchdowns. He also caught 10 receptions for 189 yards and a single score. In going over 1,000 rushing yards on the season, Herbert became the first Running Back since 2015 to go over 1,000 yards and he also set the Virginia Tech All-purpose single game yardage record in his game against Duke when he finished with 357 all-purpose yards.

Straight out of the gate, it's obvious that Herbert has never been fully utilised as a passing down Running Back. He has never logged over 10 receptions in any season, and his final year number of just 10 receptions is his career high. While he has shown some skills when thrown the ball and had good hands when catching, he has never been given a full workload as the pass catching back. He blocks well most of the time, showing keenness, but he was pretty poor in several games for The Hokies. He has exhibited all the signs of being able to pound the rock for a full 60 minutes with his high carry totals at Kansas and good carry totals in his year at VT. Herbert isn't an elite athlete, but he has superb vision and player placement observation that enables him to eradicate Defenders from tackling him by extending tackling angles. He never over-extends his skill set into what he can't do and with this trait is always slick in what he does and uses this control to work the gaps given to him well. This is no more evident than his first play as a Hokie. He uses the gap created by a shifting offensive line to burst into the secondary eliminating the Linebacker from the play by running straight ahead and then slanting away from a Safety to gain 37 yards. Angles people, it's all about the angles.

NFL Landing Spot

Landing on a Bears roster behind Montgomery and Cohen is bad news for Hill. He may not even make the team.

Rakeem Boyd

Arkansas | RB | 6'0" | 206lbs

Well, it took a little while, but we've found another of my College Fantasy Title Winning Team players. Boyd spent two seasons on my roster in both my Championship Winning seasons (humble brag). I was hugely high on Boyd coming into the 2020 season, along with so many others might I add, and he then went on to disappoint and then opt out. There are a few things that my boy Boyd needs to work on before he can be a top level guy, but he has the skills to do so and has shown it for enough time to be given a chance. Before we get into his past seasons and what he does well and what he needs to work on, we should mention his transfer from Texas A&M to a Juco School. That Juco School was none other than Independence Community College or ICC as it's better known and yes, we were treated to Boyd and what he can do in series three of the Netflix show *Last Chance U,* where he ran for 1,211 yards and 14 touchdowns in 10 games for The Pirates. Boyd wanted another shot at playing D1 football, so at Indy he improved his grades and let his Football do the talking. With offers coming in he chose to transfer to Arkansas and after three good seasons became one of the teams four Captains, only to, in the eyes of some Razorbacks fans, besmirch that captaincy by opting out of the 2020 season with two games to go.

Boyd's first year in Arkansas was a productive one and he played in 12 games, being named the starting Running Back in the last eight. At the end of the season, he would be named 'Darren McFadden Running Back of the Year' whilst also leading the team in rushing attempts by the end of the year. He instantly made his mark on the backfield as he increased his workload game by game in the first five games. He had three games over the 100 yard mark, and the best game of the year was in a loss to Vandebilt, when he logged 19 carries for 113 yards and a score. He was also part of the passing game, finishing third on the team in receptions. His final Sophomore season numbers read 123 carries, 734 yards and two scores whilst catching 23 passes for 165 yards.

As a Senior for The Razorbacks, Boyd stepped up his game in every stat column except receiving touchdowns as he failed to find paydirt as a pass catcher. He had five games over the 100 yard mark, starting in week one with 18 carries for 114 yards and a touchdown. In week three against Colorado State, he had 20 carries for 122 yards and two scores but it would be his week 10 performance that would be his game of the year. He only carried the ball eight times against Western Kentucky, yet he became the first player in program history to have two scores over 76 yards since 1997. On only his second attempt of the game he ran for 76 yards to the house and in doing so logged his longest rushing play of his career. However, in the fourth quarter he would go on to beat his own record and score from 86 yards, taking his tally of 50 yard plus touchdowns to five and see him go over the 1,000 yard mark on the season. He would end up rushing the ball 184 times on the season for 1133 yards and eight touchdowns. He also tallied 19 receptions for 160 yards as a pass catcher.

Things were trending in the right direction for Boyd and The Razorbacks, 2020 seemed like it would be Boyd's season to really make his mark on the upcoming NFL Draft and announce himself as an early picked Running Back. With Feleipe Franks now the starting Quarterback for Arkansas the dual threat ability was meant to open up lanes for Boyd to exploit and we anticipated seeing an explosion from my man Boyd. What we actually saw was a productive yet not exciting nor entertaining role from Boyd. His first two weeks were an utter disappointment and quite frankly shocking from what we had seen previously even against good competition he had been great and then in week one against Georgia he tallied just 21 yards off of 11 carries. In week two he had eight carries for just 28 yards. He did manage to find the end zone in week three but still had a low yaradge count of just 39. In week four we saw the Boyd we knew. It was unfortunately in a loss to Texas A&M which must have hurt Boyd to lose to his former School in his last year in College. He did, however, score a touchdown against The Aggies which should have helped lift his spirits. As good games went though, that was his only one of the year. He opted out as mentioned after six games and declared for the NFL Draft, finishing his Senior year with 82 carries for 309 and just three touchdowns. He also only caught 10 passes for 33 yards in the receiving game. A poor year for The Razorbacks, a down year from Boyd himself and the emergence by Trelon Smith as a rusher ultimately hurt his Draft stock.

As a Running Back, Boyd is a power back who uses his size and strength to his advantage. As we all know though, sometimes using your best trait can actually be a hindrance as occasionally Boyd will look to just run straight through Defenders and not try to avoid contact or change his running lane to gain extra yardage. This can result in being stumped from time to time and cause him to not get anything extra. Boyd is superb behind the line of scrimmage and allows the play to develop. As a result, running lanes start to open before he detonates through the opening holes. He exhibits great vision when waiting for a hole to open and if the gap isn't there but another one opens up he can use this burst to run into it. Boyd can act as a Receiver as well, and we have seen some big plays from the slot as he has natural hands. We have also seen him struggle in pass protection when being used as both a runner and a receiver. He needs to work on this aspect of his game.

NFL Landing Spot

Boyd joins a crowded Lions Backfield as a UDFA and unlikely doesn't make the roster unless he breaks out in camp.

Rhamondre Stevenson

Oklahoma | RB | 6'0" | 233lbs

Following on from the previous Juco athlete, Stevenson was just as impressive at the Juco level as Boyd was. There's something gritty about a guy who's willing to either take a cut in the tier of Football he is playing in or start in Juco with the passion and drive to want to get to D1 Football. Stevenson played for two years at Cerritos College, located in California. It has a population of just under 50,000 (if you want to know where it is and town size (if you also want to get there, BA do flights for $432, just sayin')). In small town Cali, Stevenson was prolific for The Falcons (whose logo is basically a blue version of Atlanta's logo) and after two good years he made his way onto the Oklahoma roster. Stevenson has not been without controversy in his career and before we get into his suspension from the 2019 Peach Bowl, let's go back to Juco.

As a Freshman at Cerritos, Stevenson wasn't the lead dog in the backfield. He never carried the ball more than 10 times and that only happened once. He was also rarely used in the passing game as he only caught five passes all year and his longest reception was for 13 yards, which he did twice. What Stevenson did though was knuckle down in class and work hard in training. This hard work and persistence paid off; he was given the reins to the backfield going into his Sophomore year and never looked back. He finished his Freshman year with just 501 yards off of 68 carries and three scores. Ok that isn't technically true, he didn't play in the pre-season game against Mt. San Jacinto.

In his first season as the lead Running Back Stevenson hit the ground running (excuse the pun) as in week one he tallied 13 carries for 117 yards and a touchdown. It would actually be his second lowest yardage total for the year. Then in week two he tore the doors off Moorpark, amassing three touchdowns and 200 yards off 15 carries. In week four he showed he can shoulder a workload. He carried the ball 29 times for 154 yards and a touchdown. Then came the game of his life in week five, when he made every one of his 18 carries count. He averaged 18.8 yards a carry for 339 yards and three touchdowns. Stevenson was a little more involved in the passing game in his second year when he caught 13 passes for 175 yards. His stat sheet at the end of the year was phenomenal, reading 222 rushing attempts for 2,111 yards and 16 touchdowns. That season's performance was enough for Stevenson to transfer to Oklahoma and the D1 school he was dearly after.

2019 saw Stevenson competing for carries amongst a very crowded backfield. Trey Sermon was still there, Kenedy Brooks was getting the majority of carries and Jalen Hurts was 'hurting' them all with his running abilities. Stevenson only had 64 carries for 515 yards and six touchdowns. The biggest news from Stevensons 2019 campaign was him being suspended before the Peach Bowl for a failed drugs test due to marijuana use along with two other team mates. He received a six game suspension, and this led to him only playing six games in 2020.

After serving his ban Stevenson was very productive. He only carried the ball 101 times but managed to rack up 665 yards and seven touchdowns. He averaged 6.6 yards per carry and had three games over the 100 yard mark. His first came against Kansas in his second game where he had 11 carries for 104 yards and two scores. The second of the 100 yard games came against Oklahoma State; he totalled 141 yards off 26 carries but didn't score. His final 100 yard plus game came in The Cotton Bowl against a weak Florida team. Stevenson put The Gators to the sword, rushing 18 times for 186 yards and a trip into the end zone. It was, however, his first game back for The Sooners in which he garnered attention from the onlooking world. He immediately saw action as the lead ball carrier in the Oklahoma backfield and led the team with 13 carries for 87 yards. It was his three touchdowns though that propelled him into the news and made people aware of what 'the guy back from suspension' could do. He was also used in the passing game more than he had ever been as he caught 18 passes for 211 yards. While he didn't manage to get a receiving touchdown, he showed that he has good hands and can run a route from the backfield or from the line of scrimmage.

As a Running Back Stevenson's tape is truly an intriguing watch. He is a huge man. I mean truly huge. His size means he is built for smashing through gaps created for him by the Offensive Line. To see him in action watch The Sooners against Florida. He is the first guy Spencer Rattler throws to and completes a first down on a short curl route run from the slot. He shows good awareness to catch the ball on the opposing side of his body away from the Defender, allowing him to turn and gain more yardage. Several plays later we are shown how he uses his pads well to engage in contact through the tackle and keep the legs churning to gain extra yards. He is engaged at the line of scrimmage on a rushing play, but his good low pad angle and hot stepping feet allow him to keep moving forward and gain six yards after the tackle before a second Defender manages to bring him down. He has a nasty cut that given his size takes Defenders by surprise and can be used in a combo with a heavy stiff arm to really punish a weak tackle. When all is said and done Stevenson offers huge upside as a Running Back but has he matured? Only time will tell.

NFL Landing Spot

The Patriots have another huge Running Back to add to the mix. The way Michel has fallen away and Harris hasn't shown to be who they thought he was Stevenson could end up being the primary ball carrier.

Javian Hawkins -

Louisville | RB | 5'9" | 196lbs

Javian Hawkins may well be a smaller Running Back, but he has all the skills required to be effective and has done so over his time with The Cardinals. Before he joined Louisville he played at Cocoa High School and earned the nickname Playstation, due to him moving like he was a human joystick. Hawkins is explosive and has frighteningly fast cuts and bursts of speed which led to him having over 4,000 yards and 40 touchdowns at Cocoa High. In his time at Cocoa, he was clocked running a 4.37 40-yard dash time so we know he is super quick. He was also labeled as one of the top SPARQ athletes in his class. For those who don't know what the SPARQ rating is, it is a metric created by Nike designed to measure sport-specific athleticism. SPARQ is an acronym for *Speed, Power, Agility, Reaction and Quickness*. There are various tests run to cover each of these five skills, which are then combined and weighted using a sport specific formula. Generally speaking players with a good SPARQ rating, tend to be the guys whose tape is always a fun watch and Hawkins is no exception. While he only really played two seasons as he Redshirted his Freshman year after two games, Hawkins displayed great ability in 2019 and in 2020.

In 2018 as mentioned, Hawkins Redshirted after two games. He also only had three plays from scrimmage in his Freshman year; a run and a catch against Indiana State and a solitary run against Georgia Tech. Fun fact about his three plays as a Freshman, all three were for exactly four yards. Those of you who are math wizzes amongst us will have quickly deducted that he had 12 yards on the season. The best was yet to come however, as history was to be made at Louisville.

Javian Hawkins started life as a Redshirt Freshman rapidly and jumped out the blocks fast on his way to a record setting year. He had eight games over the 100 yard mark, and one of these was over 200 yards. His first game as the starting Running Back for The Cards saw him carry the ball 19 times for 122 yards. He followed up that 100 yard plus game with another in week two against Eastern Kentucky, as he took his 11 carries and turned them into 123 yards. Then in week three he found paydirt for the first time, followed by a huge game in week five against Boston College as he carried the ball 25 times for 172 yards and a touchdown but also logged his first reception of the season with a 13 yard catch. In weeks seven and eight against two good Defences in Clemson and Virginia, he went over 100 yards in both games, 129 yards and a score against Clemson and 136 yards and two touchdowns against the Cavaliers. His best was yet to come though, as in week 11 against Syracuse he tallied 23 carries for 233 yards and a touchdown. He finished the season with 264 carries, 1,525 yards and nine touchdowns with a further four receptions for 58 yards. Hawkins ranked seventh in the nation in rushing yards, broke the school record for rushing yards by a Running Back and set a new Louisville mark for the most rushing yards in a season by a Freshman. Hawkins also totaled the third-most yards by a Freshman in ACC history, some feat for a guy who is undersized, hey?

2020 only saw The Cardinals take to the field in 10 games in a pretty putrid season where they went 3-7. Hawkins actually opted out of the season after week seven and decided to declare for the NFL Draft and forego the remaining two years of eligibility. Four of his seven games went for over 100 yards and he averaged a touchdown a game over the course of the season. The huge difference for me between 2019 and 2020 was his usage in the passing game as he saw much more action as a Receiver. In a season where The Cardinals got the luxury of not playing Clemson, Hawkins struggled on the ground against Notre Dame who were their toughest matchup. What he did do well against The Fighting Irish was catch the ball getting five receptions for 48 yards. His best game of the year, however, was in his week six game against Florida State. He carried the ball 16 times for 174 yards and three scores. His overall best game from a skill set point of view came the following week against Virginia Tech, as he carried the ball 17 times for 129 yards and a score but also had five catches for 42 yards and his first receiving touchdown of his career. He opted out after that game and as a result his final season numbers read; 133 carries, 822 yards and seven touchdowns. In his expanded role in the pass game, he caught 16 passes for 127 yards and a touchdown.

After watching his tape, I think his main weapon at the next level will be his speed and ability to make any play a huge one, most likely coming through the passing game. He is a smaller Running Back and while he has the speed and elusiveness to create big plays, he doesn't have the weight to be able to move the pile or gain extra yards by running through a Defender. His elite speed is frightening and he uses it well by eliminating incoming tackles by tacking great angles after getting into the secondary. This is no more apparent than in the game against Western Kentucky in week one of 2020 where he zooms one in from the 18 yard line. After a fast step cut into a gap opened up by the Right Guard, he's off to the races and while there is a good block by a Wide Receiver, he is too fast to the pilon that the Cornerback can't close him down fast enough. Hawkins could well be a do it all gadget Running Back if given the reps to do so.

NFL Landing Spot

Hawkins can back up Mike Davis and even push him for a part of the starting role as we know Davis can't stay fit for a full season.

Chris Evans

Michigan | RB | 5'11" | 216lbs

Here we have it Rush Nation, the first guy who genuinely tore me in half when it came to watching his tape and how I ranked him on this list. Chris Evans is as intriguing a prospect as they come from so many different angles, you don't get ranked as a top 10 all purpose Running back coming out of High School without having serious skills. He has some great tape in his locker and yet he is also labeled as a risk due to having issues at School, but he has shown the willingness to fight for his position on the team and do what is needed to get back on track. You've gotta love a guy who is willing to grind to get back in the locker room, but I also had to question why he wasn't there in the first place. Evans should have declared for the NFL Draft last year but was suspended from the team for reasons that have never been disclosed. He announced via Twitter that he had "academic issues" and planned to continue his career at Michigan. Toward the end of the 2019 season Head Coach Jim Harbaugh confirmed that Evans would be reinstated into the team and would be eligible to play in 2020. During his time away from the team, Evans worked three jobs including washing up in the back of a restaurant which had a TV in the kitchen. Evans said that he tried to watch as many games as possible but given his hectic schedule, he didn't catch all of the Wolverines games. Only six games in 2020 means we haven't really seen the previous skills that Evans showed over two years ago, which in itself is intriguing as they could still be locked away, waiting to be released.

As a Freshman in 2016 Evans started all 13 games and even made a start at Slot Receiver as he played some Wide Receiver in High School. He became only the third Wolverine to rush for over 100 yards in their debut as he notched up an impressive 112 yards from just eight carries and even found the end zone twice. Other than the week six game against Rutgers where Evans carried the ball 11 times for 153 yards 2016 was a bit of a year of mediocracy for Evans in the numbers department. De'Veon Smith was the lead back for Michigan and Evans was left to pick up the slack and carry the ball 93 times less than Smith did. Evans would finish the season with 88 carries, 614 yards and four touchdowns and also caught the ball six times for 87 yards.

The game against Minnesota is the game most highlight reels either start with or end with and is what most people remember from watching Evans' tape and with good reason, it was his best game as a Wolverine. What we also saw from Evans in 2017 was the result of Karan Higdon exploding his way into becoming the lead Running Back for Michigan. Higdon's improvement was to Evans' detriment as once again he was relegated to second in rushing attempts for the season. What Evans did do better than every other Running Back was catch the ball and he turned into the teams Receiving Back for 2017. His one good game and only game over 100 yards was THE game against The Golden Gophers where he ran for a career-high 191 yards on 13 carries with two touchdowns. I tell a lie about having one good game. His other good game was against Purdue where he tallied 14 carries for 97 yards and two touchdowns. His Sophomore year ended with him having 135 carries, 685 and six touchdowns with 16 receptions for 157 yards and a score through the air.

Evans only played in 10 games for Michigan in 2018 and was eclipsed in the Running game by Higdon once more. There really wasn't much to shout about for Evans as a Junior and his best game was sub 100 yards as he turned in a two touchdown, ten carry game for 86 rushing yards. Again he was utilized in the passing game tallying 148 yards off 16 catches and a single touchdown.

The aforementioned suspension happened in 2019 so reinstatement meant Evans could play in the shortened season for The Wolverines. While Evans was back in the vaunted Big House for Football, Michigan now had two good Running Backs in Hassan Haskins and Zach Charbonnet; Evans would have to fight for every rep. Apart from an upset win in week one against Minnesota, Michigan were bad, and Evans was left languishing on the depth chart. He never saw over five carries in a game and this was in his first game back against The Golden Gophers where he ran the ball five times for 19 yards and a touchdown. Numerically his best game was his last of the season when he carried the ball four times for 35 yards in the loss to Penn State. Evans' dismal return to Ann Arbor finished with 16 carries for 73 yards and a score whilst also catching nine balls for 87 yards. That proved enough for Evans as he declared for the NFL Draft once the season was over.

So now you've read that I'm sure you're thinking *after those two years why is he even on this list? Stocks, your son has been alive longer than it's been since Evans was productive, why will he do so in the NFL?*' Well, I think the answer to that is two fold; Evans has tread left on his tyres and has shown in the past that he can produce. I enjoyed the tape Evans produced when he was at his fluid best and has delightful balance through contact but isn't afraid to lean into a tackle and use his pads to good effect. He also offers a skillset as a pass catcher out of the backfield, which along with his physicality means he has the skills to make it at the next level. He can contribute to special teams and on third downs right away, given time he could develop into a three down back.

NFL Landing Spot

Evans has a chance to support Joe Mixon and can even take starting reps should the often injured Mixon have a prolonged period off the field.

Chuba Hubbard

Oklahoma State | RB | 6'0" | 208lbs

Growing up in Canada, all Chuba Hubbard wanted to do was play Football. His mother wasn't keen, as I imagine most aren't, and it took him ten years to persuade her to let him play contact Football. Up until this point Hubbard had been a track athlete and this background is still uber obvious in the way he plays Running Back. As soon as Hubbard was unleashed upon the High School Football world, it was obvious he was going to be a star. His High School stats at Bev Facey Community High School in Alberta Canada were nothing short of monstrous. Like when Godzilla laid waste to Tokyo, Hubbard played Football in a different stratosphere to the rest of his peers. In his three years playing Football in High School he racked up 6,880 yards on 458 attempts with 82 touchdowns. He still had a love for athletics however, and he even went to the 2015 IAAF World Youth Championships in California and placed fourth overall in the 100 meters event clocking an insanely fast 10.55 in the process. As soon as The Cowboys came knocking, Hubbard was sold and packed his bags, headed for Oklahoma State Campus.

Now before we get into his history and skillset I want to address the elephant in the room here. I have Hubbard seriously low in comparison to others. I've seen him normally ranked in the Running Back 6-9 range and I'm fine with that but for me, Hubbard is weak in one area of his game and a liability in another area and these two things mean I think his future in the NFL could be a rocky and short one. I won't tell you what they are until we get towards the end so that you do read about just how damn good he was in 2019.

After Redshirting in 2017 Hubbard started 2018 as the backup to Justice Hill. However, it wouldn't be long before we would get to see the Canadian product start to produce. Over the final four games he averaged 106 yards per contest and five yards per carry! In his first game as the featured back after Hill went down, Hubbard tore the roof off the Bedlam Game against Oklahoma. He rushed for 104 yards off of 22 attempts and had three touchdowns. The following week against West Virginia he was also heavily featured but this time found the end zone through the air, showing he can be used in the passing game while also logging 26 rushing attempts for 134 yards. Then in The Cowboys final game of the season in the Liberty Bowl against Missouri, he carried the ball 18 times for 145 yards and a score. Hubbard would end the year with 124 carries, 740 yards and seven scores while also catching 22 passes for 229 yards and another two touchdowns.

In 2019 Hubbard made us realise we were but pawns in his game of Football chess. Put simply, Hubbard was on another level to any other Running Back in College in his Sophomore year. How much better was he? Well, he averaged 64.6 yards per game more than anyone else did over the year, that's how good! I could sit here and fill an entire page of just how prolific he was but I won't, I'll give it to you straight. Hubbard played 13 games for The Cowboys; he had 12 games over 100 yards, four of these were over 200 and one of those was four yards shy of a 300 yard game. His only week under 100 yards was in the week two annihilation of McNeese State where he only had eight touches. He had a trio of three touchdown games and scored in 11 of the 13 games. Whenever Hubbard touched the ball, he looked as if he would go all the way and this was evident in the way he led the country in runs over 30 yards. In order to see just how good he was, go and have a look at the game against Kansas state or in fact, watch his whole season highlights, it really is something to behold. He would finish the year as the FBS leader in rushing yards, rushing yards per game, 200-yard rushing games and all-purpose yards per game. His numbers read 328 carries, 2,094 yards and 21 touchdowns with a further 23 catches for 198 yards. Epic stuff indeed.

Then the complete opposite happened in 2020. After not declaring for the 2020 NFL Draft as most thought he would do, Hubbard returned for his Junior year. While The Cowboys only played six games, Hubbard wasn't the same player. In three of these games he did manage to go over 100 yards though. Something was up however, and Hubbard wasn't the same player. He would finish the year with 133 carries, 625 yards and five touchdowns. He only caught eight passes for 52 yards and a score. It might not have been all his fault and the scheme let him down hugely which hurt his Draft stock dramatically in my opinion.

Hubbard is a polarising player with two very very different seasons behind him. He can be elite, but he also has an achilles heel which is why I have him so low. Go and watch the tape to see what he does well because it's beautiful. For me though, two things are a real issue. The first is that he isn't a fluid catcher of the ball and often looks like he is at war with his hands when trying, this isn't a good thing for a guy who is meant to be a three down Running Back. The biggest thing though is just how bad he is at pass protection, he simply cannot do it and when he does he doesn't look bothered or offer anywhere near the same level of effort to which he does running the ball. This will get you benched or cut in the NFL, so something needs to happen and fast for Hubbard to be considered elite. I'm happy though if he goes on to prove me wrong.

NFL Landing Spot

Chubba Hubbard slides in behind the best Running Back in Football right now in CMC. Hubbard offers some upside in the passing game but thats where CMC excels so I expect Hubbard to be CMC's handcuff and change of pace back should they need him.

C.J. Verdell -

Oregon | RB | 5'9" | 205lbs

With only two real seasons of production to go off, C.J. Verdell is a mysterious prospect to evaluate. This isn't because he hasn't had much production because he has, he's gone over 1,000 yards in his two full years. He is mysterious because we could have seen so much more from Verdell if he had the full four years in school. If he had four seasons of 1,000 yards or more then Verdell would be top 10, no doubt. Not having Justin Herbert as his on field Commander for the five games he played in during the 2020 season was fairly obvious as new Quarterback Tyler Shough took carries away from Verdell and actually led the team in carries in 2020. Verdell joined The Ducks in 2017 but Redshirted his Freshman year after being recruited from famed Footballing High School Mater Dei Catholic. Verdell had offers from Arizona, Arizona State, Baylor, Boston College, California, Colorado, Nebraska, Oregon State, UCLA, Utah, Washington State, Wisconsin and others to name a few. At Mater Dei, Verdell had three games in 2016 where he scored five touchdowns, five! That alone is a mad stat but these games all helped Mater Dei to go on and win a National Championship. Although Verdell isn't a complete prospect, he certainly has all of the intangibles I'm looking for in my Running Backs. He needs to work on a few things and hopefully the coaching at the next level can do just that.

2018 was a solid Redshirt Freshman year for Verdell as he was only one of eight FBS freshmen with 1,000 yards on the ground and just the third freshman in Ducks history to go over 1,000 yards in their first season. Not only did he accomplish those feats in his first year, but he was also the only Power 5 player in the nation with 1,000 yards rushing and 300 yards receiving, showing what he can do both on the ground but also through the air. He went over 100 yards in only his second game for The Ducks as he carried the ball 11 times for 106 yards and a touchdown. His three-week stretch from week four to six saw him get a hatrick of 100 yard plus games and he became the first Oregon Freshman ever to have three games on the spin with over 100 yards in each. His best of those three was the week six game against Washington, where he had 29 carries for 111 yards and two touchdowns. But it was his appearance in the Civil War game against Oregon State that really had Verdell a household name. His performance produced the second-best single-game rushing record by a Freshman in Ducks history on 23 carries for 187 yards and five total touchdowns. He scored four on the ground and one through the air as he had 21 yards off of his solitary catch and in doing so became the first player in the FBS since 2016 to score four rushing touchdowns and one receiving touchdown in a single game. He ended the season with 202 carries, 1,018 yards and 10 touchdowns while adding 315 yards off of 27 catches and two scores.

2019 saw Verdell once again lead the team in rushing attempts, rushing yards and rushing touchdowns and once more made his mark on Oregon history. He had three games over the 100 yard mark and two of these went over the 200 yard mark. He became the first Duck with

200 yards rushing and three touchdowns since Kenjon Barner in 2012 and also became the first player in Oregon history with 250 yards rushing and 50 yards receiving in a single game against Washington State. In his other 200 yard plus performance Verdell was named as the PAC-12's Championship MVP as he stacked up 208 yards and three scores against Utah who, up until that point, had statistically boasted the Nation's best Run Defence. After scoring a touchdown in the first two games of the season, Verdell's only other scores on the ground came in two triple touchdown games and both were in the games where he went over 200 yards. He carried the workload in week six against Colorado to the extent that his 14 carries for 171 yards were the most by a Duck ever in the longstanding rivalry of over 22 games. He would end the year with 197 carries, 1,220 yards and eight touchdowns. He also caught 14 passes for 125 yards. 2020 saw two of Verdell's five games go over 100 yards and he had three scores on the year to at least show that he still had what we all knew was in there.

As a prospect, Verdell made me sit forward in my chair at times while I watched his tape. He is a pocket rocket and offers TNT-like explosions when a gap opens up. He is quick to see a gap begin to open and fires into it, sometimes to his detriment as the gap may break down by the time he gets to it and he can be swallowed up by the tumbling bodies at the line. There are other occasions, though, when he has shown good patience in allowing his blocks to develop and it almost seems as if he has difficulty separating the two skill sets from each other in order to be able to acknowledge the sturdiness of the gap or the play design. If he can get a handle on his explosiveness and temper it with patience he will be a superb player in the running game. Although he is short, he isn't a little guy and uses his frame and bulk well when it comes to contact. He is a fierce competitor and is always willing to fight for extra yardage, he always, *always* falls forward, gaining sneaky extra yards by doing so. He isn't afraid of lowering his head and pads while charging into a Defender and often comes out of a solo tackle from the front by either flattening the guy or shedding the tackle. He is a superb finisher of runs and can punch it in when needs be by virtue of him being a north-south runner in a hurry. He has great hands in the passing game and very fairly relies on his body for the catch. He is not yet accomplished in the pass blocking game and needs some serious work in order to increase his usage on third downs. He also as I mentioned, needs to work on his gap acknowledgment so as to not get tangled up in the pile.

NFL Landing Spot

Not currently on a roster.

Larry Rountree III

Missouri | RB | 5'10" | 210lbs

One of my man Tom's guys is Larry Rountree III. He alerted me to him and once I'd watched some tape I have to admit, I was impressed. Not the kind of top 10 impressed that I was hoping for, but for a player who doesn't offer any one elite trait, Rountree is an effective Running Back who can offer a change of pace or first down work at the next level. Coming out of High School, Rountree was a bruising Running Back who wasn't scared of contact and had a superb burst which enabled him to get to his top speed quickly. This physical running style and Missouri's superb Physical Conditioning Department meant that of the team who offered him a place, becoming a Tiger was the only choice for Rountree. He was also thrown into action right away for Mizzou and never carried the ball less than 126 times in a season. He has even been involved in the passing game and was also utilised in the kick return game.

As a Freshman, Rountree sat behind Damarea Crockett until the second half of the season when Crockett unfortunately suffered a season-ending shoulder injury, releasing Rountree into the lead role. Again, like most of our prospects, Rountree found the end zone in his very first game as a college player but as mentioned it would be his second half of the season where he really came into his own. In the final seven games after Crockett was out, he averaged 82.0 yards per game, racking up five scores and 574 yards while averaging over six yards per rush. Six yards per rush hey, why didn't we think of that! His two best games came against Florida in week nine where he ran the ball 15 times for 83 yards and three touchdowns and then in the following week against Tennessee, where he carried the ball 18 times for 155 yards and a score. His Freshman year would end with him having 126 yards, 703 yards and six touchdowns. He finished as one of the top Freshman Running Backs in the conference, and nation to boot.

Rountree broke out in his Sophomore year, leading Mizzou and ranked fourth in the vaunted SEC with rushing 1,216 yards. He had five games over 100 yards and his final three weeks were pure poetry. In week three against Purdue, he carried the ball 23 times for 168 yards proving he can be a workhorse. In week seven he had a three touchdown day against Memphis that saw him rack up 118 yards off just nine carries. Then in weeks 11-13 Rountree was the bell cow for The Tigers. He had 26 carries, 135 and a score against Tennesse. 29 carries and 119 yards against Arkansas and finally he carried the ball 27 times for 204 yards and a touchdown against Oklahoma State in week 13's Liberty Bowl win. His season total numbers read 225 carries 1,216 yards and 11 touchdowns. He also chipped in through the air by catching 14 passes for 62 yards.

2019 was a slightly down year for Rountree and although he put up good numbers, he didn't continue to improve. However, 2020 saw him push up the curve. Rountree had three games over the 100 yard mark as a Junior. His first was against West Virginia in week two where he tallied 17 carries for 104 yards and a score. His best game of the year came the following week against Southeast Missouri State where he logged 18 carries for 142 yards and two touchdowns. His final 100 yard plus game came in week six against Mississippi as he carried the ball 21 times for 126 yards and another two scores. He would end up catching 13 receptions totalling 70 yards through the air while carrying the ball 186 times for 829 yards and nine touchdowns.

2020 would be when we would see, in my opinion, Rountree at his most fluid best. Five of his 10 games went over 100 yards. His two week stretch against Vandebilt and Arkansas are amongst the best two weeks you'll see on tape from any Running Back in this class. Against Vandy he carried the ball 21 times for 160 yards and three touchdowns. He then followed up with a 27 carry, 185 yard, three touchdown game against The Razorbacks. Rountree finished off his season and career as a Tiger with a 25 carry, 121 yard, two touchdown game against Mississippi State. As a Senior, Rountree set the school record for career rushing yards by a Running Back. He would finish his 2020 campaign with 209 carries, 972 yards and 14 touchdowns while catching 15 balls for 100 yards.

Although he lacks multiple gears and elite top speed, Rountree does offer good bursts and vision to attack holes that develop behind his Offensive Line. When watching his Vandebilt tape, I noticed how he sets his blocks up well and creates good running angles by being patient and allowing the game to progress just in front of him. He hasn't got a second gear to break away from Defenders, yet he does have adequate size and strength to be able to break free of tackles and create extra yardage after the contact occurs. He can be occasionally caught waiting for gaps to appear rather than bounce to the outside but given the right scheme and practice reps, this can be taught out of him. He is also adequate in the passing game but is more of a check down option than a jet sweep or wheel route guy because of his lack of speed into the secondary. He is good at most aspects of the game yet doesn't excel at any one thing. What he did show in his time as a Tiger was the willingness to play for the full 60 minutes and also the ability to take on a full workload, meaning he has more strings to his bow than just as a thumper.

NFL Landing Spot

Rountree joins the Chargers needing a huge camp performance in order to make the roster. If he can he could get some reps but will be limited because of competition.

Pooka Williams

Kansas | RB | 5'10" | 170lbs

It takes some big minerals to decide to play for The Jayhawks over some of the bigger schools that offered Pooka Williams a place on their rosters. Williams chose Kansas over LSU, Mississippi State, Memphis, Nebraska, TCU, UCLA, Tulane and Louisiana Tech. Was it to ensure he would be the alpha Running Back or was there something else? Well, it turns out that family is a big thing for Pooka and it would end up being the reason for him signing for Kansas and ultimately the reason he would leave. Upon signing, Williams said it was the family-like atmosphere that made him choose Kansas. "It's family," Williams said. "It wasn't anybody just randomly talking. It was like family." I mentioned he would leave because of family and after just four games of his 2020 campaign he opted out of the remainder games and declared for the 2021 NFL Draft He would go on to say "Family and health are the most important things to me. Right now I need to be with my mother, who is battling health issues." Born Anthony Williams Jr,. his Grandmother gave him the nickname Pooka from an early age and it just stuck. It even helped the voice of the Jayhawks, Brian Hanni, come up with an extension of Pooka when he called him Pooka the Bazooka after a big debut game in 2018. Williams was the 13 ranked all-purpose Running Back coming out of High School and it's easy to see why; he is explosive and fast, putting up huge numbers in his final year of High School that read 3,118 yards and 37 touchdowns.

Williams' first game for The Jayhawks came in week two and boy did he set the tyres on fire in his debut. He scored twice from his 14 carries and totalled 125 yards earning him the aforementioned Pooka the Bazooka nickname. Williams was superb in his 11 games as a Freshman going over 100 yards four times and one of those was over 200 yards in his huge game against The Sooners. Before that game and in just his second game for Kansas, Williams again went over 100 as he notched 163 yards and another touchdown off of 19 carries against Rutgers. In what was undoubtedly his game of the season against Oklahoma, he carried the ball 15 times for 252 yards and two touchdowns.

It should be noted that Williams also showcased his skills in the passing game as a Freshman in the game against TCU, when he caught seven passes for 102 yards and two scores. His end of season stats read 161 carries, 1,125 yards and seven touchdowns while also catching 33 passes for 289 yards and two scores. Oh, and he tossed a touchdown too against Oklahoma which made him one of only two players in the country to achieve the feat of having a passing, a rushing and a receiving touchdown in the season.

Following his superb 2018 season Williams was arrested for domestic battery and was suspended from team activities during the investigation. He was, however, granted a diversion for his arrest but would serve a one game ban for Kansas heading into his Sophomore year. He would play 12 of the 13 games for Kansas due to his suspension and was again good as he surpassed the 1000 yard mark, making him only the second Jayhawk ever to do it in back to back seasons. Williams would have five games over the 100 yard mark and was oh so close in his first game back gaining 99 yards. He would break the 100 yard mark though, in his second game back in a 22 carry, 121 yards on score performance against Boston College. He then went above 100 against Oklahoma for the second straight year and exploded against Texas the following week with 25 carries for 190 yards and two touchdowns. He would end the season with back to back 100 yard plus games but after his two touchdowns against Texas he wouldn't find paydirt again. That, for Williams, would be the down mark on the season as he only scored three times over the course of the year. What I don't think helped Williams at all in 2019 was just how bad The Jayhawks were. They won just two games over the year and playing from behind really hurt Pooka's ability to find the end zone on the ground. Again however, Williams was a weapon through the air and ended up fifth on the team in targets just five catches away from being third on the list. As a Sophomore, Williams would end the year with 203 carries, 1,061 yards and three catches adding 27 catches, 214 yards and two scores through the air.

As mentioned earlier, Williams did opt out of the season after four games in 2020 but displayed some of what we had already seen from the Kansas prospect. What we hadn't seen though, was his usage in the return game in week three. He had six kick returns for 105 yards and then in his last game as a Jayhawk he took his lone return 92 yards to the house showcasing explosive speed, good vision and fast cuts. He would end his Junior year with 51 carries, 196 yards and two touchdowns while again being targeted in the pass game he hauled in six catches for 31 yards. Size. That is what Pooka Williams lacks as a Running Back heading into the NFL. Five foot ten isn't the issue; it's the 170 lbs that means he is towards the weaker end of Running Back prospects in this year's Draft class. Although Williams has done it all through his High School and Collegiate careers, the NFL is another beast and the bigger stronger guys might stop him at the line or bring him down faster rather than Williams being able to bounce free. What he does well is play with good vision and patience and you can really see this when he is running the football. He is superb at waiting for his gaps and blocks to progress and then hits the space with ferocity. His cuts are lightning quick and allow him to gain extra yards or make Defenders miss and not get a handle on Williams.

NFL Landing Spot

Williams is a Bengal for now but faces a huge battle to make the roster.

Elijah Mitchell

Louisiana | RB | 5'10" | 215lbs

Finally, we've gotten ourselves a *Ragin' Cajun*. One of the very best college team nicknames out there, and as a player Elijah Mitchell fits the mold of a Cajun just perfectly. A shot out of a cannon, Jalapeno-like burst and aggressive kind of Running Back, Mitchell is as an enjoyable watch as any other prospect out there. Sure, there are a few limitations to his game, and he's not an athletic freak, but when you've got 41,000 crazy Louisianians screaming at you, everyone plays a little spicier. Mitchell hasn't had it all his own way in Lafayette as he has battled serious injury when he broke a foot and has been part of a backfield committee from the first time he stepped onto the field as a Ragin' Cajun. As an athlete in High School, Mitchell was prolific, and even an injury in his Sophomore year couldn't stop him posting ridiculous numbers in just eight games. In that time, he rushed for 1,903 yards and 28 touchdowns and over his whole career he ran the ball 457 times and amassed 4,045 yards and 50 touchdowns which meant he finished his time in High School as the leasing rusher in Bobcat history, averaging nine yards per carry and a touchdown every nine carries, which is just stupid.

Life in the Sun Belt didn't start as smoothly as Mitchell would have hoped. The Freshman only played in five games as a foot injury would sideline him for the rest of his season. In these five games, Mitchell went over 100 yards once, and that was in the week four clash against Louisiana-Monroe where he carried the ball 13 times for 107 yards and two touchdowns. What Mitchell did well in his Freshman year was keep a good average yard per attempt number, 6.1 YPA meant he finished the season with 42 carries, 257 yards and four touchdowns. He also caught three passes for 28 yards and a touchdown.

After rehabbing, Mitchell was fresh for the 2018 season and made an impact after a slow first three games. The Ragin' Cajuns started to get Mitchell more involved and in weeks five and six he went over 100 yards. In week five against Texas State, he carried the ball 20 times for 191 yards and three touchdowns. He followed it up with another three touchdowns and 107 yards off of 12 carries against New Mexico State. Mitchell would have another triple touchdown game in week 10 against South Alabama when he took three of his 12 carries to the house and totalled 104 yards in the process. In the week eight game against Arkansas State, he showed how good he is in the passing game as he caught six passes for 121 yards and a touchdown. He would lead the team in touchdowns and be second on the team in total yards from scrimmage. His numbers read 146 carries, 985 yards and 13 touchdowns and 20 receptions, 349 yards and three touchdowns through the air.

2019 was another good year for Mitchell, as he continued to shine in the Running Back committee. He was Louisiana's top rusher over the season, and he helped the team break the school record for total rushing yards (3,604) and total rushing touchdowns (42). Mitchell also led the team with 198 carries, 1,147 yards and 16 rushing touchdowns, meaning he was now established as the teams first player up in the Running Backs rotation. He had five games over 100 yards, with his best being the week four game against Ohio where he carried the ball 17 times for 143 yards and three touchdowns.

The shortened 2020 season meant that Mitchell only played 10 games for Louisiana but was still very effective. The Ragin' Cajuns won nine games and Mitchell was influential in the ground attack. He had two games over 100 yards and his week two performance of 16 rushing attempts, 164 yards and two touchdowns was his best game of the year. He added another string to his bow in his Senior year, where he played a role on the Special Teams unit as a kick returner, returning five kicks for 82 yards. He wasn't used quite as much in the passing game, but still had 16 receptions for 153 yards. In his last game in the glorious red of Louisiana, Mitchell carried the ball 19 times tallying up 127 yards and a score whilst also catching two passes for 45 yards in the First Responder Bowl win over Texas-San Antonio. He would end his Senior year with 141 carries, 878 yards and eight touchdowns whilst hauling in 16 passes for 153 yards.

When I sat down and went through Mitchell's tape, I was pleasantly surprised, yet ultimately left wanting a little more from him in the athletics department. He just isn't a guy who profiles as an athlete who will be breaking away from Defenders or who is explosive enough to break free of a tackle, get to the edge and cut loose along the byline whilst stiff arming a player to floor on his way to the house. He does offer a superbly built frame to act as a battering ram on early down work and has buttery smooth hands to offer a skillset in the passing game, but he doesn't have the ability to cut loose on a wheel route and gain a huge number of yards. He has good contact balance and bounces off Defenders well when given a lane to run through and uses his bulk to his advantage, but his lack of end power means he can't keep the legs churning and move the pile for those sneaky extra yards. Having said all that, if he's given a clean field to run into he offers enough speed and awareness to go all the way from 35/40 yards out but after that he may get caught by the faster Defenders in the NFL. This was evident in the game in 2019 against Alabama, when he just didn't have the juice to go all the way and was stopped on the two.

NFL Landing Spot

Mitchell joins the 49ers as a depth piece at this point in time but knowing how Shanahan uses his Running Backs Mitchell may get some useful reps.

Gerrid Doaks

Cincinnati | RB | 6'1" | 225lbs

I really struggled with where to rank Gerrid Doaks, Rush Nation. I had no idea how I should approach adding him to this list, and it turned out to be a real head and heart dilemma, but ultimately the head won out and unfortunately for Doaks, it meant that he tumbled down the list. Normally, I would wait to tell you why he fell here in my ranks but to clarify things and bring an equilibrium to the write up, I'm going to tell you now. It's the injury concerns that worry me too much with Doaks. He has missed considerable time during his Collegiate career due to injuries and while we've seen Frank Gore play forever in the NFL after two ACL injuries in college, Doaks isn't quite at Gore's level. Well, not yet anyway and therein lies my dilemma. When I flicked on Doaks' tape, I was taken aback by just how much I love how he plays Running Back. Doaks is a monster in stature and in how he runs with the ball in his possession. I won't go too much into the weeds on his skills and playing style, but let's just say he is super aggressive and runs like a bull in Pamplona after having several cans of a well known energy drink and a sniff of smelling salts. If that doesn't quite paint you a clear enough picture of the violence that occurs when Doaks runs, check out his game against Austin Peay in 2020. After driving to the one yard line he then smashes through the line on the very next play as if he was a wrecking ball for his second touchdown of the day. Physical isn't quite enough when it comes to describing his play style; there has to be a better adjective for the aggression. After Redshirting his first year in 2016, Doaks still practiced in full for The Bearcats and was awarded UC's *Co-Offensive Scout Team Player of the Year,* which shows how well he was thought of in the dressing room by the staff.

As a Redshirt Freshman, Doaks wasn't anything to write home about statistically but he managed to start to gain a handle on becoming the team's lead Running Back and even though he missed three games due to an injury, he still manages to lead the team in rushing yards while having less rushing attempts than Mike Boone and Quarterback Hayden Moore. After a largely ineffectual six carry game against Michigan in week one, his week two performance was much better and his week eight appearance against Tulane was his season best; he recorded 17 carries for 149 yards. He finished his Freshman year with 87 carries, 513 yards and two touchdowns and a further 14 catches for 135 receiving yards and a solitary score.

After missing the entire 2018 campaign with an injury suffered in pre-season, Doaks was ready to roll in 2019. He wasn't the lead back, yet he still improved on his Freshman year stats. Stuck behind Michael Warren, Doaks managed to tally 100 rushing yards over the season and played in 12 games for Cincinnati. He only went over the 100 yard mark once, and that was in week seven against Connecticut when he carried the ball 13 times for 123 yards and a touchdown. Doaks did have another good game against Tulsa, when he scored twice and reached 91 yards off of 17 carries but also caught two passes for 28 yards and another touchdown in the receiving game. He would end his year with 526 yards off of 100 carries and score five times on the ground while catching eight passes for 70 yards and a score.

2020 saw Doaks finally take over the role of lead Running Back for The Bearcats, and he played well in the nine games he suited up for. He did miss one game due to injury, however. I mentioned the Austin Peay game at the start and he blew up in his first game as lead back, carrying the ball just ten times for a meagre 20 yards yet scored three times and caught four passes for another 64 yards and a score through the air. I would like to point out that the Austin Peay game was a blowout and Doaks wasn't required to play much, not that he wasn't effective. He then had back to back 100 yard plus games against South Florida and Southern Methodist with the latter of those two games being his best. He carried the ball 20 times for 105 yards and two touchdowns. The biggest game of the year on the ground came in the week six matchup against Houston, where Doaks would carry the ball 16 times and rack up 184 yards and find paydirt once. He also had three catches for 30 yards in this game. In his final year as a Bearcat, Doaks put up his best season-long numbers of his career, posting 673 yards off of 144 carries and found the end zone seven times. He also caught the ball 14 times for 202 yards and two touchdowns. To top it off, Doaks earned his bachelor's degree in criminal justice in April 2020, showing he's not just brawn but brains too.

So here we are, the breakdowns done and I feel Doaks could well be the steal of this Draft Class from the Running Back position. Because of how littered with injuries his past is, NFL teams may be wary of him and his stock could fall making him a bargain. He has all the ability in the world when it comes to being a three down Running Back and while he hasn't had a huge number of receptions during his college career, his 2020 14.4 yards per catch is frankly ridiculous and he showed that he can run a wheel route out of the backfield but also be available in the dump off game and turn it into a big gain. As a runner, Doaks is a beast and uses his huge frame and square shoulders to level Defenders at the punt of contact. He isn't just a bruiser though; he is smart when running and uses his legs and feet to great effect when running through contact though he isn't a blazer, more of a bulldozer.

NFL Landing Spot

According to Lee, Doaks can be the RB1 in Miami next year. Has huge upside and should be your late round flier.

CHAPTER 18

Wide Receivers

Written by Chris Mitchell

Ja'Marr Chase

LSU | WR | 6'1" | 200 lbs

Aggressive competitiveness and physicality are what first hits you like a Mac Truck when you watch Ja'Marr Chase play Football. He is head and shoulders above the rest of the field in this year's draft. Only playing two years of ball at LSU hasn't hurt his draft stock one bit and opting out of the 2020 season might have done him some favours. During his record-setting 2019 season, he played alongside Justin Jefferson and Clyde Edwards-Helaire who both allowed him to get open and not see double coverage as much. If Chase had returned for the 2020 season, it is likely he would have seen almost entirely bracket coverage and this would have caused two issues. Lesser targets due to better coverage and increased injury risk due to more contact. His 2019 numbers were so good, that playing another season could have hurt his Draft stock due to his numbers regressing without that high powered offence he played in. Finally, COVID could have been a good thing for him. Chase set the SEC record for Receiving Touchdowns (20) and Receiving Yards (1,780) while winning the *Biletnikoff Award* and being a unanimous *All-American*.

When you sit down and watch Chase, it's evident he has all the tools to be an elite prospect in the NFL. 2019 proved this, and if you want to go and watch one game, watch his game against Alabama. Chase took Trevon Diggs to school. Diggs was considered one of the best man coverage defenders in the 2020 class and Chase taught him a lesson. He allowed Chase to rack up 140 yards off six receptions and one touchdown. The way Chase can analyse the Cornerbacks plans pre-snap is scary. On one play in that game, Chase was given yardage as Diggs wasn't playing press at the line of scrimmage. Chase ran a comeback and as Diggs was playing off Chase, it gave the advantage to Diggs to intercept the ball. Chase pre-jumped his route and was able to steal the ball before Diggs could jump. Later in the game, Diggs was playing press and Chase used his arms and physicality to stop Diggs blocking him at the line and allowed Chase to win over the top and gain 15 yards. The most impressive play Chase made in this game was when Diggs was playing press coverage at the line on the first play of the game. Diggs faked a step towards Chase hoping that Chase would get stuck and then not get into his route on time. Chase anticipated the fake and exploded off the line forward again using his hands to push Diggs off his step. This allowed Chase to break free down the line and take the reception to the house. A dominant display from the next Wide Receiver off the draft board?

2019 saw Ja'Marr Chase finish with 1,780 yards off 84 receptions and 20 touchdowns. As mentioned, it was a historic year for the Sophomore which was a spectacular leap from his Freshman season. He finished 2018 with 23 catches for 313 yards and three visits to the end zone. The game that put the world on notice as to just how good Chase was in 2019 was his utter obliteration of the Vanderbilt defence. In just his third game of the season, Chase scored four times and caught ten balls for 229 yards. He showed game-breaking speed before and after the catch, as well as quality crisp route running in the short and long areas of the field. Chase also has great yards after the catch ability using his physicality to gain more yards.

Ja'Marr Chase isn't the largest Wide Receiver, but he has exceptional jumping ability and hand strength that enables him to win almost every contested catch. He is rugged and tough and wants to win every catch or collision. His spring and body control are unworldly and his anticipation means he can get into position to make the catch. He shows a good ability to track the ball in flight and position himself in front of the defender to make sure he catches the ball. This positioning is what also makes his yards after the catch so good, because he is always ahead of the Defender when hitting the ground or at the catch point. Where Chase is surprisingly good is over the top on go and nine routes. Chase isn't the fastest Receiver and hasn't got Henry Rugg's speed, but he makes up for this in how he fights for the ball and uses his hands to create separation and hold Defenders at bay.

Chase doesn't need huge separation as his hands are so reliable and he knows it too, meaning he's not worried about catching the ball and then getting into free space. This normally leads to some focus drops for other Receivers, but Chase does not appear to suffer from this issue. He doesn't telegraph his routes either and can sell one route to a Defender whilst running another. We saw this in the aforementioned Alabama game where he undercut Diggs on a comeback route. He uses his hands on almost every route to keep his body free of contact from the Defender allowing him to get into position to make the catch. Double the hand fighting with his tracking ability means that Chase has translatable skills for the NFL at the next level. Ja'Marr isn't the freak athlete we have seen in recent years like DK Metcalf or some Veterans in the NFL like Julio Jones. It's this lack of athleticism that could cause some teams to fade Chase slightly. Chase looks like a 4.6 runner, not the 4.4 we expect from elite prospects but he may run slightly faster at the combine. If he can run a 4.5/4.48 then his Draft stock will be sky-high. It's his handwork, YAC and want to win that make Chase special. One other knock back is his run blocking. He sometimes looks simply disinterested, and some teams will want him to be committed on every play. Not a deal-breaker, but it could hurt his stock nevertheless.

NFL Landing Spot

Immediately becomes the Alpha Wideout for former teammate Joe Burrow and flies in with a floor of WR2 in that Bengals Offence. LSU is coming to town, hold on to your hats.

DeVonta Smith

Alabama | WR | 6'1" | 175 lbs

Ladies and Gentlemen, I give you the 2020 *Heisman Trophy* Winner and first Wide Receiver since 1991 to scoop the award: DeVonta Smith.

Separation, that's what Smith gives you in abundance. I need to start this player profile by saying the Tyreek Hill comparisons in separation and speed are down right ludicrous. While Smith is silky smooth in his route transition and explosive in his get off from the line of scrimmage like Hill, there are several reasons why I believe the comparison to be ridiculous, but we will get into those later on. After all, the winner of the *Biletnikoff Award* and record setter of the single season touchdown total (23) a year after Chase (20) has some sparkling history and skills we need to touch upon.

As a Freshman in 2017, Smith was sitting behind some of the most formidable College Wide Receivers we have seen in recent years so it seems reasonable that he only started eight games. Being down the depth chart behind players like Calvin Ridley, Jerry Jeudy and Henry Ruggs gave Smith time to develop without being thrust into the limelight, but it also allowed him to learn from some of the very best. Smith carved out 160 yards and three touchdowns off of just eight receptions in those eight games. It wasn't until the departure of Calvin Ridley that Smith started to stretch his legs in 2018.

2018 saw Smith move into a more prominent role alongside Ruggs and Jeudy. He played 13 games and saw much more action as a Sophomore with Ridley now an Atlanta Falcon. Smith caught 42 passes and took six of them to the house. He racked up an impressive 693 yards, averaging 16.5 yards per catch. It was at this point we were treated to the Ruggs/Smith speed show opening up in front of our very eyes. And what a show it was to become. It would be the week 12 game against the Oklahoma Sooners where Smith would flash his future potential. He caught six passes in that game, turning them into 104 yards and a score. The Sooners had no answer for the electric routes and sudden speed that Smith offered up.

2019 rolled around and Smith stepped up again, in my eyes becoming the number one Wide Receiver for Alabama. Whilst all the focus was on Ruggs and Jeudy in the upcoming Draft class, Smith was outstanding. The only metric in which Smith trailed Jeudy in 2019 was receptions. Jeudy had 77 whilst Smith had 68. He actually had 10 less plays from scrimmage than Jeudy did so that number could have been even closer had they played the same number of plays. All the hype about the team's speed demon was focused on Henry Ruggs. In comparison, Smith blew Ruggs away in his Junior year in all metrics except yards per reception and even then Smith trailed Ruggs by just two inches. Smith played all 13 games, hauling in 68 receptions for 1256 yards at an average of 18.5 yards per reception and finishing the season with 14 touchdowns. 14! Jeudy only had 10 and Ruggs eight. Had Smith declared for the 2020

NFL Draft would we have seen him as a Raider and not Ruggs? Who knows for certain but the way the 2020 Draft went, stranger things have happened. Smith may have been the most underrated Wide Receiver in the 2019 season to all but those hardened College Football fans. It's almost like Smith needed to go out and prove a point in the 2020 season as to why he should be selected ahead of so many others in the Draft process. Oh boy, did Smith go out and do just that. As mentioned, Smith set the single season touchdown record in 2020 with 23 scores. He amassed 117 receptions for a huge 1,856 yards, averaging 15.9 yards per catch. Jalen Waddle leaving the season early helped Smith become the Alpha but we now know he was secretly the guy anyway. He was locked in with Mac Jones this year and only had three games without a trip into the end zone. He also turned up when needed most in the two games against Notre Dame and Ohio State. He scored three times in both games, had 130 receiving yards against ND and 215 yards off 12 receptions in the National Championship win. Smith, did his draft stock no harm at all throughout the entire season and even when Waddle was playing, Smith racked up huge games against Mississippi and Georgia. Smith showed that he can go up and win the ball in contested catches but can also take any play to the house with his speed.

Studying tape on Smith made me realise just how good he is as a route runner; his explosive release is quite something. But it's his crispness of direction and suddenness of direction change that really set him apart from all but Chase. He is so fast and instant when he shifts direction, it makes running a route with him in man coverage all but impossible due to his speed. He also has a high IQ for reading Defenders when they try to set him up to break a certain way or try using the sideline as a buffer. Smith will often add a comeback or a double break into his route in order to throw off the Defender. Not only does he have the speed to burn a man over the top, but he has great hands, which means he can take smaller passes the distance too because of his yards after the catch ability. His small size makes him hard to tackle but it could also be his kryptonite at the next level. How many small Wide Receivers do we see get blasted by a Linebacker for running a crossing route into the middle of the field?

NFL Landing spot

Reunited with former teammate Jalen Hurts in Philly is a good thing. Smith is locked in as the star Wide Receiver for The Eagles and can be used all over the field as Hurts' go to guy.

Rashod Bateman

Minnesota | WR | 6'2" | 210 lbs

I fell in love with Rashod Bateman when I saw him face Purdue in the 4th game of the 2019 season. He reeled in six catches for 177 yards and two touchdowns. It wasn't his stupidly high yards per catch (29.5) that mesmerised me; it was his hands. Before this game, Bateman had already torched South Dakota State and Fresno State for over 100 yards in his first two games. Against Purdue, however, was his blow-up moment. He won the ball in all areas of the field, and his second touchdown showed his separation ability. While Bateman isn't a true burner like Henry Ruggs last year, he is still fast enough to create some separation using speed. It's his aggression and route running that mean Bateman is a top-level route runner, which the NFL scouts will lap up.

2019 was a career year for Bateman. Many expected 2020 to be a continuation of this, with Tanner Morgan still under centre. I should point out that while the Golden Gophers were in playoff contention last year going 11-2, and Morgan is a good College Quarterback, he is by no means a great Quarterback. Morgan is unlikely to make an impact in the NFL. The fact that Bateman was able to elevate the whole team along with 2019 draftee Tyler Johnson, shows what a talent he is.

During the 2019 season, Bateman put up historic numbers for the College of Minnesota. His 11 touchdowns were good enough to see him secure the most by a Sophomore in School history (third-most in a single season in School). He posted the second-most receiving yards in school history: 1,219 which was also a new Sophomore record. He was also one of the 12 finalists that were selected for the *Biletnikoff Award* and the only Big Ten player to be named a semi-finalist. He did all of this off just 60 receptions. As I said, Bateman and Johnson tore it up.

Jumping back in time quickly, Bateman was prolific as a Freshman too. He set school records in 2018 for receptions (51), yards (704) and was one touchdown (6) shy of setting the touchdown record also. He carried these hot numbers into his breakout year in 2019 and as I mentioned, the draft community expected the same transference into 2020. Then Covid happened. Bateman opted out due to health concerns and as the Big Ten wasn't playing Football either, he declared that he would be entering the 2021 NFL Draft. Once the Big Ten announced that they would be playing football, Bateman opted back in and as a fan, this was great news. The lack of training or knowing if the whole Big Ten was going to be playing ball shook up Minnesota and Bateman. Although he opted back out after five games, we were able to see his skill set on the gridiron. With Tyler Johnson operating predominantly out of the Slot in 2019, Bateman was primarily used on the outside. With Johnson gone in 2020, Bateman was allowed to move more freely across the line and showed he can play out of the Slot with ease, as well as control the outside. He finished 2020 with 36 receptions for 472 yards and two touchdowns. He averaged nearly 100 yards per game with 94.4 YPG in these five games and set a career-high in receptions (10) against Illinois. What I love most about Bateman is his catching and his hands. This is evident in the fact he has caught at least one pass in every one of his 31 career games, solid to say the least!

Hands, hands, hands. Bateman is a catch monster. When watching tape, the first thing that popped off the reel for me was how Bateman catches the ball. He isn't a body catcher at all. He always has his hands in exactly the right place and behind the balls trajectory. His finger triangle is delightful, and his hands engulf the ball as it hits his palms. Sticky mitts or not, Bateman is coming down with the ball. When catching the ball on the run, he always catches the ball in stride and ahead of him to allow him to continue the route or keep the ball away from Defenders. If going up for a jump ball, Bateman uses his physicality and hand strength to win at the point of catch and come down with the ball. These hands are among the best in the class in my opinion and will be a huge asset to any NFL team.

Bateman is built like an Alpha Receiver and while he isn't a mammoth like D.K. Metcalf, he has enough size and weight to throw down with the biggest corners. This size, coupled with his extraordinary hands means his jump ball win rate is delightfully high and it also means he is good after the catch. Bateman isn't the fastest guy, but he isn't that kind of player. He is more of a possession kind of guy with reliable hands. Saying that, I've seen him run a 4.40 40-yard dash in high school. Since then, he has added 15-20lbs so I expect him to run slower than last seen. He doesn't need that ticket speed to separate over the top. He uses his hands to fight off corners and his route running abilities to get more than enough distance between him and the Defender. Bateman's usage in the slot in 2020 meant that he added to his route tree and now runs all routes that are needed. A go or nine route isn't his strongest route. A lack of elite burst means he often doesn't run them, but if he is going up against a weaker corner he can use his size to get open over the top. One knock on Bateman is his aggression. While I'm all about it and love my Receivers to fight for every play, I can see him perhaps garnering some flags at the next level due to this physicality and handsy nature. However, this is a dream play style for me and the fact my autocorrect turned Bateman into Batman is surely saying something?

NFL Landing Spot

Finally Lamar Jackson has a Dawg on the outside. Bateman can play all over the park for The Ravens and be the other big target alongside Mark Andrews. WR2 all day for me.

Rondale Moore

Purdue | WR | 5'9" | 180 lbs

WILDCARD! Put simply, Rondale Moore has one year of explosive tape to go on and after his Freshman year, there really isn't much else to see. Moore has played just seven games since his first year and that will be the crux for many NFL teams, but when drafted Moore will offer a huge upside. Will they be getting the Freshman Moore, or the guy who seems to now be fully injured? The same thing could have and has been said about my boy Laviska Shenault, yet he finished his Rookie season with a bang and is now staring down the barrel of an Urban Meyer/Trevor Lawrence led offence at Jacksonville. Now, the talent was always there for Viska and the same can most certainly be said for Moore. Perhaps the multitude of ways that Purdue used him as a gadgety Swiss army knife type player put a bigger strain on Moore than his body could take? We have seen that Laviska can be effective if his rushing role was scaled back so why not for Moore? So many questions and as of this moment, no answers. One final question is, how do you talk about someone with only one and a half years worth of Football to breakdown? With absolute delight is how. It will mostly be based on his breakout Freshman 2018 season as that's where he put all his best stuff together. It will be the season I base my argument on for Moore to be one of the most devastating Wide Receivers in the NFL for years to come. So hold on tight Rush Nation, here we go!

After committing to Texas, Moore pulled a de-commitment and then committed to Purdue, saying he hadn't had a proper chance to choose a school due to his football commitments at High School. Moore was the first four star recruit Purdue had had in what seemed like a lifetime and it was immediately on show in his first game for The Boilermakers. Moore set a school record all purpose yards total with 313 yards and man o' man did he get them all manner of ways. Moore had 11 receptions for 109 yards and a touchdown, two rushing attempts for 79 yards and a touchdown, and then a further five kick returns for 125 yards. Just like that, Moore was a name we all knew. Week two was a bit of a come down as Moore only had three receptions for 16 yards. Undeterred, Rondale lit the afterburners again in week three against Missouri with another 11 receptions for 137 yards and a score. He was exhibiting signs that he was already NFL material with the way he was reading zone coverage and how he used his physical aggression to win collisions against Defenders. Not only this, but Moore was showing that his role as a kick returner was no joke as he had another 56 yards also against Missouri. Moore would have the game of his season and arguably one of Purdue's biggest wins in recent memory in week seven against an unbeaten Ohio State. The 'Rondale Moore Show' as I like to call it was electric, mesmerizing and a lesson in how to play Wide Receiver as a smaller-bodied guy. He finished the game with 12 catches for 170 yards and two touchdowns, 2 rushing attempts for 24 yards and four kick returns for 58 yards in the 49-20 shellacking of The Buckeyes. If you were a NFL scout at that game, you would have walked away with a notebook full of good comments and a mind full of visuals you wouldn't forget in a hurry. There was one play that exhibited all that Moore has to offer as a Wide Receiver at the next level. On a third and seven, he takes a short pass to the outside with his speed and makes a player miss a foot tackle, before getting to the first down line. Hee then keeps his feet churning while collecting two players on the forward run. He brought the fight to these two guys by keeping running right at them. He shed one and broke free of the other because of the aggression he offered into the tackle. He then turns on the jets and is able to use his ability to read the field to take the best angle into the end zone. It was also simple seven yard catches that Moore sees space on a comeback route while analysing zone or man coverage that makes his yards after the catch ability tantalising. Moore finished 2018 with 114 catches for 1,258 yards and 12 touchdowns. He also had 662 yards returning, which is a huge weapon in his arsenal.

As a smaller bodied Receiver, Moore needs to take care of his body and avoid big hits in the centre of the field. He offers teams that home run ability on any play and if fit, can be devastating. It was nice to see him bounce back in 2020, offering some big plays again after an injury riddled 2019. Moore needs to prove he can stay fit. That is his biggest hurdle in becoming a team's top weapon in the NFL. This seems to be the common theme amongst my next couple of receivers, but Moore has that X factor and I think he can win games on his own a couple of times a year in the NFL.

Moore exhibits the natural ball catching that I really look for in my Wide Receivers and then has the dangerous YAC ability to take the top off a defence. He scans the field pre-snap and spot gaps in coverage is something he doesn't have to learn in the NFL. That means one more thing he doesn't need to focus on while keeping his jersey clean. Once off the line, Moore shows a good understanding of the three levels of defence and can use his eyes to sell a route to a Linebacker or Cornerback to make better separation. If he manages to get open over the top, it's good night. If a team can exploit his Freshman years production and make the most of Moore's talents, he could be a draft steal as I think he will go much later than a couple of the guys who are after him in my list.

NFL Landing Spot

Moore lines up across from Nuke and AJ Green with Christian Kirk, Larry Fitz and Andy Issabella all still fighting for targets. Luckily Moore is a playmaker and has top level speed. Coupled with his slot play and the fact The Cardinals run the most four wide sets in the league means Moore should be just fine.

Jaylen Waddle

Alabama | WR | 5'10" | 182 lbs

The Jaylen Waddle scout beat on forums would have you believe there are folk out there who believe that Waddle is a better overall prospect than Henry Ruggs was last year. If we believe that hype, then Waddle should be drafted high, very high; top 15 high. I think his size will need to be hugely held up by his cleat stripping speed and we have seen smaller Receivers struggle to keep up with the constant hammering of the elite defenders in the NFL. What he does with exceptional skill is his route running and technical ability when catching the ball, which will look great on his scouting reports. As a Receiver, Waddle does things that most College athletes have to learn once they get drafted. His sideline technique is top drawer, and he keeps his pads and shoulders towards the ball, making an easy target for the Quarterback to hit but also makes catching the ball easier as he is primed to make the catch.

Oh, and did I mention Waddle was fast? No? Well, he is lightning quick, so much so that if you're watching on a standard definition channel he is blurry. The speed/route running combination is perfect and as Alabama used him out of the slot primarily he could break either way and caused destruction on the reg. Waddle was poised for a breakout in 2020, once Ruggs and Jeudy had departed for the NFL. However, lady luck wasn't on his side as an ankle injury in week five put his season on ice until the Natty against Ohio State, a game in which his counterpart, Devonta Smith went wild in the first half. Three receptions for 34 yards in a comeback from injury blowout in the National Title game wasn't how Waddle would have wanted his return to go, but the win helps.

As a Freshman, Waddle was behind the same stalwart names that Smith sat behind as well, and it took all of Waddle's abilities to show out in 2018. He never had more than six receptions and that was in a game versus Citadel. Waddle only had three games over 100 yards and all came off four or less receptions. Against Louisiana in week five he exploded, taking two of his three receptions to the house and ended up with 138 yards. He also had one punt return for 63 yards, proving his speed is valuable in two facets of the game; Offense and Special Teams. In week eight he turned four receptions into 117 yards and a touchdown and in week 13 against Georgia he totalled 113 yards off four receptions and had a score. Waddle finished his bit part season with 45 receptions for 848 yards and seven touchdowns, off of limited work, I'd say that was pretty good going with flashes of excellence thrown in.

2019 saw Waddle actually regress in the numbers department. There were five games where he only had one reception and had a season high five receptions against Duke and Arkansas. Waddle only went over 100 yards once against Western Carolina and that was off just three receptions. Again though, he demonstrated all the traits a scout looks for in a Slot Wide Receiver. Even though Waddle has played all over the line in his three seasons at

'Bama, he is, in my opinion, most dangerous out of the slot. He does, however, need to work a little on his intermediate route running. This could be because of his speed that he is often too fast in and out of breaks to allow things to develop and the space required to work the throw into is that much tighter that he can be off point occasionally. Waddle ended his Sophomore season with 33 receptions, 560 yards and six touchdowns. He was however, still a danger in the return game finishing the season with 662 yards and two touchdowns.

2020 as mentioned, didn't go to plan for Waddle although he finished the year with 28 receptions for 591 yards and four touchdowns. In the four games he played (not counting the game he got injured or the Natty) he went over 120 yards in them all and never had fewer than five receptions. Waddle was balling out alongside his stablemate Smith until the ankle injury ruined his year. In week one he had 134 yards and two touchdowns against Missouri and in week four against Georgia, Waddle owned the game with six receptions for 1616 yards and a score.

Waddle can be a game changing player with elite hands and speed, but he needs to stay out of trouble in the middle of the field in order to prolong his career. The lack of production is my only real concern and if 2020 had gone differently, he would be higher for me. What I do love about Waddle is his NFL readiness right now. Seeing him play again in the National Championship game was a huge bonus, as it proves he can play again before the Draft. Obviously, it's a bigger coup for Waddle as he got to show the world again that he is Football ready although he was ineffective. Waddle by name but not by nature, his ability to cut through defenses for huge yardage is invaluable, whether he caught it off a dump-off pass or it was a bob over the top. That's where Waddle is superb, his ability to play in all three levels of the defence. It's almost as if he is playing at normal speed when everyone is in slow motion. He just needs to work on developing his route running in the middle of the field when he runs out of the slot, as he can sometimes be hasty in his movements and may cause timing issues in tight windows. If he's fully healed after the injury then perhaps I'm down on Waddle too much but going on what I have, this is where he fell.

NFL Landing spot

Jalen Waddle reunites with Tua in Miami and becomes the go to guy for his former teammate. Waddle has a huge upside with his speed and big play abilities.

Tylan Wallace

Oklahoma State | WR | 6'0" | 185 lbs

Right, Rush Nation, it's time for my first public service announcement and instruction of the Playbook. Go and watch some tape of Tylan Wallace and tell me if he looks like he is six feet tall and 185 pounds? I don't think he does. We are used to Colleges enlarging their players physical traits and this could be the case right here. That shorter, slighter build in Wallace will make him more suited to the Slot Receiver position in the NFL. For The Cowboys, Wallace was mostly used on the right side of the field and occasionally from the slot. Now having said that, Wallace has a unique style of getting separation that I will get to in a little bit, but before that we have to talk some history.

2017 saw Wallace recruited from South Hills High School where he ranks among the top 15 players in Texas High School football history in terms of career receiving yards. He finished his HS career with 3,760 yards and 48 touchdowns on 182 receptions. As a Freshman for Oklahoma State, Wallace played in all 13 games, logging seven receptions for 118 yards. He also saw action as OSU's punt returner and as part of the kickoff return unit. Six of his seven receptions on the season resulted in a first down and he was also targeted on six third-down attempts and converted four of them. His big two games saw him catch three passes for 49 yards at Iowa State and two catches for 49 yards at Pittsburgh. Wallace only featured as a Wide Receiver in five games but only caught a pass or more in four of those five games. Against my Virginia Tech Hokies he didn't manage a catch but did log a tackle after an interception.

2018 was a much more productive year for The Cowboy as he was featured more heavily in the passing game. He managed to play in all 13 games in an up and down season for OSU. Wallace, however, was outstanding and made it to the final three selected players for the *Biletnikoff Award*. As impressive as his year was, in 2018 it was his games against the top ranked teams The Cowboys faced that really made Wallace stand out from the crowd. Against Texas, Wallace caught 10 passes for 222 yards and two touchdowns. Two weeks later against a good Oklahoma team he again caught ten balls for 220 yards this time and again found the end zone twice and in doing so became the first player in school history to post two games with over 200 yards against ranked opponents in a single season. Then in the following week against a ranked West Virginia, Wallace posted seven catches for 62 yards and another two touchdowns. Before this historic feat, between weeks two and five, Wallace posted over 100 yards in each game. What impressed me massively when looking into Wallace's superb season was how he led the nation with 63 receptions of 10 yards or longer showing that he has big play ability and can get open, one of the knocks on him coming out of High School. Wallace finished the 2018 campaign with 86 catches for 1,491 yards with 12 touchdowns and was primed for another huge year in 2019.

2019 saw Wallace turn on the heat for the first eight games until an ACL injury would derail the rest of his season. Through eight games Wallace led the FBS in the yards per reception category and also ranked second in the BIG 12 in touchdowns. Wallace had a huge 11 catch game against Texas Tech in which he totaled 85 yards and a score. Against McNeese State Wallace tore the roof off in week two, taking five catches to the end zone three times and racking up 180 yards. He finished his half season with 53 receptions for 903 yards and eight touchdowns, oh what could have been.

So to 2020, Wallace again played in all 10 games for the The Cowboys, showing that he had fully recovered from the ACL injury that ruined his 2019. But what Wallace lacked in 2020 was trips into the end zone. Even though there weren't many touchdowns to be had, Wallace still continued to post up a big Yards per Reception number, finishing the season with an average of 15.6. He also had the huge games his past had been littered with going over 90 yards in five of the 10 games and over 100 yards three times. Good Lord almighty, does Wallace like to play Texas. After tearing them a new one in 2018 he again put them to the sword, catching 11 passes for 187 yards and two touchdowns in week 5. He also posted up a big game against Kansas, scoring twice and amassing 148 yards off of nine catches. Overall the shortened season saw Wallace finish with 59 catches for 922 yards and six touchdowns. Coming off an ACL injury, I'd take that all day and twice on Sundays.

As a whole package, it's hard to say what Wallace can really do in the NFL. Seeing as he spent so much of his time glued to one side of the perimeter, he naturally looks as if that will be his role going forward. However, in 2020 we saw him use more across the line than in previous years and it worked well for him. He makes terrific big plays over the top and is dangerous in contested catches due to his toughness and great hands. It is these hands that are so obviously helpful in the arm fighting aspect of his game too. He isn't a fast guy at all however,, he has good bursts off the line of scrimmage and uses his body and arms well when engaging with Defensive Backs within the first ten yards of play. He often uses his arms to leverage the Defender away from him, using a good under arm technique and then has good ball locating skills to spot the ball and come down with the catch. He won't win a foot race but doesn't need to as he has such good hands and can win at the top of the route.

NFL Landing Spot

Wallace joins Bateman at the Ravens to make sure Lamar Jackson has some serious targets now. Wallace can play all over the line and be the aggressor for The Ravens.

Terrace Marshall Jr

LSU | WR | 6'4" | 200 lbs

The ultimate backup Wide Receiver, until thrust into the limelight in 2020. That perhaps isn't a fair take on a Receiver who looks as every bit NFL ready as the guys above him in this list, it's just a case of who has played behind at the Collegiate level. Marshall Jr was almost a no name in 2019, despite putting up a huge touchdown number. Why doesn't anybody really know him and what he's done, barring the 2020 campaign? Because he was playing behind the ethereal 2019 Wideouts JaMarr Chase and Justin Jefferson. Almost anyone in the College game would have trouble getting a look in with those guys ahead of them. Most thought that 2020 would be the year Marshall Jr would breakout as the number two opposite Chase. With Chase garnering all the coverage of the best Defenders, TMJ would be able to run wild and score plenty. What happened in reality was far from that; Chase held out and Terrace balled out in spectacular fashion, really bolstering his draft stock even with average Quarterback play. However, before we get to his year as the Alpha in LSU's Wide Receiver room, we need to mention the baron times. 2018 was not a good year to be Marshal Jr.

Devoid of chances and lacklustre would be how I would describe Marshall Jr's Freshman season. In an average year for LSU, Marshall Jr was never used as a weapon and was primarily a backup Wide Receiver. In fact, I will go as far as to say it was all horrendous. He never went over three receptions in the nine games, and he achieved that feat just once against Rice, turning those three receptions into 48 yards. Of the remaining eight games he played that year he had seven that were single reception games and one where he had two receptions. His best numbers for the season came against Mississippi, where he recorded one catch for 52 yards. TMJ did not find the paint once in his Freshman year. It must have been one hell of a lonely season right there. Trapped behind two of the very best can't have been easy, but Marshall forged forward and improved heading into 2019.

2019 was the year of finding the end zone for Marshall. In a year where Joe Burrow became a household name, JaMarr Chase was named the heir apparent to Julio Jones (in skill set at least) and Justin Jefferson played as an explosive a second fiddle as you could possibly ask for, Marshall managed to score 13 touchdowns. 13 in a year where he almost ghosted through the season unnoticed is a remarkable feat indeed. In a highly efficient first game of the season against Georgia Southern, Marshall had four receptions for 31 yards and three touchdowns. He then backed that up with a six catch, 123 yard, one touchdown performance against Texas. It was a year of making things count for Marshall Jr, who had a lean spell in the middle of the season with games in weeks five, six and eight with two, two and one receptions respectively. The week two performance over Texas proved to be the only week that he would go over the 100 yard mark but he would have a superb two game stretch against Georgia and Oklahoma in the two games prior to the Natty. Marshall scored twice in both games and had five for 89 yards against Georgia and six for 80 against The Sooners. In the National Championship game Marshall again found the end zone with one of his three receptions to cap off a productive season as the third Wide Receiver finishing the year with 46 receptions for 671 yards and 13 touchdowns.

Step up Senior, Chase was holding out due to Coronavirus so it was down to Marshall to embrace the number one Receiver position for LSU. After losing so much talent to the NFL, LSU was never going to be the same outfit they were in 2019. In a surprise week-one loss to Mississippi State, Marshal posted eight catches for 122 yards and two touchdowns, showing some rapport with Miles Brennan. The ever efficient Receiver only had two catches in week two but made them both count, finishing with 67 yards and two touchdowns. It was through his week three game in which he really made a statement to the watching world when he obliterated Missouri, finishing with a monster stat line of 11 receptions for 235 yards and three touchdowns. TMJ showed everything you want out of your Wide Receiver in this game. YAC for days, the ability to win jump balls, safe and reliable hands and for me a size/speed mismatch quality that is often overlooked by the casual fan. In the final game of the season for Marshall Jr, he blew up again. This time against a good Texas A&M defence, he posted numbers of 10 receptions for 134 yards and a touchdown. After this performance TMJ decided to opt out of the rest of the season and prepare for the NFL Draft.

At six feet four and 200 pounds, Marshall Jr is already a huge problem for Defensive Backs to deal with. He is fast, although not electric and has good jump ability which helps him win in those contested catch situations. His size means that he will be a big time red zone weapon and Quarterbacks will love the way he runs corner and post routes in the end zone. Not only is he tall, but he has great range which means he plucks the ball out of the sky when it could have been closer to him. Having a good wingspan will indeed be another piece of ammo to his already deadly arsenal of size and speed for the end zone targets he will surely get. Had LSU not trotted out three Quarterbacks, the offensive line was better and JaMarr Chase played, Marshall could have had a huge season in 2020.

NFL Landing Spot

The Panthers give new boy Sam Darnold a weapon to prowl along the perimeter. As Darnold improves, expect big things from the biggest target in Carolina. TMJ won't get the downfield work but targets inside the 20 and redzone should make him relevant.

Kadarius Toney

Florida | WR | 5'11" | 193 lbs

CHOMP CHOMP! Big-time athlete is Kadarius Toney, or at least that is how he was labeled coming out of High School when starting out as a Gator. Well, I think that was initially the plan for Jim McElwain as Toney was given the designation UT, utility. Not a label anyone wants, is it? You don't see Laviska labeled as UT even though he runs with the football too! The reason Toney came to be labelled UT was he played Quarterback in High School and was a big-time dual threat weapon. In his Junior year, he threw for 3,604 yards, while rushing for another 896 yards, while scoring a combined 53 touchdowns and becoming an all state selection. In his last year of High School Toney finished with 2,894 passing yards, totaling 894 rushing yards and 47 total touchdowns again being selected for the all state team. The Gators didn't recruit Toney to play Quarterback but as an athlete who would eventually find his place. It took Toney four years to finally find his place as a Wide Receiver but the story doesn't start there, he had to shed his UT tag first.

As a Freshman, Toney was used as a Running Back, a Wide Receiver and also as a Wildcat Quarterback. Toney battled through a range of injuries in 2017 and ended up only playing eight games. Technically he was only listed as a starter in two games, one as a Running Back and one at Wide Receiver. Over the eight games Toney never had more than four receptions or six rushing attempts. He scored his only touchdown, a rushing one, in the game against Kentucky. He also made just two passes from the Wildcat position; only one was completed and it went for 50 yards (also in the Kentucky game). As a Receiver in his Freshman year Toney tallied 15 receptions for 152 yards. As a Running Back Toney had 14 carries for 120 yards and one touchdown.

The game plan for Toney was much the same in his Sophomore season. He almost split his reps 50/50 between Running Back and Wide Receiver. Toney though added an evolution to his game on Special Teams as a kick returner. As a skill position player though, Toney struggled to make an impact for The Gators statistically. He never went above three receptions, except on two occasions; four times against Vanderbilt and six against Idaho. As a runner he never had more than four rushing attempts. Toney had a better season fitness wise and managed to play 12 games and as a Wildcat he made one pass for 20 yards and a touchdown. He finished his Sophomore year with 25 receptions for 250 yards and one touchdown. As a Running Back Toney carried the ball 21 times for 241 yards and never found pay dirt. As a returner, he had six returns for 133 yards.

The 2019 season was an injury riddled one for Toney. He missed large chunks of the season, managing to play only six games. He recorded the longest touchdown catch of his career in the season opener against Miami with a 66 yard catch. Toney made a few big plays in 2019 but as a whole was disappointing as both a Wideout and as a Running Back. He managed just 10 catches for 194 yards and a touchdown and 12 carries for 59 yards.

2020 was when he finally found his fire. 'Big play Toney' was in full effect and The Gators and Dan Mullen finally used him as one type of weapon (primarily):a Wide Receiver. He also showed a great connection with Kyle Trask. Toney did carry the ball but was loaded in the playbook much more as a Wideout. He also had a wild year as a kick and punt returner. He went over 100 yards four times and had a huge nine catch, 182 yard one touchdown game against LSU. He had an eight catch, 153 yard one touchdown game against the country's best defence in Alabama. Toney has such big play ability that he can turn any game on its head in an instant. As a runner Toney was effective, averaging 8.5 yards per carry yet he wasn't given enough of a shot at Running Back to make a difference. He did however, have one score in a three carry, 23 yard game against Missouri. Toney finished the year as a Receiver with 70 receptions for 984 yards and 10 touchdowns. He carried the ball 19 times for 161 yards and a score as a returner, he used his athleticism to return the 18 catches he made for 194 yards and a touchdown. Kyle Trask relied on Toney's ability to get open over the top or to use his speed to get open after using a double move on a route.

As a Wide Receiver Toney exhibits all the traits I look for in a dangerous Slot Receiver who can do damage at any point. He can be lined up anywhere along the line, even in the backfield, and will be a serious piece in the sweep game. As a pass catcher Toney is fast and is reportedly a 4.4 runner. He is smaller as a Wide Receiver but has a solid build and is slippery when trying to be tackled. His athletic background means he has a long stride and as a result tackling him is harder on the run because you can't grab both legs, leaving a body tackle as the only option. Being a track star also means he keeps his knees high, which makes tripping him harder. His thickness means he is also aggressive when engaging in contact through the tackle and he can gain extra yards by doing so. One of Toney's biggest qualities is his ability to make defences play wrong coverage or have to at least consider him as a threat on the field. He will draw coverage and mean a safety has to play slightly deeper due to his speed and big play threat, even if he doesn't catch the ball and is used as a decoy. As a Wide Receiver Toney's biggest problem will be his health, if he can stay fit he can be an electric playmaker and danger at any time.

NFL Landing Spot

Toney joins The Giants as the WR2 at best and is fighting The Shepdog and Darius Slayton for the rest of the snaps as Golladay is the clear leader in that WR room.

Marquez Stevenson

Houston | WR | 6'0" | 190 lbs

Now for my first Wide Receiver sleeper. Marquez Stevenson may be the fastest Wide Receiver you've never heard of. Whilst Waddle may have low 4.3 or even high 4.2 speed, Stevenson has acceleration in abundance and a second, third and even a fourth gear when needed and also has low 4.3 speed. The way he turns on the jets is frightening, but the best bit about his speed is that it isn't the only part of his game. While he may not be the tallest or weigh the most, his burst and explosive athleticism mean he can compete with any Defensive Back or Safety for the ball in jump situations and has natural hands. What he doesn't have is a developed route tree but some might say he doesn't need one when he can do so much with so little. Some of his highlights are stupendous.

Unusually, Stevenson has been in and around the Collegiate Game for five years. Even though he was only a modest three star recruit coming out of High School, there was enough interest in Marquez for him to choose Houston in their 2016 recruiting class. Things didn't go quite as Stevenson had planned as the blazer only played two games in 2016 after breaking his collarbone in pre-season. With two games under his belt in 2016, Stevenson was hoping that his College career would get into full swing at the start of the 2017 season. In a cruel twist of fate, he would rupture his ACL in spring practice, and that would keep him off the gridiron for the entire season, meaning he would never even see one snap in his Sophomore year.

Fully healed and ready to rumble, Stevenson played all 13 games for The Cougars in 2018. Man oh Man did he make a mark in his first Football season. Marquez had five games over 100 yards which led the ACC in games over 100 yards, he had 75 receptions which were good enough for second overall in the ACC and was third in the ACC with nine touchdowns. Stevenson showed speed that he didn't have when recruited out of High School. He was a 4.8/4.9 runner in High School but now looked like he was a four second flat runner. The kind of guy you just don't catch if he breaks free of the last man in the secondary. Stevenson put up huge numbers against Texas Tech in week three. He caught nine passes for 177 yards and two touchdowns. Again in week seven against Navy, he posted 141 yards off eight catches and two scores but also carried the ball twice for 13 yards and another touchdown, showing he had versatility and can be used as a decoy or a runner from the backfield. Stevenson was also used sparingly in the return game in 2018 and finished the season with 291 return yards. His total numbers at the end of his red shirt Sophomore year read 75 catches, 1019 yards and nine touchdowns with a further 14 carries worth 126 yards and two trips into the end zone. He accounted for 37.7% of his team's total receiving yards and 20% of his team's total receiving touchdowns. The human torch had been ignited in Houston, as if they needed more heat there, right?

In 2019 Stevenson was again prolific for The Cougars, leading the team in receptions with 50 over the year. The Cougars were not great in 2019, and that showed in Stevenson's numbers just by association with a poor team. Houston only managed four wins. In one of the losses Stevenson put up the biggest numbers of receiving yards in a single game for his career off just five catches. Marquez averaged 42.2 yards per catch against Southern Methodist. So off five receptions, Stevenson scored twice and finished with 211 yards. Again, against Navy in the final game of the season, he put up a huge game. He caught eight passes for 133 yards and two touchdowns. In an up and down year for Houston, Stevenson did fairly well, ending the season with 50 receptions for 907 yards and another nine touchdown season. He also had 17 kick returns for 473 yards and two touchdowns, highlighting his explosive plays and versatility. Due to a shortened season for UH in 2020 and two games missed due to injury, Stevenson only played five games for The Cougars. Over those five games, he still managed to average four receptions, 60.2 yards and one touchdown per game, while breaking the 100-yard mark twice.

What I like about Stevenson when watching his tape is how he does what he does so well. Most of his work is done over the top of Defenders as he is primarily used in the long ball game. He has enough size to be able to hang with Defensive Backs but not be bullied, and uses his fast twitch and long arms to get free at the line of scrimmage. You don't tend to see too many Corners playing press on him, fearing the second level speed that will burn them if he gets free. However, for Stevenson this isn't a huge problem as he is pretty fluid in his routes and sets Defenders up well with his stems. He uses his rapidness to change direction which creates enough separation so that he isn't drawn into an arm fight. It's like watching a slow-motion video; he glides past players as if they aren't even there. Have a look for one clip where he took a short eight yard slant route to the house and literally split the field in two right up the middle with all seven secondary members giving chase. He really is that fast. Unfortunately for Marquez, The Cougars used him mainly as a vertical and screen weapon which, while he does excel here, doesn't help his route tree expansion. This though, can be taught at the next level but until he shows he can offer more than that teams will know what he will be doing when on the field. His injury history might also be a niggle in the future, so let's hope he can stay fit going forward.

NFL Landing Spot

Marquez Stevenson has all the traits to push for a starting role in Buffalo alongside Diggs and company.

Amon-Ra St. Brown

USC | WR | 6'1" | 195 lbs

For those of you who aren't into your ancient Egyptian history, Amon-Ra was the God of the sun and the air, second only to Osiris who was Lord of the Underworld and judge of the dead. Fun fact: Amon-Ra St. Brown also has a brother named Osiris who plays Football for Stanford, and if the name St. Brown sounds familiar it's because his older brother already plays in the NFL as a Wide Receiver for The Green Bay Packers. Let's hope Amon-Ra exhibits slightly better hands than his brother did in the NFC Championship when he dropped one of the easiest catches he will likely ever see in Football. Luckily for us and for Amon-Ra, his hands are a delight. Like the God of the sun and the air and his namesake, our Amon-Ra is in full control when he leaves terra firma and launches into the air. He is well versed in contested catches and has superb body control when in flight, which enables him to adjust when needed. Declaring for the NFL Draft in his Junior year means we only have three years of tape to grab an opinion from but that's fine, we've seen so many other players in this portfolio with less to go off. So, let's take a look at St. Brown and his Freshman year as a Trojan for USC in 2018.

At theUniversity of Southern California, St. Brown started out faster than most of the Freshman's we've seen already. His 60 receptions led the team and as a true freshman he was just the fourth Trojan to do so in his first year. Another Trojan to do it was Bobby Trees in 2010 (that one's for you, Murf). He played in all 12 games for USC, which again, isn't something that Freshman tend to do with regularity, especially for a team with such prominence and stature as So-Cal. Amon-Ra was also fairly productive with his 60 receptions. He managed at least two or more catches in every game and was also used in the running game and even once as a punt returner. In his first game as a Trojan, Amon-Ra almost broke 100 yards as he notched up 98 yards receiving and a score off of seven catches and also had a rushing attempt for 12 yards. Then in week three Amon-Ra had his biggest game of the year against Texas. He caught nine balls for 167 yards and a touchdown. He never broke the 100 yard mark again in the season but was close in games against UCLA and Notre Dame with 98 and 94 yards respectively. He managed to finish his year turning in a team leading 60 receptions into 750 yards and three touchdowns, not too shabby for a true Freshman.

2019 saw Amon-Ra take a step forward in The Trojans offence and formed a formidable partnership with now NFL Wide Receiver Michael Pittman Jr. The pair were a constant threat for USC. However, it took St. Brown some time to get going. Well, I say that...it took one more week than in his Freshman year, as in week two against Stanford he scored twice and caught eight passes for 97 yards. It wouldn't be until week six that St. Brown would go over 100 yards receiving as he caught eight passes against Notre Dame for 112 yards and a score. Amon-Ra would then go over 100 yards in three of his last for games. He had 173 and a touchdown against Arizona State, 128 yards against UCLA and 163 yards against

Iowa. St. Brown finished his Sophomore season with 77 catches for 1,042 yards and six touchdowns. He subsequently underwent surgery for a sports hernia.

2020 was a super short season for Amon-Ra and The Trojans, playing only six games. In the six games he played, St. Brown was effective for USC. In the first two games of the season Amon-Ra went over 100 yards twice against Arizona State and Arizona. Seven receptions in both games led to 100 yards against Arizona State and 113 yards against Arizona. Those were the only two games where he went over 100 yards. He did however blow the roof off Washington State, finishing with seven receptions for 65 yards but scoring four touchdowns. Overall Amon-Ra finished 2020 with 41 receptions for 478 yards and seven touchdowns. He could well have replaced Pittman Jr. as the alpha dawg for The Trojans and his draft stock could well have been much higher for me if he blew up in 2020.

Amon-Ra is a true athlete and a superb prospect at Wide Receiver. He hasn't done as much as others in terms of numbers or doesn't have many highlight plays that pop off the film, but he has few weaknesses and is a supreme competitor. If 2020 had been a full season for him, then the rhetoric of the numbers could have been so much different but as it is it's what we have to go off. When watching St. Brown on tape, I love how he has gazelle-like agility when running his routes. He is fairly quick off the line of scrimmage and shows a good burst when catching the ball, always pointing his pads upfield as soon as he can to get those extra yards. His size is also good, and it shows when coupled with his tenaciousness in contented catches. He shows big play ability when going after the football in the air and catches the ball with his hands, not his body which is what I like to see from my Wide Receivers. He operated mostly out of the slot for The Trojans as Pittman Jr. was the bigger outside guy and that suited Amon-Ra perfectly. He is a catch monster between the numbers in the busy part of the field and uses his agility and elite hand-eye coordination to win catches and gain more yards in traffic. His agility means he can also adjust well when the ball is in flight and isn't scared to get into hand fights when doing so. Running predominantly out of the slot means he hasn't run the whole route tree so perhaps he would do well to study the play book to offer a larger service in his Wide Receiver room.

NFL Landing Spot

Amon-Ra St. Brown virtually walks into the job as one of The Lions top three guys behind veterans Williams and Perriman. Amon-Ra could be the alpha next year as those guys are on one year deals. By then St. Brown will be up to game speed and ready to produce.

Nico Collins

Michigan | WR | 6'4" | 220 lbs

After JaMarr Chase, Collins is the next Wide Receiver in my rankings to fully opt out of the 2020 season and focus on getting ready for the 2021 NFL Draft. Collins' draft stock could really have been helped by playing in 2020 but we can never really say that someone should have played or should have opted out. That decision was a personal one and one that only they could make but man I would have loved to see Collins use his mismatch size and strength in 2020. His tape from previous years was great and whilst he still has some things to work on, the way he bullies Corners and Safeties is a thing of beauty. One thing to note before we get into Nicos' tale of the tape is just how bad a spot Michigan is for Wide Receivers and their being productive. Anybody remember Donovan Peoples-Jones from this guide last year? He was the top prospect in his recruiting class and a five star recruit coming out of High School. Whilst the star rating and High School prospect system can be flawed, it is also a good barometer of overall skill. DPJ was a good Wideout as he joined The Wolverines but as soon as he became a Michigan player his ceiling was capped as they just don't use receivers enough and have streaky average Quarterbacks who can't maximise a players potential at the Wide Receiver position. Michigan predicates their game on a run first Offence and a strong Defense and now Jim Harbaugh has signed another contract, the chance a highly rated High School recruit goes to Michigan is even slimmer and if they do then prepare for them to flop at the Collegiate level. The fact Collins is even this high in my rankings shows how excited I am by his abilities and what I think he can translate skills wise to the NFL. Now to his past!

Coming out of High School ESPN had Collins ranked as the 21st Wide Receiver and the 2nd best in the State of Alabama. Typically for a Michigan Receiver Collins' College career started very very slowly. In his Freshman year he played just two games and caught three passes, one against Rutgers and two against South Carolina. Nico totaled 27 yards on the year. Not the flying start he would have liked, hell, not even a start really.

2018 was a much better year for the now Sophomore. Collins started 11 games as a Wide Receiver and appeared in the other two games. Playing in all 13 games for The Wolverines was a big step in the right direction as he was becoming a weapon in the pass game. Whilst his numbers weren't great, it was as good a year as any for the Michigan man. Collins wasn't used heavily in the pass game and never saw above six targets, this was against Northwestern in week five where he amassed 73 yards, a season and career high to that point. Against Rutgers in week 10, Collins showed his big play ability taking two of his three receptions to the house, finishing the game with 56 yards. Then again in week 12 against the sworn enemy Ohio State, he caught four passes for 91 yards and another two touchdowns. Nico finished his Sophomore year with 38 catches for 632 and six touchdowns. It's his impressive 16.6 yards per catch that shows Collins is a big play threat and moving into his Junior season he would show even more.

In 2019 Collins again progressed as a Wide Receiver in The Wolverines offence, but was still handcuffed by terrible Quarterback play and a run-first offence. Playing in all 12 games for Michigan and leading the team in touchdowns come the end of the year. Once again Collins never saw more than six catches but managed this feat twice in the year. He also improved on his yards per catch average over the year, showing superb separation at the line of scrimmage and managing to get open over the top of the defenders often. He was missed several times on deep balls that were guaranteed touchdowns by the myriad Quarterbacks that were used in 2019 by Michigan. In week six against Penn State, he caught six passes for 89 yards and two scores. Then in week 10 against Indiana, Collins had the best game of his career, he caught six balls which he shredded into 165 yards and three touchdowns. Nico would finish the season with just 37 receptions but with a yards per catch average of 19.7 he turned those few catches into 729 yards and a team leading seven touchdowns. He was named the team's Offensive player of the year and led the Big 10 with a yards per catch of 19.7 YPC.

No doubt holding out of the 2020 season hurt Collins' draft stock but we have enough tape from his time at Michigan to really see what he is capable of. It's his hugely translatable skills that mean he could be poised for a breakout in the NFL. Collins is an outside guy and uses his huge frame to box Defenders out along the sideline. We have seen this type of Wide Receiver do really well when transitioning from College to the big league; Tee Higgins was an outside guy for Clemson before being drafted. The thing Higgins had that Collins hasn't is a generational talent at the Quarterback and a coach who was willing to use him heavily in the pass game. Collins hasn't had that same luxury, however, he has shown us that his skills are there and waiting to be unleashed. His size mismatch will be a nightmare for smaller, faster Cornerbacks as he will use his leverage to create separation in the end zone and on fade and corner routes. His speed off the line of scrimmage is ok at best, but that isn't where he wins. He uses his strength and size to get open over the top. Even if someone gives him space and plays off him, he has the second gear speed that helps him to win on the go routes.

NFL Landing Spot

Aside from Brandin Cooks there isn't really anyone else to stop Collins walking straight in as a starter for the Texans. He can feast if Watson is the starter as he brings size and speed to the party in Houston.

Tutu Atwell - Louisville

Michigan | WR | 5'9" | 165 lbs

Funny story, Rush Nation. Well two stories actually. The first is a repeat of last year and this dude was my star Wide Receiver in *The 5 Yard Challenge* where I took those 5 Yard College boys to town and showed them how to do Fantasy on their own turf. If you didn't know, I took that crown and it sits perched nicely atop my head as I write this. The second story is if you Google 'Tutu Atwell stats', you get another Wide Receiver who played for The Golden Gophers in the mid nineties, this Tutu is our Tutu's father. Our Tutu's name is actually Chatarius Atwell but has been called Tutu in honor of his father for forever, as far as I can tell. This shows that our guy has pedigree, if nothing else. Atwell is our first truly undersized Wide Receiver and normally I like my guys big and strong, but Tutu is an athletic freak and has fast twitch movements for days. Atwell also impresses me in how he can be a team leader and can see the game developing before it does. This comes from his time at High School as the starting Quarterback for Miami Northwestern. Atwell was never going to play Quarterback for The Cardinals, as the talented dual threat Quarterback Malik Cunningham was also recruited in the same class as Atwell. Over his three years as a Cardinal, Atwell impressed and his biggest knock for playing at the next level is his size. Can he do it against the biggest baddest guys on the big blue marble? Well, let's see how he did in College.

As a Freshman in 2018 Atwell was a raw prospect at Wide Receiver and it showed in his usage. While he didn't have many reps under his belt at the position, he showed huge potential when given the opportunity to explode. It also didn't help Atwell that Cunningham hadn't been unboxed yet fully either and when those two got fully up to speed the lights would shine bright. Another reason why Tutu was hardly used is just how bad The Cardinals were in 2018, winning just one game. It wouldn't be until week five that Atwell had more than two catches in a game and in that game he turned four catches into 79 yards and two touchdowns against Georgia Tech. Then again he had a few down weeks with few receptions but in week seven he would go ham. Against Wake Forest, Atwell caught eight passes for 132 yards. He finished his Freshman campaign with 24 catches, 406 yards and two touchdowns. Fear not through, my Atwell lovers, as Malik Cunningham was about to be unleashed and Atwell would be given the space to reach his potential.

Once Atwell and Cunnningham had had spring training together, it became apparent that this relationship would be a blossoming one that would bear fruit for The Cards. In over 50% of Atwell's games in his Sophomore year, he went over 100 yards receiving. He scored a touchdown in over 50% of his games and went on to lead the ACC in reception yards and was also second in touchdowns. Atwell announced himself to the global stage just two years after playing Quarterback in High School. It didn't take long for him to get going and in week three against Western Kentucky he amassed 141 yards and three touchdowns off just four catches. Then in weeks eight to 11 he went berserk. Six catches, 122 yards and a score against Virginia. Six catches, 142 yards and a touchdown against Miami. Five catches, 110 yards and a score against NC State. Five catches, 152 yards and two trips into the end zone against Syracuse. In *The Music City Bowl* against Mississippi State, Tutu again went over 100 yards with a career high nine receptions for 147 yards and a score. He would finish his Sophomore season with 69 receptions, 1,272 yards and 12 touchdowns.

2020 was a shorter year for Atwell as after nine games he opted out of the rest of the season and declared he would be getting ready for the 2021 NFL Draft. Through the six games for The Cardinals as a Junior, he finished the year as the team's leading Receiver with 46 receptions for 625 yards and seven touchdowns. Only twice did he go over the 100 yard mark, once against The Miami Hurricanes when he caught eight passes for 114 yards and two touchdowns, and against Florida State where he took just three catches to the end zone once and totalled 129 yards on the day.

As an explosive athlete, Atwell has all the attributes I could ask for in a Wide Receiver. His speed and burst is ridiculous and he often breaks Defenders ankles when he shifts direction because of how sudden he is with his movements. This is no more evident than on a jet sweep against Virginia where he takes the ball to the outside, beating the Linebackers and then has all the speed he needs to glide past the Corner and stay clear of the incoming Safety to go 77 yards to the house. On another play against Kentucky, we see Atwell run a simple go route from the slot 43 yards out, where he uses his immense speed to get open over the top of the defender and has time to track the ball into his hands from 15 yards out for the score. He will be a superb Slot Receiver and a real threat in the NFL if it proves that his body can cope with the demands of playing at the next level. He is such a slight player that he simply has to add some mass if he is to survive, in my opinion. Will this slow him down too much? I don't think so, he is so fast and twitch his separation comes from movement and not fighting. He also needs to consistently work on his catching and route running as he has had some poor focus drops where he has just whiffed at balls. In his defence he is still learning his trade as a converted Quarterback. He may profile as a Special Teams returner and use this time to hone his skills further as a Wide Receiver.

NFL Landing Spot

The Rams load up on Offence by giving Stafford another playmaker. Atwell can be the gadget guy but also the field stretcher and big play guy in between Kupp and Woods.

Dyami Brown

North Carolina | WR | 6'1" | 185 lbs

I hadn't seen much of Dyami Brown until I started this project. I knew his counterpart Dazz Newsome was a solid Slot/Wide Receiver and had heard that The Tarheels had some weapons with a good Quarterback in Sam Howell under centre, but I had never really seen much North Carolina play. Man, I should have paid attention to those Tarheels and what they could do. Brown should have been on my radar sooner and if by some small miracle you're reading this Mr Brown, I can only apologise. He played Defensive Back in High School along with playing Wide Receiver so he knows the mindset of a DB and how they approach certain situations; this is evident in his game. Like any good Cornerback, he isn't afraid of being physical, which is apparent when watching his tape.

As a Freshman, Brown played in nine games and saw more than two catches in all but two of these games. In a week one loss to The North Carolina Pirates, Brown notched three catches for 24 yards. In a two catch performance in week two against Pitt, he scored his first touchdown as a Tarheel when he caught two passes for 32 yards one of them a 16 yard touchdown. As a Freshman, Brown would see limited action and would end up catching 17 passes for 173 yards and a touchdown.

Like Tutu Atwell in the previous profile, Brown would turn up as a Sophomore and become a huge part of North Carolina's game plan and a big time weapon for The Tarheels. He had at least one receiving touchdown in five-straight games to close out the season and also set a single-season school record with a receiving touchdown in 10 games. He was second in touchdowns in the ACC behind Higgins and joint with Atwell. Brown would find the end zone in each of the first three weeks of the season but it would only be weeks four and seven where he wouldn't actually score a touchdown for NC. Brown would only go over the 100 yard mark twice in 2019 and it took him a while to get to the first game in which he did so. It happened in a big way against Virginia, a team Brown would end up loving to play. He caught six passes for 202 yards and three scores. He had a yards per catch average of 33.7 YPC in that game. The second 100 yard game would come against North Carolina State when he would take one of his six catches to the house and rack up 150 yards in the process. Brown became a big-time vertical weapon for Howell and the Tarheels, finishing his Sophomore season with 51 catches, 1,034 yards and 12 touchdowns. The outlook for Brown was indeed brighter after that year.

2020 would again be a superb year for Brown and the North Carolina Offense as they would end up with a 8-3 record and he would see the 1000 yard mark broken once more in the high-powered Offence. It would be a career-making game again against Virginia where Brown would drop a MOAB (Massive Ordnance Air Blast or Mother of All Bombs) and garner some serious NFL Scout attention. In the first week of 2020 he almost hit the 100 yard mark with a six reception, 94 yard game against Syracuse. It wouldn't be until a week three matchup against Virginia Tech that Brown would find the end zone and he did so twice. He took two of his three receptions to the house and accumulated 86 yards in the process. Then in week five he had his first 100 yard game against North Carolina State, where he caught seven passes for 105 yards. Now for the big one, the home run against Virginia. Brown caught 11 passes in this game and finished with 240 yards and three touchdowns. Yes, you read that right 240 yards and three scores. In this game Brown did everything he could to bring The Tarheels back from over 20 points down. Brown exhibited an abundance of tough fighter's nature that we have come to know him for during this game. He fought hard for yards after the catch and also slipped past outstretched Defenders to gain valuable yards and first downs. He was also open many times in the short area of the field as Defenders gave him room at the line of scrimmage due to his vertical threat. Brown would then go on to have another good game against Wake Forest, with eight catches for 163 yards and two scores and another stellar performance against Miami when he turned four catches into 167 yards. He would finish 2020 being added to the *Biletnikoff Award* watch list and having final stats of 55 receptions, 1099 yards and eight touchdowns.

Something that Brown has shown he can do very well is running a vertical route. In fact, he does this with such efficiency it really enables him to actually run any route he wants when given the opportunity. The way Defenders have to give him room at the line of scrimmage means he has separation already when he breaks on a route and that allows him to get inside or outside a Defender with ease, using the buffer that is already there. This ability feeds nicely into how physical he is as a runner but also as a ball carrier. He shows willingness to get those pads down and initiate contact with a Defender to gain extra yards and shows savvy when getting out of bounds when needed. Several times in the Virginia game, Brown showed what fight he has when running and he also caught a comeback and had the awareness to spin back around and head upfield, evading a Defender who took a poor tackle angle. To improve his fighting for yardage Brown could do with adding some size and explosive power to better hide his route when releasing from the line of scrimmage.

NFL Landing Spot

Brown joins Curtis Samuel and Terry McLaurin to make a trio of weapons for Fitzmagic. Mclaurin is still the alpha in this room, but Brown is a big-time threat who can make an impact and isn't just a depth add, in my opinion.

Elijah Moore

Ole Miss | WR | 5'9" | 184 lbs

Five feet nine inches and 184 pounds in NFL numbers projects as a pure Slot Receiver, and that is where Elijah Moore predominantly played for Mississippi. But when you open up the tape, Moore has a lot more to him than a standard Slot Receiver. His skills are instantly NFL translatable and they will be very useful to him at the next level as a smaller guy. If you are brand new to the NFL and this is your first trip into Fantasy Football, then I will forgive you the next part. If not and you've just been living under a rock then you'll not know that Moore was tucked up behind a couple of NFL beasts named A.J Brown and D.K Metcalf. Both of these gentlemen are huge, so for the pocket rocket Moore, getting noticed would be an uphill struggle straight off the bat. What I find intriguing and also infuriating is Moore's clean bill of health; he has almost never been injured. For me, this is a two fold issue and bonus. He doesn't help his team block at all. I mean he can be next to the play developing and his unwillingness to block or help move the pile is downright atrocious, which is a serious issue for me. On the flip side, he gets beaten up all the time when catching balls and when being targeted he isn't afraid to throw himself into the firing line. Now for a smaller Wideout, the fact he doesn't have more of an injury history is superb and the way he was targeted in 2020 shows how tough he is. Only once did he have less than ten catches over the season. Madness for a guy to take that many hits and not be injured. I love his toughness, but want him to be more involved in team plays.

BOOM! In his first game as a Rebel, Moore explodes. Well, sort of anyway. He takes his solitary receptions to the house for fifty yards, one play, half the field and a score. As introductions to a College career go there have been many worse. Apart from that detonation in week one, Moore didn't really do much else of note over the course of his Freshman season. Oh wait! He amassed nearly 33% of his receptions over the season in one game in week 8. Against South Carolina, Moore set the School record for catches and yards for a Freshman in a single game. He caught 11 passes and totalled 129 yards in a breakout game. He ended up with 36 receptions for 398 and two scores in his Freshman year. We didn't hear more about it because he was stuck behind the beasts.

2019 saw Moore elevated up the depth chart and this was evident as he led the team in receptions, receiving yards and touchdowns. That being said, he only had four games of note and all four were over 100 yards. Week two against Arkansas saw him notch 130 yards and two touchdowns and he had a career day yardage wise against Louisiana State, when he caught nine passes for 143 yards. Excuse the shortness of his Sophomore year, but a blistering 2020 awaits. Moore finished 2019 with 67 catches for 850 yards and six scores.

2020 saw The Rebels play just eight games. That wouldn't stop Moore from doing what no other Wide Receiver in the NCAA would do, and go over 200 yards in a single game, not once but three times! In week one against Florida, Moore caught 10 passes for 227 yards.

He would again go over 200 yards against Vanderbilt as he caught 14 passes for 238 yards and three touchdowns in week six. Then in week seven he would blow the doors off South Carolina when he caught 13 balls for 225 yards and two touchdowns. A mad couple of weeks. He would cap off his season with a 12 catch, 139 yard game against Mississippi state. A year after he scored and then celebrated by pretending to be a dog and urinate on the end zone causing a yardage penalty and a last minute kick for the win by Mississippi State. In week five Moore would record just five receptions. As I have said, this would be the only game of the eight played where he wouldn't have at least ten catches. This led him to becoming the fastest player in school history to 1,000 yards in one season, achieved in just seven games. He also set the longest play in School history against the Gamecocks, when he scored a 91 yard touchdown now known as 'The Clipboard Catch.' His 14 receptions for 238 yards and three touchdowns against Vanderbilt were all career-highs and school records. Remember he was stuck behind Brown and Metcalf? No more was he held back, and he made the most of his chance. He finished his Junior year with 86 receptions, 1,193 yards and eight touchdowns.

Elijah Moore has all the intangible traits that a Slot Wide Receiver should have. His separation is unique in that he uses a combination of lethal speed and total field awareness. His ability to know where Defenders are and where they are angled means he can get upfield fast and use angles to his benefit. We saw this when he was lined up as a Running Back. His field vision is next level and his quick burst and second gear mean he can carve teams up, which he does with regularity. His willingness to be used in heavy traffic situations will mean he is targeted regularly too. His hands are safe, and his field awareness means he can focus on catching the ball, not where the hits are coming from. He can turn any play into a big time gain and will take players with him if needs be to gain a first down. Where Moore needs work is on his route tree. I picked up his direction of running almost instantly and every time he catches the ball it is on an in-route. He never runs towards the sideline but is always angled towards the traffic. He would do well to learn to run outside to protect his body from bigger hits in the busy middle of the field.

NFL Landing Spot

Well, Zach Wilson has one hell of a weapon in Moore. He will most likely operate out of the slot and will feast with Wilson's accuracy on intermediate and deep balls. Breakout candidate for sure here Gang Green.

D'Wayne Eskridge

Western Michigan | WR | 5'9" | 189 lbs

As a Cornerback knowing what a Wide receiver could do, or even better, knowing what he is going to do is a huge part of shutting people down. So what is a Cornerbacks worst nightmare? A Wide Receiver who can think like a Cornerback and use it as a weapon against them. That's what ya boy D'Wayne Eskridge is capable of, he used to be a Cornerback for Western Michigan whilst taking some reps as a Wide Receiver. He didn't fully move over to be a Wideout until his 2020 season when he unleashed a truck sized nuke on the MAC Conference. Now imagine this nightmare for Defenders, add in 4.33 speed and a burst as good as anyone else in this class and you've got yourself a serious weapon not only in the deep game but in the short game too, as Eskridge can take any pass to the house and has done so with alarming regularity. He certainly isn't the tallest, but he is well built for his size and this mass is where he generates his fast twitch and explosiveness from. He is powerfully built yet still retains a slenderness that makes him elusive enough to make Tacklers miss. He is a size/speed headache and not because he is big and fast but because he is slippery and rapid. Eskridge has played five seasons of College Football, which is unusual to see and perhaps this extended time has allowed him to transition to Wide Receiver. One thing I would say is: turn on his 2020 highlights, grab a bevvy, sit back and enjoy because it is super fun to watch.

As a Freshman, Eskridge played in ten games and was part of WMU's best ever team as they went on to win the *MAC West Division* title, *Marathon MAC Championship Game* crown and made an appearance in the *Goodyear Cotton Bowl Classic*. He only caught 17 passes for 121 yards and a solitary touchdown. That touchdown came against Northwestern in his first ever start for The Broncos. Due to Western Michigan's injuries and players transferring out, Eskridge was used predominantly as a Wideout in his Sophomore year and was more involved in the pass game. He still operated as a Cornerback and had his highest snap count of any year in 2017 with 609 across both positions. He had three games of 90+ yards and caught three touchdowns on the year. He had four games of four receptions and his highest receptions came against Akron. He caught seven passes for 93 yards and a touchdown whilst also rushing twice for seven yards. He would end his second year in College with 30 receptions, 506 yards and three touchdowns.

2018 saw Eskridge again bounce around the team, still filling the holes needed on both sides of the ball. This season however, he would go over 100 yards three times and his standout performance came in week one versus Syracuse, where he tallied eight receptions for 240 yards and two scores. His 84 yard touchdown catch tied for the fourth longest play in program history. He finished his Junior year with 38 catches 776 yards and three touchdowns.

Sadly, 2019 was a terrible year for Eskridge.He broke his Clavicle in week four after not registering a catch in weeks one or two. That would be him done for the year and he would only register three catches on the whole year for 73 yards. He was used solely as a Cornerback in weeks one and two which is why he wasn't used, don't panic.

KABOOOOOM! Just like that we all suddenly knew who D'Wayne Eskridge was and just how bleeding fast he is. WMU played just six games in 2020, Eskridge only had one game under 100 yards and he had one game over 200 yards. As a full time Wide Receiver, Eskridge fully broke out in the few games he had to do so. He put up incredible numbers and shredded all who stood before him in the MAC. He averaged 38 yards per catch in week one where he took two of his three catches to the house and racked up 114 yards. Then in week three he obliterated Central Michigan off just four catches. He scored three times and finished with 212 yards and an average YPC of 53. Monster game right there. But he wasn't done there, however, he caught seven passes for 134 yards in week four against Northern Illinois and added another 27 yards on the ground. Then finally, in week six he caught nine passes for 129 yards against Ball State. Eskridge also showed his explosiveness on Special Teams as a Kick Returner, he had three games where he had over 100 yards in the return game and one touchdown. He would finish his six games with 33 receptions, 768 yards and eight touchdowns and another one touchdown and 467 yards as a Returner.

As a prospect, Eskridge is raw in experience but as a talent has all the things you want from a speedster. He has the ball hawk skills needed to highpoint the football from playing Cornerback and has the ability to stem Defenders superbly by using his knowledge of the game and his explosive shift of direction when running his routes. Eskridge offers a safe pair of hands and doesn't body the ball when catching. His breakneck speed and change of pace allows him to play either from the Slot or on the outside where he can use his good route tree diversity to exploit Defenders using the sideline as a barrier. Where he won't win is against Corners with length, as they will be taller and higher at the catch point. But if he gets the ball fired into him, he will let his hands and feet do the talking. His speed and blocking mean he will also be useful on Special Teams, so watch out for bonus touchdowns.

NFL Landing Spot

Eskridge finds himself behind Lockett and Metcalf in Seattle as the WR3 for the Seahawks. He should still see some action but will also be a weapon on Special Teams as a returner.

Tamorrion Terry

Florida State | WR | 6'4" | 210 lbs

Tamorrion Terry plays bigger than he looks, which is really saying something - the guy is already huge. He has an enormous wing span and his catch radius makes him a delightful target for any Quarterback. He prowls along the sideline and dominates Cornerbacks with his ability to box Defenders out by using his frame as a weapon to dominate the skies. While Terry is dominating as an X or Z, he isn't without his flaws. He needs to work on his short yardage work and his reps from the Slot. As a runner, he is electric and always looks to get open over the top. His eagerness to get vertical can cause him to miss time catches and shorten off his routes in a bid to get vertical. Trying to get up to speed and vertical means he loses focus on catching the ball and has had focus drops because of this. When he is open over the top, his catching becomes much better and although he sometimes uses his body to catch the ball which isn't ideal as an outside guy as he should be high pointing the ball, he more often than not produces clean catches when running the go or nine routes. Look at me, Rush Nation I've gone off on a tangent there and brought the final paragraph screaming into the first. Ok so getting back on track, Terry also has a slight knock on him regarding playing time. He Redshirted in his first year in 2017 meaning he has only provided us with two full seasons of production as he left the 2020 campaign due to a knee injury which he would later have surgery on to fix. While it was only a minor procedure, it is believed that it was on the same knee as he had an operation on prior to the 2019 season. Although this injury and surgery didn't make Terry miss any time, a recurrence of an injury is no small matter, and this could flare up again if he is asked to run fast and far often. A little something to keep an eye on going forward.

After Redshirting his 2017 season, Terry broke into the teams Wide Receiver room and immediately became a starter. His reception total was low for the year, but he tied for the most receiving yards and led the team in touchdowns. His total yards for the season would break an FSU record for most receiving yards by a Freshman, a record that had previously stood for 41 years! Terry was used sparingly as a Receiver in 2018 but that didn't stop him having two games over the 100 yard mark and his average yards per catch was a huge 21.3, meaning he was a big play guy all year. His first game over the 100 yard mark came against North Carolina State when he caught five passes, racked up 142 yards and two touchdowns. His second was in week 11 against Boston College where he caught just three passes but tallied up 112 yards and a score. He would finish his season catching just 35 passes but totaling 744 yards and eight touchdowns.

If 2018 was a good year for Terry, then 2019 was a breakout for the young Redshirt Sophomore and it's no wonder that after his record setting campaign our very own Tom from 5 Yard College had Terry as his *Plant Your Flag Wide Receiver* for the 2020 season. While that didn't pan out, Terry was outstanding for The Seminoles in his second year. He led the NCAA in yards per touchdown reception at 57.89 yards which was the highest in 15 years when a Receiver had over nine touchdowns. He also had six touchdown receptions of at least 60 yards tied for the highest total in NCAA since at least 2010, a record which Dede Westbrook set at Oklahoma. He only had three games over the heralded 100 yard mark, but keep in mind the majority of his games were over the 60 yard mark and he was a constant threat to take any pass to the house. This was all after that aforementioned knee surgery that limited him in training camp. He again took North Carolina State to the cleaners when he caught five passes for 77 yards and two touchdowns. He then once more bullied the life out of the Boston College Defence as he caught seven passes for a huge 157 yards and a solitary touchdown. It would be in his final two weeks as a Redshirt Sophomore that Terry would do some of his finest work as a Seminole. In the final game of the regular season, he took on The Gators and now NFL Cornerback C.J. Henderson and torched them to within an inch of being barbecued Gators. He caught seven passes and although he didn't manage a trip into the paint, he tallied a huge 131 yards on a Cornerback who was meant to be superb in man coverage. Then in the close *Sun Bowl* loss to The Arizona State Sun Devils, Terry was elite. He caught a career high nine passes for 165 yards and a touchdown. He would end the year with figures of 60 receptions for 1,188 yards and nine touchdowns.

2020 was meant to be the year, but things transpired against Terry and the Noles. After five games he left the LSU program and declared for the NFL Draft. His only game of note was a record setter against Notre Dame. He caught a career tying nine receptions for 146 yards and a touchdown. It was the most yards by a visitor at Notre Dame Stadium since 2011 and this was against a good ND Defence. He would end the year with 23 catches, 289 yards and a solo touchdown. He left the program after week six and Tweeted "it breaks my heart that I cannot finish what I started here at Florida State." As an outside prospect, Terry is a monster and can use his skills to ply a trade in the NFL. He needs to develop his route tree and improve on his concentration and catching but as a raw prospect, I love what he offers. He is the kind of guy who has the talent to become a dominant Wide Receiver in the NFL but needs the right coaching to become great. He can dominate the outside for years to come and that in itself is super exciting.

NFL Landing Spot

Terry was signed as an UDFA by Seattle and whilst he appears to be impressing he will have some work to do to make the active roster due to the depth the Hawks have at WR.

Seth Williams

Auburn | WR | 6'2" | 224 lbs

In a Draft where Auburn would lose not one but two of their best Wide Receivers, it was hard to pick between speed and production. In the end, Williams was the clear guy to pick as volume is king as we all know. The fact that there are even two Wide Receivers from Auburn that have the possibility to be drafted is a rare thing indeed. Auburn has only had two Wideouts drafted in the last five years and you have to go back to 2006 to find a Draft class where there were another pair of Tigers past-catchers drafted in the same year . 247 Sports had Williams as the fifth best rated player in his home state of Alabama and he was generally seen as a four star prospect across other platforms. He was also ranked as the tenth best Athlete in the nation and also participated in the Long Jump and High Jump. Now we know why this kid has hops. The first thing you see is how good at jumping Williams is and how he will be a superb red zone weapon because of his ability to climb the ladder and get above Defenders in the end zone. But more on that later, as we have three years of production to take a look at. Before we do, however, Williams could be the first Wide Receiver we see in my rankings that actually could have hurt his Draft stock by having a poor year in 2020. He was slated to be a 2021 first rounder after his Sophomore year and much was expected in his Junior year. Williams (and Auburn to be fair) didn't live up to the hype that was buzzing around in the pre-season. Bo Nix was going to break out, and Willaims and Schwartz would follow suit. However, what we actually saw was the emergence of a Running Back by the name of Tank Bigsby, and you'll have to wait for the next Playbook to hear about him.

As a Freshman Williams played in 10 games and was listed as a starter in nine of them. Williams would have one or two receptions in all but three of his ten games for The Tigers. After an average first three weeks Williams would find the end zone in a two catch, 60 yard performance against Southern Mississippi. Williams would have his first of two, five reception games in week five against Tennessee where he would record 85 yards and a touchdown. The only other game of note from his Freshman year was the week nine matchup against Liberty. Williams would record his first 100 yard plus game after catching five passes for 109 yards and a trip into the end zone. A slow and steady start to his College career would see Williams finish the year with 26 receptions, 534 yards and five touchdowns.

2019 and Williams' Sophomore year would see him put some of the biggest numbers ever by an Auburn Wide Receiver. He would end up with the eleventh most yards and sixth most touchdowns in School history. A tale of two halves of the season with touchdowns for Williams saw him score all eight before week eight and then never see pay dirt again, oh what could have been.

Bo Nix would find Williams in the end zone in his first game as a Sophomore against a good Oregon Defense as Williams would go on to catch four passes for 41 yards and a touchdown. Two games stood out for Williams in 2019, one against Mississippi State and the other against Georgia. Both Bulldogs too, must be something in that name I recon. Against Mississippi State Williams had a breakout game and caught eight passes for 161 yards and two scores on a day he did everything we want to see from our X Receiver. Then against Georgia he caught a whopping 13 passes for 121 yards, again showcasing that big play ability and jump ball skillset. Williams finished his Sophomore season with 59 receptions, 830 yards and eight touchdowns and was primed for a big Junior year in 2020. That didn't happen though as Williams struggled to be productive and was often outclassed by Defenders in what was a very different year for The Tigers star. The first game was a stonker for Williams as he caught six passes for 112 yards and two touchdowns and set a huge precedent. The rest of the season was a damp squib, however, as he only went over 100 yards once more in a win at Mississippi where he caught eight passes for 150 yards and a touchdown. Otherwise, for Williams he struggled to get over three receptions in most games and dropped a howler of a long touchdown against Bama in what was a poor season for the hot prospect. All in all he was still Bo Nixs' favorite target and showed why he specialises in being a jump ball guy. He would finish his Junior year with 47 receptions, 760 yards and just four touchdowns.

2020 was a terrible year for our boy Williams and it did dent his stock a little in my opinion. He proved in 2019 that he had what we want from our outside guy and if he had improved further in 2020 then he would have risen to top 12 for me. But he isn't and we're here so what do I think of Williams when watching tape? He is a monster in the air and has hang time like no other. He attacks the ball trajectory at his highest point meaning he towers above Defenders when making the catch. He also shows good tracking ability when the ball is coming into his zone, which allows him to get his leap right, which he showed with a spectacular one handed grab along the sideline against Mississippi State. That being said he will be the perfect red zone weapon when targeted in the end zone because of his ability to box out Defenders and win on fades and corner routes. He isn't a burner so don't expect him to beat NFL Cornerbacks over the top but be a possession guy with touchdown upside. He could also do well to learn how to sell routes better off the line of scrimmage so as to not be so one dimensional.

NFL Landing Spot

Williams joins Denver as a depth piece as of now and faces a battle to stay on the roster.

Amari Rodgers

Clemson | WR | 5'10" | 210 lbs

As a player who has played all four years for The Clemson Tigers, Rodgers is a guy who knows his way round a gridiron, and more specifically he knows his way round the middle of the field as an explosive Slot Receiver. A veteran of the Trevor Lawrence experience in Death Valley, Rodgers has been effective in his limited role behind some big time Wide Receivers at Clemson. Hunter Renfrow, Deon Cain, Tee Higgins, Justyn Ross and Travis Etienne are all guys who have had the lion's share of receptions ahead of Rodgers, yet Rodgers has been a stalwart for T Law and flourished finally in his Senior year in 2020. If Rodgers was in a body type lineup, you would instantly align him to the Running Back group. He is stocky and solid but with burst and superior vision just like a good ball carrier out of the backfield. Then you see Rodgers lineup in the Slot and explode off the line. He is similar to a diamond, small yet multi faceted, he shows many skills that will translate perfectly to the NFL and has shown these throughout his career at the Tigers so it's no fluke that when you see him go to work he is productive. He isn't just an inside guy either as he has one hell of a leap for a smaller framed Wide Receiver. Through his four years at Clemson, Rodgers has made explosive plays and at times has made grabs he straight up shouldn't have.

As a Freshman Rodgers was used sparingly as a new piece in his first year for The Tigers. Even though he played in all 12 games, he never found the end zone. He saw a season high three receptions in his first game for Clemson. In week one against Kent State, he caught three receptions for 19 yards. The best week as a Freshman came in week nine against Citadel where he only caught one pass for seven yards but had a superb kick return game. He returned one punt for eight yards and a kick return for 36 yards. Rodgers would end up with just 19 receptions for 123 yards and zero trips into the end zone.

Aa a Sophomore Rodgers was used in a much higher capacity from the Slot. He again played in all 15 of Clemson's games on the way to winning the National Championship. In a fairly modest season where he would see an uptick in receptions, he would average 3.6 receptions a game. He found the end zone in week one in a four catch 49 yard game against Furman. His standout game of the season was in week eight against Florida State where he caught six passes for 156 yards and two touchdowns and had three punt returns for 62 yards. Rodgers would finish the season ranked second on the team with 55 receptions, record 575 yards and score four touchdowns. He was again dangerous in the punt return game taking 39 returns 299 yards and scoring one touchdown.

2019 was a bit of a step back for Rodgers after tearing his ACL. He returned in week two of the season for The Tigers but had limited usage throughout the season perhaps due to his injury and reinjury concerns. His standout game was in week three at Syracuse where he caught four passes for 121 yards and two scores. Against Florida State in week six he scored a rushing score on a 29-yard attempt. Rodgers would end his Junior season catching

30 passes for 426 yards and four touchdowns through the air and adding that score on the ground to boot.

2020 was Rodgers' year to explode for Clemson as he set career highs in receptions, yards gained and touchdowns whilst also being named a Biletnikoff Award semifinalist. He had three games where he went over 100 yards and was under 50 yards just twice. A huge game against Georgia Tech in week five saw him reel in six catches for 161 yards and two touchdowns in a career high yardage game. He was barely used in the punt return game, but he found the end zone on one of his nine attempts. He recorded eight catches in the loss to Notre Dame gaining 134 yards in the process and then in the return fixture again caught eight passes for 121 yards. His Senior year ended with Rodgers catching 77 balls for 1,020 yards and seven touchdowns.

As a Slot Receiver Rodgers has the perfect traits to move his game to the next level. Slot Receivers thrive from taking manufactured plays for big-time catches and yardage. Rodgers build and Running Back style of play means he is perfectly suited to be used from the Slot. He knows how to use his size and address' contact with his tough physicality. He has superb vision when running through a crowd and can see coverage breaking don or gaps that might occur in zone coverage. Being five foot ten also gives him a lower centre of gravity which means he has good contact balance and can fight for extra yardage using his powerful legs and physical nature. Where Rodgers excels through all this is creating yards after the catch. His vision allows him to see gaps, and he has good soft hands so catching isn't a focus thing allowing him to concentrate on getting those extra yards. His speed and burst also make him a threat in short yardage situations as he can turn and stop on a dime creating separation for quick throws and fast outs to the sideline. This burst and speed luckily wasn't affected by his ACL injury and having the shorter height and thick frame means he is built tough for those big hits that will be coming in the NFL. Rodgers could do with extending his route tree and his shorter length means he does struggle on occasion in contested catches due to a small wing span and overall length.

NFL Landing Spot

Aaron Rodgers finally gets another weapon to play with in Rodgers. Rodgers walks straight into the WR2 spot in Green Bay in my opinion and will put up Fantasy Numbers from the get go.

Sage Surratt

Wake Forest | WR | 6'3" | 215 lbs

This story needs to start way back, when Sage Surratt was deciding where to commit to. His intentions were to go to Harvard as he has committed there, but he wasn't the biggest fan of their Football program. After visiting Wake Forest and falling in love with their business program, he found the allure of playing in the *Power 5 Conference* along with a superior Football program too much and moved his commitment to The Demon Deacons. To be honest, just the team's nickname had me hooked. Surratt had one hell of a High School football career and as a senior, Sage would set state records with 129 receptions, 2,104 yards and 28 touchdowns for a player in their Senior year. This though, would only help him achieve a three star rating by ESPN and 247 Sports as he was, at the time, a dual sports athlete excelling in Basketball as well. We are pretty lucky he chose to recommit though, as his exposure to the Football world would have been much more limited at Harvard and we wouldn't have been witness to some of his exciting plays. Sage is a big boy, his frame is well filled out and he uses his levers well, but he isn't a top end athlete. He doesn't have breakaway speed and is a target to be caught after making a long catch and run effort. There is also the issue that we have only seen two seasons of football from Surratt and the last time we saw him play was in week nine of 2019. By the time he hits the Football field, it will be almost two full years since he has played a competitive snap. Does this mean he is fresh though? Let's find out.

Even though Surratt Red-shirted his Freshman year, he was productive from the moment he stepped onto the field in those oh so sweet matte black and gold uniforms. In his first game as a Deacon he set a School record for the most receptions and receiving yards by a Freshman at Wake Forest. He caught 11 passes for 150 yards against Tulane. Except for one other game in 2018, Surratt had a modest year and didn't see above 4 receptions or 67 yards. Considering he had blown the barn doors off in week one you would have thought they would have gotten him more involved. Surratt would get his first touchdown as a Deacon in week three against Boston College, on a corner route in the red zone he would be uncontested on the catch for his first score. By week seven The Demon Deacons had had enough of mediocre play at the Quarterback position and unleashed Jamie Newman into the starting line-up. In Newman's first game, Surratt would catch eight passes for 109 yards in a win against North Carolina State. He would score in his last two games of the year, one against Duke and the other against Memphis. The touchdown against Memphis would be the catalyst for Wake Forest to go on and win the Birmingham Bowl as Surratt would finish his Freshman year with 41 catches, 581 yards and four touchdowns.

2019 would start well again for Surratt as he showed his full intentions to get onto NFL Scouts radars nice and early. He was now a well embedded part of the passing game and would go onto set a School record for most consecutive games with a touchdown (8), two in

2018 and six in 2019. In the first game of the year, Surratt again started his campaign with an over 100 yard game. He caught seven passes for 158 yards and a score in a win against Utah State. Then in week three he would catch nine balls for 169 yards and another touchdown. Against Elon in week four, Surratt caught eight passes for 112 yards and two scores. In week six however, Sage would have a career day against Louisville. He caught 12 passes for 196 yards and three touchdowns and was electric for the full 60 minutes. The very next week he caught seven balls for 170 yards against Florida State. Unfortunately, for Surratt he picked up a season ending shoulder injury against Virginia Tech and that would be the last time we would see him in the black and gold. He would finish the season with 66 receptions for 1,001 yards and 11 touchdowns.

Although Wake Forest said that Surratt was healthy and ready to play in 2020, he opted out before the season began and declared for the 2021 NFL Draft. Even though he had only played nine games as Sophomore, Surratt did enough to propel him up the draft board in what is a very deep Wide Receiver class. His 11 touchdowns were enough for the second most in School history and his 111.2 receiving yards per game average turned out to be an eighth-best in ACC history. He was also named as one of the 12 semi-finalists in the prestigious *Biletnikoff Award*.

As a Wide Receiver, the first thing that stands out about Surratt is his physicality when playing on the outside. He very rarely runs from the slot as he doesn't offer much in the separation game so will be easily covered in man coverage and also in zone by Defences covering the middle of the shallow field. What Sage does very well is use his size and strength to engage in physical battles with Defenders. He doesn't use too much force and never extends his arms to push Defenders away, he just uses his frame well to hold Defenders off when engaged in arm battles. As an outside route runner he runs very clean routes and hardly gets stumped at the line of scrimmage due to his good use of his levers and his explosive movement. What he does not offer is downfield speed; he gets open over the top and wins jump balls, but doesn't offer long yards after the catch bonus as he is prone to being caught from behind. Where our boy does his damage is in contested catches. He uses his large frame to box Defenders out and then lets his hands do the work, as a red zone weapon he could be lethal.

NFL Landing Spot

Surrat can surprise many as he joins The Lions as an UDFA with high upside.

Demetric Felton

UCLA | WR | 5'8" | 188 lbs

As prospects go, Demetric Felton is as difficult to describe as any. In his time for The UCLA Bruins, Felton played as both Running Back and as a Wide Receiver primarily from the Slot. In fact, over his duration at UCLA there is only a difference of 150 yards between his rushing total and receiving totals. He carried the ball more than he caught it, but it was only in his final year that he played one position much more than the other. Up until his Senior year, he was almost at a 50/50 split for carries to receptions. I didn't know whether to rank him as a Running Back or as a Wide Out and it came down to me watching his tape and where I thought he would best fit into the NFL that I ranked him as a Receiver. I think his size and shiftyness means he will provide a gadget-like ability to the Slot Receiver position and possibly on Special Teams as well. Interestingly, I don't know if evaluators actually really know where he should play either, as he was recruited out of High School as a Wide Receiver yet played as a three down back in High School. Not only that, but he was also a Special Teams star in his years before UCLA, so actually is he a jack of all trades and yet is he a master of none? Well, let's find out.

Felton didn't see any action in his first year of College as he enrolled in the spring quarter. His first game came in 2017 where he played in 12 games but only recorded stats in four of the games. As most of our prospects tend to do, he found the end zone in his first ever game in College. Felton's first career touchdown came against Hawaii when he found pay dirt off of one of his three carries and he tallied 37 yards in the process. That would be his best game of the year as although he would record four catches against Kansas State, he would only take them for 21 yards. He averaged 7.5 yards per carry as a Freshman and would look to increase his workload heading into 2018.

2018 saw Felton used more in the passing game and he logged more catches than carries. Strangely though, of the 12 games Felton saw action, in eight of these he was listed as a starting Wide Receiver which headed away from his previous season as being primarily used as a Running Back. Over the season he only logged five carries and three of these came in a game against Arizona, where he had his best game of the season. Felton turned those three carries into 18 yards but caught the ball four times for 36 yards and a touchdown. As a pass catcher, statistically his best game was in week two where he caught three passes for 49 yards. Felton saw multiple receptions in all but two of his nine games where he logged action and he wound up with season ending numbers of 20 receptions for 207 yards and a touchdown. He also carried the ball just five times for 27 yards with no trips into the paint.

2019 saw Felton's numbers swing back to being more of a Running Back as he logged more carries than catches but it was in the passing game where he did most of his damage. As a runner, his best game was against Oregon State where he had 11 carries for 111 yards and a score. As a pass catcher his best game was undoubtedly against Washington State where he caught seven passes for 150 yards and two touchdowns. He was electric in the passing game and averaged 10.8 yards per reception on the limited work he got. Felton was becoming a devastation option from the Slot with Running Back capabilities and was exploiting Defenders tackle angles for fun as a Junior. He would end up carrying the ball 86 times for 331 yards and a score but his damage was done when lined up as a Slot Receiver. He caught 55 passes for 594 yards and four scores, yet as things had already done for Felton, a swing the other way was about to happen.

2020 saw Felton heavily used in the run game for The Bruins. He became the lead guy for UCLA and carried the ball over 20 times in four of the six games he played in. He started out with just 10 carries for 57 yards and a score but also logged a season best seven carries for 46 yards and a touchdown in the passing game. He would then have his first of three 100 yard plus rushing games with a 25 carry 105 yard performance in week two. His week three game against Oregon was outstanding as a ball carrier as he rushed for 167 yards off of 34 carries and two touchdowns. He also returned five kicks for 105 yards. His week four game against Arizona was also superb as he rushed for 206 yards and a score off of 32 carries. Felton would lead the Bruins in carries over the season and would end up with figures of 132 carries for 668 yards and five touchdowns while catching 22 passes for 159 yards and three scores.

Felton is a shifty pass catcher, who offers excellent yards after the catch ability due to his elusiveness and skills as a Running Back. He is surprisingly patient at allowing his route to develop and uses his fast cut skills from being a Running Back to make covering him hard. He has superb hands and as a pass catcher will offer the Quarterback a safety net or dump off valve should he get into trouble. He also excels on sweeps and bubble screens where he can use his small frame and elusiveness to get up field in a hurry. As a Running Back, he offers something in the run game but his small size means at the next level he could get stuffed at the line more often than not. His size also means he could get overshadowed by outside Corners if they come into the box playing man or by a Linebacker who is playing spy on Felton if he is lined up in the backfield. He offers some intriguing skills as a pass catcher at the next level.

NFL Landing Spot

Felton was drafted by The Browns and apparently will be used as a Running Back!

CHAPTER 19

Tight Ends

Written by **Chris Mitchell**

Kyle Pitts

Florida | TE | 6'6" | 243lbs

How does someone who has logged just 100 receptions over his entire Collegiate career end up ahead of someone nicknamed Baby Gronk on everyone's Tight End list? There is one simple answer and there is no point in being cute about it. Kyle Pitts is the best Tight End prospect to come out of College since some believe Gronkowski or Kelce. He is as generational at the position as Trevor Lawrence is at Quarterback and how Pitts is overlooked because of how he is a Tight End is preposterous. In the modern game the Tight End is much more of a weapon than those of yesteryear and as a pass catcher Pitts is as dangerous as any player outside of ja'Marr Chase and Rashod Bateman for me. I would have no hesitation to take Pitts as the third player off the Wide Receiver list if he was listed as one. There are even some analysts who claim he isn't a Tight End and we will see him deployed as a Wide Receiver. Regardless of where we see Pitts lined up he will be a nightmare for the opposition. He is as an explosive athlete as there is in this Draft class and what separates him from most of the other Offensive players drafted this year is his explosiveness and ball catching skills from someone who is six foot six. He just shouldn't be able to move the way he does, yet he shreds Linebackers and Defensive Backs when running routes and has concentration skills second to none which means he is always focused on the ball and the point of catch which in turn makes poorly thrown balls in his vicinity almost auto catches. Kyle Trask leaned on Pitts in the 2020 season and I'm sure we can expect much more of the same at the next level.

Normally I would write all of this at the end but Pitts is so good it all came spewing out before we got to his history. He is as versatile as they come when it comes to his placement on the field. He can play as an X, Y or Z and is even superb when playing from in-line with a hand in the dirt. He sells delay blocks as well as Gronk did at his best and explodes off the line in instant release faster than a Tight End should. He has delightfully soft hands to go with his mammoth catch radius and coupled with his athleticism means he has top tier body control and flexibility when high pointing catches or moving of his centre to adjust for a poorly thrown ball. He isn't afraid to get his hands dirty in the run blocking game either and if there is something he does need some work on, it's in this area of his game. Whilst he is a good blocker occasionally he is slow to engage with his hands and can be beaten by a handsy Edge Rusher. This is a small part of his elite game that can be worked on and isn't a killer by any stretch of the imagination. Pitts is as good as they come as a Tight End and it wouldn't surprise me if we are talking about him for the next 10 years.

Pitts' career in Gainesville started slowly. I mean really slowly as he was used primarily on special teams and only logged three receptions as a Freshman. Coming out of High School, Pitts was ranked behind Brevin Jordan in his recruitment class. Whilst he was still an intriguing prospect he was only the 150th overall in the ESPN list and wasn't ranked as five-star prospect either. This may have fueled him to show what he was capable of and he did so instantly as a Freshman. In just his third game he caught one pass for 52 yards and a touchdown, showing his atheltesoms and exploviness straight off the bat. It would end up being his last reception of the year but it showed just what he can do.

As a Sophomore, Pitts became a huge focal point for The Gators and truly turned into the beast we see today. He started 12 of the 13 games and scored five touchdowns, the second most by a Tight End since 1995. He finished third amongst all FBS Tight Ends in receptions and seventh in receiving yards. He averaged 12 yards per catch in 2019 and was a constant threat to break off a huge play. In week five Pitts had his first two score game where he caught four passes for 28 yards and a pair of touchdowns. He caught a career high eight receptions in week eight against Auburn where he tallied 65 yards off those catches. His best game of the year was against Louisiana State where he caught five passes for 108 yards showing just how dangerous he could be. Pitts would end up with final year numbers of 54 receptions, 649 yards and five touchdowns. The best however was yet to come.

In 2020 Pitts played just eight games for The Gators yet finished second on the team behind Kadarius Toney in receptions. Pitts was the focal point for Kyle Trask and Dan Mullens and was THE red zone weapon when it came to the crunch. We all knew Pitts was special but his week one annihilation of Ole Miss was truly breathtaking. He recorded eight catches for 170 yards and four touchdowns. One was from the one yard line showing that he can be effective when given limited area to operate in. Two were from inside the redzone and the other was a 71 yard catch and run showing he has gas to get to the paint from wherever he catches the ball. He scored another two touchdowns in week two against South Carolina. Then against Kentucky he caught five passes for 99 yards and three touchdowns. He finished off his season with two games over 100 yards against Tennessee and Alabama. In almost identical games he caught seven passes for 128 and 129 yards respectively. The only difference being a score against Bama. Before he would forgo his Senior year and declare for the NFL Draft he would log 43 catches for 770 yards and 12 touchdowns. Pitts will make his mark on the NFL for sure.

NFL Landing Spot

Kyle Pitts joins all the other talent in the pass-catching room in Atlanta. He immediately becomes a top 8 TE for Fantasy and has top 5 Upside.

Pat Freiermuth

Penn State | TE | 6'5" | 258lbs

Two years ago when I was invited to a College Fantasy Football League by none other than our very own Ash, Pat Freiermuth was the guy to grab in the Draft. He came with the nickname Baby Gronk and the hype was real. He ultimately ended up having a fairly decent season in 2019 and I was happy I'd grabbed him late in the Draft process. Whilst all the hype this Draft season is about Pitts, Freiermuth himself can be a serious weapon at the next level. Whilst perhaps the 'Baby Gronk' moniker is maybe a little strong, Pat is everything you want from your Tight End. He has size, speed, superb hands, runs good routes and can block to a decent standard. That's where he will need to improve his game for the NFL but considering Travis Kelce was used more as a receiving Tight End than a blocking one shows how the NFL is beginning to use their big guys.

Whilst we rapidly forget players after all the Draft hype has vanished, Pat Freiermuth joined Penn State at exactly the right time. Mike Gesicki has just left for the NFL after being Drafted by The Dolphins and we all salivated over Mike as a prospect coming into the League. Freiermuth was approached by some of the huge Schools in the recruitment process, Notre Dame and Ohio State to name the big ones, but ultimately Pat chose to stay as close to home as he could and decide Penn State would be his new home. As Gesicki left a gaping hole in the Tight End room, Freiermuth more than filled it with his huge frame. Even coming out of High School, Freiermuth was huge, six feet five and nearly 250 pounds and he put it straight to use in the first year for The Nittany Lions.

As a Freshman Freiermuth got straight down to business. He ended the season with the most touchdown receptions (8) by a Penn State Freshman since Deon Butler (9) in 2005. Just like that big Pat had made a mark on the game and was instantly recognised as a nightmare for Defences due to his size/speed mismatch. He ran a sub five second 40 Yard Dash when he was in High School, which is scary fast for a lad of his stature. He was consistently targeted throughout 2018 but he that consistency never went above three in a single game. He averaged just over two receptions a game and his best game was in his tenth game of the season against Rutgers where he caught three passes for 47 yards and found the endzone twice. Freiermuth would end his Freshman season catching 26 passes, scoring eight touchdowns and racking up 368 yards. Things were looking rosey for big Pat and 2019 would be no different.

As a Sophomore Freiermuth showed again how he can be a threat on any play. There are three games that stand out from a statistical view point in 2019. His week two demolition of Buffalo, the week eight hatrick of touchdowns against Michigan State and the over 100 yard game in week nine against Minnesota. The game against Buffalo came out of nowhere as in week one he didn't exactly light it up with just one reception. He then exploded against Buffalo when he caught eight passes for 99 yards and two scores. The eight catches were nearly 25% of his Freshman season reception total in one game. He then scored three times against The Spartans as he averaged 12 yards per catch off of six receptions, totaling 60 yards. His week nine game against The Golden Gophers was odd in the respect he didn't find the end zone. He caught seven passes for 101 yards, averaging 14.4 yards per reception. Then in the huge rivalry game against The Buckeyes, Freiermuth caught six passes but only managed 40 yards as the tough Ohio State Defence made life hard for Freiermuth and co. He would finish the season with 43 receptions, 507 yards and seven touchdowns. He would end up being second on the team in receptions and yards and was primed to have a breakout third year.

2020 didn't exactly go to plan for the Junior. For the first four games of the season it was evident that Freiermuth was a big part of Penn State's passing game plan. He caught seven passes for 60 yards and a touchdown in week one against Indiana. He then caught just three passes in week two but averaged 15.3 yards per reception. He then caught six passes in week three totalling 91 yards. In his final game of the year he caught seven balls for 113 yards averaging 16.1 yards per catch. A shoulder injury would shut his season down and he would ultimately end up having surgery on the joint. He caught 23 passes over the four games, totaled 310 yards and scored just once. Until his injury he led all Tight Ends in the FBS in receptions per game with an average of 5.8 per game. What could have been for Pat? We will never know but what we do know is what he is capable of.

As a prospect Freiermuth has everything the modern Tight End needs to excel in the NFL. He runs well and creates space off of Defenders by using his physicality and aggressive route running. He can be used from anywhere across the line and is perhaps a better blocker than Pitts is. He excels in playing from inline where he can block and release into a delayed route. He bullies Defenders in the Secondary with his size and creates havoc when being part of the forward blocking unit. That being said he does need to work on his blocking in order to be truly considered a three down player. He can get caught square on and doesn't engage his hands fast enough to stop the upward push. As a pass catcher he offers huge upside and we know how the NFL loves a pass catching Tight End.

NFL Landing Spot

Freiermuth joins a Steelers team that needed the big-bodied Tight End once more. Big Pat can be effective for the next decade for the Steelers and has some upside in the passing game.

Brevin Jordan

Miami | TE | 6'2" | 247lbs

Brevin Jordan is of NFL bloodstock, his father Darrell Brevin was drafted in 1990 by The Atlanta Falcons. Players who come from a family of past players in the NFL tend to do very well themselves, especially when it's the player's father who has been a pro. In his recruiting class Jordan was the highest rated Tight End prospect according to 24/7 Sports and received a monstrous 31 offers from Colleges trying to make Jordan their man. Perhaps it was the outrageous Senior season in High School that meant he had so many offers after all he posted up 1,111 yards and 13 touchdowns off just 63 receptions, High School kids just couldn't hang with Jordan. In the end he decided to commit to The Hurricanes and as a player has improved every year at Miami. Like many of our top prospects, Jordan started his Collegiate career with a bang.

Jordans Freshman season couldn't have started any better. He was targeted alot for a first game by a Tight End. Jordan caught seven passes for 52 yards and also scored twice on his debut for The Hurricanes. He then had another superb game in week two against Florida International when he caught five passes for 67 yards and another touchdown. The best Tight End prospect in the 2018 recruiting class was showing the world what he was capable of early doors. The following week against North Carolina caught just one pass for four yards. The following week he only caught two passes but they went for 51 yards and a touchdown showing that he can be a big play threat at any moment. Two weeks later against Boston College, Jordan had his season high in receptions when he caught eight psses for 36 yards. Jordan wouldn't find the end zone again and would end up finishing his Freshman season with 32 catches for 287 yards and four touchdowns. Better was yet to come for the flashy Tight End.

In 2019 the Sophomore again started the season on fire in a tough week one matchup against Florida, Jordan again found the end zone. He caught five passes for 88 yards. Again in week two he caught another high number of passes as he reeled in six catches for 73 yards. In a scarily parallel week three game to his week three Freshman game, Jordan only caught two passes for two yards. Then again he bounced back with a big week four as he only caught three passes but amassed 70 yards. Then in week five he blew away Virginia Tech with a seven catch, 136 yard performance and he also found the end zone for his second score of the season. In the final game of his nine game season, Jordan was again good against a team from Florida as he caught six passes for 48 yards against Florida State. His Sophomore season would end up with final numbers of 35 catches, 495 yards and 2 scores.

In a year that saw Jordan step forward hugely in his route running, an interesting stat from Jordans 2020 season was that he had the best yards per route run of any Tight End. He had 2.42 yards per route run; Kyle Pitts was 2.24 in 2020 (per PFF). Yards per route run is finding out how effective a player is with the opportunities given to him by dividing the total receiving yards a player accumulated by how many routes on passing plays he actually ran. Why this is important for a guy like Brevin is that Yards per route run is a very good identifier in Rookie Wide Receivers as to how they will fare into their Sophomore year. It's a great outliner as to whether they will be productive in their second year and anyone with a number over 2.00 is considered to be going to have a good second year. Now for sure there are exceptions that prove the rule wrong and it isn't hard and fast but when the NFL is using Tight Ends more and more as weapons and not just the occasional catch, this bodes very well for Jordan going forward. 2020 was obviously a great year for Jordan as I've said and his stand out games were in weeks two, seven and eight. Against Louisville in week two he caught seven targets for a massive 120 yards and a touchdown. He then had a 140 yard, six catch game against North Carolina in which he found the end zone again. He finished off his season with a eight catch, 96 yard, two touchdown game against Oklahoma State in The Cheez-It Bowl (terrible name I know). He would end up ranking second in team in receptions and receiving yards and was tied for team lead in touchdown receptions despite missing three games. His end of season numbers read, 38 catches, 576 yards and seven touchdowns, Jordan then declared for the NFL.

As a weapon at the next level Brevin Jordan projects to be a very dangerous and tricky customer for NFL Defences. He is a yard after the catch machine and has proven to be almost unstoppable against Cover Defence in the College game. He has some areas of concern that he will need to work on inorder to maximise his potential however. He loses focus on contested catches and there were times where I thought he was too worried/focused on the Defender and what he was doing rather than on catching the Football. He also needs to gain some core strength to be a fully dependable blocker, he gives his all but needs to have a better understanding of how to block so that he doesn't get squared up and move off his point due to poor footwork, at times he appears statuesque. Jordan can be that next Tight End monster we all love if he just knuckles down and gets to work on those issues. He has electric pace when engaging his second gear and can shred Secondaries if they aren't in the right place or get their tackle angles wrong.

NFL Landing Spot

Jordan joins a Texans team who have never really utilized the Tight End and are currently in no-man's land with the Watson situation. Take caution if drafting now.

Hunter Long

Boston College | TE | 6'5" | 253lbs

Whilst Hunter Long isn't perhaps a name you may have heard in this Draft Class he is a Quarterbacks dream at the position. Long is a monster of a man and trying to cover him has proven difficult for many a Defender who has attempted it. Coming out of High School, Long was already a big lad. He was already six foot five and weighed a staggering 235 pounds. He had some mass to add to his huge frame but that would be the easy bit for Long. Getting an offer from a big School would be where he would end up struggling. Eventually Boston College came knocking and they were the best of the bunch as most of his offers came from FCS Schools.

Long would Redshirt his Freshman year after playing in just four games. What's crazy about those four games is he had one reception in all of them and averaged a healthy 25.8 yards per catch before redshirting. He displayed all his athletic prowess over these four games amassing 103 yards and had two touchdowns in the process. His solitary catch in the game against Holy Cross went for 35 yards and a touchdown and then in the following game against Louisville he again took his solitary catch to the house on a 26 yard reception. Long had flashed what he was capable of before Redshirting and people were put on high alert after seeing him make four big catches.

After his Redshirt season the Sophomore stepped onto the field and into a larger role straight from the get go. So much so in fact, he would lead the team in receiving yards come the end of the season. He would record a season and career high four receptions in week one when he would total 53 yards off of those four catches. He would actually record more than one reception in all but one of his 11 games played and that solitary catch game came in week eight against Syracuse. Long found the end zone for the first time in week five against Louisville as he averaged 33 yards per catch as he only caught three passes but tallied 99 yards. Thenn in the following week against North Carolina State, Long caught three passes for 84 yards but did not find the end zone. His second touchdown came in week 10 against Pitt as he only caught two passes in that game but one of them a 25 yard touchdown. Long finished his first season proper with 28 receptions, 509 yards and just the two touchdowns. After his first four games in his Freshman year Long would have wanted more trips into the end zone but they didn't come to fruition as Boston College had a coaching change and also finished 63rd in the country in points scored and ended the season with a 6-7 record which ultimately hurt Long's touchdown chances.

If 2020 was anything to go by then Hunter Long should have been talked about much higher in Draft discussions than he was. Long had a record setting year as an Eagle, in which he led the nation in receptions at the Tight End position and was also second in receiving yards. He had a breakout campaign for Boston College as he also notched up the second highest reception number in School history trailing only Pete Mitchell's 66 receptions in 1993.

Long started the year with back to back touchdowns in weeks one and two. He also had a career high receptions in week one against Duke where he racked up seven catches for 93 yards and one score. Then in the very next game he would eclipse that reception record as he caught nine passes for 81 yards and a score in a win against Texas State. Long would then get even closer to having a 100 yard game in week three as he again caught nine passes totalling 96 yards. That 100 yard game was coming, Long just didn't know it yet. In a season which flip flopped wins and losses for The Eagles, Long was fairly consistent with his participation as part of the passing game. He had two down weeks receptions wise as he logged just two receptions per game in weeks eight and ten and then just three receptions per game in weeks six and seven. He did, however, find the end zone in week five when he caught a 20 yard pass from Phil Jurkovec (a name to watch out for in the coming years). His career performance came against Virginia in the last game of the season and now what we know to be his final game at Boston College. He caught eight passes for 109 yards and a score as The Eagles would eventually end up losing 43-32. After the season was over Long would declare for the NFL Draft a year early.

When watching Long he comes across as extremely reliable and a powerful player who is always turning upfield to gain a few extra yards on the play. Long caught many passes with his back to the goal posts and would often be covered by one or two defenders. He would more often than not be able to turn round after the catch and either use his mass to fall forward or run forward dragging a Defender or two with him for a few extra yards after the catch. One play I noted of Longs was against Duke where he caught a ball in a contested catch situation in which one of his arms was being held down by the Defender. He and the Defender went up and Long displayed superb concentration and catching ability to reel it in with one hand whilst having the other hand held down. He has good hands and superb focus whilst runs the majority of routes well. He doesn't have breakaway speed though so wont be a huge yards after the catch guy at the next level. He also needs to work on his blocking to be used on all downs in the NFL.

NFL Landing Spot

Long joins Gesiki making for a formidable Tight End room at The Dolphins. Long isn't really a blocker so look for him to be open alot in the middle of the field for Tua.

CHAPTER 20

Thank You(s)

Written by Chris Mitchell & Adam Murfet

We gave some thank you's at the front of the book. However, there are certainly some here at the back of the book that are required. These are the unsung heroes who helped contribute to the book.

Firstly, for the data side, we would like to thank FantasyPros, Expand the Boxscore and Fantasy Data. There is also special thanks to Fantasy Football Calculator and Fantasy Alarm for help on the ADP side. At the end of this section are links to their websites. Please do use them as they are fantastic resources. The majority of the data came from FantasyPros and Fantasy Data, so thank you so much.

We would also like to thank Richard Price as well. Richard helped Murf with the construction of the data sheets for the Fantasy Mock Drafts so thank you for all your help in putting that together.

Thanks also to the Mock Draft Committee. To SFB9 Champ Gary Haddow of Fighting Chance Fantasy, Kevin Tompkins of Fighting Chance Fantasy, Joe Pepe of Fantasy Data, Ben Rolfe of Pro Football Network, 2020 Warrior Bowl Champion (curses!!) Steven Perkins of Dynasty Football Digest, Bob Lung, creator of the Kings Classic and the Consistency Guide, Lewis Glover of DFF Dynasty, Drew Davenport of Football Guys, Gage Bridgford of Rotoballer and Dynasty Nerd, JB Barry of Razzball and Rich Cooling of 5 Yard Rush for helping with one of the mock draft committees and the time you have spent to make content for this book as a result.

Many thanks also to Christopher Pinto of Fantasy First Rounders and Rumboyz, Ger O'Callaghan who is a 4 time SFB players, Martin Weeks, Greg Boyland the creator of Warrior Bowl, Corey Rosynek, Jeff Tindall, Paddi Cooper of Fake Teams, Jorge Edwards of Fantasy in Frames, Jonas Hurbin, Peter Gent the creator of Shark Tank and Eurovision FF, and Dave Gray of Betfair and First and Ten for the second mock draft committee and the time you have spent to help make content for this book as a result.

To Peter Melia for being a sounding board early on in this book and giving me some advice and recommendations that have been added to this as a result. Thank you my friend.

Thank you to 4for4 Fantasy Football for the subscription for data, as well as to Pat Fitzmaurice, Bob Lung, Gary Haddow, Dwain McFarland and Brian Drake for reviewing the early edit of the book and coming up with some useful suggestions and insight.

Thank you to anyone who has been a guest on the show. We appreciate your time and helping us to create great content.

Thank you to our Patreons. You have been invaluable at keeping us going. We will forever be in your debt.

FantasyPros- www.fantasypros.com

Fantasy Data- https://fantasydata.com

Fantasy Football Calculator- https://fantasyfootballcalculator.com

Fantasy Alarm- www.fantasyalarm.com

4for4- https://www.4for4.com/

Expand the Boxscore- https://expandtheboxscore.com/

CHAPTER 21

Appendix - Charts & Research

Written by Adam Murfet

This section is the charts section of the book, with full tables and charts to add additional context to the chapters in the book.

PAS Metric Tables

All these metrics are worked out on PPR scoring.

Quarterbacks

Rank	Name	Total Points	Games Played	PPG Average	PAS
1	Patrick Mahomes	374.4	15	24.96	7.18
2	Josh Allen	395.56	16	24.72	6.94
3	Aaron Rodgers	382.76	16	23.92	6.14
4	Kyler Murray	378.74	16	23.67	5.89
5	Deshaun Watson	369.32	16	23.08	5.30
6	Russell Wilson	359.78	16	22.49	4.71
7	Justin Herbert	332.84	15	22.19	4.41
8	Lamar Jackson	332.78	15	22.19	4.41
9	Ryan Tannehill	343.86	16	21.49	3.71
10	Tom Brady	337.92	16	21.12	3.34
11	Kirk Cousins	306.2	16	19.14	1.36
12	Ben Roethlisberger	267.22	15	17.81	0.03
13	Gardner Minshew II	160.16	9	17.80	0.02
14	Matt Ryan	280.44	16	17.53	-0.25
15	Drew Brees	209.48	12	17.46	-0.32
16	Joe Burrow	173.72	10	17.37	-0.41
17	Cam Newton	259.98	15	17.33	-0.45
18	Ryan Fitzpatrick	153.24	9	17.03	-0.75
19	Derek Carr	272.12	16	17.01	-0.77
20	Carson Wentz	198.4	12	16.53	-1.25
21	Matthew Stafford	260.56	16	16.29	-1.50
22	Teddy Bridgewater	241.22	15	16.08	-1.70
23	Jared Goff	239.98	15	16.00	-1.78
24	Baker Mayfield	248.12	16	15.51	-2.27
25	Mitchell Trubisky	153.7	10	15.37	-2.41
26	Philip Rivers	239.96	16	15.00	-2.78
27	Drew Lock	181.32	13	13.95	-3.83

28	Tua Tagovailoa	135.46	10	13.55	-4.23
29	Daniel Jones	180.02	14	12.86	-4.92
30	Andy Dalton	136.36	11	12.40	-5.38
31	Nick Mullens	116.28	10	11.63	-6.15
32	Nick Foles	104.18	9	11.58	-6.20
33	Sam Darnold	134.02	12	11.17	-6.61
34	Taysom Hill	152.62	16	9.54	-8.24
35	Alex Smith	71.58	8	8.95	-8.83
36	Jalen Hurts	108.94	15	7.26	-10.52

Running Backs

Rank	Name	Total 0.5 PPR Points	Games Played	PPG Average	PAS
1	Dalvin Cook	315.8	14	22.56	10.50
2	Alvin Kamara	336.3	15	22.42	10.36
3	Derrick Henry	323.6	16	20.23	8.17
4	Aaron Jones	235.4	14	16.81	4.75
5	Nick Chubb	199.7	12	16.64	4.58
6	James Robinson	225.9	14	16.14	4.08
7	David Montgomery	237.8	15	15.85	3.79
8	Jonathan Taylor	234.8	15	15.65	3.59
9	Myles Gaskin	143.7	10	14.37	2.31
10	Josh Jacobs	214.8	15	14.32	2.26
11	Chris Carson	169.3	12	14.11	2.05
12	Austin Ekeler	138.3	10	13.83	1.77
13	David Johnson	163	12	13.58	1.52
14	Ezekiel Elliott	197.7	15	13.18	1.12
15	Antonio Gibson	184.2	14	13.16	1.10
16	Miles Sanders	156.4	12	13.03	0.97
17	D'Andre Swift	166.8	13	12.83	0.77
18	Kareem Hunt	199.5	16	12.47	0.41
19	Jeff Wilson Jr.	135.8	11	12.35	0.29
20	Ronald Jones II	172.3	14	12.31	0.25

21	Melvin Gordon III	182.4	15	12.16	0.10
22	Clyde Edwards-Helaire	158	13	12.15	0.09
23	Kenyan Drake	179.7	15	11.98	-0.08
24	Mike Davis	177	15	11.80	-0.26
25	Raheem Mostert	91.7	8	11.46	-0.60
26	James Conner	147.1	13	11.32	-0.74
27	J.K. Dobbins	159.5	15	10.63	-1.43
28	Nyheim Hines	161.7	16	10.11	-1.95
29	Todd Gurley II	150.7	15	10.05	-2.01
30	Rex Burkhead	95.1	10	9.51	-2.55
31	J.D. McKissic	151.4	16	9.46	-2.60
32	Damien Harris	88.8	10	8.88	-3.18
33	Chase Edmonds	141.5	16	8.84	-3.22
34	Leonard Fournette	114	13	8.77	-3.29
35	Giovani Bernard	134.6	16	8.41	-3.65
36	Wayne Gallman	126.1	15	8.41	-3.65
37	Latavius Murray	124.7	15	8.31	-3.75
38	Darrell Henderson Jr.	122.3	15	8.15	-3.91
39	Sony Michel	71.8	9	7.98	-4.08
40	Jamaal Williams	111.6	14	7.97	-4.09
41	Devin Singletary	124.6	16	7.79	-4.27
42	Gus Edwards	123.7	16	7.73	-4.33
43	Carlos Hyde	76.9	10	7.69	-4.37
44	Cam Akers	96.3	13	7.41	-4.65
45	Adrian Peterson	118.5	16	7.41	-4.65
46	Zack Moss	94.6	13	7.28	-4.78
47	Kalen Ballage	79.4	11	7.22	-4.84
48	Jerick McKinnon	109.7	16	6.86	-5.20
49	Tony Pollard	106.7	16	6.67	-5.39
50	James White	92.1	14	6.58	-5.48
51	Duke Johnson	70.4	11	6.40	-5.66
52	Justin Jackson	55.8	9	6.20	-5.86
53	Alexander Mattison	80.4	13	6.18	-5.88
54	Frank Gore	92.2	15	6.15	-5.91
55	Malcolm Brown	97.6	16	6.10	-5.96

56	Le'Veon Bell	66.6	11	6.05	-6.01
57	Phillip Lindsay	62.5	11	5.68	-6.38
58	Boston Scott	83.1	16	5.19	-6.87
59	Brian Hill	82.9	16	5.18	-6.88
60	Joshua Kelley	69.7	14	4.98	-7.08
61	Devontae Booker	77.2	16	4.83	-7.24
62	La'Mical Perine	47	10	4.70	-7.36
63	Mark Ingram II	49.9	11	4.54	-7.52
64	Kyle Juszczyk	72.1	16	4.51	-7.55
65	Benny Snell Jr.	69.9	16	4.37	-7.69
66	Alfred Morris	39.2	9	4.36	-7.70
67	Ty Johnson	55.3	13	4.25	-7.81
68	Josh Adams	33.6	8	4.20	-7.86
69	Chris Thompson	32.6	8	4.08	-7.99
70	DeeJay Dallas	48.4	12	4.03	-8.03
71	Kerryon Johnson	62.3	16	3.89	-8.17
72	Samaje Perine	60.2	16	3.76	-8.30
73	Jordan Wilkins	55.3	15	3.69	-8.37
74	A.J. Dillon	39.3	11	3.57	-8.49
75	Darrel Williams	45.5	13	3.50	-8.56
76	Ito Smith	48.8	14	3.49	-8.57
77	Peyton Barber	53	16	3.31	-8.75
78	Jalen Richard	41.6	13	3.20	-8.86
79	Matt Breida	37.5	12	3.13	-8.94
80	Dion Lewis	47.7	16	2.98	-9.08
81	Jeremy McNichols	37.9	16	2.37	-9.69
82	Royce Freeman	31.1	16	1.94	-10.12

Wide Receivers

Rank	Name	Total 0.5 PPR Points	Games Played	Total PPG	PAS
1	Davante Adams	300.9	14	21.49	12.09
2	Tyreek Hill	285.4	15	19.03	9.63

3	Stefon Diggs	265.1	16	16.57	7.17
4	Calvin Ridley	236.5	15	15.77	6.37
5	Will Fuller V	162.4	11	14.76	5.36
6	A.J. Brown	206.5	14	14.75	5.35
7	Adam Thielen	217	15	14.47	5.07
8	DeAndre Hopkins	230.3	16	14.39	4.99
9	Justin Jefferson	230.2	16	14.39	4.99
10	DK Metcalf	229.8	16	14.36	4.96
11	Keenan Allen	195.1	14	13.94	4.54
12	Tyler Lockett	215.4	16	13.46	4.06
13	Julio Jones	120.6	9	13.40	4.00
14	Mike Evans	213.6	16	13.35	3.95
15	Allen Robinson II	211.9	16	13.24	3.84
16	Chris Godwin	158.5	12	13.21	3.81
17	Brandon Aiyuk	154.5	12	12.88	3.48
18	Brandin Cooks	191.5	15	12.77	3.37
19	Robert Woods	200.1	16	12.51	3.11
20	Terry McLaurin	180.3	15	12.02	2.62
21	Amari Cooper	190.8	16	11.93	2.53
22	D.J. Moore	178.5	15	11.90	2.50
23	Jamison Crowder	142.52	12	11.88	2.48
24	Marvin Jones Jr.	189.8	16	11.86	2.46
25	Diontae Johnson	177.8	15	11.85	2.45
26	Antonio Brown	94.6	8	11.83	2.43
27	JuJu Smith-Schuster	185.6	16	11.60	2.20
28	Curtis Samuel	173.6	15	11.57	2.17
29	Chase Claypool	183.9	16	11.49	2.09
30	Corey Davis	158.9	14	11.35	1.95
31	Cole Beasley	166.5	15	11.10	1.70
32	Robby Anderson	176.6	16	11.04	1.64
33	CeeDee Lamb	174.7	16	10.92	1.52
34	Cooper Kupp	162.7	15	10.85	1.45
35	Sterling Shepard	129.5	12	10.79	1.39
36	Tyler Boyd	153.14	15	10.21	0.81
37	Jarvis Landry	151.96	15	10.13	0.73

38	Nelson Agholor	161.6	16	10.10	0.70
39	Tee Higgins	161.1	16	10.07	0.67
40	DJ Chark Jr.	127.1	13	9.78	0.38
41	DeVante Parker	134.8	14	9.63	0.23
42	Marquise Brown	154	16	9.63	0.23
43	Emmanuel Sanders	134.3	14	9.59	0.19
44	Laviska Shenault Jr.	128.1	14	9.15	-0.25
45	T.Y. Hilton	136.2	15	9.08	-0.32
46	Russell Gage	145.06	16	9.07	-0.33
47	Tim Patrick	135.7	15	9.05	-0.35
48	Michael Gallup	143.8	16	8.99	-0.41
49	John Brown	80.3	9	8.92	-0.48
50	Keke Coutee	70.5	8	8.81	-0.59
51	Christian Kirk	122.4	14	8.74	-0.66
52	Mike Williams	129.7	15	8.65	-0.75
53	Jerry Jeudy	131.6	16	8.23	-1.18
54	Preston Williams	65.8	8	8.23	-1.18
55	Allen Lazard	81.3	10	8.13	-1.27
56	Randall Cobb	81.1	10	8.11	-1.29
57	Jakobi Meyers	113.02	14	8.07	-1.33
58	Rashard Higgins	102.4	13	7.88	-1.52
59	Keelan Cole Sr.	121.9	16	7.62	-1.78
60	Darnell Mooney	121.6	16	7.60	-1.80
61	Marquez Valdes-Scantling	120.8	16	7.55	-1.85
62	Gabriel Davis	119.4	16	7.46	-1.94
63	Travis Fulgham	96.9	13	7.45	-1.95
64	Darius Slayton	116	16	7.25	-2.15
65	Zach Pascal	114.9	16	7.18	-2.22
66	Kendrick Bourne	105.2	15	7.01	-2.39
67	Breshad Perriman	84.1	12	7.01	-2.39
68	Sammy Watkins	68.9	10	6.89	-2.51
69	Greg Ward	106.6	16	6.66	-2.74
70	Hunter Renfrow	103.6	16	6.48	-2.93
71	Mecole Hardman	101.6	16	6.35	-3.05
72	David Moore	101.3	16	6.33	-3.07

73	Tre'Quan Smith	86.1	14	6.15	-3.25
74	Josh Reynolds	98.3	16	6.14	-3.26
75	Michael Pittman Jr.	78.9	13	6.07	-3.33
76	Willie Snead IV	77.7	13	5.98	-3.42
77	Jalen Reagor	65.7	11	5.97	-3.43
78	Danny Amendola	83.4	14	5.96	-3.44
79	Tyron Johnson	69.5	12	5.79	-3.61
80	K.J. Hamler	75.1	13	5.78	-3.62
81	Golden Tate	69.02	12	5.75	-3.65
82	Damiere Byrd	91.4	16	5.71	-3.69
83	Larry Fitzgerald	73.9	13	5.68	-3.72
84	A.J. Green	87.8	16	5.49	-3.91
85	Henry Ruggs III	71.1	13	5.47	-3.93
86	Denzel Mims	49.2	9	5.47	-3.93
87	Scotty Miller	86	16	5.38	-4.03
88	Demarcus Robinson	85.1	16	5.32	-4.08
89	Richie James Jr.	52.9	10	5.29	-4.11
90	James Washington	84.2	16	5.26	-4.14
91	Anthony Miller	84.2	16	5.26	-4.14
92	Jalen Guyton	83.1	16	5.19	-4.21
93	Chris Conley	77.1	15	5.14	-4.26
94	Braxton Berrios	78.8	16	4.93	-4.48
95	Isaiah McKenzie	78.58	16	4.91	-4.49
96	Jakeem Grant Sr.	63.3	14	4.52	-4.88
97	Cam Sims	70.2	16	4.39	-5.01
98	Quintez Cephus	56.9	13	4.38	-5.02
99	Donovan Peoples-Jones	51.4	12	4.28	-5.12
100	Marvin Hall	51.3	12	4.28	-5.13
101	N'Keal Harry	57.4	14	4.10	-5.30
102	Miles Boykin	60.1	16	3.76	-5.64
103	Collin Johnson	50.2	14	3.59	-5.81
104	Cordarrelle Patterson	52.9	16	3.31	-6.09
105	DaeSean Hamilton	50.8	16	3.18	-6.23

Tight Ends

Rank	Name	Total 0.5 PPR PPG	Games Played	Total PPG	PAS
1	Travis Kelce	260.26	15	17.35	8.29
2	Darren Waller	225.1	16	14.07	5.01
3	George Kittle	101.1	8	12.64	3.58
4	Mark Andrews	141.1	14	10.08	1.02
5	Robert Tonyan	150.6	16	9.41	0.35
6	T.J. Hockenson	141.8	16	8.86	-0.20
7	Mike Gesicki	132.8	15	8.85	-0.21
8	Logan Thomas	140.62	16	8.79	-0.27
9	Dallas Goedert	93.4	11	8.49	-0.57
10	Hunter Henry	115.3	14	8.24	-0.82
11	Jonnu Smith	119.7	15	7.98	-1.08
12	Rob Gronkowski	126.8	16	7.93	-1.14
13	Noah Fant	118.3	15	7.89	-1.17
14	Eric Ebron	113.8	15	7.59	-1.47
15	Hayden Hurst	121.1	16	7.57	-1.49
16	Jimmy Graham	118.6	16	7.41	-1.65
17	Jared Cook	108.9	15	7.26	-1.80
18	Dalton Schultz	115	16	7.19	-1.87
19	Tyler Higbee	106.2	15	7.08	-1.98
20	Austin Hooper	90.5	13	6.96	-2.10
21	Evan Engram	109.5	16	6.84	-2.22
22	Irv Smith Jr.	83.5	13	6.42	-2.64
23	Jordan Reed	60.1	10	6.01	-3.05
24	Zach Ertz	59.5	11	5.41	-3.65
25	Trey Burton	69.3	13	5.33	-3.73
26	Dan Arnold	81.3	16	5.08	-3.98
27	Jordan Akins	65.2	13	5.02	-4.04
28	Dawson Knox	54.8	12	4.57	-4.49
29	Gerald Everett	72.4	16	4.53	-4.54
30	Mo Alie-Cox	64.9	15	4.33	-4.73
31	Tyler Eifert	64.9	15	4.33	-4.73
32	Kyle Rudolph	51.4	12	4.28	-4.78
33	Richard Rodgers	58.5	14	4.18	-4.88

34	**Darren Fells**	65.7	16	4.11	-4.95
35	**Anthony Firkser**	64.2	16	4.01	-5.05
36	**Greg Olsen**	41.9	11	3.81	-5.25
37	**Jack Doyle**	52.6	14	3.76	-5.30
38	**Drew Sample**	58.9	16	3.68	-5.38
39	**Chris Herndon**	58.2	16	3.64	-5.42
40	**Tyler Kroft**	35.9	10	3.59	-5.47
41	**Cameron Brate**	54.2	16	3.39	-5.67
42	**Nick Boyle**	30.3	9	3.37	-5.69
43	**Jacob Hollister**	53.4	16	3.34	-5.72
44	**Harrison Bryant**	49.8	15	3.32	-5.74
45	**David Njoku**	42.8	13	3.29	-5.77
46	**Will Dissly**	49.1	16	3.07	-5.99
47	**Durham Smythe**	45.8	15	3.05	-6.01
48	**Cole Kmet**	48	16	3.00	-6.06
49	**Donald Parham Jr.**	38.9	13	2.99	-6.07
50	**Pharaoh Brown**	35.3	13	2.72	-6.34
51	**James O'Shaughnessy**	40.2	15	2.68	-6.38
52	**Ross Dwelley**	40	16	2.50	-6.56
53	**Adam Shaheen**	39	16	2.44	-6.62
54	**Marcedes Lewis**	33.7	15	2.25	-6.81
55	**Tyler Conklin**	34.9	16	2.18	-6.88
56	**Adam Trautman**	30.6	15	2.04	-7.02
57	**Ryan Izzo**	24.4	12	2.03	-7.03
58	**Jesse James**	31.9	16	1.99	-7.07
59	**Ian Thomas**	30.5	16	1.91	-7.15
60	**Foster Moreau**	29.5	16	1.84	-7.22
61	**Jason Witten**	25.4	16	1.59	-7.47

Kickers

Rank	Name	Total 0.5 PPR Points	Games Played	PPG Average	PAS
1	Younghoe Koo	160	15	10.67	3.26

Rank	Name	Points Week 1-16 Total		Total PPG	PAS
2	Jason Sanders	160	16	10.00	2.59
3	Daniel Carlson	152	16	9.50	2.09
4	Tyler Bass	149	16	9.31	1.90
5	Greg Zuerlein	141	16	8.81	1.40
6	Rodrigo Blankenship	141	16	8.81	1.40
7	Ryan Succop	138	16	8.63	1.22
8	Brandon McManus	128	15	8.53	1.12
9	Justin Tucker	136	16	8.50	1.09
10	Harrison Butker	131	16	8.19	0.78
11	Cairo Santos	130	16	8.13	0.72
12	Wil Lutz	128	16	8.00	0.59
13	Ka'imi Fairbairn	126	16	7.88	0.47
14	Jason Myers	125	16	7.81	0.40
15	Graham Gano	124	16	7.75	0.34
16	Randy Bullock	93	12	7.75	0.34
17	Joey Slye	122	16	7.63	0.22
18	Stephen Gostkowski	114	15	7.60	0.19
19	Zane Gonzalez	90	12	7.50	0.09
20	Mason Crosby	115	16	7.19	-0.22
21	Dustin Hopkins	115	16	7.19	-0.22
22	Chris Boswell Q	93	13	7.15	-0.26
23	Matt Prater	113	16	7.06	-0.35
24	Nick Folk	112	16	7.00	-0.41
25	Michael Badgley	112	16	7.00	-0.41
26	Cody Parkey	100	15	6.67	-0.74
27	Samuel Sloman	53	8	6.63	-0.79
28	Robbie Gould	97	15	6.47	-0.94
29	Sam Ficken	53	9	5.89	-1.52
30	Dan Bailey	86	16	5.38	-2.04
31	Jake Elliott	70	16	4.38	-3.04

D/STs

Rank	Name	Points Week 1-16 Total	Total PPG	PAS
1	Indianapolis Colts	151	9.44	2.20

2	Pittsburgh Steelers	150	9.38	2.14
3	Los Angeles Rams	149	9.31	2.07
4	Baltimore Ravens	143	8.94	1.70
5	Miami Dolphins	139	8.69	1.45
5	Washington Football Team	127	7.94	0.70
7	New Orleans Saints	122	7.63	0.39
8	Buffalo Bills	118	7.38	0.14
9	Tampa Bay Buccaneers	117	7.31	0.07
10	Kansas City Chiefs	110	6.88	-0.37
11	Arizona Cardinals	107	6.69	-0.55
12	New England Patriots	104	6.50	-0.74
13	Philadelphia Eagles	103	6.44	-0.80
14	Seattle Seahawks	103	6.44	-0.80
15	New York Giants	103	6.44	-0.80
16	Carolina Panthers	97	6.06	-1.18
17	Cleveland Browns	94	5.88	-1.37
18	Green Bay Packers	94	5.88	-1.37
18	Chicago Bears	90	5.63	-1.62
20	San Francisco 49ers	88	5.50	-1.74
21	Dallas Cowboys	78	4.88	-2.37
22	Denver Broncos	74	4.63	-2.62
22	Los Angeles Chargers	72	4.50	-2.74
22	Atlanta Falcons	72	4.50	-2.74
25	Tennessee Titans	70	4.38	-2.87
26	New York Jets	65	4.06	-3.18
27	Minnesota Vikings	57	3.56	-3.68
28	Jacksonville Jaguars	52	3.25	-3.99
29	Houston Texans	48	3.00	-4.24
30	Cincinnati Bengals	45	2.81	-4.43
31	Las Vegas Raiders	39	2.44	-4.80
32	Detroit Lions	27	1.69	-5.55

The Perfect Draft by Position and ADP

As mentioned in the "The Value of Each Round of a Fantasy Football Draft" chapter, here is all the data based on 2020, 2019, and 2018 ADP. This data comes from Fantasy Alarm, Fantasy Football Calculator and Fantasy Pros.

Quarterbacks

Round	QB-2020	QB-2019	QB-2018	Average per Round 2020-2018	Average Difference Pts per Round
1	-	-	-		
2	23.99	-	-	23.99	NA
3	-	21.54	20.77	21.15	-2.84
4	-	-	-		
5	26.76	22.13	18.80	22.56	1.41
6	23.47	17.49	19.94	20.30	-2.26
7		17.10	17.51	17.31	-2.99
8	21.85	19.31	19.20	20.12	2.81
9	18.93	15.13	15.82	16.63	-3.49
10	20.27	22.73	23.39	22.13	5.50
11	13.40	16.98	19.09	16.49	-5.64
12	17.29	16.96	13.15	15.80	-0.69

Running Backs

Round	RB-2020	RB-2019	RB-2018	Average per Round 2020-2018	Average Difference Pts per Round
1	17.96	15.61	17.28	16.95	-
2	14.10	15.12	14.36	14.52	-2.43
3	10.48	13.44	8.76	10.89	-3.63
4	11.18	12.82	11.44	11.81	0.92
5	9.70	9.92	8.13	9.25	-2.56
6	11.23	11.38	10.26	10.96	1.71
7	9.39	13.30	8.80	10.50	-0.46
8	9.21	7.45	11.78	9.48	-1.02
9	5.87	5.91	4.60	5.46	-4.02
10	5.49	8.97	8.59	7.68	2.22
11		-	-	-	-

12	-	-	-	-

Wide Receiver

Round	WR-2020	WR-2019	WR-2018	Average per Round 2020-2018	Average Difference Pts per Round
1	15.61	14.53	17.04	15.73	-
2	14.81	13.44	15.93	14.73	-1.00
3	12.28	11.97	14.16	12.80	-1.93
4	13.36	12.53	9.79	11.89	-0.91
5	11.48	12.41	7.51	10.47	-1.43
6	11.90	11.61	11.08	11.53	1.06
7	10.99	9.29	11.30	10.53	-1.00
8	9.78	9.62	8.35	9.25	-1.28
9	10.68	9.33	8.92	9.64	0.39
10	9.49	9.79	6.63	8.64	-1.01
11		-	-	-	-
12		-	-	-	-

Tight Ends

Round	TE-2020	TE-2019	TE-2018	Average per Round 2020-2018	Average Difference Pts per Round
1	-	13.46	-	13.46	
2	15.16	-	8.69	11.93	-1.53
3	-	12.15	15.63	13.89	1.96
4	7.24	-	14.62	10.93	-2.96
5	13.53	10.93	6.63	10.36	-0.57
6	-	5.15	7.51	6.33	-4.03
7	7.15	10.18	7.81	8.38	2.05
8	8.24	5.13	7.14	6.84	-1.54
9	7.77	12.18	7.73	9.23	2.39
10	6.73	6.29	7.92	6.98	-2.25
11	8.74	6.70	-	7.72	0.74
12	-	4.09	12.62	8.36	0.64

2020 ADP Raw Data (RD) Values and Breakdown

Year	Name	Pos	ADP	ADP Round	Fantasy Points 0.5 PPR	Game Played	PPG	RD Points Average Per Game	Difference from Previous Round	Notes
2020	Christian McCaffrey	RB	1.09	1	81.9	3	27.30	17.96	N/A	
2020	Saquon Barkley	RB	2.17	1	12.4	2	6.20	15.61	N/A	
2020	Ezekiel Elliott	RB	3.32	1	184.1	14	13.15			
2020	Alvin Kamara	RB	5.09	1	336.3	15	22.42			
2020	Michael Thomas	WR	5.9	1	63.9	7	9.13			
2020	Dalvin Cook	RB	6.27	1	315.8	14	22.56			
2020	Derrick Henry	RB	7.72	1	288.6	15	19.24			
2020	Joe Mixon	RB	10.68	1	89.1	6	14.85			
2020	Davante Adams	WR	11.94	1	287.3	13	22.10			
2020	Tyreek Hill	WR	15.45	2	285.4	15	19.03			
2020	Josh Jacobs	RB	15.53	2	193.9	14	13.85			
2020	Kenyan Drake	RB	15.6	2	173.1	14	12.36			
2020	Miles Sanders	RB	15.75	2	156.4	12	13.03	14.81	-0.80	
2020	Nick Chubb	RB	15.77	2	199.7	12	16.64	14.10	-3.86	
2020	Travis Kelce	TE	16.37	2	260.3	15	17.35	15.16	N/A	
2020	DeAndre Hopkins	WR	16.79	2	224	15	14.93	23.99	N/A	
2020	Aaron Jones	RB	17.02	2	218.9	13	16.84			
2020	Austin Ekeler	RB	17.32	2	124.2	9	13.80			
2020	Julio Jones	WR	17.79	2	120.6	9	13.40			
2020	Clyde Edwards-Helaire	RB	18.61	2	158	13	12.15			
2020	Lamar Jackson	QB	19.74	2	316.56	14	22.61			
2020	Patrick Mahomes	QB	19.82	2	380.4	15	25.36	10.48	-3.62	
2020	George Kittle	TE	21.15	2	90.8	7	12.97	12.28	-2.53	
2020	Chris Godwin	WR	21.71	2	130.7	11	11.88			
2020	Kenny Golladay	WR	29.03	3	55.8	5	11.16			
2020	Mike Evans	WR	30.87	3	207.5	15	13.83			
2020	Allen Robinson	WR	33.36	3	207.2	15	13.81			
2020	Todd Gurley	RB	33.81	3	146.7	14	10.48			

2020	Odell Beckham	WR	33.81	3	75.3	7	10.76			
2020	D.J. Moore	WR	35.18	3	165.9	14	11.85			
2020	Amari Cooper	WR	37.7	4	183.7	15	12.25			
2020	JuJu Smith-Schuster	WR	38.37	4	170.1	15	11.34			
2020	Adam Thielen	WR	39.99	4	209.3	14	14.95			
2020	James Conner	RB	40.01	4	138.4	12	11.53			
2020	Melvin Gordon	RB	40.3	4	163.4	14	11.67			
2020	Mark Andrews	TE	40.4	4	136.4	13	10.49			
2020	Jonathan Taylor	RB	40.62	4	196.9	14	14.06	13.36	1.07	
2020	Cooper Kupp	WR	40.88	4	162.7	15	10.85	11.18	0.70	
2020	Leonard Fournette	RB	41.04	4	110.3	12	9.19	7.24	-7.92	
2020	Chris Carson	RB	42.04	4	160	11	14.55			
2020	A.J. Brown	WR	42.63	4	186.4	13	14.34			
2020	Zach Ertz	TE	45.01	4	39.9	10	3.99			
2020	Calvin Ridley	WR	46.47	4	229.9	14	16.42			
2020	Le'Veon Bell	RB	47.77	4	66.6	11	6.05			
2020	David Johnson	RB	50.46	5	143.5	11	13.05			
2020	Robert Woods	WR	55.26	5	194.5	15	12.97	9.70	-1.47	
2020	DK Metcalf	WR	56.04	5	226.2	15	15.08	11.48	-1.88	
2020	Dak Prescott	QB	56.3	5	138.64	5	27.73	12.61	-0.75	(without Courtland Sutton)
2020	Raheem Mostert	RB	57.76	5	91.7	8	11.46	13.53	6.29	
2020	Courtland Sutton	WR	57.83	5	8.1	1	8.10	26.76	2.78	
2020	Kyler Murray	QB	58.61	5	386.96	15	25.80			
2020	Darren Waller	TE	59.48	5	202.9	15	13.53			
2020	Mark Ingram	RB	59.5	5	46	10	4.60			
2020	D.J. Chark	WR	59.97	5	127.1	13	9.78			
2020	Devin Singletary	RB	60.6	6	124.6	16	7.79			
2020	Keenan Allen	WR	61.09	6	195.1	14	13.94			
2020	Tyler Lockett	WR	62.5	6	188.4	15	12.56	11.90	0.42	
2020	Russell Wilson	QB	62.62	6	354.64	15	23.64	23.47	-3.29	
2020	Terry McLaurin	WR	64.89	6	166.8	14	11.91	0.00	N/A	

2020	Cam Akers	RB	65.11	6	96.3	13	7.41	**11.23**	**1.53**	
2020	David Montgomery	RB	65.18	6	214.1	14	15.29			
2020	Deshaun Watson	QB	66.33	6	349.52	15	23.30			
2020	D'Andre Swift	RB	67.88	6	152.3	12	12.69	**9.39**	**-1.84**	
2020	DeVante Parker	WR	70.46	6	119.7	13	9.21	**10.99**	**-0.92**	
2020	Kareem Hunt	RB	70.64	6	194.9	15	12.99	**7.15**	**-6.38**	
2020	Stefon Diggs	WR	73.5	7	254	15	16.93			
2020	T.Y. Hilton	WR	74.62	7	124	14	8.86			
2020	J.K. Dobbins	RB	80	7	131.5	14	9.39			
2020	Marquise Brown	WR	80.55	7	135.4	15	9.03			
2020	Tyler Higbee	TE	80.96	7	100.6	14	7.19			
2020	Evan Engram	TE	82.05	7	106.8	15	7.12			
2020	Michael Gallup	WR	83.68	7	136.9	15	9.13			
2020	Tyler Boyd	WR	85.44	8	151.4	14	10.81			
2020	A.J. Green	WR	86.39	8	87.8	15	5.85			
2020	Will Fuller	WR	86.71	8	162.4	11	14.76			
2020	Hunter Henry	TE	87.96	8	115.3	14	8.24	**9.78**	**-1.20**	
2020	Jarvis Landry	WR	89.55	8	138.1	14	9.86	**8.24**	**1.08**	
2020	Josh Allen	QB	89.8	8	384.8	15	25.65	**21.85**	**-1.62**	
2020	Matt Ryan	QB	93.04	8	270.74	15	18.05	**9.21**	**-0.18**	
2020	Julian Edelman	WR	94.38	8	45.7	6	7.62			
2020	Ronald Jones	RB	94.81	8	158.5	13	12.19			
2020	James White	RB	95.06	8	81	13	6.23			
2020	Marlon Mack	RB	97.34	9	7.1	1	7.10			
2020	Deebo Samuel	WR	98.22	9	64.2	7	9.17			
2020	Drew Brees	QB	100.1	9	195.44	11	17.77			
2020	Tom Brady	QB	100.26	9	318.66	15	21.24			
2020	Diontae Johnson	WR	102.08	9	166.7	14	11.91	**5.87**	**-3.34**	
2020	Hayden Hurst	TE	102.61	9	110.3	15	7.35	**5.26**	**-3.95**	**(Without Mack)**
2020	Jordan Howard	RB	103.95	9	30.2	7	4.31	**10.68**	**-0.29**	
2020	Tarik Cohen	RB	104.5	9	14.5	3	4.83	**18.93**	**-2.92**	
2020	Phillip Lindsay	RB	105.72	9	62.5	11	5.68	**7.77**	**-0.46**	

2020	Carson Wentz	QB	106.59	9	213.4	12	17.78		
2020	Marvin Jones	WR	106.91	9	155.8	15	10.39		
2020	Brandin Cooks	WR	107.8	9	157.4	14	11.24		
2020	Rob Gronkowski	TE	107.93	9	122.9	15	8.19		
2020	Jared Cook	TE	110.26	10	96.6	14	6.90		
2020	CeeDee Lamb	WR	110.98	10	173.6	15	11.57		
2020	Christian Kirk	WR	111.84	10	122.4	14	8.74		
2020	Matt Breida	RB	112.34	10	37.5	10	3.75		
2020	Sony Michel	RB	112.36	10	50.7	7	7.24	5.49	-0.38
2020	Zack Moss	RB	113.01	10	92	12	7.67	20.27	1.34
2020	Kerryon Johnson	RB	113.83	10	62.3	14	4.45	9.49	-1.18
2020	Aaron Rodgers	QB	115.2	10	361.26	15	24.08	6.73	-1.04
2020	Darius Slayton	WR	117.04	10	112.8	15	7.52		
2020	Jerry Jeudy	WR	117.25	10	107.1	15	7.14		
2020	Matthew Stafford	QB	117.42	10	246.94	15	16.46		
2020	Austin Hooper	TE	117.95	10	78.8	12	6.57		
2020	Latavius Murray	RB	118.44	10	124.7	15	8.31		
2020	Jamison Crowder	WR	119	10	137.4	11	12.49		
2020	Tevin Coleman	RB	120.3	10	10.7	7	1.53		
2020	Noah Fant	TE	124.23	11	111.5	14	7.96		
2020	Mike Gesicki	TE	124.49	11	125.6	14	8.97		
2020	T.J. Hockenson	TE	128.42	11	137.8	15	9.19	8.74	2.01
2020	Daniel Jones	QB	131.1	11	174.16	13	13.40	13.40	-6.88
2020	Dallas Goedert	TE	132.22	11	93.4	11	8.49		
2020	Jonnu Smith	TE	137.25	12	118.4	13	9.11		
2020	Ben Roethlisberger	QB	137.46	12	277.22	15	18.48		
2020	Baker Mayfield	QB	138.62	12	239.38	15	15.96	0.00	NA
2020	Jared Goff	QB	140	12	252.98	15	16.87	17.29	3.90
2020	Joe Burrow	QB	144.72	12	178.72	10	17.87		

2019 ADP Raw Data (RD) Values and Breakdown

Year	Name	Pos	ADP	ADP Round	Fantasy Points 0.5 PPR	Game Played	PPG	RD Points Average Per Game	Difference from Previous Round	Notes
2019	Saquon Barkley	RB	1.55	1	198.9	12	16.58	15.61	N/A	
2019	Christian McCaffrey	RB	2.42	1	393.5	15	26.23			
2019	Alvin Kamara	RB	3.38	1	189.3	13	14.56			
2019	Ezekiel Elliott	RB	3.66	1	258.8	15	17.25			
2019	DeAndre Hopkins	WR	6.63	1	217.5	15	14.50	14.53	N/A	
2019	David Johnson	RB	7.3	1	123.5	13	9.50			
2019	Le'Veon Bell	RB	8.44	1	171.8	14	12.27			
2019	Davante Adams	WR	10.29	1	152.4	11	13.85			
2019	Julio Jones	WR	12.41	1	213.3	14	15.24			
2019	Travis Kelce	TE	12.97	1	201.9	15	13.46	13.46	N/A	
2019	James Conner	RB	12.98	1	128.5	10	12.85			
2019	Michael Thomas	WR	13.52	2	294.4	15	19.63	13.44	-1.09	
2019	Odell Beckham	WR	13.78	2	148.7	15	9.91			
2019	Nick Chubb	RB	14.55	2	232.5	15	15.50	15.12	-0.49	
2019	Dalvin Cook	RB	14.99	2	269.5	14	19.25			
2019	Todd Gurley	RB	16.44	2	194	14	13.86			
2019	JuJu Smith-Schuster	WR	17.22	2	90.6	11	8.24			
2019	Joe Mixon	RB	17.5	2	177.8	15	11.85			
2019	Antonio Brown	WR	22.64	2	14.1	1	14.10			
2019	Mike Evans	WR	23.94	2	199.2	13	15.32			
2019	Patrick Mahomes	QB	25.98	3	279.98	13	21.54	21.54	N/A	
2019	Melvin Gordon	RB	26.76	3	138.6	11	12.60	13.44	-1.68	
2019	Zach Ertz	TE	27.27	3	171.6	15	11.44	12.15	-1.31	
2019	Keenan Allen	WR	28.2	3	190.8	15	12.72	11.97	-1.47	
2019	George Kittle	TE	28.32	3	167.2	13	12.86			
2019	Leonard Fournette	RB	29.85	3	221.4	15	14.76			

2019	Damien Williams	RB	29.99	3	96.7	10	9.67			
2019	Adam Thielen	WR	30.1	3	99.4	10	9.94			
2019	Aaron Jones	RB	30.43	3	275	15	18.33			
2019	Tyreek Hill	WR	31.35	3	151.2	11	13.75			
2019	Marlon Mack	RB	31.48	3	154.6	13	11.89			
2019	Kerryon Johnson	RB	31.98	3	68.7	7	9.81			
2019	T.Y. Hilton	WR	32.37	3	93.9	9	10.43			
2019	Derrick Henry	RB	32.88	3	246.5	14	17.61			
2019	Amari Cooper	WR	33.02	3	195.2	15	13.01			
2019	Devonta Freeman	RB	33.26	3	159.8	13	12.29			
2019	Josh Jacobs	RB	36.93	3	181.6	13	13.97			
2019	Stefon Diggs	WR	37.65	4	180.6	15	12.04	**12.53**	**0.56**	
2019	Kenny Golladay	WR	43.74	4	206.8	15	13.79			
2019	Julian Edelman	WR	44.14	4	202.2	15	13.48			
2019	Brandin Cooks	WR	44.73	4	91	13	7.00			
2019	Mark Ingram	RB	44.78	4	229.5	15	15.30	**12.82**	**-0.62**	
2019	Chris Godwin	WR	45.75	4	233.1	14	16.65			
2019	Sony Michel	RB	46.25	4	133.2	15	8.88			
2019	Chris Carson	RB	48.29	4	214.1	15	14.27			
2019	Robert Woods	WR	48.84	4	170.8	14	12.20			
2019	David Montgomery	RB	51.75	5	140.6	15	9.37	**9.92**	**-2.9**	
2019	Phillip Lindsay	RB	51.83	5	174.9	15	11.66			
2019	Cooper Kupp	WR	54.68	5	204.1	15	13.61	**9.93**	**-2.6**	
2019	A.J. Green	WR	55.03	5	0	1	0.00	**12.41**	**-0.12**	**(without AJ Green)**
2019	Calvin Ridley	WR	57.32	5	165.5	13	12.73			
2019	Tyler Lockett	WR	57.81	5	180.1	15	12.01			
2019	Evan Engram	TE	58.26	5	87.4	8	10.93	**10.93**	**-1.22**	
2019	James White	RB	58.95	5	155	14	11.07			
2019	Tyler Boyd	WR	59.5	5	169.5	15	11.30			

Year	Player	Pos								
2019	Deshaun Watson	QB	60.69	5	331.98	15	22.13	**22.13**	**0.59**	
2019	Tarik Cohen	RB	60.92	5	113.5	15	7.57			
2019	D.J. Moore	WR	62.36	6	187	15	12.47	**11.61**	**-0.8**	
2019	Aaron Rodgers	QB	66.45	6	262.36	15	17.49	**17.49**	**-4.64**	
2019	Allen Robinson	WR	66.74	6	194.1	15	12.94			
2019	O.J. Howard	TE	68.09	6	66.9	13	5.15	**5.15**	**-5.78**	
2019	Kenyan Drake	RB	71.01	6	173.4	13	13.34	**11.38**	**1.46**	
2019	Mike Williams	WR	71.33	6	132	14	9.43			
2019	Tevin Coleman	RB	72.5	6	122.6	13	9.43			
2019	Derrius Guice	RB	74.08	7	53.9	5	10.78	**13.30**	**1.92**	*Ekeler
2019	Jarvis Landry	WR	74.31	7	180.7	15	12.05	**9.29**	**-2.32**	
2019	Hunter Henry	TE	75.9	7	110	11	10.00	**10.18**	**5.03**	
2019	Sammy Watkins	WR	78.04	7	111.2	13	8.55			
2019	Austin Ekeler	RB	78.82	7	249.6	15	16.64			
2019	Alshon Jeffery	WR	78.91	7	100.7	10	10.07			
2019	Miles Sanders	RB	79.8	7	187.1	15	12.47			
2019	Corey Davis	WR	81.48	7	87.2	14	6.23			
2019	Baker Mayfield	QB	82.76	7	227.12	15	15.14	**17.10**	**-0.39**	
2019	Matt Ryan	QB	82.97	7	266.82	14	19.06			
2019	Will Fuller	WR	84.42	7	109.5	11	9.95			
2019	Jared Cook	TE	84.46	7	134.6	13	10.35			
2019	Robby Anderson	WR	84.64	7	133	15	8.87			
2019	Christian Kirk	WR	85.05	8	124.1	12	10.34	**9.62**	**0.33**	
2019	Eric Ebron	TE	87.15	8	71	11	6.45	**5.13**	**-5.05**	
2019	David Njoku	TE	89.01	8	12.6	3	4.20			
2019	Rashaad Penny	RB	89.05	8	71.3	10	7.13	**7.45**	**-5.85**	
2019	Vance McDonald	TE	89.6	8	61.6	13	4.74			
2019	Latavius Murray	RB	91.76	8	132.2	15	8.81			

2019	Carson Wentz	QB	92.97	8	265.8	15	17.72	**12.87**	**-4.73**	
2019	Darrell Henderson	RB	93.21	8	20.4	13	1.57			
2019	Russell Wilson	QB	94.37	8	313.38	15	20.89	**19.31**	**2.21**	(without Luck)
2019	Royce Freeman	RB	95.26	8	159.8	13	12.29			
2019	Andrew Luck	QB	96	8	0	1	0.00			
2019	Larry Fitzgerald	WR	96.29	8	133.4	15	8.89			
2019	Jordan Howard	RB	98.2	9	106.4	9	11.82	**5.91**	**-1.59**	
2019	Dante Pettis	WR	98.6	9	29	11	2.64	**9.33**	**-0.29**	
2019	Dede Westbrook	WR	100.04	9	105	14	7.50			
2019	Courtland Sutton	WR	101.51	9	179.2	15	11.95			
2019	Lamar Miller	RB	102.92	9	0	1	0.00			
2019	Sterling Shepard	WR	102.99	9	106.9	9	11.88			
2019	Jared Goff	QB	103.62	9	238.36	15	15.89	**15.13**	**-4.18**	
2019	Curtis Samuel	WR	103.73	9	142.4	15	9.49			
2019	Drew Brees	QB	107.6	9	206.74	10	20.67	**18.28**	**-1.03**	(without Newton)
2019	Austin Hooper	TE	107.73	9	146.2	12	12.18	**12.18**	**7.05**	
2019	Cam Newton	QB	107.92	9	17.68	2	8.84			
2019	Marvin Jones	WR	107.94	9	162.9	13	12.53			
2019	LeSean McCoy	RB	110.25	10	104.6	13	8.05	**8.97**	**3.06**	
2019	Kyler Murray	QB	111.08	10	282.28	15	18.82	**22.73**	**4.45**	
2019	Emmanuel Sanders	WR	111.21	10	133.3	16	8.33	**9.79**	**0.46**	
2019	Matt Breida	RB	112.72	10	92.2	12	7.68			
2019	Duke Johnson	RB	116.11	10	117.8	15	7.85			
2019	Lamar Jackson	QB	116.41	10	421.68	15	28.11			
2019	Devin Singletary	RB	118.55	10	133.4	12	11.12			
2019	Delanie Walker	TE	119.22	10	44	7	6.29	**6.29**	**-5.89**	
2019	Carlos Hyde	RB	119.54	10	146.9	15	9.79			
2019	Ronald Jones	RB	119.68	10	140.2	15	9.35			

2019	Golden Tate	WR	119.95	10	112.4	10	11.24			
2019	Jameis Winston	QB	120.07	10	318.82	15	21.25			
2019	Ben Roethlisberger	QB	121	11	13.74	1	13.74	16.98	-5.75	
2019	Mark Andrews	TE	121.1	11	175.2	15	11.68	6.70	0.41	
2019	Dak Prescott	QB	122.1	11	319.16	15	21.28	18.06	-4.67	(without Roethlisberger)
2019	Tom Brady	QB	127.19	11	255.84	15	17.06			
2019	Philip Rivers	QB	128.9	11	237.76	15	15.85			
2019	Trey Burton	TE	132.46	11	15.4	9	1.71			
2019	Kyle Rudolph	TE	134.53	12	94.2	15	6.28	4.09	-2.61	
2019	Kirk Cousins	QB	137.37	12	250.42	15	16.69	16.96	-1.12	
2019	T.J. Hockenson	TE	137.46	12	64.7	12	5.39			
2019	Mitchell Trubisky	QB	138.66	12	206.44	14	14.75			
2019	Josh Allen	QB	140.18	12	297.36	15	19.82			
2019	Jimmy Garoppolo	QB	140.42	12	248.52	15	16.57			
2019	Chris Herndon	TE	141.09	12	1.2	2	0.60			

2018 ADP Raw Data (RD) Values and Breakdown

Name	Pos	ADP	ADP Round	Fantasy Points 0.5 PPR	Game Played	PPG	RD Points Average Per Game	Difference from Previous Round	Notes
Todd Gurley	RB	1.02	1	342.6	14	24.47	17.28	N/A	
LeVeon Bell	RB	1.02	1	0	1	0.00	19.44	N/A	(without Bell)
David Johnson	RB	1.04	1	211.4	15	14.09			
Ezekiel Elliott	RB	1.04	1	290.7	15	19.38			
Antonio Brown	WR	1.05	1	271.7	15	18.11	17.04	N/A	
Alvin Kamara	RB	1.06	1	313.7	15	20.91			
Saquon Barkley	RB	1.07	1	318.1	15	21.21			
Melvin Gordon	RB	1.08	1	242.4	11	22.04			
Leonard Fournette	RB	1.09	1	109.4	8	13.68			

Player	Pos	Pick	Round	Points	Games	Avg			
DeAndre Hopkins	WR	1.1	1	255.3	15	17.02			
Kareem Hunt	RB	1.11	1	217.2	11	19.75			
Odell Beckham Jr	WR	1.12	1	191.9	12	15.99			
Christian McCaffrey	RB	2.01	2	327.5	15	21.83	14.36	-2.92	
Julio Jones	WR	2.02	2	245	15	16.33	15.93	-1.11	
Dalvin Cook	RB	2.03	2	124	10	12.40			
Michael Thomas	WR	2.04	2	247.6	15	16.51			
Keenan Allen	WR	2.06	2	203.2	14	14.51			
Jordan Howard	RB	2.07	2	146.1	15	9.74			
Davante Adams	WR	2.07	2	274.1	15	18.27			
Devonta Freeman	RB	2.07	2	11.6	1	11.60			
Rob Gronkowski	TE	2.09	2	104.3	12	8.69	8.69	N/A	
A.J. Green	WR	2.1	2	126.4	9	14.04			
Joe Mixon	RB	2.11	2	210.7	13	16.21			
Mike Evans	WR	3.01	3	215.8	15	14.39	14.16	-1.77	
Stefon Diggs	WR	3.02	3	200.6	14	14.33			
Tyreek Hill	WR	3.02	3	258.4	15	17.23			
Jerick McKinnon	RB	3.03	3	0	1	0.00	7.01	-7.35	
T.Y. Hilton	WR	3.04	3	193.9	13	14.92			
LeSean McCoy	RB	3.05	3	98.8	13	7.60	8.76	5.6	(without McKinnon)
Alex Collins	RB	3.06	3	101.1	10	10.11			
Royce Freeman	RB	3.07	3	80	13	6.15			
Travis Kelce	TE	3.07	3	234.4	15	15.63	15.63	6.94	
Doug Baldwin	WR	3.08	3	113.1	12	9.43			
Adam Thielen	WR	3.1	3	245.6	15	16.37			
Aaron Rodgers	QB	3.1	3	311.54	15	20.77	20.77	N/A	
Amari Cooper	WR	3.1	3	174.3	14	12.45			
Kenyan Drake	RB	3.1	3	167.7	15	11.18			
Derrick Henry	RB	4.01	4	182.7	15	12.18	11.44	2.68	
Larry Fitzgerald	WR	4.02	4	139.6	15	9.31	9.79	-4.37	
Lamar Miller	RB	4.03	4	147.5	13	11.35			

Name	Pos							
JuJu Smith-Schuster	WR	4.05	4	229.2	15	15.28		
Zach Ertz	TE	4.06	4	219.3	15	14.62	14.62	-1.01
Jarvis Landry	WR	4.06	4	157.9	15	10.53		
Jay Ajayi	RB	4.07	4	40.9	4	10.23		
Josh Gordon	WR	4.08	4	118.2	12	9.85		
Chris Hogan	WR	4.09	4	79.3	15	5.29		
Mark Ingram	RB	4.11	4	126.7	11	11.52		
Marshawn Lynch	RB	4.12	4	71.5	6	11.92		
Demaryius Thomas	WR	4.12	4	127.2	15	8.48		
Golden Tate	WR	5.02	5	140.6	14	10.04	7.51	-2.28
Deshaun Watson	QB	5.02	5	309.74	15	20.65	18.80	-1.97
Brandin Cooks	WR	5.03	5	182.5	14	13.04		
Allen Robinson	WR	5.04	5	125.8	13	9.68		
Jimmy Graham	TE	5.05	5	99.5	15	6.63	6.63	-7.99
Marquise Goodwin	WR	5.05	5	75.9	11	6.90		
Kerryon Johnson	RB	5.07	5	123.4	10	12.34	8.13	-3.31
Tom Brady	QB	5.07	5	254.3	15	16.95		
Dion Lewis	RB	5.08	5	127.4	15	8.49		
Carlos Hyde	RB	5.09	5	90.5	13	6.96		
Marvin Jones	WR	5.1	5	98.3	9	10.92		
Rex Burkhead	RB	5.12	5	33	7	4.71		
Greg Olsen	TE	6.01	6	66.6	9	7.40	7.51	0.88
Russell Wilson	QB	6.02	6	290.54	15	19.37	19.94	1.14
Corey Davis	WR	6.02	6	143.8	15	9.59	11.08	3.57
Jamaal Williams	RB	6.02	6	97.4	15	6.49	10.26	2.13
Emmanuel Sanders	WR	6.04	6	162.7	12	13.56		
Julian Edelman	WR	6.07	6	152.6	11	13.87		
Chris Carson	RB	6.08	6	172	13	13.23		
Cam Newton	QB	6.08	6	282.6	14	20.19		
Tevin Coleman	RB	6.09	6	165.7	15	11.05		
Trey Burton	TE	6.1	6	114.3	15	7.62		
Alshon Jeffery	WR	6.1	6	138.4	12	11.53		
Drew Brees	QB	6.11	6	303.98	15	20.27		

Name	Pos							
Michael Crabtree	WR	6.12	6	102.7	15	6.85		
Evan Engram	TE	7.02	7	85.2	10	8.52	**7.81**	**0.3**
Rashaad Penny	RB	7.02	7	65.3	12	5.44	**8.80**	**1.46**
Will Fuller	WR	7.04	7	90.3	7	12.90	**11.30**	**0.28**
Peyton Barber	RB	7.05	7	133	15	8.87		
Sony Michel	RB	7.05	7	130.6	12	10.88		
Kyle Rudolph	TE	7.08	7	115.5	15	7.70		
Delanie Walker	TE	7.08	7	7.2	1	7.20		
Sammy Watkins	WR	7.09	7	95.1	10	9.51		
Carson Wentz	QB	7.1	7	192.66	11	17.51	**17.51**	**-2.43**
Isaiah Crowell	RB	7.11	7	130.2	13	10.02		
Jamison Crowder	WR	7.11	7	67.1	8	8.39		
Cooper Kupp	WR	7.12	7	115.1	8	14.39		
Chris Thompson	RB	8.01	8	66.2	9	7.36	**11.78**	**-2.98**
Robby Anderson	WR	8.01	8	127.5	13	9.81	**8.35**	**-2.95**
Andrew Luck	QB	8.04	8	303.82	15	20.25	**19.20**	**1.69**
Tarik Cohen	RB	8.04	8	188.2	15	12.55		
Kirk Cousins	QB	8.05	8	272.14	15	18.14		
Marlon Mack	RB	8.05	8	152.3	11	13.85		
Devin Funchess	WR	8.06	8	100.9	14	7.21		
Aaron Jones	RB	8.07	8	158.5	12	13.21		
Jordan Reed	TE	8.07	8	92.8	13	7.14	**7.14**	**-0.67**
Randall Cobb	WR	8.1	8	64.2	8	8.03		
Adrian Peterson	RB	8.11	8	179	15	11.93		
Ronald Jones II	RB	9.01	9	17.2	8	2.15	**4.60**	**-7.18**
Duke Johnson	RB	9.02	9	105.6	15	7.04		
Jordy Nelson	WR	9.02	9	112.9	14	8.06	**8.92**	**0.57**
Mike Williams	WR	9.04	9	144.8	15	9.65		
Nelson Agholor	WR	9.04	9	114.9	15	7.66		
Robert Woods	WR	9.06	9	219.1	15	14.61		
Matthew Stafford	QB	9.07	9	193.74	15	12.92	**15.82**	**-3.38**
Jimmy Garoppolo	QB	9.07	9	48.02	3	16.01		

David Njoku	TE	9.07	9	108.2	14	7.73	7.73	0.59
Pierre Garcon	WR	9.09	9	46.6	8	5.83		
Kenny Stills	WR	9.1	9	107.6	14	7.69		
Philip Rivers	QB	9.12	9	277.98	15	18.53		
Kelvin Benjamin	WR	10.01	10	55.1	14	3.94	6.63	-2.29
James White	RB	10.01	10	218.2	15	14.55	8.59	3.99
Nick Chubb	RB	10.02	10	181.5	15	12.10		
Sterling Shepard	WR	10.05	10	139.9	15	9.33		
Matt Ryan	QB	10.05	10	325.6	15	21.71	23.39	7.57
Ben Roethlisberger	QB	10.07	10	327.08	15	21.81		
Corey Clement	RB	10.08	10	70.1	11	6.37		
Ty Montgomery	RB	10.1	10	56	12	4.67		
CJ Anderson	RB	10.11	10	42	8	5.25		
Jack Doyle	TE	10.11	10	47.5	6	7.92	7.92	0.19
Pat Mahomes	QB	10.11	10	399.74	15	26.65		
Jared Goff	QB	11.08	11	286.36	15	19.09	19.09	-4.30
Alex Smith	QB	12.04	12	138	10	13.80	13.15	-5.94
George Kittle	TE	12.04	12	189.3	15	12.62	12.62	4.7
Marcus Mariota	QB	12.05	12	174.92	14	12.49		

Consistency by Position in 2020

We have referenced consistency a fair bit in this book. However, there are two schools of thought. One is to sacrifice overall points for a player to be consistent and perform at a certain level every week. The other is to chase the highest overall points totals for players. I have seen plenty of research to back up both approaches. Bob Lung, who we mentioned earlier, is the King of Consistency and we are a massive fan of his work. It certainly helps to have consistency in your teams to ensure you make the playoffs. However, Jordan McNamara in his Analytics of Dynasty book also shows the merit of going for the most points overall.

Either way, whatever school of thought you subscribe to, we thought it was key to identify the amount of MVP weeks players achieved. We classed an MVP week as an average top 3-4 performer in their position every week by setting a point average it would take to score a top 3 to 4 performance for their position in a given week. Having the knowledge of those players who won you weeks and how frequently, and those that finished outside the top 24 in a week on average points (or top 18 for QBs and TEs) or busted in weeks.

Knowing this information will help to make key decisions in the draft. It can be a great tiebreaker or information that will help you set tiers. All points are worked out on 0.5pt PPR Scoring.

Quarterbacks

Rank	Name	Total Pts 1-17	GP	Average	ADP	MVP 26.5+ Pts	Solid 18-26.49 Pts	Bust 17.99 below	GP	MVP%	Solid%	Bust%	Last Years Rank
1	Josh Allen	395.56	16	24.72	7	7	4	5	16	43.75	25.00	31.25	6
2	Aaron Rodgers	382.76	16	23.92	12	5	10	1	16	31.25	62.50	6.25	11
3	Kyler Murray	378.74	16	23.67	4	6	7	3	16	37.50	43.75	18.75	7
4	Patrick Mahomes	374.4	15	24.96	2	6	8	1	15	40.00	53.33	6.67	8
5	Deshaun Watson	369.32	16	23.08	6	4	10	2	16	25.00	62.50	12.50	2
6	Russell Wilson	359.78	16	22.49	5	5	7	4	16	31.25	43.75	25.00	5
7	Ryan Tannehill	343.86	16	21.49	21	6	3	7	16	37.50	18.75	43.75	21
8	Tom Brady	337.92	16	21.12	10	5	5	6	16	31.25	31.25	37.50	12
9	Justin Herbert	332.84	15	22.19	36	5	5	5	15	33.33	33.33	33.33	n/a
10	Lamar Jackson	332.78	15	22.19	1	4	6	5	15	26.67	40.00	33.33	1
11	Kirk Cousins	306.2	16	19.14	22	1	9	6	16	6.25	56.25	37.50	13
12	Matt Ryan	280.44	16	17.53	8	3	4	9	16	18.75	25.00	56.25	9
13	Derek Carr	272.12	16	17.01	27	1	8	7	16	6.25	50.00	43.75	17
14	Ben Roethlisberger	267.22	15	17.81	15	1	7	7	15	6.67	46.67	46.67	53
15	Matthew Stafford	260.56	16	16.29	13	0	7	9	16	0.00	43.75	56.25	29
16	Cam Newton	259.98	15	17.33	18	2	5	8	15	13.33	33.33	53.33	52
17	Baker Mayfield	248.12	16	15.51	16	3	2	11	16	18.75	12.50	68.75	19
18	Teddy Bridgewater	241.22	15	16.08	26	1	6	8	15	6.67	40.00	53.33	32
19	Jared Goff	239.98	15	16.00	17	1	4	10	15	6.67	26.67	66.67	15
20	Philip Rivers	239.96	16	15.00	23	0	4	12	16	0.00	25.00	75.00	16
21	Drew Brees	209.48	12	17.46	9	0	7	5	12	0.00	58.33	41.67	24
22	Carson Wentz	198.4	12	16.53	11	2	3	7	12	16.67	25.00	58.33	10
23	Drew Lock	181.32	13	13.95	24	1	3	9	13	7.69	23.08	69.23	37
24	Daniel Jones	180.02	14	12.86	14	0	2	12	14	0.00	14.29	85.71	22

Running Backs

Rank	Name	Total Pts 1-17	GP	Average	ADP	MVP 21 Pts	Solid 20.9-10.5 Pts	Bust 10.49pts & below	GP	MVP%	Solid%	Bust%	Last Years Rank
1	Alvin Kamara	336.3	15	22.42	4	5	9	1	15	33.33	60.00	6.67	13
2	Derrick Henry	323.6	16	20.23	6	6	6	4	16	37.50	37.50	25.00	6
3	Dalvin Cook	315.8	14	22.56	5	7	6	1	14	50.00	42.86	7.14	3
4	David Montgomery	237.8	15	15.85	27	5	5	5	15	33.33	33.33	33.33	24
5	Aaron Jones	235.4	14	16.81	12	3	8	3	14	21.43	57.14	21.43	2
6	Jonathan Taylor	234.8	15	15.65	19	3	8	4	15	20.00	53.33	26.67	n/a
7	James Robinson	225.9	14	16.14	95	3	7	4	14	21.43	50.00	28.57	n/a
8	Josh Jacobs	214.8	15	14.32	9	3	5	7	15	20.00	33.33	46.67	15
9	Nick Chubb	199.7	12	16.64	8	4	6	2	12	33.33	50.00	16.67	7
10	Kareem Hunt	199.5	16	12.47	29	2	6	8	16	12.50	37.50	50.00	50
11	Ezekiel Elliott	197.7	15	13.18	3	2	7	6	15	13.33	46.67	40.00	4
12	Antonio Gibson	184.2	14	13.16	46	1	7	6	14	7.14	50.00	42.86	n/a
13	Melvin Gordon III	182.4	15	12.16	17	2	7	6	15	13.33	46.67	40.00	26
14	Kenyan Drake	179.7	15	11.98	10	2	7	6	15	13.33	46.67	40.00	18
15	Mike Davis	177	15	11.80	100	2	5	8	15	13.33	33.33	53.33	116
16	Ronald Jones II	172.3	14	12.31	30	2	5	7	14	14.29	35.71	50.00	25
17	Chris Carson	169.3	12	14.11	16	2	5	5	12	16.67	41.67	41.67	10
18	D'Andre Swift	166.8	13	12.83	28	2	6	5	13	15.38	46.15	38.46	n/a
19	David Johnson	163	12	13.58	23	1	7	4	12	8.33	58.33	33.33	38
20	Nyheim Hines	161.7	16	10.11	52	2	3	11	16	12.50	18.75	68.75	49
21	J.K. Dobbins	159.5	15	10.63	36	1	7	7	15	6.67	46.67	46.67	n/a
22	Clyde Edwards-Helaire	158	13	12.15	11	0	8	5	13	0.00	61.54	38.46	n/a
23	Miles Sanders	156.4	12	13.03	14	2	5	5	12	16.67	41.67	41.67	14
24	J.D. McKissic	151.4	16	9.46	94	1	5	10	16	6.25	31.25	62.50	57

Wide Receivers

Rank	Name	Total Pts 1-17	GP	Average	ADP	MVP 21.7 Pts	Solid 21.6-13.2 Pts	Bust 13.1pts & below	GP	MVP%	Solid%	Bust%	Last Years Rank
1	Davante Adams	300.9	14	21.5	2	6	5	3	14	42.86	35.71	21.43	24
2	Tyreek Hill	285.4	15	19	3	4	7	4	15	26.67	46.67	26.67	30
3	Stefon Diggs	265.1	16	16.6	27	3	7	6	16	18.75	43.75	37.50	21
4	Calvin Ridley	236.5	15	15.8	17	4	7	4	15	26.67	46.67	26.67	25
5	DeAndre Hopkins	230.3	16	14.4	5	4	5	7	16	25.00	31.25	43.75	5
6	Justin Jefferson	230.2	16	14.4	49	4	4	8	16	25.00	25.00	50.00	n/a
7	D.K. Metcalf	229.8	16	14.4	23	3	5	8	16	18.75	31.25	50.00	n/a
8	Adam Thielen	217	15	14.5	12	4	3	8	15	26.67	20.00	53.33	62
9	Tyler Lockett	215.4	16	13.5	19	3	3	10	16	18.75	18.75	62.50	14
10	Mike Evans	213.6	16	13.4	9	2	8	6	16	12.50	50.00	37.50	12
11	A.J. Brown	212.5	14	15.2	15	2	7	5	14	14.29	50.00	35.71	15
12	Allen Robinson II	211.9	16	13.2	8	3	4	9	16	18.75	25.00	56.25	11
13	Robert Woods	200.1	16	12.5	22	2	5	9	16	12.50	31.25	56.25	17
14	Keenan Allen	195.1	14	13.9	20	2	5	7	14	14.29	35.71	50.00	8
15	Brandin Cooks	191.5	15	12.8	37	3	2	10	15	20.00	13.33	66.67	
16	Amari Cooper	190.8	16	11.9	13	1	4	11	16	6.25	25.00	68.75	9
17	Marvin Jones Jr.	189.8	16	11.9	36	2	3	11	16	12.50	18.75	68.75	27
18	JuJu Smith-Schuster	185.6	16	11.6	11	1	7	8	16	6.25	43.75	50.00	66
19	Chase Claypool	183.9	16	11.5	84	1	5	10	16	6.25	31.25	62.50	n/a
20	CeeDee Lamb	180.7	16	11.3	40	2	3	11	16	12.50	18.75	68.75	n/a
21	Terry McLaurin	180.3	15	12	21	1	5	9	15	6.67	33.33	60.00	27
22	D.J. Moore	178.5	15	11.9	14	1	5	9	15	6.67	33.33	60.00	18
23	Diontae Johnson	177.8	15	11.9	41	1	6	8	15	6.67	40.00	53.33	41
24	Robby Anderso	176.7	16	11	57	1	6	9	16	6.25	37.50	56.25	39

Tight Ends

Rank	Name	Total Pts 1-17	GP	Average	ADP	MVP 13.6+ Pts	Solid 13.5-9.2 Pts	Bust 9.1pts & below	GP	MVP%	Solid%	Bust%	Last Years Rank
1	Travis Kelce	260.26	15	17.35	1	11	2	2	15	73.33	13.33	13.33	1
2	Darren Waller	225.1	16	14.07	5	7	4	5	16	43.75	25.00	31.25	5
3	Robert Tonyan	150.6	16	9.41	N/A	3	6	7	16	18.75	37.50	43.75	64
4	T.J. Hockenson	141.8	16	8.86	15	2	6	8	16	12.50	37.50	50.00	31
5	Mark Andrews	141.1	14	10.08	3	5	3	6	14	35.71	21.43	42.86	2
6	Logan Thomas	140.62	16	8.79	N/A	3	5	8	16	18.75	31.25	50.00	50
7	Mike Gesicki	132.8	15	8.85	14	3	2	10	15	20.00	13.33	66.67	12
8	Rob Gronkowski	126.8	16	7.93	6	4	2	10	16	25.00	12.50	62.50	n/a
9	Hayden Hurst	121.1	16	7.57	12	2	5	9	16	12.50	31.25	56.25	34
10	Jonnu Smith	119.7	15	7.98	16	2	4	9	15	13.33	26.67	60.00	19
11	Jimmy Graham	118.6	16	7.41	34	3	3	10	16	18.75	18.75	62.50	21
12	Noah Fant	118.3	15	7.89	13	3	1	11	15	20.00	6.67	73.33	16
13	Hunter Henry	115.3	14	8.24	8	1	6	7	14	7.14	42.86	50.00	8
14	Dalton Schultz	115	16	7.19	N/A	2	2	12	16	12.50	12.50	75.00	113
15	Eric Ebron	113.8	15	7.59	22	1	5	9	15	6.67	33.33	60.00	27
16	Evan Engram	109.5	16	6.84	7	1	4	11	16	6.25	25.00	68.75	18
17	Jared Cook	108.9	15	7.26	9	1	7	7	15	6.67	46.67	46.67	7
18	Tyler Higbee	106.2	15	7.08	10	2	1	12	15	13.33	6.67	80.00	9

Top Scores by Position Over the Past 5 Season

This section has all the top points scorers, by position, over the past 5 seasons. This allows you to see the change at the position, who is consistently performing at an elite level, and who is a flash in the pan, or needs everything to break right for them to have an elite finish. All scoring is done in 0.5 PPR Point Scoring.

I make reference to this earlier in the book about common mistakes of fantasy players. If you can take the consistency charts above and mix it in with the information below, as well as keeping tiers and ranks, you will be in a great position heading into 2021.

Quarterbacks

2020 Rank	Name	Total points 0.5PPR	Games Played	PPG Average
1	Kyler Murray	386.96	15	25.8
2	Josh Allen	384.8	15	25.65
3	Patrick Mahomes II	380.4	15	25.36
4	Aaron Rodgers	361.26	15	24.08

5	Russell Wilson	354.64	15	23.64
6	Deshaun Watson	349.52	15	23.3
2019 Rank	**Name**	**Team**	**Games Played**	**PPG Average**
1	Lamar Jackson	421.68	15	28.11
2	Deshaun Watson	331.98	15	22.13
3	Dak Prescott	319.16	15	21.28
4	Jameis Winston	318.82	15	21.25
5	Russell Wilson	313.38	15	20.89
6	Josh Allen	297.36	15	19.82
2018 Rank	**Name**	**Team**	**Games Played**	**PPG Average**
1	Patrick Mahomes II	399.74	15	26.65
2	Ben Roethlisberger	327.08	15	21.81
3	Matt Ryan	325.6	15	21.71
4	Aaron Rodgers	311.54	15	20.77
5	Deshaun Watson	309.74	15	20.65
6	Drew Brees	303.98	15	20.27
2017 Rank	**Name**	**Team**	**Games Played**	**PPG Average**
1	Russell Wilson	327.48	15	21.83
2	Alex Smith	295.18	15	19.68
3	Cam Newton	288.38	15	19.23
4	Carson Wentz	283.74	13	21.83
5	Tom Brady	280.24	15	18.68
6	Kirk Cousins	270.1	15	18.01
2016 Rank	**Name**	**Team**	**Games Played**	**PPG Average**
1	Aaron Rodgers	345.82	15	23.05
2	Matt Ryan	318.02	15	21.2
3	Drew Brees	312.32	15	20.82
4	Kirk Cousins	289.2	15	19.28
5	Andrew Luck	289.16	14	20.65

| 6 | Dak Prescott | 284.5 | 15 | 18.97 |

Running Backs

2020 Rank	Name	Total points 0.5PPR	Games Played	PPG Average
1	Alvin Kamara	336.3	15	22.4
2	Dalvin Cook	315.8	14	22.6
3	Derrick Henry	288.6	15	19.2
4	James Robinson	225.9	14	16.1
5	Aaron Jones	218.9	13	16.8
6	David Montgomery	214.1	14	15.3
7	Jonathan Taylor	196.9	14	14.1
8	Kareem Hunt	194.9	15	13
9	Josh Jacobs	193.9	14	13.9
10	Ezekiel Elliott	184.1	14	13.2
11	Nick Chubb	182.9	11	16.6
12	Mike Davis	177	15	11.8
2019 Rank	Name	Total points 0.5PPR	Games Played	PPG Average
1	Christian McCaffrey	393.9	15	26.3
2	Aaron Jones	275	15	18.3
3	Dalvin Cook	265.9	14	19
4	Ezekiel Elliott	258.8	15	17.3
5	Austin Ekeler	249.6	15	16.6
6	Derrick Henry	246.5	14	17.6
7	Nick Chubb	232.5	15	15.5
8	Mark Ingram II	229.5	15	15.3
9	Leonard Fournette	221.4	15	14.8
10	Chris Carson	214.1	15	14.3
11	Saquon Barkley	198.9	12	16.6
12	Todd Gurley II	194	14	13.9
2018 Rank	Name	Total points 0.5PPR	Games Played	PPG Average

		Total points 0.5PPR	Games Played	PPG Average
1	Todd Gurley II	342.6	14	24.5
2	Christian McCaffrey	327.5	15	21.8
3	Saquon Barkley	318.1	15	21.2
4	Alvin Kamara	313.7	15	20.9
5	Ezekiel Elliott	290.7	15	19.4
6	Melvin Gordon III	242.4	11	22
7	James Conner	241.6	12	20.1
8	James White	218.2	15	14.6
9	Kareem Hunt	217.2	11	19.8
10	David Johnson	211.4	15	14.1
11	Joe Mixon	210.7	13	16.2
12	Phillip Lindsay	205.3	15	13.7
2017 Rank	Name	Total points 0.5PPR	Games Played	PPG Average
1	Todd Gurley II	351.3	15	23.4
2	Le'Veon Bell	299.1	15	19.9
3	Kareem Hunt	259.2	15	17.3
4	Alvin Kamara	252.6	15	16.8
5	Melvin Gordon III	243.7	15	16.3
6	Mark Ingram II	241.6	15	16.1
7	LeSean McCoy	229.9	15	15.3
8	Leonard Fournette	196.6	12	16.4
9	Jordan Howard	186.1	15	12.4
10	Carlos Hyde	183.5	15	12.2
11	Christian McCaffrey	180.7	15	12.1
2016 Rank	Name	Total points 0.5PPR	Games Played	PPG Average
1	David Johnson	361.9	15	24.1
2	Ezekiel Elliott	309.4	15	20.6
3	Le'Veon Bell	279.9	12	23.3
4	LeSean McCoy	271.7	14	19.4
5	DeMarco Murray	264.9	15	17.7
6	Devonta Freeman	230.9	15	15.4
7	Melvin Gordon III	230.1	13	17.7
8	LeGarrette Blount	218.3	15	14.6

9	Jordan Howard	202.1	14	14.4
10	Mark Ingram II	197	15	13.1
11	Jay Ajayi	192.4	14	13.7
12	Latavius Murray	188.7	13	14.5

Wide Receivers

2020 Rank	Name	Total points 0.5PPR	Games Played	PPG Average
1	Davante Adams	287.3	13	22.1
2	Tyreek Hill	285.4	15	19
3	Stefon Diggs	254	15	16.9
4	Calvin Ridley	229.9	14	16.4
5	D.K. Metcalf	226.2	15	15.1
6	DeAndre Hopkins	224.8	15	15
7	Justin Jefferson	212.4	15	14.2
8	Adam Thielen	209.3	14	15
9	Mike Evans	207.5	15	13.8
10	Allen Robinson II	207.2	15	13.8
11	Keenan Allen	195.1	14	13.9
12	Robert Woods	194.5	15	13

2019 Rank	Name	Total points 0.5PPR	Games Played	PPG Average
1	Michael Thomas	294.4	15	19.6
2	Chris Godwin	233.1	14	16.7
3	DeAndre Hopkins	217.5	15	14.5
4	Julio Jones	213.3	14	15.2
5	Kenny Golladay	206.8	15	13.8
6	Cooper Kupp	204.1	15	13.6
7	Julian Edelman	202.2	15	13.5
8	Mike Evans	199.2	13	15.3
9	Amari Cooper	195.2	15	13
10	Allen Robinson II	194.1	15	12.9
11	DeVante Parker	192.5	15	12.8
12	Keenan Allen	190.8	15	12.7

2018 Rank	Name	Total points 0.5PPR	Games Played	PPG Average
1	Davante Adams	274.1	15	18.3
2	Antonio Brown	271.7	15	18.1
3	Tyreek Hill	258.4	15	17.2
4	DeAndre Hopkins	255.3	15	17
5	Michael Thomas	247.6	15	16.5
6	Adam Thielen	245.6	15	16.4
7	Julio Jones	245	15	16.3
8	JuJu Smith-Schuster	229.2	15	15.3
9	Robert Woods	219.1	15	14.6
10	Mike Evans	215.8	15	14.4
11	Keenan Allen	203.2	14	14.5
12	Stefon Diggs	200.6	14	14.3
2017 Rank	Name	Total points 0.5PPR	Games Played	PPG Average
1	DeAndre Hopkins	261.8	15	17.5
2	Antonio Brown	259.8	14	18.6
3	Keenan Allen	203.4	15	13.6
4	Tyreek Hill	201.7	15	13.5
5	Julio Jones	197.4	15	13.2
5	Larry Fitzgerald	197.4	15	13.2
7	Michael Thomas	194.1	15	12.9
8	A.J. Green	186.6	15	12.4
9	Davante Adams	185.5	14	13.3
10	Adam Thielen	185.2	15	12.4
11	Jarvis Landry	184.3	15	12.3
12	Marvin Jones Jr.	178.5	15	11.9
2016 Rank	Name	Total points 0.5PPR	Games Played	PPG Average
1	Antonio Brown	254.3	15	17
2	Jordy Nelson	246.6	15	16.4
3	Mike Evans	241.1	15	16.1
4	Odell Beckham Jr.	239.2	15	16
5	T.Y. Hilton	215.8	15	14.4

6	Brandin Cooks	203.9	14	14.6
7	Doug Baldwin	201.2	15	13.4
8	Julio Jones	199.3	13	15.3
9	Davante Adams	189.1	15	12.6
10	Michael Crabtree	187.6	15	12.5
11	Michael Thomas	183.1	14	13.1
12	Larry Fitzgerald	178.1	15	11.9

Tight Ends

2020 Rank	Name	Total points 0.5PPR	Games Played	PPG Average
1	Travis Kelce	260.3	15	17.4
2	Darren Waller	202.9	15	13.5
3	Robert Tonyan	141.8	15	9.5
4	T.J. Hockenson	137.8	15	9.2
5	Mark Andrews	136.4	13	10.5
6	Logan Thomas	129.4	15	8.6
7	Mike Gesicki	125.6	14	9
8	Rob Gronkowski	122.9	15	8.2
9	Jonnu Smith	118.4	13	9.1
10	Jimmy Graham	117.1	15	7.8
11	Hunter Henry	115.3	14	8.2
12	Eric Ebron	113.8	15	7.6

2019 Rank	Name	Total points 0.5PPR	Games Played	PPG Average
1	Travis Kelce	201.9	15	13.5
2	Mark Andrews	175.2	15	11.7
3	Zach Ertz	171.6	15	11.4
4	George Kittle	167.2	13	12.9
5	Darren Waller	162.3	15	10.8
6	Austin Hooper	146.2	12	12.2
7	Jared Cook	134.6	13	10.4
8	Hunter Henry	110	11	10
9	Tyler Higbee	107.5	14	7.7
10	Dallas Goedert	107.2	14	7.7

11	Jason Witten	104	15	6.9
12	Mike Gesicki	99.1	15	6.6
2018 Rank	**Name**	**Total points 0.5PPR**	**Games Played**	**PPG Average**
1	Travis Kelce	234.4	15	15.6
2	Zach Ertz	219.3	15	14.6
3	George Kittle	189.3	15	12.6
4	Eric Ebron	175.2	15	11.7
5	Jared Cook	155.3	15	10.4
6	Austin Hooper	118.3	15	7.9
7	Kyle Rudolph	115.5	15	7.7
8	Trey Burton	114.3	15	7.6
9	David Njoku	108.2	14	7.7
10	Rob Gronkowski	104.3	12	8.7
11	O.J. Howard	103.5	10	10.4
12	Vance McDonald	102.6	14	7.3
2017 Rank	**Name**	**Total points 0.5PPR**	**Games Played**	**PPG Average**
1	Rob Gronkowski	192.8	13	14.8
2	Travis Kelce	192	15	12.8
3	Zach Ertz	162	13	12.5
4	Evan Engram	141.6	15	9.4
5	Jimmy Graham	136.5	15	9.1
6	Delanie Walker	134.1	15	8.9
7	Kyle Rudolph	128.9	15	8.6
8	Jack Doyle	117.2	14	8.4
9	Cameron Brate	113.9	15	7.6
10	Jason Witten	112.8	15	7.5
11	Eric Ebron	104.5	15	7
12	Hunter Henry	104.4	12	8.7
2016 Rank	**Name**	**Total points 0.5PPR**	**Games Played**	**PPG Average**
1	Travis Kelce	179.2	15	12
2	Greg Olsen	163.6	15	10.9

3	Delanie Walker	149.6	14	10.7	
4	Jimmy Graham	148.4	15	9.9	
5	Kyle Rudolph	144.3	15	9.6	
6	Cameron Brate	142.5	15	9.5	
7	Martellus Bennett	129.8	15	8.7	
8	Jordan Reed	125.1	11	11.4	
9	Jason Witten	116.3	14	8.3	
10	Zach Ertz	112.2	13	8.6	
11	Dennis Pitta	111.3	15	7.4	
12	Jack Doyle	107.9	15	7.2	

Mock Draft ADP 2021

In January 2021 I created some mock draft communities to determine set ADP prices with the same players drafting in the same spot once per month. The idea was to capture early off season sentiments, Rookie pre-draft and Free Agency sentiments, post NFL draft rookie rankings and trends through the offseason. As a thank you for buying this book, you will get a link to this sheet displaying all this data, tracking this data month on month. Thank you to everyone for contributing to this and a massive thank you to Richard Price for helping me create the sheet and making sure it's easy to portal all the info through.

Here is all the data. This first chart is the draft results of all mock drafts (rookies at the bottom of the draft).

Player Name	Team	Position	5 Yard Rush Mock	Rankers Mock Jan21	Rankers Mock Feb 21	Rankers Mock Mar 21	Non Rankers Mock Jan21	Non Rankers Mock Feb21	Non Rankers Mock Mar21
Christian McCaffrey	CAR	RB	1	1	1	1	2	2	2
Derrick Henry	TEN	RB	2	3	2	4	3	5	4
Saquon Barkley	NYG	RB	3	2	3	2	5	1	5
Dalvin Cook	MIN	RB	4	5	4	3	4	4	3
Alvin Kamara	NO	RB	5	6	5	6	1	3	1
Ezekiel Elliott	DAL	RB	6	4	8	8	9	9	9
Jonathan Taylor	IND	RB	7	9	9	5	13	8	8
Josh Jacobs	LV	RB	8	14	15	15	16	16	16
Nick Chubb	CLE	RB	9	8	6	11	8	10	13
Clyde Edwards-Helaire	KC	RB	10	27	34	32	11	35	34
Davante Adams	GB	WR	11	7	10	9	6	7	7
David Montgomery	CHI	RB	12	38	35	38	17	20	29
D'Andre Swift	DET	RB	13	31	13	13	27	19	18

DeAndre Hopkins	ARI	WR		14	11	14	14	10	18	17

	KC	WR	15	10	12	10	7	12	10
Stefon Diggs	BUF	WR	16	17	21	18	20	11	22
Calvin Ridley	ATL	WR	17	21	27	40	28	28	23
James Robinson	JAX	RB	18	35	19	22	26	23	26
Mike Evans	TB	WR	19	22	32	35	44	46	40
Austin Ekeler	LAC	RB	20	15	11	12	15	15	15
Patrick Mahomes	KC	QB	21	25	30	30	18	22	51
J.K. Dobbins	BAL	RB	22	32	23	23	29	30	27
Michael Thomas	NO	WR	23	20	25	28	23	26	28
Travis Kelce	KC	TE	24	16	7	7	12	6	6
A.J. Brown	TEN	WR	25	13	18	26	19	37	19
Joe Mixon	CIN	RB	26	26	24	21	34	25	31
Aaron Jones	GB	RB	27	19	17	19	14	13	14
DK Metcalf	SEA	WR	28	18	22	27	22	29	11
Chris Godwin	TB	WR	29	23	41	41	30	42	35
George Kittle	SF	TE	30	30	28	17	31	27	12
Cam Akers	LAR	RB	31	28	16	16	35	17	20
Antonio Gibson	WAS	RB	32	39	20	20	21	31	33
Keenan Allen	LAC	WR	33	29	36	34	41	34	32
Adam Thielen	MIN	WR	34	44	39	45	32	44	45
Kenny Golladay	DET	WR	35	43	43	43	45	51	52
Justin Jefferson	MIN	WR	36	12	26	29	37	32	24
Terry McLaurin	WAS	WR	37	40	40	51	38	41	47
Chris Carson	SEA	RB	38	34	45	42	33	14	21
Miles Sanders	PHI	RB	39	24	29	24	25	21	25
Allen Robinson	CHI	WR	40	33	31	31	39	39	37
D.J. Moore	CAR	WR	41	36	46	47	56	43	30
Tyler Lockett	SEA	WR	42	58	58	61	57	74	75
Russell Wilson	SEA	QB	43	75	75	75	70	71	77
Darren Waller	LV	TE	44	41	33	33	40	24	36
Ronald Jones	TB	RB	45	61	69	79	36	36	76
Cooper Kupp	LAR	WR	46	51	54	49	48	63	80
Julio Jones	ATL	WR	47	47	44	36	47	38	42
CeeDee Lamb	DAL	WR	48	57	57	53	24	60	44
Amari Cooper	DAL	WR	49	45	37	37	46	54	43
Josh Allen	BUF	QB	50	56	56	55	54	48	54
Lamar Jackson	BAL	QB	51	68	48	63	49	52	63
Mark Andrews	BAL	TE	52	60	51	69	43	50	46
JuJu Smith-Schuster	PIT	WR	53	37	49	48	60	62	73
D.J. Chark	JAX	WR	54	50	77	71	74	87	74
Robert Woods	LAR	WR	55	42	52	54	51	45	39
Deshaun Watson	HOU	QB	56	78	66	65	61	57	48
Kyler Murray	ARI	QB	57	63	64	57	63	55	64

Melvin Gordon	DEN	RB	58	54	61	60	83	56	59
Courtland Sutton	DEN	WR	59	55	55	66	62	79	50
Joe Burrow	CIN	QB	60	132	148	138	94	101	99
Justin Herbert	LAC	QB	61	88	87	64	69	75	71
Diontae Johnson	PIT	WR	62	64	53	81	52	47	49
Odell Beckham	CLE	WR	63	65	47	62	66	85	72
Brandon Aiyuk	SF	WR	65	59	62	77	79	67	67
Aaron Rodgers	GB	QB	66	83	68	100	53	68	84
DeVante Parker	MIA	WR	67	70	72	74	80	81	94
Tee Higgins	CIN	WR	68	76	42	78	72	65	66
Brandin Cooks	HOU	WR	69	67	67	82	81	64	82
Deebo Samuel	SF	WR	70	73	85	96	59	83	79
Kenyan Drake	ARI	RB	71	48	63	72	50	33	70
Dak Prescott	DAL	QB	72	74	74	68	71	61	69
Kareem Hunt	CLE	RB	73	46	50	50	42	49	41
Tyler Boyd	CIN	WR	74	53	71	76	75	53	53
Marvin Jones	DET	WR	75	94	104	110	117	88	86
T.Y. Hilton	IND	WR	76	131	128	182	116	105	106
Chase Claypool	PIT	WR	77	79	79	93	68	73	61
Laviska Shenault	JAX	WR	78	104	81	148	92	97	109
A.J. Dillon	GB	RB	79	66	38	59	82	72	78
Raheem Mostert	SF	RB	80	52	60	52	55	58	58
David Johnson	HOU	RB	81	49	73	39	58	66	56
Zach Ertz	PHI	TE	82	133	130	154	0	155	96
James Conner	PIT	RB	83	112	93	99	64	69	142
Zack Moss	BUF	RB	84	86	80	104	67	95	91
Marquise Brown	BAL	WR	85	62	59	83	73	92	81
Tom Brady	TB	QB	86	137	110	131	130	131	136
Henry Ruggs	LV	WR	87	95	122	98	105	167	0
Jerry Jeudy	DEN	WR	88	91	88	88	85	78	90
Jamison Crowder	NYJ	WR	89	96	96	113	100	93	114
Robby Anderson	CAR	WR	90	89	76	111	95	76	100
Todd Gurley	ATL	RB	91	87	113	167	102	94	138
Tarik Cohen	CHI	RB	92	127	111	106	91	140	154
Nyheim Hines	IND	RB	93	90	90	114	108	82	117
Devin Singletary	BUF	RB	94	85	97	86	76	124	155
Jalen Reagor	PHI	WR	95	108	108	90	135	115	144
Corey Davis	TEN	WR	96	93	102	101	126	98	123
Curtis Samuel	CAR	WR	97	97	100	124	114	90	110
Julian Edelman	NE	WR	98	82	106	132	87	99	107
Jarvis Landry	CLE	WR	99	72	82	91	84	80	85

Damien Harris	NE	RB	100	80	99	107	86	70	102
Michael Gallup	DAL	WR	101	71	95	95	107	77	92
Christian Kirk	ARI	WR	102	99	146	0	109	108	147
Michael Pittman	IND	WR	103	114	103	103	112	112	115
T.J. Hockenson	DET	TE	104	100	84	102	77	104	98
Chase Edmonds	ARI	RB	105	77	83	92	90	103	62
Leonard Fournette	TB	RB	106	102	78	67	101	40	65
Mike Williams	LAC	WR	107	122	0	0	119	141	112
Ke'Shawn Vaughn	TB	RB	108	0	166	158	0	0	0
Marlon Mack	IND	RB	110	147	118	142	132	157	0
Tony Pollard	DAL	RB	111	84	94	118	103	144	164
Mike Gesicki	MIA	TE	112	121	144	147	93	117	88
Nelson Agholor	LV	WR	113	172	192	121	178	0	0
Dallas Goedert	PHI	TE	114	107	92	125	99	135	118
Darius Slayton	NYG	WR	115	120	158	0	88	129	105
Hunter Henry	LAC	TE	116	125	91	144	148	114	97
Latavius Murray	NO	RB	117	130	136	115	0	148	0
John Brown	BUF	WR	119	106	115	150	106	165	148
Myles Gaskin	MIA	RB	120	81	65	56	65	59	38
Darrell Henderson	LAR	RB	121	144	123	134	0	187	0
Alexander Mattison	MIN	RB	122	143	127	143	137	120	0
Parris Campbell	IND	WR	123	140	125	164	169	145	0
Robert Tonyan	GB	TE	124	0	139	130	111	111	113
James White	NE	RB	125	113	120	97	0	151	0
Cole Beasley	BUF	WR	127	110	107	149	141	142	130
Phillip Lindsay	DEN	RB	128	109	133	108	121	163	0
J.D. McKissic	WAS	RB	129	0	117	0	123	100	141
Sterling Shepard	NYG	WR	130	98	98	120	138	86	143
Mecole Hardman	KC	WR	131	115	121	0	129	166	129
Lynn Bowden	MIA	RB	132	145	0	0	115	0	0
Blake Jarwin	DAL	TE	134	141	164	141	157	143	160
Russell Gage	ATL	WR	135	135	126	126	0	159	0
Rashaad Penny	SEA	RB	136	92	86	117	168	121	150
Allen Lazard	GB	WR	137	150	150	166	133	132	180
Salvon Ahmed	MIA	RB	138	0	0	0	0	0	0
Evan Engram	NYG	TE	139	119	89	119	153	118	124
Matt Ryan	ATL	QB	140	138	145	122	163	134	120
Jerick McKinnon	SF	RB	141	0	0	0	0	0	0
Le'Veon Bell	KC	RB	142	118	143	178	124	0	0

Name	Team	Pos							
Kerryon Johnson	DET	RB	143	0	0	0	0	0	0
Benny Snell	PIT	RB	144	0	0	0	154	182	166
La'Mical Perine	NYJ	RB	145	101	101	152	159	119	146
Rob Gronkowski	TB	TE	146	154	154	109	142	128	151
Hunter Renfrow	LV	WR	147	128	0	0	0	0	0
Anthony Miller	CHI	WR	148	0	0	0	0	0	0
Preston Williams	MIA	WR	149	123	0	0	125	162	0
Mike Davis	CAR	RB	150	183	159	0	0	123	121
Quintez Cephus	DET	WR	151	180	0	0	146	0	0
Sony Michel	NE	RB	152	155	162	151	149	109	0
Antonio Brown	TB	WR	153	0	124	0	113	89	128
Justin Jackson	LAC	RB	154	0	147	0	0	158	158
Joshua Kelley	LAC	RB	155	0	0	0	176	161	185
Bryan Edwards	LV	WR	156	156	0	0	97	0	0
Irv Smith	MIN	TE	157	149	151	0	150	133	133
Mark Ingram	BAL	RB	158	166	132	84	0	0	0
Eno Benjamin	ARI	RB	159	0	0	0	0	0	0
Darnell Mooney	CHI	WR	160	153	131	156	139	122	156
Ryan Tannehill	TEN	QB	161	117	109	0	89	96	127
Darrynton Evans	TEN	RB	162	0	0	0	0	0	0
Tua Tagovailoa	MIA	QB	163	160	0	0	145	146	182
Ben Roethlisberger	PIT	QB	164	159	165	0	0	185	0
Kirk Cousins	MIN	QB	165	0	0	0	136	136	165
Jalen Hurts	PHI	QB	166	139	105	139	165	106	111
Baker Mayfield	CLE	QB	126	0	157	0	134	113	179
Gus Edwards	BAL	RB	168	124	116	140	122	147	95
Steven Sims	WAS	WR	171	0	0	0	0	0	0
Jakobi Meyers	NE	WR	172	0	0	0	155	0	0
Anthony McFarland	PIT	RB	173	152	0	159	0	179	0
Jeffery Wilson	SF	RB	174	116	114	116	96	110	134
N'Keal Harry	NE	WR	175	0	0	0	0	0	0
Boston Scott	PHI	RB	176	0	0	0	170	0	0
A.J. Green	CIN	WR	177	168	0	128	0	125	0
Matthew Stafford	DET	QB	178	129	112	133	156	102	116
Austin Hooper	CLE	TE	179	0	155	0	120	164	0
Sammy Watkins	KC	WR	180	0	0	146	151	0	0
Antonio Gandy-Golden	WAS	WR	181	0	0	0	0	0	0
Carson Wentz	PHI	QB	182	171	135	153	0	139	126
Derek Carr	LV	QB	183	0	0	0	173	156	0

Player	Team	Pos							
Jamaal Williams	GB	RB	184	164	137	0	0	127	162
Eric Ebron	PIT	TE	185	167	156	0	0	0	159
Van Jefferson	LAR	WR	186	161	0	0	0	153	0
Tyler Johnson	TB	WR	187	0	0	0	0	0	0
Jonnu Smith	TEN	TE	188	142	167	0	110	126	163
Greg Ward	PHI	WR	189	0	0	0	0	0	0
Giovani Bernard	CIN	RB	190	0	0	0	0	0	0
Devonta Freeman	NYG	RB	191	0	0	0	0	0	0
Ito Smith	ATL	RB	192	0	138	0	0	0	0
Breshad Perriman	NYJ	WR	193	148	141	0	140	0	0
Marquez Valdes-Scantling	GB	WR	194	0	0	0	166	0	0
K.J. Hamler	DEN	WR	195	0	0	0	0	0	0
Brian Hill	ATL	RB	196	0	0	0	0	130	0
Devin Duvernay	BAL	WR	197	0	0	0	0	0	0
Dante Pettis	NYG	WR	198	0	0	0	0	0	0
DeeJay Dallas	SEA	RB	199	134	0	0	0	0	0
Zach Pascal	IND	WR	200	0	0	0	0	0	0
Ryquell Armstead	JAX	RB	201	0	0	0	0	0	0
Daniel Jones	NYG	QB	202	0	176	161	160	0	0
James Washington	PIT	WR	203	157	0	0	0	0	0
Emmanuel Sanders	NO	WR	204	163	161	163	0	0	0
Washington Football Team	DEF	WAS	0	136	168	168	187	174	152
Duke Johnson	HOU	RB	0	146	180	0	0	0	0
Gabriel Davis	BUF	WR	0	151	152	0	147	137	119
Miles Boykin	BAL	WR	0	158	0	0	0	0	0
Cole Kmet	CHI	TE	0	162	160	0	0	177	153
Pittsburgh Steelers	DEF	PIT	0	165	172	180	184	0	171
New Orleans Saints	DEF	NO	0	169	174	0	0	181	0
San Francisco 49ers	DEF	SF	0	170	171	171	0	0	0
Baltimore Ravens	DEF	BAL	0	173	0	0	171	0	0
Harrison Butker	KC	K	0	174	186	174	174	171	168
Miami Dolphins	DEF	MIA	0	175	173	0	186	186	186
Tampa Bay Buccaneers	DEF	TB	0	176	170	170	181	0	0
Los Angeles Rams	DEF	LAR	0	177	175	183	158	0	0

New England Patriots	DEF	NE		0	178	178	172	0	0	0

Player	Team	Pos							
Justin Tucker	BAL	K	0	179	169	173	175	150	174
Younghoe Koo	ATL	K	0	181	181	175	177	183	161
Los Angeles Chargers	DEF	LAC	0	182	0	0	189	0	0
Tyler Bass	BUF	K	0	184	185	189	190	152	188
Rodrigo Blankenship	IND	K	0	185	184	191	182	0	190
Greg Zuerlein	DAL	K	0	186	182	169	0	175	175
Indianapolis Colts	DEF	IND	0	187	177	185	0	170	169
Wil Lutz	NO	K	0	188	187	0	180	180	189
Robbie Gould	SF	K	0	189	190	190	185	0	191
Matt Breida	MIA	RB	0	190	0	0	0	0	0
Zane Gonzalez	ARI	K	0	191	183	0	0	0	0
Matt Gay	LAR	K	0	192	0	0	0	191	0
Javonte Williams	FA	RB	0	0	0	44	0	0	57
Denzel Mims	NYJ	WR	133	111	140	165	143	0	122
Will Fuller	HOU	WR	64	69	70	70	78	91	83
Hayden Hurst	ATL	TE	118	126	134	155	164	116	140
Logan Thomas	WAS	TE	170	103	129	160	104	107	135
Jared Cook	NO	TE	0	0	0	137	131	0	0
O.J. Howard	TB	TE	0	0	0	0	144	0	0
Noah Fant	DEN	TE	109	105	119	123	98	84	101
Tre'Quan Smith	NO	WR	0	0	0	0	152	0	0
Damien Williams	KC	RB	169	0	142	0	0	160	0
Tyler Higbee	LAR	TE	0	0	153	157	161	0	139
Wayne Gallman	NYG	RB	0	0	0	0	162	138	0
Jared Goff	DET	QB	167	0	0	0	0	154	0
Scott Miller	TB	WR	0	0	0	0	172	0	0
Donovan Peoples-Jones	CLE	WR	0	0	0	0	179	0	0
Cairo Santos	CHI	K	0	0	0	0	188	188	0
Jason Sanders	MIA	K	0	0	189	176	191	189	181
Buffalo Bills	DEF	BUF	0	0	0	0	192	173	170
Keke Coutee	HOU	WR	0	0	0	0	0	149	0
Ryan Succop	TBB	K	0	0	0	0	0	169	183
Travis Fulgham	PHI	WR	0	0	0	0	0	176	0
Mike Badgley	LAC	K	0	0	0	0	0	184	184
Green Bay Packers	DEF	GBP	0	0	0	0	0	190	0
Kansas City Chiefs	DEF	KCC	0	0	0	186	0	192	0
Najee Harris	FA	RB	0	0	0	25	0	0	55
Travis Etienne	FA	RB	0	0	0	46	0	0	60
Ja'Marr Chase	FA	WR	0	0	0	58	0	0	68
DeVonta Smith	FA	WR	0	0	0	73	0	0	93
Jaylen Waddle	FA	WR	0	0	0	80	0	0	149

Name	Team	Pos							
Rashod Bateman	FA	WR	0	0	0	85	0	0	125
Kenneth Gainwell	FA	RB	0	0	0	87	0	0	87
Tylan Wallace	FA	WR	0	0	0	89	0	0	0
Rondale Moore	FA	WR	0	0	0	94	0	0	104
Kyle Pitts	FA	TE	0	0	0	105	0	0	89
Chuba Hubbard	FA	RB	0	0	0	112	0	0	108
Terrace Marshall	FA	WR	0	0	0	127	0	0	131
Jermar Jefferson	FA	RB	0	0	0	129	0	0	145
Trevor Lawrence	FA	QB	0	0	0	135	0	0	132
Michael Carter	FA	RB	0	0	0	136	0	0	103
Dyami Brown	FA	WR	0	0	0	162	0	0	0
Rhamondre Stevenson	FA	RB	0	0	0	177	0	0	0
Demetric Felton	FA	RB	0	0	0	179	0	0	0
Kylin Hill	FA	RB	0	0	0	0	0	0	137
Justin Fields	FA	RB	0	0	0	0	0	0	176
Pooka Williams	FA	RB	0	0	0	0	0	0	192

Printed in Great Britain
by Amazon

61549307R00194